QUICK ESCAPES®
San Francisco

Help Us Keep This Guide Up to Date

Every effort has been made by the authors and editors to make this guide as accurate and useful as possible. However, many things can change after a guide is published—establishments close, phone numbers change, facilities come under new management, etc.

We would love to hear from you concerning your experiences with this guide and how you feel it could be improved and kept up to date. While we may not be able to respond to all comments and suggestions, we'll take them to heart and we'll also make certain to share them with the author. Please send your comments and suggestions to the following address:

The Globe Pequot Press
Reader Response/Editorial Department
P.O. Box 480
Guilford, CT 06437

Or you may e-mail us at:
editorial@globe-pequot.com

Thanks for your input, and happy travels!

Quick Escapes® Series

QUICK
ESCAPES®

San Francisco

*26 Weekend Getaways
From the Bay Area*

FIFTH EDITION

by
KAREN MISURACA

Revised and updated by
Donna Peck

The
Globe
Pequot
Press

GUILFORD, CONNECTICUT

Quick Escapes is a registered trademark of The Globe Pequot Press.

Photo credits: Pp. 1, 6: courtesy Sonoma County Convention and Visitors Bureau; p. 19: courtesy Sonoma Valley Visitors Bureau; p. 58: courtesy Don Leonard; p. 101: courtesy Fort Bragg/Mendocino Convention and Visitors Bureau; pp. 123: courtesy National Park Service; pp. 129, 156: courtesy Richard G. Averitt; p. 133: courtesy California Office of Tourism; p. 144: courtesy Santa Cruz County Convention and Visitors Bureau; pp. 193, 197: courtesy Sacramento Convention and Visitors Bureau; p. 208: courtesy Dave Carter/Nevada City Chamber of Commerce; p. 219: courtesy Bear Valley Lodge; p. 232: courtesy Incline Village/Crystal Bay Visitors and Convention Bureau; p. 257: courtesy Incline Village Visitors Bureau; p. 265: courtesy Keith Walklet/National Park Service; p. 281: courtesy Mammoth Mountain. All other photos are by the author.

Text design by Casey Shain
Maps by Maryann Dubé © The Globe Pequot Press

ISSN 1542-2526
ISBN 0-7627-2426-9

Manufactured in the United States of America
Fifth Edition/First Printing

ACKNOWLEDGMENTS

Thanks to Jan Austerman, Arianne Bautista, Ellie Billings, Julie Brady, Mary Ann Brandt, Nina Laramore, Terry Marburger, LaVerne Richmond, Ellen Stepheus, Lucy Steppens, Stephanie Wood, and Karen Racer.

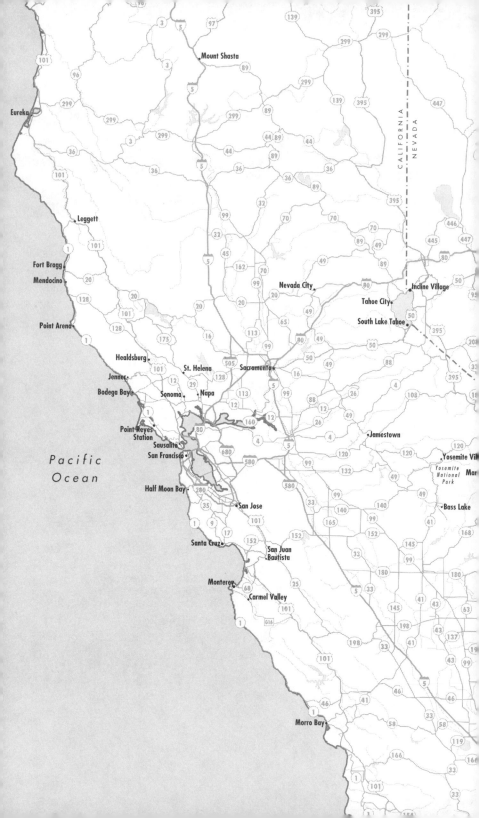

CONTENTS

INTRODUCTION

This guidebook honors that staple of American travel: the car trip. Here are twenty-six detailed trips, providing everything you need to know for a perfect getaway from San Francisco. Every escape is a driving tour, with sight-seeing, recreation, restaurants, and lodging located and described. To give you a variety of activities from which to choose, each weekend itinerary is quite lively, packed with sights and side trips. Annual special events are listed, as are recommended restaurants and lodgings. There's More gives you reasons to return another time. For advance planning, check out the more than twenty-six maps and, listed under For More Information, the visitors bureaus.

If you favor weekends tucked away in one peaceful spot, use the chapters to book a quiet bed-and-breakfast inn, choose romantic restaurants, and read about what all the other tourists are doing.

Within easy distance are the Wine Country, '49er gold rush towns, redwood forests, villages by the sea, cabins in the Sierras, and houseboats on the Sacramento Delta. It's hard to avoid clichés when describing the wide choice of places to go within a few hours.

From the historic missions of the Salinas Valley to the gleaming gem of Lake Tahoe, honky-tonk beach towns, and wilderness, High-Sierra trails, you can escape every weekend for a year and still have a hundred places to see.

For maximum enjoyment of your sojourns, take care to avoid heavy traffic times—Friday and Sunday afternoons and commuting hours. Keeping California's microclimates in mind, be prepared for weather changes throughout the year, particularly in the coastal and mountain regions. Fog, rain, or snow may not be what you expected, but discoveries made on a wintry weekend could turn you into a California lover, in more ways than one.

If you're looking forward to a particular bed-and-breakfast inn or a restaurant, be sure to call well in advance. And remember that in some resort communities, businesses may not be open every month of the year.

Most restaurants and lodgings listed are in the midrange pricewise; a few special places are expensive. Rates and prices are not noted because they can be counted on to change.

In this fifth edition, you will find more Web site addresses, reflecting the tremendous tide of information now available on-line, not to mention the benefits of browsing beforehand. Even the tiniest inn is likely to have a Web site, with a virtual tour of each room. On-line, you can make restaurant and lodging reservations, get driving instructions, and print out maps to specific street addresses. Not like the old days, when we had to phone and write for brochures and maps!

If you have comments on how the escapes worked out for you, please drop me a note care of The Globe Pequot Press. Thanks is due to the travelers who made useful suggestions and contributions to this fifth edition of *Quick Escapes: San Francisco.*

It's a good idea to include the following items in your getaway bag:

- Jacket, long pants, and walking shoes for trail hiking and beachcombing in any weather.

- Binoculars (so as not to miss bald eagles circling and whales spouting).

- Corkscrew, a California necessity.

- Day pack or basket with picnic gear.

- Maps: The directions and maps provided herein are meant for general information—you'll want to obtain your own maps.

- California State Park Pass: Most state parks charge a day fee of several dollars. Frequent visitors to the state parks will save money by purchasing an annual car pass and/or boat launching pass (discounts are available for seniors and those with a limited income). Call (916) 653–6995; www.cal-parks.ca.gov.

- Golden Eagle Passport: For any person, and their accompanying private party, an annual pass is available to national parks and federally operated tourist sites for a $50 fee (888–467–2757; www.nationalparks.org). This will save you $20 on Tioga Pass in Yosemite National Park.

For more information on northern California destinations, write or call the California Division of Tourism, P.O. Box 1499, Sacramento, CA 94812-1499; (800) 862–2543; www.gocalif.ca.gov.

NORTHBOUND
ESCAPES

Wine Road to the Sea 1

The Russian River Route, Healdsburg

1 Night

In the mid-1800s tourists from San Francisco rode ferries across the bay and hopped onto a narrow-gauge railroad to reach summer resorts on the Russian River. The arrival of the motorcar and the decline of lumbering caused the towns along the river to fall into a deep sleep for a few decades. The town of Guerneville never missed a beat, however, thriving through the big band era when Benny Goodman and Harry James kept the weekenders coming. In the 1970s the tremendous growth of wineries began a new era of tourism. Now more than fifty Sonoma County wineries can be discovered on the back roads of the Russian River and Dry Creek Valleys.

☐ Wineries

☐ Farms trails

☐ Antiquing

☐ Redwoods

☐ River rambling

☐ Victorian town

The Russian River winds through redwood canyons; past sandy beaches, orchards, and vineyards; sliding calmly all the way to the Pacific Ocean at Jenner. Rustic inns, casual cafes, leafy walking trails, great fishing holes, and magnificent redwood groves are reason to spend several weekends following its path.

Canoeing, kayaking, and tubing on the Russian are very popular activities. A good paddling route is the scenic 10-mile stretch from Forestville to Guerneville, where you find many beaches and stopping points for fishing and picnicking. It takes a half day, including rest stops. Osprey, blue herons, deer, and turtles are some of the wildlife that accompany your trek. Canoe and kayak companies shuttle you back to your starting point. Bring plenty of water, secure your car keys with a safety pin in your pocket, and beware of sunburn on the top of your legs.

Your weekend begins in the Victorian town of Healdsburg. The westernmost destination of your Russian River Wine Road escape is the tiny town of Jenner, on a high bluff overlooking a marshy bird sanctuary at the mouth of the river.

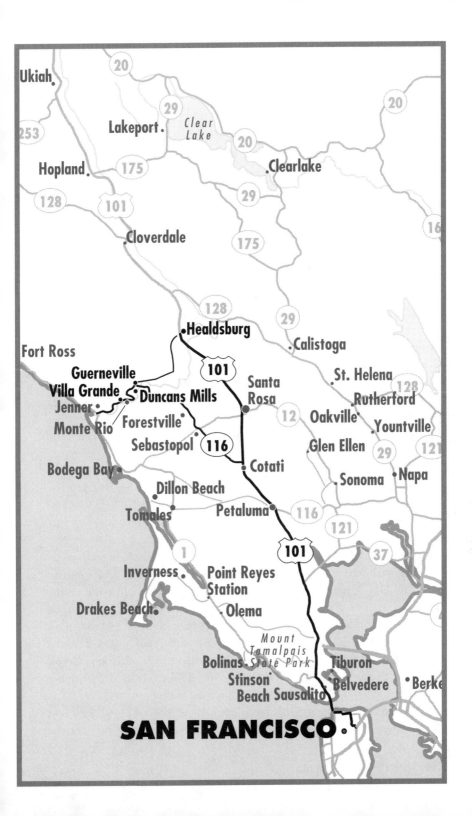

Day 1 / Morning

Head north from the Golden Gate Bridge on Highway 101 to Healdsburg, about one and a quarter hours, taking the central Healdsburg exit into the center of town, parking on the **Healdsburg Plaza,** a lovely, tree-shaded Spanish-style plaza built when the town was established in 1867. The plaza is surrounded by shops, restaurants, and a new hotel: **Hotel Healdsburg.** Band concerts and outdoor festivals are held on the plaza green on many weekends.

Between the Alexander Valley and the Dry Creek Valley, the small town of Healdsburg is prime wine country. Grown here are some of California's finest Zinfandels, a hearty red of Italian heritage. The Dry Creek Valley also produces excellent Sauvignon Blanc, a dry but fruity white wine. At the **Russian River Wine Company,** 132 Plaza Street (707–433–0490), you can taste and collect wines from more than sixty wineries. Also nearby are the Healdsburg Public Library and the **Sonoma County Wine Library,** 139 Piper at Center Street (707–433–3772), and the **Healdsburg Historical Museum,** 221 Matheson (707–431–3325). Get a walking-tour map at the **Chamber of Commerce,** 217 Healdsburg Avenue (707–433–6935).

Among the shops on and nearby the plaza is **Options,** 126 Matheson Street (707–431–8861), where exceptional ethnic and American crafts are the main attractions. Fifty antiques dealers hold court in the big blue building at **Mill Street Antiques,** 44 Mill Street (707–433–8409).

At **Healdsburg Classics,** 226 Healdsburg Avenue (707–433–4315), are fourteen antiques shops selling everything from country pines to garden pieces, estate jewelry, and Native American artifacts.

On weekday afternoons, linger at Recreational Park, where town regulars practice bocce, a form of lawn bowling popular in Italian communities.

The **Dry Creek Valley** west of town is top biking and wine tasting territory. A nice 20-mile loop on gently rolling hills starts at the town plaza, heads south to Mill Street, crosses under the highway, and joins Dry Creek Road going north. Endless vineyards and rows of low, forested mountains remain in view throughout the ride. At the old **Dry Creek General Store** (3495 Dry Creek Road; 707–433–4171), buy sandwiches and picnic here or take provisions in your bike basket.

Ferrari-Carano, at 8761 Dry Creek Road (707–433–6700; www. ferraricarano.com), comes as a surprise in the valley, where most of the wineries are small, country places. Don and Rhonda Carano, second-generation Italian-Americans who ran the Eldorado Hotel and Casino in Reno, Nevada, recreated Tuscany in their Dry Creek Valley winery estate. Voluptuous gardens surround the Villa Fiore tasting room where the Mediterranean ambience echoes the character of their wines. Because their vineyards range from valley to foothill to mountain vineyards, they have great fruit to work with. *Wine Spectator* rated Ferrari-Carano wines fifth on a list of the top one hundred.

If Zinfandel is your passion, be sure to stop at **Quivira Winery,** 4900 West Dry Creek Road (707–431–8333; www.quivirawine.com), where picnic grounds overlook the valley.

Founded in 1876, **Simi Winery** (16275 Healdsburg Avenue; 707–433–6981) offers one of the most comprehensive and enjoyable tours in the valley; the shady terrace here is pleasant on hot days.

On the south end of town on a bend of the Russian River, **Healdsburg Memorial Beach Park** (13839 Old Redwood Highway; 707–433–1625) is a popular place to sun and swim.

LUNCH: Bistro Ralph, 109 Plaza Street, Healdsburg; (707) 433–1380. Locally raised produce, meats, and poultry are used to create miracles: roasted garlic and polenta with baby lamb, Hog Island oysters, peach shortcake, crème brûlée. Ask for the Local Stash, a special wine list of older vintages from the Dry Creek and Alexander Valley wineries.

Afternoon

Proceed southwest out of town on Westside Road, stopping at the sharp left turn and driving through the arch to see **Madrona Manor,** 1001 Westside Road (707–433–4231), one of California's largest and finest Victorian masterpieces. Built in 1881, the huge manor is now an inn and restaurant surrounded by magnificent gardens. Walk in and ask for a tour of the museumlike rooms and outbuildings; depending on their bookings, it may or may not be possible but is definitely worth a try.

Mill Creek Vineyards, at 1401 Westside Road (707–431–2121), is a small, family-owned winery on a knoll overlooking the valley; it's fun to see their wooden mill wheel turning beside the creek. Two picnic areas offer panoramic views of the valley and beyond. Mill Creek Vineyards makes several wines, from a good "Old Mill Red" table wine to a superb Cabernet Sauvignon.

A bridge spans the beautiful Russian River.

You'll be following the Russian River now, all the way to the ocean. Valley foothills become mountains, oaks give way to dark redwood and fir forests, and the roadsides become ferny and damp. Along the riverbank in freshwater marshes grow silvery gray-green willows and cottonwoods.

Take a left onto Wohler Road, passing more than a half-dozen wineries on your way to River Road, then turn west. Stop at **Korbel Champagne Cellars,** 13250 River Road (707–824–7000), for a tour of the winery and the gardens. Founded in 1886 by Czech immigrants, the ivy-covered stone winery is a piece of Old Europe tucked into the rolling, vineyard-carpeted hills of the Russian River Valley. The guided winery tour, including museum, film, garden walk, and champagne tasting, is one of the most complete and enjoyable of all California wineries. In-depth garden tours show off antique roses and hundreds of spring bulbs. You can also taste Russian River Brewing Company beer at Korbel and choose from an astonishing variety of gourmet deli items in the market/deli/ espresso bar.

You'll follow the river and the redwoods a few minutes farther down the road to the summer-vacation town of **Guerneville,** chock-full of souvenir shops, cafes, and art galleries. In the middle of town, turn north onto Armstrong Woods Road a mile or so to **Armstrong Grove Redwoods State Reserve** (707–869–2015), 750 acres of glorious redwood groves along Fife Creek. Easy paths lead to sunny picnic areas and old-growth trees up to 300 feet tall. For a half-day horseback ride into the wilderness bordering Austin Creek State Recreation Area, call the **Armstrong Woods Trail Rides and Pack Station** (707–887–2939). Even beginning riders will love the lunch ride, which meanders gently out of the redwood forest through a variety of wildlife habitats to ridgetops overlooking the Russian River Valley.

Accessed from Armstrong Grove, the **Austin Creek Recreation Area** (707–869–2015) is 4,200 acres of hills, canyons, and river glens that campers, hikers, and horseback riders love to explore. Wildflowers in the spring, deep forests, good birding, bluegill and black bass fishing in Redwood Lake, and primitive camping sites are a few of the attractions. It is hot and dry in summer, glorious in spring with blooming wild azaleas, rushing creeks, and maples, ash, and alder in full leaf.

LODGING: Applewood Inn, 13555 Highway 116, Guerneville; (707) 869–9093; www.applewoodinn.com. An elegant 1920s California Mission Revival mansion in the redwoods, featuring a heated swimming pool, six acres of gardens and forest, hot tub, in-room Jacuzzis and double showers, and verandas. Sixteen romantically decorated rooms with down comforters, garden views. You could forget the sight-seeing and just settle in here.

DINNER: Applewood Inn. Candlelight gourmet dinners by the fireplace. Think about sea bass with chive and quinoa crust, and roasted chicken with bing-cherry mustard reduction.

Day 2 / Morning

BREAKFAST: Brie omelettes, eggs Florentine, and more fresh, hot entrees in the beautiful new dining room at Applewood Inn.

Ten minutes west of Guerneville, bear left across the bridge onto Moscow Road and through the tiny burg of Monte Rio to **Villa Grande,** a small river-bend village that's changed little since the 1920s, when it was built as a summer encampment for vacationers from San Francisco. There is a beach here and a delightful array of early Craftsman-style cottages.

Back on the main road, it's not far to **Duncans Mills,** where a dozen or so shops nestle in a Victorian-era village, another 1880s railroad stop. Take a look at the only remaining North Pacific Coast Railroad station. The **Duncans Mills General Store** (707–865–1240) stocks fishing gear, groceries, and antiques. The **Gold Coast Coffee Co. Cafe and Bakery,** Steelhead Boulevard (707–865–1441), offers a selection of freshly baked goods from their wood-fired brick oven. Shops in Duncans Mills sell everything from fishing gear and fine jewelry to top-notch wildlife art. A worldly surprise in this bucolic village, the aromatic, elegant **Sanctuary** shop (25185 Main Street; 707–865–0900) specializes in beautiful Asian imports.

Farther west, the Russian River meets the sea at Bridgehaven, the junction of Highways 116 and 1. In winter, ocean waves and the river clash here in a stormy drama. In summer the mouth of the river is cut off from the ocean by temporary dunes. Salmon and steelhead runs attract crowds of seals hoping for delicious bites of their favorite food. In spring, seals hide in the river's mouth to give birth away from the sharp eyes of hungry sharks and whales.

Fabulous, easily accessible beaches are located just to the north and the south, off Highway 1. Have a picnic on the beach or head back to Duncans Mills for lunch.

LUNCH: Cape Fear Cafe, 25191 Highway 116, Duncans Mills; (707) 865–9246. African tribal masks are dramatic accents at this charming little place. The North Carolinian chefs turn out wonderful fresh seafood dishes, homemade pasta, and vegetarian specialties.

Afternoon

Drive back on Highway 116 to Guerneville, turning south on 116 past Forestville to **Kozlowski Farms,** 5566 Gravenstein/Highway 116 (707–887–1587), for luscious berries, jams, fresh fruits, and pies—the ultimate Sonoma County farm store. Pick up a **Sonoma County Farm Trails** map at Kozlowski's to locate the many produce outlets and nurseries in these verdant rolling hills. Nearby are the **Green Valley Blueberry Farm,** 9345 Ross Station Road (707–887–7496); **Carriage Charter,** 3325 Gravenstein

Highway (707–823–7083), offering horse-drawn carriage rides; and **Bennett Valley Farm,** 6797 Giovanetti Road (707– 887–9557), with dried flowers, garlic, and wreaths.

Between Sebastopol and Highway 101 are dozens of antiques shops on Gravenstein Highway.

Proceed south on Highway 101 and back to the Golden Gate Bridge.

There's More

Canoeing. Trowbridge Canoes, 13840 Old Redwood Highway, Healdsburg; (707) 433–7247.

Burke's Canoe Trips, 8600 River Road, Forestville; (707) 887–1222.

Fishing. An excellent map to fishing access in the entire Russian River area is available from the Russian River Chamber of Commerce & Visitor Center, P.O. Box 255, Guerneville 95446; (707) 869–9000.

Jimtown Store, 6706 Highway 128, a few miles northeast of Geyserville, just north of Healdsburg off Highway 101; (707) 433–1212; www.jim town.com. A destination in itself, this is an upscale general store/souvenir and antiques shop/gourmet deli/refreshment stand.

Northwood Golf Course, 19400 Highway 116, Guerneville; (707) 865–1116. Eighteen holes in a spectacular redwood grove. There is a pleasant cafe here with a shady deck overlooking the fairways.

Special Events

January. Winter Wineland, Healdsburg; (800) 723–6336. A weekend of tasting, live entertainment, and celebrity events at the wineries.

March. Russian River Wine Road Barrel Tasting; (800) 723–6336.

April. Passport to Dry Creek, Healdsburg; (707) 433–3031. Wine tastings, winery and vineyards tours, food pairings, entertainment at several wineries.

May. Memorial Day Weekend Antiques Fair, Healdsburg; (707) 433–4315. An extravaganza of antiques displays and sales.

September. Russian River Jazz Festival; (707) 869–3940. Huge crowds at the beach in Guerneville; big-name performers.

October. Sonoma County Harvest Fair, Sonoma County Fairgrounds, Santa Rosa; (707) 545–4203. A three-day salute to the wine harvest with tastings, annual judging of the wines, demonstrations, exhibits, art, music, and food.

Other Recommended Restaurants and Lodgings

Forestville

Topolos at Russian River Vineyards, 5700 Gravenstein/Highway 116, Forestville; (707) 887–1562. Greek and California cuisine in a circa 1870 estate home, in the dining room by the wood-burning stove or outside on the garden patio. Local seafood, duckling in black currant Madeira sauce, souvlaki, spanakopita, seasonal specialties; adjacent to Russian River Vineyards.

Guerneville

Ridenhour Ranch House Inn, 12850 River Road; (707) 887–1033. Next to Korbel Champagne Cellars. A century-old redwood ranchhouse with comfortable rooms and a cottage; European chef and owner cooks incredible breakfasts.

Sweet's Cafe and Bakery, 16251 Main; (707) 859–3383. The best place for Belgian waffles, omelettes, homemade croissants, espresso, and lunch.

Healdsburg

Belle de Jour Inn, 16276 Healdsburg Avenue; (707) 431–9777; www.belledejourinn.com. On a hilltop on six acres, white garden cottages have king or queen beds, fireplaces, whirlpool tubs, refrigerators, and country charm.

Costeaux French Bakery and Cafe, a block from the plaza at 417 Healdsburg Avenue; (707) 433–1913. Award-winning breads and pastries, scrumptious sandwiches, and picnic items to stay or to go; breakfast and lunch.

The Haydon Street Inn, 321 Haydon Street; (707) 433–5228. A 1912 Queen Anne Victorian on a quiet, tree-shaded street. French and American antiques, down comforters, designer touches. Claw-foot and Jacuzzi tubs, full breakfasts, air-conditioning. Separate two-room cottage.

Healdsburg Charcuterie, 335 Healdsburg Avenue; (707) 431–7213. An upscale restaurant where locals love the eccentric, pig-inspired decor and the dazzling Provence-inspired food: bouillabaisse, monkfish soup with artichokes, rabbit Provençal, house-cured pork, rib-eye steak in roasted garlic sauce, and more rib-sticking, fabulous food; including the best hamburger in the Wine Country. Lunch and dinner.

Healdsburg Inn on the Plaza, 110 Matheson Street; (707) 433–6991 or (800) 431–8663. Victorian bed-and-breakfast with ten antiques-chocked rooms, private baths, fireplaces, afternoon wine and tea, full breakfast.

Hotel Healdsburg, 25 Matheson Street, off Healdsburg Avenue; (707) 431–2800. With the arrival of Hotel Healdsburg on the square, the town has achieved a level of chic unmatched in the Wine Country. Ask for a room on the third floor overlooking the town square. The hotel offers a full-service spa and complimentary continental breakfast from Dry Creek Kitchen, off the lobby.

Madrona Manor, 1001 Westside Road; (707) 433–4231 or (800) 258–4003. California cuisine, French and Italian classic dishes, a much heralded restaurant in one of the most elegant Victorian mansions in California. Reservations absolutely necessary. Twenty elaborately decorated inn rooms in the mansion, plus stunning traditional decor, large rooms and suites in a carriage house, and other cottages. Swimming pool, fireplaces, private baths.

Manzanita, 366 Healdsburg Avenue; (707) 433–8111. Chef Bruce Frieseke features seasonal ingredients and Russian River wines in this award-winning restaurant located in a one-hundred-year-old building north of the town square.

Oakville Grocery, 124 Matheson Street; (707) 433–3200. In the old city hall, an upscale market and deli with scrumptious take-out food, local wine, and cheese from around the world.

Raford House, 10630 Wohler Road; (707) 887–9573. On five acres of vineyards, an 1880 Victorian with seven lovely rooms, two with fireplaces. Full breakfast.

Ravenette Cafe, in a corner of the foreign-film Raven Theater, 117 North Street; (707) 431–1770. Hearty bistro fare, faux-tiger banquettes, tiny and terrific.

Jenner

Jenner Inn and Cottages, 10400 Coast Highway 1; (707) 865–2377. Comfortable bed-and-breakfast rooms with antiques and wicker, fireplaces, hot tubs, private baths, sea views.

For More Information

Healdsburg Chamber of Commerce, 217 Healdsburg Avenue, Healdsburg, CA 95448; (707) 433–6935 or (800) 648–9922; www.hbg.sonoma.net.

Redwood Empire Association and North Coast Visitor Center, 2801 Leavenworth, San Francisco, CA 94133-1117; (415) 394–5991; www.red woodempire.com. Brochures and information on the Wine Country, the North Coast, and Redwood Country.

Russian River Chamber of Commerce and Visitor Center, 14034 Armstrong Woods Road, Guerneville, CA 95446; (707) 869–9212.

Sonoma County Tourism Program; (800) 380–5392; www.sonomacounty. com; e-mail: info@sonomacounty.com. Free sixty-five-page visitors guide to entire county.

Southern Sonoma Valley

On Country Roads

2 Nights

Between the rugged Mayacamas Mountains and the Sonoma Mountains, the 17-mile-long Sonoma Valley is a patchwork of vineyards and rich farmlands. Two-lane roads meander along rivers and creeks, through oak-studded meadows and foothills to country villages and to towns with entire neighborhoods that are National Historic Monuments. The Victorian and early California Mission eras come alive in museums and in hundreds of restored homes, inns, and buildings all over the valley.

More than thirty premium wineries are located here, the birthplace of the California wine industry. Their production facilities and tasting rooms, in many cases, are of significant architectural and historical interest. Thousands of acres of vineyards create a tapestry of seasonal color and texture that cascades across the hills and streams out onto the valley floor.

☐ Early California history

☐ Wineries

☐ Shopping

☐ Hiking, biking, golf

☐ Cheese, wine, produce

☐ Mountain and valley parks

Moderate climate and rich soil produce world-famous gourmet foods—cheeses, sausages, foie gras, orchard fruits and berries, nuts, and sourdough French bread. California Wine Country cuisine, a gastronomic genre all its own, attracts diners and chefs from afar.

Exploring the Sonoma Valley on quiet back roads by car, foot, or perhaps bike, you'll enjoy the landscape and discover some of old California. After a day of wine tasting, browsing in the shops, gourmet dining, and maybe a round of golf, a cozy bed-and-breakfast inn will be a welcome refuge.

Day 1 / Morning

From the Golden Gate Bridge, drive north on Highway 101 to the Highway 37/Napa/Vallejo exit, driving east to the Highway 121/Sonoma left turn.

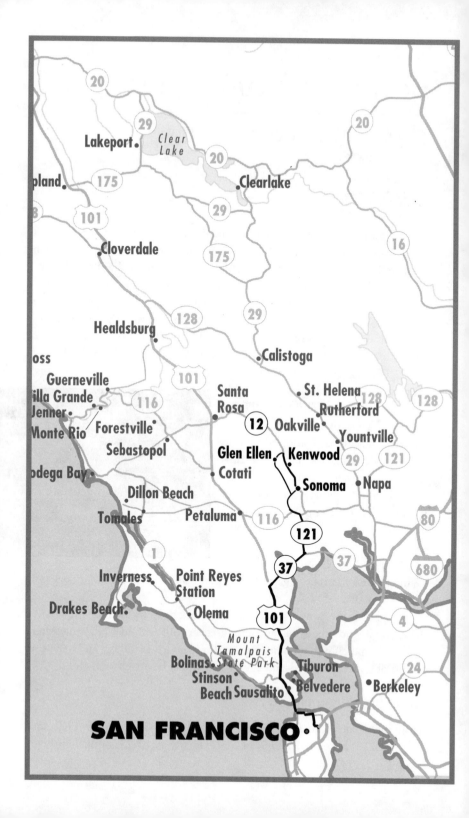

Drive north on this road to Schellville (four-way stop) and continue to the Arnold Drive right turn; stay on Arnold for 8 miles to the foresty village of Glen Ellen.

This is the **Valley of the Moon,** named by its most famous (sometimes infamous) resident, Jack London, author of the classic adventure tales *Call of the Wild* and *The Sea Wolf.* You'll pass the **Jack London Bookstore,** 14300 Arnold Drive (707–996–2888), across the road from a wonderful old gristmill, still creaking slowly over a rushing creek. Across the road is a small shopping complex including **Carmenet Marketplace** (707–929–6277). **Mucca** (707–938–3451) is a new restaurant in the old mill building, with a nice deck under the trees. Try the house-made pasta, the smoked salmon pizza, or the luscious T-bone chop with crispy, roasted new potatoes. At the **Olive Press** (707–939–8900), watch the fruit being pressed, taste olive oils, and browse for linens and ceramics from Provence.

When you see the large **London Lodge** banner, you've arrived in Glen Ellen, just a few blocks long. Turn left at the lodge, driving 1 mile up into dense oak forests to **Jack London State Historic Park** (707–938– 1519). Once London's home ranch, the park is 800 magnificent acres of walking trails through groves of oaks, madrones, Douglas fir, redwoods, ferns, and explosions of wildflowers. There are shady picnic sites, mountain and valley views, a romantically spooky ruin, and a museum. Remnants of **Wolf House,** London's gigantic stone mansion, lie deep in a forest glade, at the end of a delightful short path through the trees (handicapped accessible by golf cart). Only walls and chimneys remain of the elaborately decorated and furnished home, which burned to the ground before London and his wife, Charmian, could enjoy it. Filled with London memorabilia and most of the original furnishings, his smaller home, the **House of Happy Walls,** is open to visitors daily except holidays. You can view the exhibits free of charge.

On the way back to Glen Ellen, make a wine-tasting and -touring stop at **Benziger Family Winery,** 1883 London Ranch Road (707–935–3000). Beautiful valley oaks and gardens, an art gallery, and picnic grounds are here, in addition to the tasting room. This is the only winery in the valley to offer a motorized tram tour of the vineyards. Call ahead for reservations.

In Glen Ellen, cross the stone bridge, bear left, and turn left onto Warm Springs Road for a 6-mile drive. First you'll see **Glenelly Inn,** 5131 Warm Springs Road (707–996–6720), a peach-and-white confection built in 1916 as a railroad inn for train passengers from San Francisco who gamboled their summers away at nearby mineral springs resorts. Feeling lazy and warm? Stop at **Morton's Sonoma Springs Resort**

(707–833–5511) for a picnic on sweeping lawns or a swim in one of three heated pools. Just beyond, you'll come into Kenwood, a tiny, overgrown hamlet of cabins and rustic homes, and then meet up with Highway 12; still a two-lane country road, it's a main route through the county.

LUNCH: Turn left onto Highway 12 and stop for a late lunch at **Cafe Citti,** 9049 Sonoma Highway, Glen Ellen; (707) 833–2690. A deli cafe with tables outdoors under the trees. Fresh, fabulous salads are ready to take out, or you can stay here and enjoy homemade pasta entrees and a glass of wine.

Afternoon

You'll see signs on Highway 12 for wineries: **Château St. Jean** (707– 833–4134), **Landmark** (707–833–1144), and **Kunde Vineyards** (707– 833–5501). One of Château St. Jean's Cabernet Sauvignons has been listed by the *Wine Spectator* as one of the best wines in the world. A tasting room for seven of the valley's finest small wineries is **Family Wineries of Sonoma Valley** (9200 Sonoma Highway, Kenwood; 707–833–5504).

Go north on Highway 12 for 0.5 mile; then turn right on Adobe Canyon Road and drive 3 miles to **Sugarloaf Ridge State Park** (707– 833–5712), a 3,000-acre green and golden jewel of mountains, redwood groves, creeks, wildflower-strewn meadows, and views. You may take a short walk or a hike, picnic in the pines, park your RV overnight, or camp out in your tent. In the late afternoon, cool off with strawberry margaritas, alcoholic or non-, under a grape arbor at **Vineyards Inn,** 8445 Sonoma Highway (707–833–4500), a Mexican cantina and restaurant at the corner of Highway 12 and Adobe Canyon Road.

DINNER: **Kenwood Restaurant,** 9900 Sonoma Highway, Kenwood; (707) 833–6326. One of the most celebrated of Wine Country restaurants, with a vineyard-surrounded terrace and a cool, elegant dining room. Go for the top-drawer Petaluma duck with brandied cherries, Bodega Bay bouillabaisse, or a hearty Kenwood burger; save room for fresh berry cobbler. The wine list will not disappoint. Reservations absolutely necessary, lunch and dinner.

LODGING: **Sonoma Mission Inn and Spa,** 18140 Highway 12, Sonoma/ Boyes Hot Springs; (707) 938–9000 or (800) 862–4945; www.sonoma missioninn.com. A glamorous, pink-and-white, 1920s-style extravaganza of a hotel guarded by tall palms and surrounded with lush gardens. An elegant lobby with cushy furnishings and a huge fireplace greets upscale guests.

Rooms in the historic building are beautiful but small; rooms and suites in the annex buildings are spacious and luxurious, some with fireplaces and terraces. A fabulous $20 million spa is world-famous, with exotic and traditional treatments and pampering beauty and health regimes, including weight loss. Ayurvedic "revitalizers," grape-seed body polishes, and special couples programs are popular. The spa was named one of the top ten in the United States by the *Zagat Survey* and "Best Resort Spa" by *Gourmet* magazine.

The glassed-in, elegant Santé dining room overlooks a beautiful swimming pool terrace. The bold, bright, flavorful international cuisine that Toni Robertson creates begins with her daily rounds to Sonoma's farms and gardens. Her specialties include grilled ostrich filet with heirloom potatoes and baby artichoke, Sonoma grilled quail with rosemary polenta, scallop dumplings, and a delicate goat cheese soufflé. Ask about spa and golf packages; the resort owns the Sonoma Mission Golf Club.

Day 2 / Morning

BREAKFAST: Breakaway Cafe, 19101 Highway 12, Sonoma, in the Albertson's shopping plaza; (707) 996–5949. Relax in a big booth and dig into an all-American breakfast of omelettes, platter-size hotcakes, or sausage and eggs. This is a popular locals' place for breakfast, lunch, and dinner. Come back later for pork chops and mashed potatoes, roasted chicken, burgers and salads, comforting soups, veggie specials, luscious desserts, and smoothies.

Highway 12 runs into West Napa Street, where you take a left and head north to the **Sonoma Plaza,** a typical Spanish town square, the largest and one of the oldest in California, laid out by Gen. Mariano Guadalupe Vallejo in 1834. The site of many annual festivals and historical events, it's a National Historic Landmark, and a beautiful one—huge bay and eucalyptus trees, a meandering stream with chattering ducks, a playground, picnic tables, and the monolithic stone **City Hall,** which houses the **Visitors Bureau,** 453 First Street East (707–996–1090). If you are here on a Tuesday, be sure to take a walk through the plaza during the Farmer's Market in the early evening, when locals get together to picnic and purchase their weekly veggies and fruits, baked goods, cheeses, flowers, honeys, and more, all locally produced.

Surrounding the plaza, and for several blocks around, are many historic buildings, including the **Mission San Francisco Solano de Sonoma,** circa 1841, the last of the California missions built, with a beautiful small chapel and museum. The commandant who held sway in the Sonoma area when Mexico owned California, Gen. Mariano Vallejo constructed a barracks compound for his soliders, which is now a state park and a museum on the plaza (707–938–1519). The museum shop is a great place to find educational and entertaining things for children, from paper dolls in period dress to small toys. Thick-walled adobes, Victorians, and Classic Revival and Mission Revival structures line the plaza and adjacent streets. Park your car, get out your camera, and explore the plaza and the streets and alleyways for a block or so in each direction. The visitors bureau has good walking-tour maps.

Not to be missed on the plaza: **The Wine Exchange of Sonoma,** at 452 First Street (707–938–1794), to taste and buy the wines of almost every winery in the Sonoma and Napa Valleys, and **Kaboodle,** 447 First Street (707–996–9500), a feminine fairyland of country French gifts and accessories.

On the corner, in a historic building topped by a dome, **The Corner Store** is upscale and delightfully crowded with European and Wine Country accessories and gifts, from Italian ceramics and pewter to fine linens, bath products, and French posters. In the store is a popular wine-tasting bar (498 First Street East; 707–996–2211; www.sonomacorner store.com).

Just off the plaza, **Viva Sonoma** is a warren of Mediterranean gifts, one-of-a-kind accessories for your Wine Country villa, and women's clothing, with a lovely garden (180 East Napa Street; 707–939–1904).

Look for the replica of a San Francisco cable car for a free ride around the plaza and to **Sebastiani Vineyards,** a few blocks away. Behind the winery are shaded picnic tables with vineyard and hillside views (707–938–5532).

The **Spirits in Stone Gallery** at 452 First Street displays dramatic African Shona stone sculpture, and there are interesting large photographs of Africa and a video to watch (707–935–6254). Next door at **Artifax International,** 450 First Street, take a look at African and Asian carvings, masks, jewelry, and doodads of great color and variety in an exotic incensed environment (707–996–9494).

LUNCH: Dig into homemade pasta salad, a frittata, or a foccacia sandwich at **Cucina Viansa,** on the corner of First and Spain Streets, Sonoma (707–935–5656), a cafe and wine bar in the prettiest historic building in town. Live jazz is performed here on weekend nights.

City Hall in Sonoma Plaza.

Afternoon

Even if you're not interested in wine tasting, you'll want to walk, bike, or drive 1.5 miles (take East Napa Street south to Lovall Valley Road, then go left onto Old Winery Road) from the plaza to the **Buena Vista Winery** (707–938–1266), an enchanting Wine Country estate with vine-covered stone buildings, ancient trees, and rampant flower gardens. Tasting rooms are stocked with guidebooks, artwork, and museum-quality antiques. Buena Vista's Hungarian founder, Count Agoston Haraszthy, engaged in friendly wine-making competition with General Vallejo in the mid-1800s. The interconnected small roads on this eastern outskirt of town are pretty and quiet for walks, drives, and bike rides to several other wineries.

Also in this area, **Ravenswood** winery is perched above a quiet, winding road that is a perfect 1-mile walking route through vineyard lands. Ravens-wood's low-slung, stone tasting room is one of the most interesting for souvenir and wine shopping. They vow, "No wimpy wines allowed," and their famous Zinfandel and spicy Early Harvest Gewürztraminer prove the point. Weekend gourmet barbecues at the winery are held on a leafy terrace; reservations are not necessary (18701 Gehricke Road, 888–669–4679; www.ravenswood-wine.com).

Another paved path for walking and biking, accessed near the plaza, winds 1.5 miles, east-west, from Fourth Street East to Highway 12, passing by parks, playing fields, and the historic Vallejo Home. A block from the plaza on the walking path, **Depot Park** has a playground, barbecue grills, and picnic tables under the trees, a good choice when the plaza is crowded. If you are hooked on local history, visit the small **Depot Park Museum** to see a restored stationmaster's office, re-creations of Victorian households, and photos of early Sonomans (707–938–1762).

Near the walking path at 315 Second Street East, the **Vella Cheese Company** is one of the best of the great Sonoma County cheese makers (800–848–0505). In this stone building, jack, blue, and cheddar have been made since 1931. Try the pepper jack and the garlic cheddar. Across the street look for **The Patch,** a vegetable stand beside a huge garden, where produce is picked fresh every day.

Accessible by the walking path and by car, the **General M. G. Vallejo Home** is a classic, Yankee-style, two-story Gothic Revival shipped around the Horn and erected in 1851 (707–938–1519). You can tour the home, which is called *Lachryma Montis,* meaning "Tears of the Mountain." Original and period furnishings in every room re-create the days when Vallejo and his daughters lived here. The glorious garden has huge magnolia, fig, and oak trees, and a fish pond with turtles and koi. The home is part of the state park property, so one admission ticket is good at the mission, the barracks compound, and the Vallejo home.

DINNER: Della Santina's, 133 East Napa Street, East Sonoma; (707) 939–1266. The fireplace creates a cozy atmosphere for fancifully prepared fresh seafood from both coasts; intimate in winter, popular and fun on the patio in summer.

LODGING: Sonoma Mission Inn.

Day 3 / Morning

BREAKFAST: Basque Boulangerie Cafe, 400 First Street East, Sonoma; (707) 935–7687. At a sidewalk table or indoors in the tiny, busy cafe on the plaza, enjoy luscious European pastries, quiche, coffee drinks, and light breakfasts, plus snacks and sandwiches all day.

Leaving Sonoma, head south from the plaza on Broadway/Highway 12 for less than 1 mile, then turn left onto Napa Road, another view-filled country byway. If you're extending your trip to the lower Napa Valley (see Northbound Escape Three), turn left at the Highway 121 junction; otherwise, turn right at the junction. Go straight on through the Schellville–Highway 121 intersection and down the road to **Schug Carneros Estate** (707–939–9363), a winery tucked up against a low range of hills, a lost little corner of the valley. German-owned Schug makes a traditional California Chardonnay, a sparkling red wine, and a German-style Gewürztraminer, unusual for this area.

Continue on Highway 121 south at a slow pace along a 10-mile stretch of rolling hills. You can take a scenic ride in an antique biplane at **Aero-Schellville** (707–938–2444). Turn right at the **Gloria Ferrer Champagne Caves** sign and drive up toward the hills to the tile-roofed Spanish hacienda built by the largest sparkling wine company in the world—Freixenet, based in Spain—at 23555 Highway 121 (707–996–7256). Gloria Ferrer has a luxurious tasting salon with a fantastic view. Many annual events are scheduled here, such as Catalan cooking classes and fireside concerts.

Back on Highway 121 heading south, a vine-draped arbor leads to **Viansa Winery and Marketplace** (707–935–4700), a red-tiled, terra-cotta–colored Italian winery on a hill above the highway. There is much to enjoy at Viansa besides their unusual Italian wine varieties. Sangiovese, Vernaccia, Nebbiolo, Aleatico, Trebbiano, and Chardonnay are the grapes blended into their traditional wines. At the huge gourmet delicatessen and Italian marketplace you can buy a sandwich, a salad, packaged gourmet foods, cookbooks, ceramics, and waterfowl-related gifts. Barbecues and special events open to the public are held here in the summertime.

Viansa has restored the ninety-acre wetlands below the winery, one of the largest private waterfowl preserves in the state; more than 10,000 birds have been spotted in a single day.

On weekends there are stock car and motorcycle races at **Sears Point Raceway** (800–870–7223) at the junction of Highways 121 and 37, where you turn right, head west toward Marin County, and take Highway 101 south to the Golden Gate.

There's More

Balloon rides. Aerostat Adventures Hot Air Ballooning; (800) 579–0183; www.aerostat-adventures.com. Fly over the Sonoma County vineyards. Air Flambuoyant; (800) 456–4711.

Bike rental. Sonoma Cyclery in Sonoma; (707) 935–3377.

Horseback riding. Sonoma Cattle Company; (707) 996–8566. Sugarloaf Ridge State Park; (707) 833–5712.

Ledson Winery and Vineyards, 7335 Highway 12, Santa Rosa; (707) 833–2330. A half-mile from Kenwood, this beautiful castle stands at the beginning of the Valley of the Moon, as Jack London called this stretch of Highway 12.

Matanzas Creek Winery and Estate Gardens, 6097 Bennett Valley Road, Santa Rosa; (800) 590–6464; www.matanzascreek.com. Make an appointment to tour this unique winery in a magical corner of the countryside. There are aromatic, truly stunning lavender fields, and you can buy estate-grown lavender products.

Ramekins Sonoma Valley Culinary School, 450 West Spain Street, Sonoma; (707) 933–0450; www.ramekins.com. For adventurous home cooks, an annual schedule of more than 300 hands-on classes presented by renowned chefs from around the country, from traditional Provençal recipes to wine and food pairing, Southwestern and California cuisine, artisan bread baking, and much more. Upstairs are six lovely bed-and-breakfast rooms with views of the surrounding hills. This is a beautiful "rammed earth" building with a Spanish adobe look.

Sonoma Valley Regional Park, Highway 12 between Arnold Drive and Madrone Road, near Glen Ellen; (707) 539–8092. A mostly flat, paved path winding a mile one way through an oak forest, with a pretty creek along the way. You can bike and picnic; dogs must be leashed. Across the highway the tiny **Garden Court Cafe** serves hearty breakfasts and lunches (13875 Sonoma Highway; 707–935–1565).

Special Events

January. Art of the Olive, Sonoma; (707) 996–1090.

February. Taste of the Olive, Sonoma Barracks, Sonoma; (707) 996–1090.

March. Heart of the Valley Barrel Tasting, Sonoma; (707) 996–1090.

April. "Barreling into Spring" annual barrel tasting of Family Wineries of Sonoma Valley; (707) 833–5504. Two days of tastings, meet the wine makers, gourmet food, live entertainment.

June. Ox Roast, Sonoma Plaza; (707) 996–1090. Visitors are welcome at this locals' fund-raising event. Scrumptious beef barbecue, wine and beer, live entertainment.

Vintage Racecar Festival, Sonoma Plaza; (707) 996–1090.

July. Salute to the Arts, Sonoma Plaza; (707) 938–1133; www.winery.com/ salute. The biggest and best of the annual art festivals in the plaza, with two days of displays and sales of some of the highest-quality art, fine crafts, and gift items by county artisans; plus wine tasting, concerts, and lots of food.

Fourth of July Parade, Sonoma Plaza; (707) 996–1090. The mother of all hometown parades, with every kid in town, antique cars, fire engines, the town band, cops on bikes, and more. Food, live music, and art in the plaza all day, and evening fireworks.

Sonoma Valley Wine Festival, Sonoma; (707) 996–1090.

July–August. Jazz Series, Bartholomew Park Winery; (707) 935–9511. At a beautiful outdoor winery site, top-notch jazz performers in concert.

September. Valley of the Moon Vintage Festival, Glen Ellen; (707) 996–1090.

Sonoma Valley Harvest Wine Auction, Boyes Hot Springs; (707) 935–0803.

December. Blessing of the Olives, Mission San Francisco Solano de Sonoma; (707) 996–1090.

Holiday Concert Series, Sonoma Valley Chorale; (707) 935–1576.

Other Recommended Restaurants and Lodgings

Glen Ellen

Gaige House Inn, 13540 Arnold Drive; (707) 935–0237; www.gaige.com. An Italianate Victorian on the outside, a mix of styles and periods on the inside. Thirteen spectacular inn rooms with Ralph Lauren linens, eclectic art, some canopy beds, and giant whirlpool tubs; garden rooms within steps of a 40-foot swimming pool, fireplaces. Big country breakfast. Unique among Wine Country inns. You can enjoy a full array of spa treatments in your room or poolside, from massage to wraps and scrubs.

The Girl and the Gaucho, 13690 Arnold Drive; (707) 938–2130. The fresh produce, poultry, and seafood of Sonoma County are prepared with Southwestern and Latin panache. Especially tasty are the empanadas, grilled prawns, and fried yucca. The grilled swordfish with roasted red pepper and saffron rice recalls a trip to Barcelona. A small, quite popular cafe with a well-deserved, top-notch reputation.

Kenwood

Kenwood Inn, 10400 Sonoma Highway; (707) 833–1293. Vine-covered, Tuscan-style villas around a walled courtyard with a pool and Jacuzzi, herb and flower gardens, gorgeous antiques-filled suites with feather beds, fireplaces, balconies, and vineyard views. Sumptuous breakfasts and an in-house spa with beauty and body treatments—a place for honeymoons and romantic getaways.

Sonoma

Lodge at Sonoma, 1325 Broadway; (707) 935–6600. A large luxury hotel, within several blocks of the plaza, with cottages, spacious hotel rooms with some sitting areas and fireplaces, a swimming pool terrace and beautiful gardens, restaurants, and a full-service beauty and fitness spa.

MacArthur Place, 29 East MacArthur Street; (800) 722–1866; www.macarthurplace.com. Anchored by a smashing 1850s main house and surrounded by gardens and a clutch of large cottages with plush accommodations, MacArthur Place is a full-service spa with bicycles to borrow, and a large swimming pool; plus, Saddles, a dinner house.

Piatti, 405 First Street West; (707) 996–2351. Lively dining room and a gracious tree-shaded patio, wood-fired pizza ovens, rotisserie roasting, contemporary Northern Italian food.

Rob's Rib Shack, 18709 Arnold Drive, on the west side of Sonoma; (707) 938–8520. A casual cafe at the golf practice range, serving yummy ribs and BBQ specialties, really good Caesar salad, microbrews, fun roadhouse decor, outdoor tables.

Swiss Hotel, 18 West Spain Street; (707) 938–2884. In one of Sonoma's oldest historic buildings on the plaza, a lively locals' bar and a lovely dining room and garden patio. Homemade pasta, local lamb, and fresh fish; dazzling desserts; great Sunday brunch, lunch, and dinner.

Thistle Dew Inn, 171 West Spain Street; (800) 382–7895. Five antiques-filled rooms and a suite, garden hot tub, fireplaces, private decks and private entrances, free use of bicycles, lovely gardens, gourmet breakfast, afternoon refreshments. Book well in advance.

Victorian Garden Inn, 316 East Napa Street; (707) 996–5339. A dream of a century-old home a block from the plaza; pool, fireplaces, and full breakfast.

For More Information

Bed and Breakfast Association of Sonoma Valley; (800) 969–4667.

Sonoma County Tourism Program; www.sonomacounty.com.

Sonoma Reservations; (800) 576–6662. Motels, inns, spas, homes.

Sonoma Valley Visitors Bureau, on the plaza, 453 First Street East, Sonoma, CA 95476; (707) 996–1090; www.sonomavalley.com.

The Carneros, Napa, Yountville, and Rutherford

1 Night

Thirty miles long, just one-sixth the size of Bordeaux, the Napa Valley is home to the densest concentration of wineries in North America and to some of the state's most highly regarded California-cuisine restaurants, several championship golf courses, dozens of charming bed-and-breakfast inns, and scenery that attracts visitors from all over the world.

☐ Art and architecture

☐ Wineries

☐ Shopping

☐ California cuisine

☐ Vineyard walks

☐ Gourmet picnics

☐ Country lanes

Your escape begins in the Carneros wine-growing district at the top of San Pablo Bay, cooled by ocean breezes and summer fogs. Grapes ripen more slowly here than in the hot, dry upper valley, creating notable Chardonnays and Pinot Noirs. Vineyards and wineries here are relatively new in Napa's 150-year history of wine making, and many tourists are unaware of the quiet lanes of the Carneros.

There is time for some lesser-known sights near the town of Napa, a day in Yountville, and a meander down the Silverado Trail. Stretching from Napa 35 miles north to Calistoga, the trail winds along at the foot of high mountain ridges. Sprinkled along the way are wineries and champagne cellars, gargantuan mansions, small stone cottages, luxurious hotels, and quaint inns, each in its own idyllic corner of the Wine Country.

Day 1 / Morning

From the Oakland Bay Bridge, drive forty-five minutes north on Highway 80, *past* the Napa/Highway 37 exit, to the American Canyon exit a few miles north of Vallejo, turning west and connecting with Highway 29

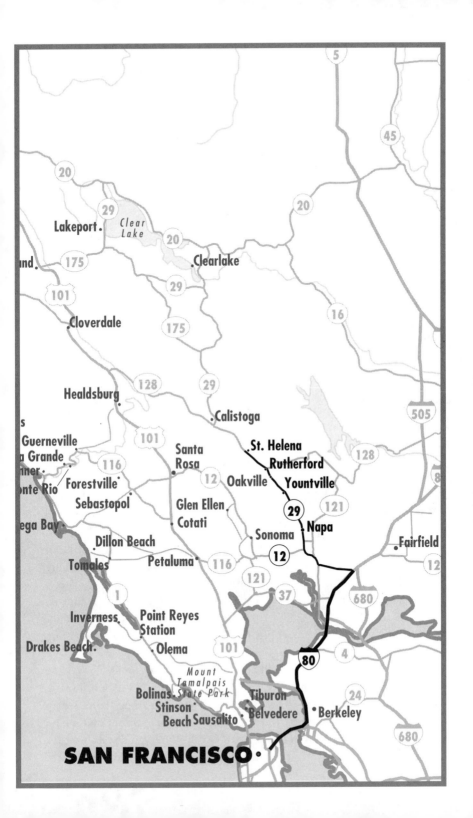

north into Napa; you'll be on Soscol Avenue. From Soscol take a left onto Third Street, crossing the Napa River, and park a few blocks down, across from a bright blue Victorian at 1517 Third Street.

BREAKFAST: Alexis Baking Company, 1517 Third Street, Napa; (707) 258–1827. Inventive breakfasts, the best pastries and desserts in the county, cappuccino, local color.

Need maps and brochures? The **Napa County Visitors Center,** 1310 Napa Town Center (707–226–7459), where you can talk to the knowledgeable volunteers, is accessed from First Street, within a few blocks of the bakery.

Just behind the bakery cafe, charming Victorian neighborhoods are bounded by Franklin, Division, Elm, and Riverside Drives; for just a peek, behind the bakery, drive up Franklin and down Randolph.

Head west on First Street to Highway 29, then south two minutes to Highway 12, turning west. Within a minute turn left onto Cuttings Wharf Road and get lost for a while in the rolling vineyards and country roads of Carneros; biking is great on these empty lanes.

Although a brandy distillery, not a winery, **RMS Vineyards** makes an interesting stop at 1250 Cuttings Wharf Road; (707) 253–9055. You can take a guided tour in a lovely garden setting to see the huge copper pots, a labyrinth of equipment, and the cellars, and learn about how brandy is made. Rather than tasting, as you do at the wineries, you participate in an aroma sampling.

Going west on Las Amigas, take a left onto Buchli Station Road to **Bouchaine** (707–252–0401), a winery specializing in Chardonnay and Pinot Noir; an appointment will be necessary. Farther west on Las Amigas, **Acacia Winery** (707–226–9991) produces superb Chardonnays; make an appointment to taste here, too—it's well worth it. Going right onto Duhig Road, you'll wind up back on Highway 12.

The supercolossal French château on the hill is **Domaine Carneros,** 1240 Duhig Road (707–257–0101), a French-American winery producing sparkling wines. Scamper up the quadruple staircase to the tasting room for a tour.

Cross Highway 12 onto Old Sonoma Road; go left onto Dealy Lane to **Carneros Creek Winery,** 1285 Dealy Lane (707–253–9463), a small, friendly place with picnic tables under a vine-covered arbor. If you are up for a walk on a quiet country lane, past vineyards, cow pastures, and rolling hills, park across the road from Carneros Creek Winery and walk west for a couple of miles until you reach a private property sign, and then return.

Connect again with Highway 29 and head north five minutes to a left onto Redwood Road, then 6.5 miles through redwood and oak forests to **Hess Collection,** 4411 Redwood Road, Napa (707–255–1144). A large and important European and American contemporary art collection resides here in a historic winery building. Take the self-guided tour and enjoy the gardens, the views, and the wine.

Return to Napa and head north on Highway 29 for ten minutes to **Yountville.** Park at Vintage 1870, 6525 Washington Street, in the middle of town. The few streets of this tiny town are lined with vintage cottages in overgrown country gardens. On Washington, the main drag, a blizzard of shops, restaurants, and inns makes this a popular Wine Country destination.

The landmark building in Yountville is **Vintage 1870,** a huge former winery sheltering a big toy store, import and clothing shops, a great T-shirt store, outdoor cafes, and more (707–944–2451; www.vintage1870.com).

LUNCH: Pacific Blues Cafe, in front of Vintage 1870, Yountville (707–944–4455). Indoors or on the deck, gourmet burgers and sandwiches, veggie specialties, fresh seafood, homemade soups, big salads, microbrews on tap.

Afternoon

Take a rest on a garden bench at Vintage 1870, or rush the stores! **The Toy Cellar** is a treasure house of dolls and games, with a toy train zipping around the ceiling (707–944–2144). In the **Vintage 1870 Wine Cellar** more than one hundred locally produced wines are available to taste; (707) 944–9070 or (800) 946–3487.

Other shops sell Victorian gewgaws, gourmet cooking accessories, fashions, art—more than enough to wear the numbers off your credit cards.

Near Vintage 1870, the **Overland Sheepskin Company** (707–944–0778) has sheepskin coats, leather jackets, and Western hats. **Blue Heron Gallery,** 6526 Washington (707–944–2044), has for more than three decades displayed the best of local artists' works. **Raspberry's,** at Beard Plaza, 6540 Washington (707–944–9211), is one of the loveliest art-glass galleries you will ever see. My favorites are the vibrantly glowing, hand-blown, foot-long tropical fish that are "swimming" in the window.

At the north end of town, **Yountville Park** is a grassy, oak-shaded commons with a fantastic children's playground and picnic tables. For a 3-mile round-trip walk or bike ride, go east from the park through the fascinating old cemetery to Yount Mill Road and follow it north to Highway

29 and back. Running along a tributary of the Napa River, the road is shady and bedecked with lovely views of the mountains and vineyards. Watch for a plaque about George Calvert Yount, the first white settler in the valley. Yount wangled from Mexico the huge land grant of Rancho Caymus in the 1850s—comprising much of the heart of the valley, including Yountville—and built grist- and sawmills on the river. You will see the remains of one of his large wooden barns.

From the intersection of Yount Mill and Yountville Cross Roads, you can head east a couple of miles to connect with the Silverado Trail. On Yountville Cross Road at the bridge, the **Napa River Ecological Reserve** is a place to walk beside the river under oaks and sycamores. You can wade and fish here, too.

Few people know that you can take an easy, pleasant walk on paved paths around the grounds of the old **Yountville Veterans Home,** on the west side of Highway 29 from Yountville (707–944–4600). It's a veritable botanical garden, with magnificent, huge trees that were planted well before the turn of the twentieth century.

On the grounds of the Yountville Veterans Home is an architectural surprise, the new **Napa Valley Museum** of contemporary art and the history of the valley, with indoor and outdoor exhibits and a garden terrace (55 Presidents Circle; 707–944–0500; www.napavalleymuseum.org).

Just below the museum off Highway 29, **Domaine Chandon** is a French-owned sparkling-wine cellar where you can wander the oak-studded grounds and learn about *méthode champenoise* wine making. A flute of champagne awaits in the tasting salon; try the Blanc de Noirs, a blossomy pink bubbly. The airy, contemporary-design restaurant here is one of the most celebrated in the valley, headed by a distinguished chef who produces miracles of California and French cuisine.

Arrive at your lodgings in time to enjoy the gardens and perhaps a dip in the pool before dinner.

DINNER: For a snazzy, upscale atmosphere and renowned California cuisine, try **Mustard's** (707–944–2424), two minutes north of Yountville on the highway. Go for inventive pastas, grilled and spit-roasted poultry and meats, and the supercolossal wine list. This is a very popular, fun place, and you may need to make reservations several days ahead.

LODGING: **Villagio Inn and Spa,** 6541 Washington Street, Yountville; (800) 351–1133. An eighty-room luxury garden hotel; elegant, spacious rooms with fireplaces, spa baths; 60-foot lap pool, tennis, buffet breakfast.

Day 2 / Morning

BREAKFAST: Villagio Inn. After breakfast head north on Highway 29 and, just past Oakville Cross Road, stop at the **Oakville Grocery** (707–944–8802) for the makings of a French country picnic: pâtés, baguettes, quiches, *fromages,* charcuterie, baby vegetables, salads. There are hundreds of northern California wine selections and specialty foods from this region and around the world; fresh, rustic hearth breads; and the famous oversize cookies.

If you have time for only one winery visit (say it isn't true), this is the one (1991 St. Helena Highway, Rutherford; 707–968–1100; www. niebaum-coppola.com). In addition to making dazzling wines, **Niebaum-Coppola Estate Winery** has a Hollywood connection. The renowned movie maker Francis Ford Coppola restored one of the oldest winery estates in the valley (Inglenook) to its former glory and had his Hollywood designers create an extravaganza of a winery, gift store, museum, and park. Drive down a long allée between vineyards and trees to his spectacular park modeled after the Luxembourg Gardens, complete with bubbling fountains, promenades, and lawns.

Separate from the main tasting room, the cozily elegant, on-site Mamarella Café is a cozy wine and cigar bar. Walk from the cafe through cool caves, where wine is stored behind iron bars, into two high-ceilinged rooms full of Wine Country–style home accessories, clothing, art and books, and the main wine tasting bar. Notice the gleaming exotic woods, huge stained-glass windows, and the glamorous, curving main stairway leading to the museum. Ever see real Oscars up close? Here they are: Coppola's golden beauties, along with photos and other cool stuff from his movies, including the *Tucker* auto, the boat from *Apocalypse Now,* costumes from *Bram Stoker's Dracula,* and charming artifacts from his family history. Italian opera music drifts through the winery.

Out of this world are the stunning contemporary architecture and the Bordeaux-style reds of superluxe **Opus One,** owned by the two most famous wine makers on the planet—Robert Mondavi and Baron Philippe de Rothschild. Don't even think about dropping in without an appointment (7900 St. Helena Highway, Oakville; 707–944–9442).

Up the road at **St. Supery Vineyards and Winery,** 8440 St. Helena Highway, Rutherford (707–963–4507), you can walk through a demonstration vineyard, see an art show, tour a lovely Queen Anne Victorian farmhouse, and enjoy elaborate exhibits about grape growing and wine making. And taste wine, too.

Drive to the Silverado Trail and turn left; then turn right up the hill to **Auberge du Soleil Resort** (180 Rutherford Hill Road, Rutherford 94573; 707–963–1211 or 800–348–5406; www.aubergedusoleil.com), where you'll feel as though you've dropped suddenly into an olive grove in the south of France. Wisteria-draped arbors and riots of flowers beckon you past fat stucco walls into a tile-floored entry, flooded with light from the terraces where beautiful people dine al fresco on California cuisine. Enjoy the heartstopping view, take a look at the sculpture garden, and ask to see a villa, for future getaways. This is one of the most luxurious and beautiful resorts in the Wine Country, if not the world. Rooms and suites have huge, elegant, comfortable furnishings; French doors opening onto private terraces; giant, fabulous bathrooms; and amenities galore. *Gourmet, Travel and Leisure,* and *Condé Nast Traveler* call it one of the world's best and most romantic small resorts.

For a rare personal experience, visit **Anderson's Conn Valley Vineyards,** a short drive off the Silverado Trail near St. Helena (707–963–8600). The owners are the winemakers and the tour guides to their caves, small winery, and vineyards; make an appointment in advance.

L U N C H : Picnic under the oaks at **Rutherford Hill Winery;** (707) 963–1871; www.rutherfordhill.com. Just up the hill from Auberge du Soleil, with the same panoramic view, this winery has 40,000 square feet of cool, underground caves, seen on thirty-five-minute tours. Enjoy your Oakville Grocery picnic at tables under the oaks or in the olive grove.

A little south of Rutherford Hill, **Mumm Napa Valley,** at 8445 Silverado Trail (707–963–1133), is a French-American sparkling-wine cellar with a tasting terrace, vineyard views, and a great gift shop.

A little south of Mumm, **Pine Ridge Winery,** at 5901 Silverado Trail (707–253–7500), is a small but top-notch winery where you can tour the caves, taste medal-winning Chardonnay, and picnic in a grassy grove under tall pines. There are swings for the kids and a nice walking trail through the vineyards and along the ridge overlooking the winery.

Afternoon

Watch for the left turn to the **Silverado Country Club and Resort,** 1600 Atlas Peak Road, Napa (707–257–0200), a 1,200-acre resort famous for its two eighteen-hole Robert Trent Jones golf courses. Towering eucalyptus, palm, magnolia, and oak trees line the drive leading to a huge, circa-1870 mansion. A curving staircase and period chandeliers grace the lobby; a terrace bar overlooks sweeping lawns, waterways, and gardens. Silverado has several restaurants and one of the largest tennis complexes in northern California. Scattered about the lush gardens and quiet courtyards are condominium units and cottages, some with fireplaces; nine swimming pools, and a glamorous new beauty and fitness spa. Popular with nongolfers at the spa is the "Golf Widow"—three hours of massage, facial, manicure, and pedicure. Golfers like the hydromassage with a hundred air and water jets, and the old-fashioned Swedish massage.

Take tea in the lounge, then head south to Napa and back to the Bay Area.

There's More

Ballooning. Floating silently in a hot-air balloon is an unforgettable way to see the Wine Country. Always scheduled for the early morning, balloon trips are usually accompanied by champagne, breakfast, and much revelry. Rates average $185 per person.

Adventures Aloft, P.O. Box 2500, Yountville 94599; (707) 255–8688.

Balloons Above the Valley, P.O. Box 3838, Napa 94558; (707) 253–2222 or (800) 464–6824; www.balloonrides.com. Departs from Domaine Chandon Winery in Yountville.

Bonadventura Balloon Company, P.O. Box 78, Rutherford 94573; (800) FLY–NAPA; www.bonadventuraballoons.com.

Napa Valley Balloons, P.O. Box 2860, Yountville 94599; (707) 253–2228 or (800) 253–2224; www.napavalleyballoons.com. Launches at sunrise from Domaine Chandon Winery.

Biking. The Napa Valley can be divided into three moderately strenuous bike trips: a circle tour around the spa town of Calistoga, a mid-valley tour in and around St. Helena and Yountville, and a third tour in the Carneros region. The mostly flat Silverado Trail, running along the east side of the valley, is a main biker's route. Crisscrossing the valley between Highway 29 and the Silverado Trail are myriad leafy country roads. You can arrange to have the bike rental company deliver bikes to your hotel and pick up you and your bikes at a winery or other destination.

Bicycle Trax, 796 Soscol Avenue, Napa; (707) 258–8729.

Napa Valley Cyclery, 4080 Byway East, Napa; (800) 707–BIKE. Pick-up service, scheduled and private tours, rentals.

Copia, the American Center for Wine, Food and the Arts, 500 First Street, Napa; (707) 257–3606; www.copia.org. Copia celebrates American achievements in the culinary, wine making, and visual arts and commands twelve acres along the Napa River in Napa Valley. Wine icon Robert Mondavi and American chefs Julia Child, Alice Waters, and R. W. Apple Jr. have been involved in creating the food forum, cafe, and exhibit spaces. Monday evening performances range from jazz to pop to classical.

Di Rosa Preserve, 5200 Carneros Highway, Napa; (707) 226–5991; www. dirosapreserve.org. Call well ahead to see a fantabulous contemporary art collection, one of the largest and most valuable ever assembled in California, in a nineteenth-century manor house beside a lake, outdoors, and in a big gallery.

Golf. Chardonnay Club, 2555 Jameson Canyon, Napa; (707) 257–8950; www.chardonnayclub.com. On the south end of Napa, two links-style, eighteen-hole courses in a challenging landscape of ravines, hills, and vine-yards; predictably windy. The private course here, with a demanding 74.4 rating, is open to members of other private clubs; a new public course, Eagle Vines, opened here in 2001.

J. F. Kennedy Municipal Golf Course, just north of Napa; (707) 255–4333. Eighteen challenging holes, water on fourteen; reasonable rates.

Yountville Golf Course, 7901 Solano Avenue, Yountville; (707) 944–1992; www.YountvilleGC.com. A new, walkable nine-holer in a beautiful site at the foot of Mount Veeder. Giant redwoods loom along fairways dotted with young trees and watered by a small creek and ponds.

Napa Valley Wine Train, 1275 McKinstry Street, Napa; (707) 253–2111 or (800) 427–4124; www.winetrain.com. Elegant restored dining and observation cars, a relaxing way to see the valley; lunch and dinner; no stops on the slow, three-hour chug from Napa to St. Helena and back.

Six Flags Marine World, at Highways 80 and 37, 2001 Marine World Parkway Way, Vallejo 94591; (707) 643–6722; www.sixflagsmarineworld. com. An oceanarium and wildlife and amusement park with $40 million worth of roller coasters and rides. Among the highlights are the live shows: Dolphin Harbor, the Batman Waterthrill show, the killer whale show, Tiger Splash Attack, and the sea lion, elephant, and tropical bird shows. Hold your breath on the Boomerang and the Kong roller coasters, and on the DinoSphere TurboRide.

Skyline Park, East Imola Avenue, Napa; (707) 252–0481. Hilly woodlands and meadows for hiking, horseback riding, picnicking, and RV and tent camping. Great for winter mushroom expeditions and springtime wildflower walks; find the waterfalls for a summer splash.

Wine education. Robert Mondavi Winery's three-and-a-half-hour tour and wine essence tasting is one of the most comprehensive of the free educational tours offered by wineries. For reservations call (707) 226–1395, ext. 4312. Located at 7801 St. Helena Highway (Highway 29) in Oakville.

Merryvale Vineyards holds a beginner's wine-tasting seminar in the cask room on Saturday mornings. For reservations call (800) 326–6069. Located at 1000 Main Street in St. Helena.

Franciscan Winery has a hands-on blending seminar. Call (707) 963–7111.

Wine Plane, P.O. Box 4074, Napa 94558; (888) 779–6600 or (707) 747–5533; www.wineplane.com. For the sightseers and wine aficionados who would like to see the appellations, the benches, and the wine valleys from the air, while snacking and sipping.

Special Events

June. Napa Valley Wine Auction; (707) 963–5246. Wine aficionados from all over the world come for three days of parties, barrel tastings, and events at wineries; auction benefits local hospital.

August. Music in the Vineyards, Napa Valley wineries; (707) 578–5656. Noted chamber music artists from across the country assemble to play in beautiful winery settings; wine tasting, too.

September. Harvest Fest, Charles Krug Winery, St. Helena; (707) 253–2353.

River Festival, Third Street Bridge, Napa; (707) 226–7459. Napa Valley Symphony performs at the riverside.

October. Yountville Days Festival; (707) 944–0904. Parade, music, entertainment, food.

November. Napa Valley Wine Fest; (707) 253–3563.

December. Napa Valley Jazz Festival, Yountville; (707) 944–0310.

Other Recommended Restaurants and Lodgings

Napa

Bistro Don Giovanni, 4110 St. Helena Highway, five minutes north of Napa; (707) 224–3300. Rub elbows with the beautiful Wine Country people in a lively cafe atmosphere. Country Italian cuisine, risotto, wood-fire roasted chicken, eclectic pasta, one of the valley's best wine lists. A little noisy but never boring.

Blackbird Inn, 1755 First Street; (888) 567–9811; www.foursisters.com. Built as a private residence in 1910, the inn is a virtual gallery of California's Arts and Crafts period. The stained-glass front doors depict autumn-gold gingko leaves; the staircase banister resembles a tree limb. Hallways and public areas are lined with early California landscape art. They add a delightful feature to the parlor where guests meet for early-evening wine and hors d'oeuvres, then again in the morning for a hearty country breakfast. Many of the inn's eight rooms have fireplaces and private decks. A good place to headquarter while visiting wineries and Copia, the American Center for Wine, Food and the Arts.

La Residence, 4066 St. Helena Highway, on the north end of Napa; (707) 253–0337. A romantic inn in a French barn and a circa-1870 mansion surrounded by gardens on two oak- and pine-studded acres. Rooms are elaborately decorated with antiques, designer fabrics and linens, and four-poster beds, and have fireplaces, patios, and verandas. Full breakfast, wine and hors d'oeuvres, swimming pool.

Oak Knoll Inn, 2200 East Oak Knoll Avenue; (707) 255–2200. In the middle of 600 acres of Chardonnay vines, four huge, elegant guest rooms with private entrances, fireplaces, king-size brass beds, hot tub, swimming pool. Full gourmet breakfast, wine and cheese in the evening.

Pasta Prego, 3206 Jefferson Street; (707) 224–9011. A best-kept secret, one of the best restaurants in the area: 1990s-style Northern Italian cuisine, like polenta with mushroom sauce, smoky grilled veggies, rich risottos, fresh local fish, poultry, meats, and many pastas. Noisy and fun, patronized by the "in crowd" of local winery families. Dining is indoors in the small dining room, at the counter, or on the heated patio.

Rutherford

Rutherford Grill, 1880 Rutherford Road; (707) 962–1782. Go for the smoky baby back ribs, mountains of feathery onion rings, grilled and spit-roasted poultry and meats, garlic mashed potatoes, and jalapeño corn bread. Big booths inside, umbrella tables and a wine bar outside. The bad news: It is a very popular place, and you may have to wait on weekends. The good news: The attractive patio where you wait has a wine bar and a bubbling fountain.

Yountville

Bistro Jeanty, 6510 Washington Street; (707) 944–0103. An upscale French country bistro with wonderful, hearty dishes prepared by a famous Frenchman.

Bouchon, 6534 Washington Street; (707) 944–8037. The $1 million interior resembles an elegant Parisian brasserie, with a stunning bar and ceiling fixtures from Grand Central Station. Its bistro food is celebrated throughout the land.

Compadres, next to Vintage 1870; (707) 944–2406. Delightful outdoor patio under giant palms and oaks, zowie margaritas, good Mexican food.

The French Laundry, 6640 Washington Street; (707) 944–2380. Said to be one of the best restaurants in the world, a veritable temple of country French and California cuisine, so revered and desired it has no sign out front (reserve weeks, even months, in advance). In a vine-covered stone building in a garden, as if in the south of France. The food, the service, and the wine list are astounding.

Gordon's Cafe and Wine Bar, 6770 Washington Street; (707) 944–8246. In a former stagecoach stop, the small, noisy, popular place for exotic picnic fare to go and casual, quick meals here. Breakfast (cinnamon buns!) and lunch every day, prix fixe dinner on Friday.

Maison Fleurie, 6529 Yount Street; (707) 944–1388 or (800) 522–4140; www.foursisters.com. An ivy-covered stone inn with the look of southern France; lush gardens and a swimming pool, bountiful breakfasts, afternoon wine, bikes. Thirteen guest rooms have vineyard views; some have fireplaces and spa tubs.

Napa Valley Lodge, 2230 Madison Street; (707) 944–2468 or (800) 368–2468; www.woodsidehotels.com. In a great location near the city park, with a heated pool on a sunny terrace, this upscale, Mediteranean-style lodge has recently renovated, spacious rooms and suites with balconies or patios in a garden setting; a champagne breakfast buffet is complimentary. Sauna, fitness center. This is one of a small chain of particularly comfortable, plush, small hotels in California. Ask here for a Historic Yountville walking tour guide.

Ristorante Piatti, 6480 Washington Street; (707) 944–2070. One in an upscale chain of Northern Italian places in northern California. It's fun to watch the chefs in the open kitchen prepare pastas, roasted and rotisseried poultry and meats, and vegetable specialties galore. Outdoors under the arbor is the place to be.

Yountville Inn, 6462 Washington Street; (707) 944–5600 or (800) 972–2293; www.yountvilleinn.com. A nice, new, small inn on the creek, with fire-place rooms, pool, and continental breakfast, conveniently located on the south end of town.

For More Information

B&B Style, P.O. Box 298, Calistoga, CA 94515; (707) 942–2888.

Napa Valley Conference and Visitor Bureau, 1310 Napa Town Center, Napa, CA 94559; (707) 226–7459.

Napa Valley Reservations Unlimited, 1819 Tanen, Suite B, Napa, CA 94559; (707) 252–1985 or (800) 251–6272; www.napavalleyreservations.com.

Napa Valley Vintners Association, P.O. Box 141, St. Helena, CA 94574; (800) 982–1371. Ask for the excellent, free winery touring map.

Tourist information: www.napavalley.com; e-mail: info@freeruntech.com; (707) 265–1835. Free information about wineries, lodgings, dining, events, recreation, and shopping.

Yountville Chamber of Commerce, 6795 Washington Street, Yountville, CA 94599; (707) 944–0904. In Washington Square Center, north end of town.

Upper Napa Valley 4

Heart of the Wine Country

2 Nights

"Up valley," as the northern half of the Napa Valley is called, is anchored by Calistoga, a hot springs resort town founded in the 1840s. Steam rises from 200-degree mineral springs at a dozen or so health resorts; some are scatterings of historic clapboard cottages with simple facilities, whereas others are Roman-style spas with luxurious lodgings. This is the place for rest and rejuvenation, for massages, mud baths, beauty treatments, and slow swims in warm pools. The mud-bath experience must be tried, at least once; be warned that après mud bath you won't feel like moving for quite a spell.

☐ Hot springs

☐ Art galleries

☐ Winery architecture tour

☐ Shopping

☐ Mud baths

☐ Vineyard picnic

As you drive to Calistoga, through the valley bordered by the Mayacamas Range on the west and the Howell Mountain Range on the east, the tremendous variety of Napa Valley soils and microclimates becomes evident. It's fun to try the diverse wines produced from grapes grown on the dry hillsides, those from the valley floor, and especially the wines from grapes grown on the "benches," the alluvial fans of soil and rocks eroded down from the mountainsides into triangles of rich bedding for vineyards whose grapes have produced wines besting the best in France.

Besides wine tasting and hot-bath soaking "up valley," there's tons of shopping to do in St. Helena, plus biking, hiking, golfing, and ballooning; perhaps you'll be forced to return for another weekend or two.

Day 1 / Morning

From the Golden Gate Bridge, drive north on Highway 101 to the Napa/Highway 37 exit, connecting with Highway 121 east to Highway 29 at Napa, then driving thirty minutes north to **St. Helena**—about ninety minutes altogether.

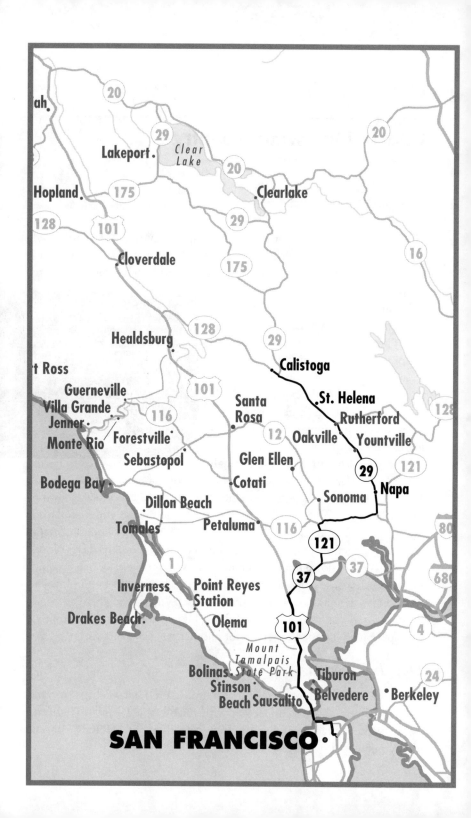

BREAKFAST: Gillwoods, 1313 Main Street, St. Helena; (707) 963–1788. Unique breakfast specialties and all-American favorites. Enjoy the plethora of specialty shops on Main. **Main Street Books,** 1371 Main (707–963–1338), is stocked with regional guidebooks. The **Gallery on Main Street,** 1359 Main (707–963–3350), shows the best of local artwork.

Showplace North at 1350 Main (707–963–5556) is worth a stop to see the beautiful stone-walled interior hung with tapestries and the view out the back through wavy windows to the mountains on the east side of the valley. European-style feather comforters ride high over custom-designed pine and iron beds.

The **St. Helena Wine Center,** 1321 Main (707–963–1313), will ship mixed cases of local wines, from Schramsburg Blanc de Blanc to Marilyn Merlot, and they sell fine cigars, too.

Get your pet a rubber frog, a doggie futon, or some gourmet biscuits at the ultimate dog and cat store, **Fideaux** (1312 Main Street; 707–967–9935).

Anchoring the north end of town on Main Street is tiny Lyman Park, for almost a century a grassy spot for reclining under the oaks, with a gazebo and a stone water fountain for dogs and horses. Across the street at 1429 Main, **Vanderbilt and Company** is a huge store with ceramics, linens, glassware, and myriad accessories from France and Italy (707–963–1010).

If you're a Robert Louis Stevenson aficionado, you'll find 8,000 pieces of his memorabilia at the **Robert Louis Stevenson Museum,** 1490 Library Lane (707–963–3757). Next door, the **Napa Valley Wine Library** (707–963–5145) houses 6,000 books, tapes, and reference materials on the art of wine making and the history of the valley.

A block off the main drag, take a step back in time at the retro **Big Dipper** old-fashioned ice cream parlor, decorated with old Coke signs and other fun relics. Have a thick shake or a banana split, or some penny candy (1336A Oak Avenue; 707–963–2616).

Driving north from St. Helena, you'll see redwood forests grow darker and deeper, maples and oaks crowd closer to the roadside, creating canopies of leaves and branches overhead, brilliant canyons of color in the fall. Watch for **Beringer Winery's Rhine House** on the left, built in 1883 as a reminder to the winery founder of his family home in Germany. This is a good place to take a full winery tour, which includes the huge cellar caves carved into the hillside by Chinese laborers more than a hundred years ago.

LUNCH: Wine Spectator Greystone Restaurant, just north of Beringer on Highway 29 at the Culinary Institute of America (CIA) in St. Helena; (707) 967–1010. From 1889 until about a century later, the Christian Brothers Winery inhabited Greystone, a massive, multistory, European-style château with 22-inch-thick, hand-cut volcanic stone walls guarded by towering palm trees. Greystone is now the western outpost of the CIA, the prestigious culinary college in Hyde Park, New York.

The stunning, contemporary Mediterranean (rather noisy) restaurant turns regional cuisine into high art. The outdoor dining terrace overlooks an ancient oak forest and rolling vineyards. Tours of the state-of-the-art kitchens and demonstration in the culinary theater are a few dollars a person; call ahead.

Plan an hour after lunch to wander around, see the food and wine museum, and browse the school store, a blockbuster of a gourmet emporium, where CIA-logo attire and 1,500 cookbook titles are just part of an unbelievable inventory of tools and gifts in an environment reminiscent of southern Europe.

Afternoon

Two minutes north of the CIA on Highway 29 at the Freemark Abbey sign, turn right into the parking lot and go into the **Hurd Beeswax Candle Factory and Store** (707–963–7211) to see wild and colorful handmade beeswax candles of every description being created for shipment worldwide.

Just up the road, **Bale Grist Mill State Park** (707–963–2236) is a wooded glade with a 36-foot waterwheel beside a rushing creek. Walk from here into **Bothé–Napa Valley State Park** (707–942–4575) to find a lovely campground in Ritchie Creek canyon, a swimming pool, and shady picnic sites under redwoods and firs along the creek. Both of these parks are home to the endangered spotted owl. You can take a one- or two-hour guided horseback ride along Ritchie Creek and up along the ridges overlooking the valley. Call **Napa Valley Trail Rides** at (707) 996–8566.

Proceed another ten minutes to Calistoga and have a predinner glass of wine at the trendy **Hydro Bar and Grill,** 1403 Lincoln Avenue (707–942–9777). The exotic bistro menu here changes daily and may include red wine–fennel sausage with potato and artichoke hash or roasted mushroom and goat cheese lasagna. The wine and microbrew list is extensive.

DINNER: All Season's Cafe, 1400 Lincoln, Calistoga; (707) 942–9111.

A classically trained chef holds forth in the kitchen, inventing American versions of Mediterranean food with all locally grown and produced ingredients. Home-smoked salmon and chicken, grilled Petaluma duck breast, pizzettas, pasta, fresh fish, killer pies. Salads are tops here, such as warm spinach with smoked chicken and lemon dressing.

LODGING: Scott Courtyard, 1443 Second Street, Calistoga; (707) 942–0948. Private, roomy suites (some with full kitchens) in circa-1940 bungalows surrounded by lush gardens. Swimming pool, hot tub, library with fireplace, fully equipped art studio, separate video/TV room. Full breakfasts served in a bistro setting, evening wine and cheese.

Day 2 / Morning

BREAKFAST: Scott Courtyard.

Set off on a walking tour of town, a compact grid of tree-shaded streets. The architecture is an eclectic conglomeration of Victorian, art deco, 1950s funky, Craftsman, and Greek and Mission Revival. Get a map and some orientation at the **Sharpsteen Museum,** 1311 Washington (707–942–5911), where an elaborate diorama re-creates the 1800s resort town. Exhibits are lifelike and colorful, and a huge collection of old photos recalls the people who came here more than a hundred years ago to "take the waters." Ben Sharpsteen was one of Walt Disney's original animators and you can see his Oscar in the museum.

Just off the main street on Cedar, the green oasis of **Pioneer Park** on the Napa River has lawns, a gazebo, and a great kids' playground. Next door to the park, **The Elms,** 1300 Cedar (707–942–9476), is a bed-and-breakfast inn in a fanciful French Victorian mansion.

Lee Youngman Galleries, at 1319 Lincoln (707–942–0585), displays large collections of well-known California artists' works.

The **Evans Ceramics Gallery,** at 1421 Lincoln (707–942–0453), sells one-of-a-kind, fine ceramic art. Don't miss **Ca'Toga Galleria d'Arte,** where a noted Venetian artist and muralist showcases his fabulous glazed ceramics, painted furniture, and garden sculpture, which have been *faux* painted to echo ancient Pompeian, Roman, and sixteenth-century Venetian originals. The beautiful building itself and the spectacular ceiling mural inside are worth a special visit (1206 Cedar Street; 707–942–3900).

The work of some of the best artisans in northern and southern California is shown and sold at the **Artful Eye:** jewelry, wine glasses, ceramics, glass, clothing, and more (1333A Lincoln; 707–942–4743).

Zenobia (1410 Lincoln Avenue; 707–942–1050) has everything from Z to A: jewelry, glass art, folk art, clothing, and metal artwork—anything that is colorful and bright. If you are a wine aficionado and want to add to your wine book collection or pick up guidebooks to the Wine Country, stop in at the **Calistoga Bookstore,** 1343 Lincoln (707–942–4123).

LUNCH: Wappo Bar Bistro, 1226B Washington Street, Calistoga; (707) 942–4712. A small cafe with patio tables beside a fountain, serving ethnic-inspired inventions such as Middle Eastern pomegranate-glazed pork, Ecuadorean hornada, Central American duck carnitas, Asian noodle salads, and homemade ice cream. Try to arrive either before or after the traditional mealtimes, or you may wait for a table.

Afternoon

A restored 1868 Southern Pacific train station on Lincoln houses the visitors bureau and the **Calistoga Wine Stop,** 1458 Lincoln Avenue (707–942–5556), where you can choose from more than 1,000 Napa and Sonoma Valley wines and arrange for them to be shipped. **American Indian Trading Company** (1458 Lincoln Avenue; 707–942–9330; www.spiritfeather.com) has artifacts, beadwork, books, jewelry, pottery, sculpture—work representing the Cherokee, Lakota, Sioux, Paiute, Zuni, Hopi, and Navajo.

Spend the rest of the day at one of Calistoga's health resorts being herbal-wrapped, enzyme-bathed, massaged, and soaked in mineral-rich mud; expect to feel like warm Jell-O when it's over.

Calistoga Spa Hot Springs, at 1006 Washington Street (707–942–6269), is one of the largest. You come for the day or stay overnight in spacious motel units equipped for light housekeeping. Float blissfully in three large, naturally heated mineral pools and take advantage of full spa services.

One of the oldest resorts in town, founded in 1865, **Indian Springs Hot Springs Spa and Resort,** at 1712 Lincoln Avenue (707–942–4913), has an old-fashioned air about it, but it offers all the spa treatments that the newer resorts do. Built in 1913 and still restoring the spirits of bathers is the Olympic-size pool filled with mineral water from three natural geysers, heated to 92 degrees in summer and 101 in winter. From a studio cottage to a large house, accommodations are simple and comfortable, including gas fireplaces, soft terry robes, and air-conditioning. Amenities include a clay tennis court, bicycles and bike surreys, croquet, hammocks, and barbecue grills.

The elegant **Lavender Hill Spa** (1015 Foothill Boulevard at Hazel; 707–942–4495) specializes in treatment for couples, offering everything from massage to acupressure, aromatherapy, and "Vibra Sound" in addition to the traditional mud baths.

Not in the mood for mud and massage? Take a hike in **Robert Louis Stevenson State Park,** 7 miles north of Calistoga on Highway 29, or on the **Oat Hill Mine Trail,** a historic landmark that starts at the junction of Lincoln Avenue and the Silverado Trail. Mountain bikers, horseback riders, and hikers like this rocky, rigorous, 5-mile climb to China Camp.

DINNER: **Catahoula Restaurant and Saloon,** in the **Mount View Hotel and Spa** at 1457 Lincoln Avenue, Calistoga; (707) 942–2275. Louisiana-born Jan Birnbaum adds Cajun spice and lots of love to his cooking. Try the rooster gumbo, pecan-crusted catfish, zippy sausages, and poultry and meats smoked in a wood-fired oven. Gooey desserts to die for. Reservations absolutely necessary.

Rooms at the Mount View overlook the town or the palm-shaded courtyard; room decor may be art deco or Victorian. There is a heated outdoor pool, a whirlpool filled with mineral water from the inn's own hot springs, and an upscale spa facility with beauty and health treatments. Ask about the private spa rooms with double-size Jacuzzis (707–942–6877).

LODGING: Scott Courtyard.

Day 3 / Morning

BREAKFAST: Scott Courtyard.

Proceed a few minutes north on the Silverado Trail, north of Calistoga to **Château Montelena** (707–942–5105), at the foot of Mount St. Helena. Secluded in a piney wood, the winery is a spectacular castle built of French limestone brought around the Horn in 1880, enchantingly poised above a small lake surrounded by gardens and weeping willows, with a vineyard view. A Chinese junk floats serenely, and red lacquered gazebos provide private places for conversation and sipping of the renowned estate-grown Cabernets and Reislings, available only here. In 1972 a Château Montelena Chardonnay exploded the myth that French wines are best by winning a blind tasting against France's finest.

Head south on the Silverado Trail and turn right onto Dunaweal Lane to **Clos Pegase** (707–942–4982), a russet-colored, postmodern extravaganza of a winery, the result of an international architectural competition.

Besides wine tasting here, you'll enjoy the vineyard views, sculpture garden, frescoed murals, and a slide show about the history of wine making.

A minute farther on Dunaweal, the sparkling white Moroccan aerie of **Sterling Vineyards** (800–726–6136) floats like an appartition high on a hilltop. For a small fee, a tram will take you on a four-minute gondola ride to a sky-high terrace with valley views. The winery tour is self-guided, and there are outdoor tables up here for picnicking with your own provisions, or you can buy simple deli items on-site.

Back on the Silverado Trail, continue south through the valley to a left onto Meadowood Lane for a stroll on the grounds of the **Meadowood Napa Valley** (707–963–3646), a posh country lodge reminiscent of the 1920s, residing regally on a rise overlooking 250 densely wooded acres, a golf course, and tennis and croquet courts. Meadowood is the home of the annual Napa Valley Wine Auction, a spectacular four-day event attended by deep-pocket bidders and wine lovers from all over the world. The complete health and beauty spa offers fitness and relaxation classes, aromatherapy, reflexology, Swedish massage, salt glow, and facials.

LUNCH: The Grill, on the terrace at Meadowood. Or, for a picnic lunch, take a right onto Zinfandel Lane, crossing over to Highway 29, and head south a few minutes to Oakville, stopping for gourmet goodies at **Oakville Grocery** (707–944–8802), at Oakville Cross Road. Drive two minutes up this road to **La Famiglia di Robert Mondavi,** where you will find an Italian marketplace of gifts, gourmet foods and wines, and a wonderful, viewful picnic deck (1595 Oakville Grade; 707–944–2811; www.lafamigliawines.com).

Or try **V. Sattui Winery,** at 111 White Lane south of St. Helena (707–963–7774), which has a pretty, shady picnic grove on two acres of lawn around a stone-walled 1885 winery. The gourmet deli sells literally hundreds of varieties of cheeses and meats, fresh breads, and juices and drinks. Disadvantages here are the sight of the busy highway and the arrival of tour buses. Don't be concerned if you miss the wine tasting here; there are better choices for wine.

Afternoon

Head south to the Bay Area.

There's More

Biking. Getaway Adventures, 1117 Lincoln Avenue, Calistoga; (707) 942–0332, and 620 East Washington, Petaluma; (800) 499–BIKE or (707) 763–3040; www.getawayadventures.com. Guided biking and hiking day trips and overnights in the Napa Valley, with gourmet picnics and wine tasting. Try the thrilling Downhill Cruise guided bike descent from the top of Mount St. Helena, with stops on the way down for photo ops and catching your breath. It's perfectly safe, even for kids nine years old and older and for toddlers in bike trailers.

Las Posadas Bike and Hike Trail: Drive 6 miles up Deer Park Road to Angwin, go right on Cold Spring Road, and take the left onto Las Posadas Road to the parking area. Cruise on bike or stroll on a leafy trail through dense redwood and oak groves, a cool place to be on a hot day.

Palisades Mountain Sports, 1330B Gerrard Street, behind the fire department; (707) 942–9687. Rentals. Mountain bike specialists, rock climbing equipment.

Spring Mountain Road: Bike on Madrona for 3 blocks, west of Main Street in St. Helena; then turn right on (paved) Spring Mountain for a steep ride up (about an hour) and a thrilling ride down.

Giuseppe's Truck, 865 Silverado Trail North; (707) 942–6295. Almost a century ago, health addicts drove their horse-drawn carriages from San Francisco to Calistoga to drink the waters. Bubbling up out of the ground with intense carbonation and more than sixty-five minerals essential for good health, Calistoga Mineral Water is now one of the premier bottled waters in the world. To commemorate the founding of the water company, and to have some fun, a larger-than-life sculpture of the founder's 1926 truck was erected on the roadside: six tons, 14 feet tall, and 35 feet long— a great photo op.

Lake Berryessa, east of Napa off Highway 128. Lake Berryessa is one of the state's most popular recreation lakes, with 165 miles of hilly, oak-covered shoreline. Year-round fishing for trout and bass, warm water for waterskiing and swimming, complete resort, camping, and water-sports facilities and rentals.

Old Faithful Geyser, 1299 Tubbs Lane, Calistoga; (707) 942–6463. Blows its top every fifteen minutes.

Petrified Forest, 4100 Petrified Forest Road, Calistoga; (707) 942–6667. Six million years ago a volcanic explosion turned redwoods to stone.

Safari West, 3115 Porter Creek Road, Santa Rosa; (707) 579–2551 or (800) 616–2695; www.safariwest.com. Giraffes in Napa? Yes, at the far northern end of the valley on open grasslands and rolling hills in a wildlife preserve with more than 400 exotic animals and birds, and African plains animals, including zebras, elands, endangered antelope, giraffe, impala, and Watusi cattle. Private half-day tours in safari vehicles. A once-in-a-lifetime expedition; advance reservations required. Many animals at Safari West are either members of an endangered species or are already extinct in the wild.

Spas. Calistoga Village Inn and Spa, 1880 Lincoln Avenue, Calistoga 94515; (707) 942–0991; www.greatspa.com. Complete spa facilities in a country setting with vineyard views.

Golden Haven Hot Springs, 1713 Lake Street, Calistoga; (707) 942–6793; www.goldenhaven.com. Complete spa facilities, mineral pool.

Health Spa Napa Valley, 1030 Main Street, St. Helena; (707) 967–8800; www.NapaValleySpa.com. In the town center, a full-service, very pretty day-use beauty and fitness spa offering complete skin and body care, ayurvedic treatments, and massage and couples packages, with a lap pool, whirlpool, steam, and more.

Lincoln Avenue Spa, 1339 Lincoln Avenue, Calistoga; (707) 942–5296; www.lincolnavenuespa.com. Mud baths, body and beauty treatments, pools.

Roman Spa, 1300 Washington Street, Calistoga; (707) 942–4441; www. romanspahotsprings.com. Mineral pools, beauty treatments, mud baths, enzyme baths, saunas, rooms around a tropical garden.

White Sulphur Springs Resort and Spa, 3100 White Sulphur Springs Road, St. Helena; (707) 963–8588; www.whitesulphursprings.com. The oldest hot springs resort in the state, in a wooded canyon with hiking trails, with a warm, outdoor sulfur soaking pool; a nice swimming pool; museum; hammocks; and barbecues. Creekside cottages and inn rooms have simple decor; complimentary continental breakfast. There is a full-service spa with beauty and health treatments; spa guests are welcome to enjoy the facilities along with inn guests.

Special Events

September. Hometown Harvest Festival, Oak Street, St. Helena; (707) 963–4456. Dancing, parade, arts and crafts, music, food, wine.

October. Old Mill Days, Bale Grist Mill State Park; (707) 963–2236. Costumed docents grind grain and corn on the millstones and make bread; demonstrations of traditional trades and crafts, games, entertainment.

Calistoga Beer, Sausage and Chili Fest; (707) 942–6333. More than 50 microbreweries participate. Music and tastings; www.calistogafun.com.

Other Recommended Restaurants and Lodgings

Calistoga

Cafe Pacifico, 1237 Lincoln Avenue; (707) 942–4400. A Mexican motif is the backdrop for incredible breakfasts, lunches, and dinners. Try the blue-corn buttermilk pancakes and chili rellenos.

Calistoga Inn, 1250 Lincoln Avenue; (707) 942–4101. In a charming circa-1880 building with a splendid outdoor dining terrace on the Napa River. Breakfast, lunch, and dinner. Hearty country fare: chili, burgers, *huevos rancheros,* crab cakes, fresh fish, and award-winning homebrewed beers and ales. Also eighteen comfortable rooms.

Carlin Country Cottages, 1623 Lake Street; (707) 942–9102. Nice, simple cottages in a wide courtyard, with Shaker-style furnishings. Some have Jacuzzi tubs; some have one or two separate bedrooms. Spring-fed swimming pool.

Cottage Grove Inn, 1711 Lincoln Avenue; (707) 942–8400 or (800) 799–2284. One of the most commodious, private, and romantic of Wine Country accommodations; separate cottages with luxurious furnishings, fireplaces, deep whirlpool tubs, front porches with wicker rockers, and perfectly wonderful breakfasts, all within a short stroll of town.

Garnet Creek Inn, 1139 Lincoln Avenue; (707) 942–9797; www.garnet creekinn.com. Five charming rooms, one with a lift to a handicap room. Large country-style wraparound porch.

Silver Rose Inn, 351 Rosedale Road; (707) 942–9581 or (800) 995–9381; www.silverrose.com. Large, very comfortable rooms with valley views, some with fireplaces, whirlpool tubs, and private balconies. Particularly attractive are the lofty public rooms, where sumptuous breakfasts are served and guests linger to chat and read. Rose gardens, tennis courts, pitching and putting greens, and a swimming pool terrace complete the amenities. Beauty treatments and massage are available at the spa facility or in your room.

St. Helena

Adagio Inn, 1417 Kearney Street; (707) 963–2238 or (888) 8ADAGIO; www.adagioinn.com. On a quiet street just off the main drag, a charming, small, Victorian bed-and-breakfast inn. A full breakfast is served on the shady veranda or before the fireplace in the dining–common room. Private baths, robes, down comforters, refrigerators, and more amenities.

Cantinetta Tra Vigne (at Tra Vigne); (707) 963–8888. Cozily residing in a nineteenth-century sherry distillery, an Italian deli, market, and wine bar. Fresh pizzettas, salads, sandwiches, sweets, house-brand oils and vinegars. Eat here or take out.

Dean and DeLuca, 601 Highway 29; (707) 967–9980. Huge gourmet market, wine shop, produce mart, and deli, a welcome new offshoot of the famous New York store. Incredible variety of cheeses and meats, rotisserie chicken, and wonderful salads and entrees to go, plus packaged foodstuffs of all kinds, from fig balsamic vinegar to olive oil pressed in the most obscure orchard in Tuscany. Enjoy sandwiches, fresh-fruit smoothies, and espresso drinks in the back on the sunny patio. Expensive and worth it.

El Bonita, 195 Main Street; (707) 963–3216 or (800) 541–3284. Hidden behind the original 1930s art deco motel are new two-story motel units with private balconies looking into the trees and over the gardens. Large, two-room suites have microkitchens. Small pool, sauna; reasonable rates.

Harvest Inn, 1 Main Street, just south of town; (707) 963–9463; www. coastal hotel.com. Antiques, four-posters, elaborate furnishings in luxury rooms and suites surrounded by acres of lush English gardens, a labyrinth of shady pathways, lawns, and bowers. Private balconies, fireplaces, two pools. Expanded continental breakfast.

Inn at Southbridge, 1020 Main Street; (800) 520–6800. New and quite lovely, a small inn with spacious, luxurious rooms with fireplaces, sitting areas, private balconies with vineyard views, down comforters, and more amenities. Guests have access to the top-notch spa and sports facilities at Meadowood Napa Valley. Listed in *Small Luxury Hotels of the World*.

Pinot Blanc, 641 Main Street; (707) 963–6191. Exotic French and California cuisine prepared by one of the country's young star chefs in a luxe country bistro, with a smashing wine list.

Terra, 1345 Railroad Avenue; (707) 963–8931. In a historic stone building, warm and romantic; exotic California cuisine with French and Japanese accents, miraculous wine list. Chef Hiro Sone made a name for himself at Spago in Los Angeles.

Tomatina, 1016 Main Street; (707) 967–9999. Yummy brick-oven pizza and pasta are served at long wooden tables and to go. And more: polenta, *piadines* (a pee-uh-dee-nee is a salad-sandwich-pizza), and amazing desserts. Look for the big tomato out front.

Tra Vigne, 1050 Charter Oak Avenue at Highway 29; (707) 963–4444. At stone-topped tables under the trees and umbrellas, keep your eyes peeled for movie stars and winery owners. It's easy to imagine you are at a villa in the Italian countryside. The terra-cotta–toned stone walls are rampant with vines, and a glimpse through iron-framed windows discloses a vibrantly painted, high-ceilinged bar and restaurant. A rich balsamic vinegar game sauce blankets roasted polenta; house-cured prosciutto melts in your mouth. Exciting varieties of homemade ravioli, roasted poultry rubbed with exotic spices, and more.

For More Information

Bed and Breakfast Inns of the Napa Valley; (707) 944–4444.

Calistoga Chamber of Commerce, Old Depot, 1458 Lincoln Avenue, Calistoga, CA 94515; (707) 942–6333; www.calistogafun.com.

St. Helena Chamber of Commerce, 1080 Main Street, St. Helena, CA 94574; (707) 963–4456; www.sthelena.com.

The Redwood Route 5

Seacoast Towns, Path of the Giants

2 Nights

On your drive up Highway 101 to the seaside logging town of Eureka, stop along the way to see the redwoods and play on the Eel River. California's coastal redwoods are the world's tallest living things. Walking beneath a 300-foot forest canopy among these silent giants from the age of the dinosaurs is an unforgettable experience.

Eureka and smaller coastal towns look much as they did in their Victorian heyday—streets lined with gracious old homes and elaborate gingerbread-trimmed hotels. Settled during the California gold rush in the mid-1800s, the county's founding coincided with the birth of Victorian architecture, and in every town are glorious examples of the era.

From partaking of bed-and-breakfast inns, fresh seafood, logging and Indian history, wildlife sanctuaries, and sea air to fishing for the mighty salmon, biking on forest paths, and going river rafting or beachcombing, you'll find more than a weekend's worth of enticements here. In addition, Humboldt County is home to nearly 8,000 artists—more artists per capita than any other county in California. Recently named the "Number One Best Small Art Town in America," Eureka is a uniquely creative community, as demonstrated in many art-, music- and culture-related events, festivals, and galleries. Take note of the flamboyant murals around town; ask for a mural walk map at the chamber of commerce.

- ☐ Logging towns
- ☐ Rivers and seacoast
- ☐ Victorian village
- ☐ Ancient redwoods
- ☐ Seafood cafes
- ☐ California history

Expect foggy mornings, even in summer, and winter rains December through March. These tremendous northern woods are true rain forests, thriving on drizzle and damp. But don't let drippy weather keep you at

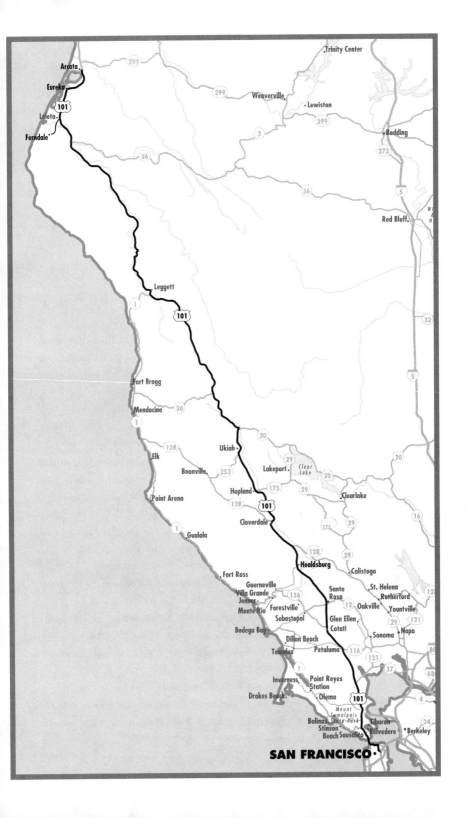

home. Fishing is best from October through March, and Eureka is misty and romantic then, too.

Day 1 / Morning

Begin the 280-mile trip at the Golden Gate Bridge, going north on Highway 101 for 80 miles to **Healdsburg.** Take the Central Healdsburg exit and go 2 blocks north to the plaza, the palm-shaded heart of the wine regions of the Alexander and Dry Creek Valleys.

BREAKFAST: Costeaux French Bakery and Cafe, a block from the plaza at 417 Healdsburg Avenue, Healdsburg; (707) 433–1913. Award-winning breads and pastries, scrumptious sandwiches, and picnic items to stay or go.

Back on 101, head north. Between Cloverdale and Leggett you'll share the road with logging trucks as the highway winds along the rugged, forested spine of the Coast Range. Above Leggett, watch for the **Redwood Tree House,** a fun tourist trap with a good collection of guidebooks and maps. The vestibule is formed from the burned-out shell of a giant sequoia; the tree, however, is still alive and thriving.

Twenty-three miles north of Leggett, the **Benbow Inn,** built in 1925, is a Tudor-style monolith overlooking a twenty-six-acre summer lake (445 Lake Benbow Drive, Garberville; 707–923–2124). You can stay at the historic inn in antiques-filled rooms, some with fireplaces, and have afternoon tea and scones in the parlor; the excellent restaurant overlooks the lake, and there is a nine-hole golf course across the road. Here you can fish and rent a canoe; for a refreshing side trip, go with the park rangers (707–946–2263) on a one-hour interpretive canoe tour to absorb some natural history and see osprey, turtles, herons, and belted kingfishers in the springtime.

Now on to the **Avenue of the Giants,** a world-famous, 33-mile scenic drive, a highlight of your visit to Redwood Country. The avenue bypasses the highway, and its many attractions are well marked; turnouts and parking areas access short loop trails into the forest. Some 51,222 acres of spectacular redwood groves along the Eel and its south fork are contained here in **Humboldt Redwoods State Park** (707–946–2263). These are the biggest of the 2,000-year-old beauties remaining in a 30-mile-wide belt of coastal redwoods stretching from Monterey to Oregon.

Pick up picnic goodies at one of the small groceries along the first few miles of the avenue; then begin your tour at the **Humboldt Redwoods Visitors Center** (707–946–2263), about 4 miles from the south end of the avenue. Here you'll get oriented by a movie, exhibits, and trail maps. Ask for advice on the lengths and types of walks and drives you'd like to take in the park. Docents will show you a special binder of trail maps, pointing out new trails and those that may be closed due to weather or maintenance.

Not to be missed is the **Rockefeller Forest** in the **Big Trees** area, a 5-mile drive in on Mattole/Honeydew Road. Tiptoeing along boardwalks and spongy pathways in the damp, cool stillness at the foot of these magical giants, you'll hear only the bustle of chipmunks. Under a fragrant green canopy hundreds of feet above your head, the shade on the forest floor is deep, even on a hot summer's day. Wildflowers—trillium, wild iris, and redwood orchid—spring from a carpet of moss and fern, while brilliant blue Steller's jays flash through the branches overhead. A spooky rush of air signals the flight of a black raven; the shiny and silent 2-foot-long ravens are aggressive guardians of their thousand-year-old forest. A short trail leads to a sandy riverbank, for sunbathing, wading, picnicking, and fishing.

LUNCH: Have your picnic here or at Bull Creek Flats.

Afternoon

Returning toward the highway on the Mattole/Honeydew Road, watch for the sign to **Bull Creek Flats,** a sunny pebbled beach and picnic area at a lovely bend in the river; wild lilacs bloom here in great purple clouds in spring. In the rainy season the river runs with salmon and steelhead. Summer fishing—carp and eels—is for fun, not for food.

One hundred miles of trails in Humboldt Redwoods State Park are maintained for walkers, backpackers, bikers, and horseback riders. Meanderings will turn up old homesteaders' cabins and a plethora of campgrounds. Apple blossoms bloom in orchards planted by early settlers. In the fall big-leaf maples, alders, and buckeyes turn red and gold. In the farthest outback are bobcats, black-tailed deer, foxes, ring-tailed cats, and even black bears.

Reaching Eureka by day's end, you'll be warmly welcomed in the lobby of the Hotel Carter, with wine and hors d'oeuvres before the fireplace.

DINNER: Restaurant 301, Hotel Carter, 301 L Street, Eureka; (707) 444–8062 or (800) 404–1390. *Bon Appetit* and other magazines rave about the cuisine and the wine list. At your table beside sky-high windows overlooking Old Town, try fresh Humboldt Bay oysters with teriyaki/wasabi crème fraîche, sesame-seared salmon, portabello chevre lasagna, or other perfectly fresh seafood, local poultry, and game dishes; seasonal produce is featured, including the vast array of veggies from the kitchen gardens. Special dinners with top wine makers are popular occasions booked well in advance. The wine list was chosen by *Wine Spectator* as one of the world's best; oenophiles make pilgrimages here to taste the rare vintages. In spite of it all, the atmosphere is comfortable, welcoming, and understated.

LODGING: Carter House Victorians, 301 L Street, Eureka; (707) 445–1390 or (800) 404–1390; www.carterhouse.com. A stunning four-building complex in Old Town: a magnificent replica of a San Francisco Victorian, the Bell Cottage, and the Hotel Carter, each housing plush, ultracomfortable accommodations. Marble fireplaces, whirlpool tubs, four-poster beds, cushy armchairs and couches, spacious parlors, and even some common kitchens. No lacy kitsch here, just understated elegance and top personal service, enjoyed by such notables as Steven Spielberg and Rene Russo and their families. Named the "Best B&B/Small Hotel in Northern California" and "the find of the year," the restaurant and the lodgings here are exceptional in their ambience and comfort.

Day 2 / Morning

BREAKFAST: A sumptuous breakfast at the Hotel Carter. Take time to browse the kitchen gardens, one of the most extensive at any inn on the West Coast; guests are often invited to join in the daily harvest.

With an architectural/scenic walking-tour map, start the day with an exploration of the surrounding Victorian neighborhood, between C and M Streets and about 5 or 6 blocks south of Second Street, ending up under the gaslights in Old Town. For a short waterfront stroll, park at the Carson Mansion on the north end of town, enjoy glimpses of the mansion gardens, then walk a block south on Second Street and turn right into the Adorni Center parking lot. A paved path extends in both directions along the waterfront, for beautiful views of the bay and the boats. On the waterfront, home port to more than 500 fishing boats, are several blocks of 1850–1904 Queen Anne, Eastlake, and Classic Revival buildings. The Victoriana is enhanced by parks, fountains, playgrounds, and shaded benches for resting between shopping, photo snapping, and museum discoveries along the brand-new Eureka Boardwalk, extending four blocks along the bay from G to C Streets.

Not to be missed are the nautical art and artifacts, collectibles, and unique gifts at **Many Hands Gallery,** 438 Second Street; (707) 445–0455. The **Humboldt Bay Maritime Museum** displays nautical relics, old navigation equipment, an early radar unit, a lighthouse lens, and fragments of wrecked ships; admission is free (122 First Street; 707–444–9440). The **Clarke Memorial Museum,** at Third and E Streets (707–443–1947), a 1920s Italian Renaissance–style former bank with a glazed terracotta exterior, houses an extraordinary collection of Indian basketry, antique weapons, maritime artifacts and photos, furniture, and memorabilia of early Humboldt days. **Humboldt's Finest** displays fine art glass, sleek woodwork and furnishings, and a variety of other locally produced home accessories and gifts; not craftsy or cute, simply elegant (405 Second Street; 707–443–1258). The **William Carson Mansion,** at Second and M Streets, said to be the most photographed home in America, is a wedding cake of an Italianate/Queen Anne mansion built in the 1880s by a lumber baron; it's a private club, and the interior is off-limits to the public.

LUNCH: Cafe Waterfront Oyster Bar and Grill, 102 F Street at First, Eureka; (707) 443–9190. On the waterfront with a water view, fresh seafood for breakfast, lunch, and dinner. Fish burgers, clam and oyster specialties, lively bar, casual Victorian decor. Or, for a picnic lunch, go to **Sequoia Park,** Glatt and W Streets, in fifty-two acres of virgin redwoods with a zoo, a kids' playground, formal gardens, walking paths, and a duck pond.

Afternoon

From June through September, a seventy-five-minute cruise of the bay, departing from the foot of L Street, can be had on the **MV** *Madaket* (707–444–9440), a wooden steamer built in the 1920s. You'll get a narrated tour of historical and natural sights around the bay, passing oyster farms, aquatic birds, and the third largest colony of harbor seals in the West. If it's a clear, mild day, try the cocktail cruise, leaving at 4:00 P.M. Another choice for touring the bay is at **Hum Boats,** at Woodley Island Marina, where on weekends you can rent kayaks and sailboats or get a water ride (707–443–5157).

One of the magical places in Eureka is the **Blue Ox Millworks and Historic Park** (800–248–4259; www.blueoxmill.com), an old mill at the foot of X Street, 3 blocks north of Fourth. This is a museumlike job shop and sawmill that makes custom trim for Victorian buildings, using the same machines that were used to create the originals. Take a self-guided tour on catwalks above the workers or call ahead for a guided tour. A loggers' camp, a blacksmith shop, a gift shop, a bird sanctuary, and other attractions make this a worthy stop.

The William Carson Mansion, Old Town Eureka.

DINNER: Sea Grill, 316 E Street, Eureka; (707) 443–7187. Voted "Best Seafood Restaurant" in the county for several years. Sea Grill is a noisy, popular place. Come early to avoid the crowds and enjoy choosing from a huge seafood menu; great salad bar, steaks, and luscious desserts, too. Reservations are usually necessary; lunch and dinner.

LODGING: Carter House Victorians.

Day 3 / Morning

BREAKFAST: The **Samoa Cookhouse,** on the Samoa Peninsula, Eureka; (707) 442–1659. Reached by the Highway 255 bridge on the north edge of Old Town, this is the last surviving lumber camp cookhouse in the West. At long oilcloth-covered tables with charmingly mismatched chairs, giant American breakfasts are served from 6:00 A.M., including biscuits with sausage gravy, platters of pancakes, and scrambled eggs. Lunch and dinner are served family-style: huge loaves of bread, cauldrons of soup, big bowls of salad and vegetables, baked ham, and roast beef are followed by wedges of homemade pie. Prices are quite reasonable, and kids four and younger eat free.

Even if you don't eat here, stop in to see the delightful museum of logging equipment, artifacts, and fantastic photos of early days. A short walk from behind the cookhouse is a quiet bayside village and a nice playground. From here you can walk or bike along the edge of Humboldt Bay for 6 miles north to Arcata. Bird life is extraordinary, from marbled godwits to curlews, dowitchers, falcons, and many more.

From the Samoa Cookhouse, drive scenic Highway 255 north fifteen minutes around Humboldt Bay to **Arcata,** home of Humboldt State University. This is another old logging town with unique attractions, such as the **Historic Logging Trail** in Arcata's 600-acre **Community Forest,** Fourteenth Street and Union (707–822–7091). On foot, take Nature Trail #1 on the west side of the parking lot and follow signs and a map to see logging sites and equipment from a century ago.

Arcata Marsh and Wildlife Sanctuary, 600 South G Street in Arcata (707–826–2359), is a bird-watcher's mecca. Spend a couple of hours here on 4.5 miles of quiet footpaths in a stunning bayside setting, with freshwater ponds, a salt marsh, tidal mudflats, and winding water channels alive with birds and ducks. This is also a good place to jog or have a picnic; leashed dogs are allowed. You would never guess this is a wastewater reclamation project and, in fact, a model for the nation. Stop at the interpretive center here for maps and information about birding walks throughout the region, and ask about guided walks at the marsh. In April, the annual spring migration bird festival, called Godwit Days, is a big event, bringing birders from across the country (800–908–WING). For daily bird sightings call (707) 822–LOON.

Another area for good walking and biking is **Arcata Bottoms,** just west of town, bordered by Humboldt Bay and Lamphere-Christensen Dunes Preserve.

In this town committed to sustainable environmental practices, an interesting manufacturer puts on a show. From recycled glass bottles, **Fire and Light** produces a successful line of tabletop accessories and dinnerware (1499B Tenth Street; 707–825–7500 or 800–844–2223). Call ahead for a tour to see the spectacular operation of transforming, by hand, 4,200-degree molten glass into luminous, jewel-colored dinnerware. From bins of broken jars and bottles to the beautiful end products, it's a fascinating process. For information on the White House Task Force on recycling, where Fire and Light is one of the featured companies, go to www.ofee. gov. Look for the dinnerware at **Pacific Flavors** shop in Eureka (516 Second Street; 707–442–2900).

At the **HSU Natural History Museum and Store** are million-year-old fossils, live tidepools and native animals, and exhibits about the natural history of the region (1315 G Street; 707–826–4479). If you visit Trinidad north of here, stop in at the Humboldt State University Marine Lab and Aquarium (570 Ewing Street, Trinidad).

Twenty-two miles north of Arcata and stretching for more than 40 miles, **Redwood National Park** is a World Heritage Site encompassing three state parks: **Prairie Creek Redwoods, Del Norte Coast Redwoods,** and **Jedediah Smith Redwoods.** The National Park Visitors Center (707–464–6101) is between the park entrance and the town of Orick. You will need to get a (free) permit to drive the steep, 17-mile road to Tall Trees Grove, where a 3-mile round-trip walking trail leads to the world's first-, third-, and fifth-tallest redwoods. There are more than 300 developed campsites in the park, shoreline trails, and swimming beaches in the Smith River and Redwood Creek.

For an afternoon of antiquing and a walk in the country, drive 22 miles south of Eureka and take the Ferndale exit, driving 5 miles west across the Eel through flat, green dairylands to **Ferndale.** Just two long streets of glorious Victorian buildings, the entire tiny town is a State Historic Landmark. Art galleries, antiques shops, ice cream parlors, and cafes abound. The **Gingerbread Mansion,** at 400 Berding Street (707–786–4000; www.gingerbreadmansion.com), is one of the premier Victorian masterpieces on the West Coast. Dressed in bright yellow and peach with cascades of lacy white trim and surrounded by whimsical formal gardens, the gigantic hundred-year-old beauty is ½ block long. Nine elaborately decorated rooms have claw-foot tubs (one room has two tubs, toe to toe), and the mansion has four parlors.

It will take a couple of hours to stroll Main Street, take pictures of the old buildings, and browse in the shops. (On the way into town, watch for a large, light green building with striped awnings and a red door: the **Fernbridge Antiques Mall,** a veritable bazaar of forty dealers selling everything from estate jewelry to Victorian furniture, at 597 Fernbridge Drive; 707–725–8820.)

At **Golden Gait Mercantile** (421 Main Street; 707–786–4891), time is suspended in the 1850s with barrels of penny candy, big-wheeled coffee grinders, and glass cases lined with old-fashioned restoratives and hair pomades. Step into the **Blacksmith Shop** to see the largest collection of modern-day iron accessories in the West, including fanciful chandeliers, lamps, and furnishings (445 Main Street; 707–786–4216).

Take a peek at the **Ferndale Museum** to see a small but mighty exhibit of the history and the agriculture of the "Cream City," with complete room settings, an operating seismograph, and a blacksmith shop (Shaw and Third Streets across from Main; 707–786–4466).

At the **Kinetic Sculpture Museum** are strange, handmade, people-powered machines that travel over land, mud, and water (393 Main Street; 707–786–9259). These were driven in the World Championship Great Arcata to Ferndale Cross-County Kinetic Sculpture Race, which is held annually in May. Called the "triathlon of the art world," the three-day event is great fun to watch, as the fantastical contrivances are driven, dragged, and floated over roads, sand dunes, Humboldt Bay, and the Eel River. Among the machines in past races were "Nightmare of the Iguana" and "Tyrannosaurus Rust," which was powered by cavemen.

Ferndale sparkles all over and decorates to the max at Christmastime. The lighting of the tallest living Christmas tree in America, a parade, a Dickens Festival, and concerts are among the blizzard of holiday activities.

LUNCH: Curley's Grill, 460 Main Street in the Victorian Inn, Ferndale; (707) 786–9696. California cuisine, homemade soup and foccacia, local fresh fish, grilled sandwiches, and more, indoors in an old-fashioned dining room or on the patio; lunch and dinner.

Afternoon

On the south end of Main, go left onto Ocean Street to **Russ Park** to stretch your legs in a 110-acre closed-canopy spruce and redwood forest with more than 3 miles of wildflower trails.

On the edge of the Eel River Delta, a resting point on the Pacific Flyway, Ferndale is within minutes of great bird-watching and some nice walks. Running 5 miles west out of town, Centerville Road leads to the beach, where a wide variety of bird life and animals can be seen on walks north and south—swans, geese, sandpipers, pelicans, and cormorants, as well as seals and whales.

On the east side of town are country lanes leading to the Eel River Estuary, great routes for walking and biking, and you can launch canoes and kayaks here in quiet waters or take a guided boat tour of the estuary (Camp Weoh Guide Service; 707–786–4187). Loons, cormorants, harriers, egrets, and more than 150 feathered species live in or pass through these wetlands. Where the Eel meets the sea, watch for sea lions, seals, and river otters.

Head back to the Bay Area, stopping along the way to walk again under the great redwoods.

There's More

Humboldt Bay National Wildlife Refuge, 1020 Ranch Road, Loleta, just south of Eureka; (707) 733–5406. Take the Hookton Road exit from Highway 101 and drive 1.2 miles to the Hookton Slough trailhead, a 1.5-mile path along the south edge of Humboldt Bay. Thousands of birds and ducks migrate through these beautiful grasslands, freshwater marshes, and mudflats, including 25,000 black brants that fly from their nesting grounds in the Arctic to Baja. Look for herons, owls, ospreys, mallards, egrets, terns, and more. Rest rooms.

King Range National Conservation Area. Maps and information at BLM headquarters, 1695 Heindon Road, off Janes Road in Arcata; (707) 825–2300. Rugged and largely inaccessible, the "Lost Coast" between Mattole Point and Shelter Cove is 24 miles of shoreline, mountain streams, trails, and forests for camping, hiking, and fishing, with five campgrounds. Two-lane Mattole Road is a corkscrew called "Wild Cat" that winds through spectacular mountainous countryside. The easiest route in is from Redway to Shelter Cove, where you can wander on a black sand beach, have lunch in a cafe, camp in your RV or tent, and fish off the shore.

Loleta Bottoms. For an easy walk or bike ride on quiet, coastside roads, drive or bike from Loleta (just south of Eureka) west on Cannibal Island Road to Crab Park, at the mouth of an arm of the Eel River. You can scramble around the edge of the estuary and walk back east on the quiet road, watching for plovers, tundra swans, and curlews. Go right on Cock Robin Island Road, where mudflats attract masses of shorebirds. Continue back to your car or on toward Loleta, where the Loleta Cheese Factory (800–995–0453) is a good place to stop for sandwiches, snacks, and cheese tasting (fabulous organic cheese). There is a network of two-lane roads in this area, between the highway and the ocean.

Morris Graves Museum of Art, 636 F Street, Eureka; (707) 442–0278. Newly renovated and spectacular, a stunning library building donated to the town by Andrew Carnegie early in the twentieth century is now an exceptional art museum showing a wide variety of works in seven galleries. Call ahead for information on musical and theatrical performances held here.

Prairie Creek Redwoods, 50 miles north of Eureka on Highway 101, a World Heritage Site; (707) 488–2171. Twelve thousand acres of magnificent coastal redwoods, mountain biking and hiking trails, Roosevelt elk, museum, beaches, campgrounds, Fern Canyon.

Richardson's Grove State Park, 8 miles south of Garberville on Highway 101; (707) 247–3318. Walk or bike on 10 miles of trails to see old-growth redwoods along the south fork of the Eel River. Swim, fish, picnic, and camp; three leafy, pretty campgrounds are near the river.

SkyTrail Gondola at Trees of Mystery, 15500 Highway 101 North, Klamath; (707) 482–2251 or (800) 638–3389; www.treesofmystery.net. For a bird's eye view of some of the world's oldest and tallest coastal redwoods, ride the only six-passenger forest gondola on the continent to an elevation of nearly 750 feet. You disembark at SkyTrail Summit for breathtaking mountain, forest, and ocean views.

Tours. Aurora River Adventures, P.O. Box 938, Willow Creek 95573; (530) 629–3843; www.rafting4fun.com. Day trips on the wild and scenic Klamath River.

Pride Enterprises Tours; (800) 400–1849. Guided tours of redwoods and Victorian homes by local historian Ray Hillman.

Special Events

April. Redwood Coast Dixieland Jazz Festival, Eureka; (707) 445-3378; www.redwoodjazz.org. Put on your zoot suit and kick up your heels to big band, Dixieland, zydeco, and swing music from some of the top bands in the country; all over town and on the waterfront. Arrive a day early for the Taste of Main Street, when twenty area restaurants show off their specialties.

Rhododendron Festival, Eureka; (707) 442–3738. Home and garden tours, parade, and more.

Dolbeer Steam Donkey Days, Fort Humboldt State Historic Park; (707) 445–6567. Logging competition; operation of steam donkeys, locomotives, and equipment; rides.

May. Bebop and Brew, Arcata; (707) 826–6059. Big-name jazz and twenty-five microbrew varieties; food, too.

June. Arcata Bay Oyster Festival, Arcata; (707) 822–4500. Oysters and other foods prepared by more than twenty local chefs; live entertainment.

Scandinavian Festival and Barbecue, Main Street, Ferndale; (707) 444–8444. Dancing, food, a parade, and festivities for descendants of Scandinavian lineage and for visitors; food, music, and fun.

August. Humboldt County Fair and Horse Races; (707) 786–9511.

September. Bigfoot Days, Willow Creek; (530) 629–2693. Celebration of the Bigfoot legend with a parade, barbecue, music, vendors, and more.

Festival on the Bay, Eureka; (707) 443–7252. Boat tours, carriage rides, arts and crafts, food, music, and live entertainment.

November. Humboldt County's Coastal Christmas celebrations begin, two months of festivites; (800) 346–3482.

December. Truckers' Parade, downtown Eureka; (707) 443–9747. Some 150 big rigs decorated in Christmas lights; logger-style floats. You've never seen anything like this parade.

Other Recommended Restaurants and Lodgings

Arcata

Abruzzi's, in historic Jacoby's Storehouse on the town plaza, 780 Seventh Street; (707) 826–2345. Homemade pasta and Italian specialties in an upscale atmosphere; make reservations for lunch and dinner. Stained-glass glows, and brick and old beams create ambience in this lovely, upscale restaurant in a circa-1850 building. Contemporary and traditional Italian specialties, housemade pasta and veal dishes, plus steak and wonderful fresh fish; try the sweet potato crab cakes and the blackened salmon.

Larrupin Cafe, 1658 Patrick's Point Drive, 2 miles north of Trinidad; (707) 677–0230. In a two-story yellow house in the country is an art-filled space with masses of fresh flowers and a fireplace, California cuisine and seafood, barbecued oysters, Cajun ribs; dinner only.

Plaza Grill, 780 Seventh Street in Jacoby's Storehouse; (707) 826–0860; www.abruzzicatering.com. A casual cafe with a fireplace and town views. Terrific burgers, sandwiches, and fish platters; lunch and dinner.

Wildflower Cafe and Bakery, 1604 G Street; (707) 822–0360. Yummy muffins and pastries, homemade soup, Mexican and Chinese food, hearty daily specials like quiche and stroganoff; breakfast, lunch, and dinner.

Eureka

Campton House, 305 M Street; (707) 443–1601 or (800) 772–1622. A charming Craftsman-style cottage with three spacious, comfortable bedrooms; two baths; parlor; dining room; and a kitchen—perfect for a big family or a family reunion. You can also book just one room. Across the street from the Carson Mansion and within walking distance of all the sights and restaurants in town. A plain continental breakfast and afternoon tea are included, as are use of the pool and sauna at the adjacent motel.

Cornelius Daly Inn, 1125 H Street; (707) 445–3638 or (800) 321–9656. A beautiful bed-and-breakfast mansion built in 1905, with elegant antiques; three rooms, one with fireplace; and two suites, each very private and very pretty. Full breakfast.

Elegant Victorian Mansion, 1406 C Street; (707) 444–3144. Perhaps the finest of Eureka's great treasure trove of Victorian bed-and-breakfast inns, built in 1888, it's an extravagantly antiques-filled Queen Anne surrounded by a garden of 150 antique roses; there are four large, comfortable rooms, plus croquet, vintage movies, fireplace chats, and a library of guidebooks.

Eureka Inn, 518 Seventh Street; (707) 442–6441 or (800) 862–4906; www. eurekainncom. A fabulous English Tudor–style, half-timbered hotel built in the 1920s. In the lobby before the huge fireplace, guests loll in cushy leather couches and armchairs during the week and dance their socks off when swing bands play on the weekends. Red leather booths are cozy in the Rib Room dinner house; the Bristol Rose casual cafe and a poolside dining area serve exceptional California cuisine, American comfort food, and plenty of fresh seafood; the extensive wine list, featuring some of the best California and European wines, gets top marks from serious wine buffs. A lively pub and a cocktail lounge are popular gathering spots. Christmastime is festive, when a towering, glittering tree is the backdrop for nightly live entertainment. Rooms are spacious, with traditional decor.

Lost Coast Brewery, 617 Fourth Street; (707) 445–4480. At this friendly microbrew pub, try some AlleyCat amber ale or a rugged glass of Downtown Brown; hearty pub food at lunch and dinner. Owned by a woman who was one of the first females to found a microbrewery in the United States.

Red Lion Inn, 1929 Fourth Street; (707) 445–0844 or (800) 547–8010; www.redlion.com. One hundred seventy-five nice motel rooms in town, plus pool, restaurant, and bar.

Hopland

Fetzer Vineyards Bed & Breakfast, 13601 Eastside Road; (707) 744–7600 ext. 604 or (800) 846–8637 ext. 604; www.fetzer.com. Fetzer's is just ¾ mile east of Hopland on Highway 175. The Tasting Room & Visitors Center is open daily 9:00 A.M. to 5:00 P.M., and features Five Rivers Ranch Cabernet Sauvignon from California's central coast. Overnight guests can choose a suite in the Carriage House with an oversized whirlpool bath, one of the grand bedrooms in the Haas House, or a more private experience in the Valley Oaks cottage. Complimentary breakfast.

Loleta

Southport Landing, 444 Phelan Road; (707) 733–5915; www.northcoast. com/southport. Once a haven for ship captains, Southport Landing is a historic landmark beside the Humboldt Bay National Wildlife Refuge in a quiet, idyllic country setting. Seven charming, smallish bedrooms with garden and water views, bikes to borrow for exploring the surrounding countryside, kayaks to borrow for paddling the bay, a pool table, Ping-Pong, games, and a library; sumptuous breakfast.

For More Information

Arcata Chamber of Commerce, 1635 Heindon Road, Arcata, CA 95521; (707) 822–3619; www.arcata.com/chamber.

Eureka Chamber of Commerce, 2112 Broadway, Eureka, CA 95501; (800) 356–6381; www.eurekachamber.com. Visitors center has an extensive display of local information.

Humboldt County Convention and Visitors Bureau, 1034 Second Street, Eureka, CA 95501; (800) 346–3482; www.redwoodvisitor.org. Call for a copy of *Destination Redwood Coast,* an excellent guide to the area.

Victorian Village of Ferndale, 248 Francis Street, Ferndale, CA 95536; (707) 786–4477; www.victorianferndale.org/chamber.

Bodega Bay 6

A Weekend at the Coast

1 Night

From the Gravenstein Apple Capital of Sebastopol through Sonoma County's rolling pastures to the major fishing port of Bodega Bay, there is much to fill a weekend. Some of the warmest and most beautiful of the northern California beaches are found near Bodega Bay, where sea lions, boats, sailboarders, and thousands of birds share a harbor. Some of the best weather days are in October, November, and December, when other places in the Bay Area are chilly. Dense fog occurs only about twenty days annually. On the way to the wild Sonoma County beaches and the lively harbor town, relaxing meanders on country roads are enlivened with frequent stops for antiques and art-gallery browsing, sight-seeing, and coastal contemplation in cafes.

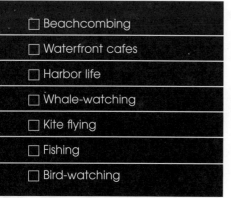

- ☐ Beachcombing
- ☐ Waterfront cafes
- ☐ Harbor life
- ☐ Whale-watching
- ☐ Kite flying
- ☐ Fishing
- ☐ Bird-watching

Day 1 / Morning

Drive north from the Golden Gate on Highway 101 for forty-five minutes to Cotati, turning west onto Highway 116 to Sebastopol. You'll pass more than a dozen antiques shops on the way into town; stop if you dare at the **Antique Society,** 2661 Gravenstein Highway South (707–829–1733), the county's largest antiques collective. **Sebastopol Antiques Mall,** at 755 Petaluma Avenue (707–823–1936), has rooms of goodies.

BREAKFAST: East West Cafe, 128 North Main, Sebastopol; (707) 829–2822. Simply the best local produce in inventive breakfasts; vegetarian specialties.

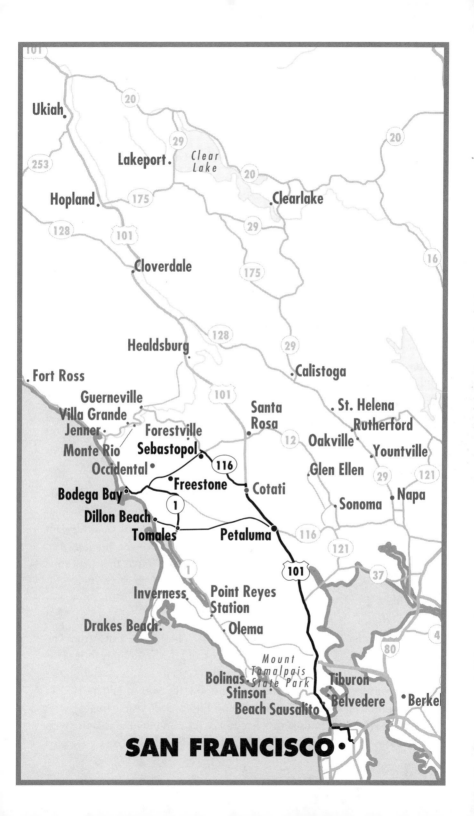

Set off through the orchardlands of western Sonoma County on the Bodega Highway; after 6 miles take a right turn onto the Bohemian Highway to **Freestone.** **The Wishing Well Nursery,** 306 Bohemian Highway (707–823–3710), is like no other nursery. Surrounding a 200-year-old hotel are acres of fabulous plants and flowers, outdoors and in greenhouses. Exotic birds, fancy chickens, ducks, swans, peacocks, and pheasants twitter in cages, glide on ponds, and strut around as if they owned the place. Decorating the grounds are statuary remnants of the century-old Palace of Fine Arts in San Francisco. The nursery is open Friday through Monday. **Trude's Antiques** (707–823–3710) is in the same building; a player piano accompanies your antiques discoveries in the large shop.

For picnics and on-the-road snacks, stop in at **Wild Flour Bread** (140 Bohemian Highway, Freestone; 707–874–2938). Several kinds of fabulous breads are baked daily, plus sticky buns, and pizzas on Friday and Monday.

Continue on the Bodega Highway a few miles to the wide-spot-in-the-road town of **Bodega,** 2 miles west of Bodega Bay; take a left onto Bodega Lane. The old school on the hill that looks vaguely familiar is the **School House.** Currently a private residence, the house is open for tours Saturday and Sunday at 2:00 P.M. and 3:00 P.M. There is no public phone number. When Alfred Hitchcock filmed *The Birds* in 1962, this was the school where the black beauties lined up menacingly on the schoolyard jungle gym and chased the children down the road. Near the house is St. Teresa's Church, circa 1860, and a few antiques and gift shops.

LUNCH: **The Tides Wharf and Restaurant,** 825 Highway 1, midtown Bodega Bay; (707) 875–3652. Dine at a sunny window table overlooking the action of the wharf and the harbor. Fresh local seafood: clam chowder, Dungeness crab, salmon, mussels, sand dabs—the list goes on. Breakfast, lunch, and dinner; snack bar. Shop for gizmos at the small souvenir shop.

Afternoon

Whale-watching cruises and deep-sea fishing party boats leave from the wharf, headquarters for Bodega Bay's harbor and the home port for northern coast fishing vessels. Fishermen unload their catch, and shoppers choose from local and imported fresh seafood. It's crab in fall, herring in spring, salmon in summer—and rock and ling cod all year. Mingled with weathered clapboard houses are a handful of seafood restaurants along with a few shops and motels scattered around the edges of the large, protected harbor where pleasure boats from all over the world come to anchor away from the open sea.

On the north end of town, turn left onto Eastshore Road, then right onto Westshore Road, circling the bay. Fishing boats and sailboats are lined up at **Spud Point Marina** (707–875–3535), and there's a long fishing pier where you can try your luck. At **Westside Park** (707–875–2640), you can picnic, dig for clams and bait, and launch a boat. Most days sailboarders flit like butterflies in the harbor breezes. Every April, thousands of visitors come to the park for the **Bodega Bay Fisherman's Festival** to see the blessing of the fleet and a decorated boat parade and to enjoy a big outdoor fair with food and entertainment, arts and crafts (707–875–3422).

There's a sign for the **UC Davis Marine Laboratory,** which is open for free drop-in tours on Friday afternoons; call ahead to tour other days. A half-mile of coastline and surrounding marine habitat is protected and studied by the university. Exhibits and working research projects such as aqua farming are fascinating (2099 Westside Road; 707–875–2211).

At the end of the road, park and get out onto the bluffs of **Bodega Head** (707–875–3483), a prime whale-watching site. Hundreds of whales migrate north along the coast from December through April. Footpaths from here connect to 5 miles of hiking and horseback-riding trails in grassy dunes. Rangers and docent volunteers are on hand during whale-watching months to lead walks along the bluff trail and to answer questions.

Back on Eastshore Road near the highway, stop in at **Branscomb's Inn and Art Gallery,** 1588 Eastshore Road (707–875–3388). There are three floors of galleries with sea views, featuring local and internationally known artists, wildlife etchings, seascapes, and vineyard scenes; one of the best galleries in gallery-rich Sonoma County. At **Candy and Kites,** 1415 Highway 1 (707–875–3777), get you-know-what for your beach walks. The **Ren Brown Collection,** 1781 Highway 1 (707–875–2922), features works from California and Japan—wood blocks, etchings, silkscreens—the largest collection of contemporary Japanese prints in California. The only wine-tasting room on the Sonoma Coast, **Gourmet Au Bay** features wines by the glass as well as fine crafts and gifts (913 Highway 1; 707–875–9875; www.gourmetaubay.com). The shop is owned by Grammy-winning record producer Ken Mansfield (ask him about the Beatles) and his wife, Connie. You can choose here from more than 1,000 bottles of Sonoma County wines.

The **Bodega Bay Surf Shack** is headquarters for rentals, maps, and advice on biking, beachcombing, kayaking, surfing, and sailboarding, with lessons and guided tours available; plus beachwear. Go to the Web site for fascinating satellite reports, maps, and forecasts about waves and weather (Pelican Plaza; 707–875–3944; www.bodegabaysurf.com).

From Bodega Bay north to Bridgehaven, the **Sonoma Coast State Beach** (707–875–3483) is 13 miles of sandy beaches and coves accessible in a dozen or so places; dramatic rocky promontories and sea-stacks, tidepools, and cliffsides make this a thrilling drive. You can camp at **Wright's Beach** or **Bodega Dunes** (800–444–7275). On the north end of the Bodega Bay area, the Bodega Dunes comprise more than 900 acres of huge sand dunes, some as high as 150 feet. There is a 5-mile riding and hiking loop through the dunes and a hiking-only trail to Bodega Head. In a spectacular show of color, thousands of monarch butterflies flock to a grove of cypress and eucalyptus trees adjacent to the dunes every October through February. There are rest rooms here, and a campground.

For rock fishing and surf fishing, **Portuguese Beach** is a good choice; for beachcombing and tidepooling, try **Shell Beach.** Across Highway 1 from Shell Beach, a trail runs up and over the hills to a small redwood forest.

Surf fishing is good at **Salmon Creek Beach** (campsite reservations: 800–444–7275), a beautiful dune area planted with European grasses. At the north end of the beaches, **Goat Rock,** a notoriously dangerous place to swim, is popular for seashore and freshwater fishing at the mouth of the Russian River; seals like it, too.

DINNER: **Duck Club** at Bodega Bay Lodge, Highway 1 on the south end of Bodega Bay, near Bodega Harbour Golf Links; (707) 875–3525. Fresh Sonoma County seafood, poultry, cheeses, and produce on a California cuisine menu. One of the top dining experiences on the northern California coast.

LODGING: **Bodega Bay Lodge,** 103 Highway 1, Bodega Bay; (707) 875–3525 or (800) 368–2468; www.woodsidehotels.com. Among pines and grassy, landscaped dunes overlooking the Pacific, Doran Beach, bird-filled marshes, and the bluffs of Bodega Head. Spacious, deluxe rooms and luxury suites with views, terraces, or decks; comforters; Jacuzzi tubs; robes; fireplaces. The lobby has a giant stone fireplace and two 500-gallon aquariums filled with tropical fish. Sheltered swimming pool with sea view; spa; sauna; fitness center; bikes; golf packages. You can park your car here and just settle in for a blissful getaway weekend, using your feet or bikes to get around, slipping into the spa for beauty and health treatments, and sampling the fine food at the Duck Club.

Day 2 / Morning

BREAKFAST: Complimentary continental breakfast in the Duck Club restaurant at Bodega Bay Lodge. Later in the morning, the **Sandpiper Dockside Cafe,** on the water at 1410 Bay Flat Road, Bodega Bay (707–875–2278), is the place to tuck into eggs with home fries, *huevos rancheros,* or crab omelettes.

From the lodge, take a morning walk in **Doran Beach Regional Park** (707–875–3540), a 2-mile curve of beautiful beach separating Bodega Bay and Bodega Harbor. Clamming in the tidal mudflats and sailboarding in the harbor waters are two popular activities. The combination of freshwater wetlands, salt marshes, and the open sea attracts a great variety of shorebirds and waterfowl; you may even see pond turtles, harbor seals, or sea lions. RV and tent camping sites are breezy (707–875–3540). Reservations: (707) 565–CAMP.

Head out of town, south on Highway 1 through Bodega Bay to the Valley Ford cutoff/Highway 1 road just west of Bodega, to Valley Ford. You'll drive past lush green hills, dairy farms, and ranches to the town of **Tomales,** a 2-block-long headquarters for crabbing, clamming, and surf fishing at **Dillon Beach** and in the skinny finger of **Tomales Bay,** between the mainland and the peninsula of Point Reyes National Seashore. A number of nineteenth-century buildings remain near the intersection of Main Street and Dillon Beach Road; the Church of the Assumption, just south of town, was built in 1860.

The town of Dillon Beach, 4 miles west of Tomales, consists of a collection of Craftsman-style beach cottages from the 1930s; on the beach are some of the richest tidepools on the entire coastline. You can walk on the dunes or drive 1 mile south to Lawson's Landing, where hang gliders often ride the winds. Camping, boating, and fishing equipment and advice are available at **Lawson's Landing Resort** (707–878–2443).

LUNCH: Emily B's Deli, 27000 Highway 1, Tomales; (707) 878–2732. This quaint Victorian-style eatery, decorated with original Victorian tin print, serves up sandwiches, soups, lasagna, chili, and daily specials.

Afternoon

To connect with Highway 101 south to the Golden Gate, drive east on Tomales Road, a eucalyptus-lined lane winding through coastal farmlands; it's 15 miles to **Petaluma.** If you have some of the afternoon remaining, pick up a walking-tour map at the Chamber of Commerce, 215 Howard (707–762–2785), and sightsee in the riverport town.

There's More

Golf. Bodega Harbour Golf Links, 21301 Heron, off Highway 1 on the south end of Bodega Bay, Bodega Bay; (707) 875–3538. One of the most beautiful courses in the state, with all the characteristics of a traditional links layout, including sand, sea, and breezes. Islands of gorselike scrub and a huge freshwater marsh add challenge and beauty.

Sportfishing. New Sea Angler and Jaws, at the Boathouse, 1145 Highway 1, Bodega Bay; (707) 875–3495.

The Nicholas Effect. Behind the Brisas Del Mar, through the RV park (Nicholas Green Foundation, P.O. Box 937, Bodega Bay 94923; 707–875–2263; www.nicholaseffect.com). The children's bell tower is a memorial for a young boy from the town, Nicholas Green, who was killed by highway robbers while vacationing in Italy with his family. His parents donated his organs to seven Italians waiting for transplants. On the tower are 140 bells, almost all sent by Italians—school bells, church bells, ships' bells, mining bells, and cow bells—which chime when the wind blows. This is a lovely setting near cypress trees and green hills, with a glimpse of the ocean.

Special Events

April. Bodega Bay Fisherman's Festival, Bodega Bay; (707) 875–3422. Thousands come for the blessing of the fleet and boat parade, outdoor fair, food, entertainment, and arts and crafts.

August. Sebastopol Apple Fair: (707) 586–FARM.

Sonoma County Wineries Association Auction: (707) 586–3795.

September. Bodega Bay Allied Arts Show, Bodega Harbour Yacht Club; (707) 875–2585. Large, annual exhibition of the work of the regional arts community.

Bodega Bay Sandcastle Building Festival, Doran Beach; (707) 875–3540.

December. Heritage Homes of Petaluma annual holiday parlor tour: (707) 762–3456.

Victorian Tea, Petaluma Woman's Club, 518 B Street, Petaluma; (707) 762–4247 or (707) 778–4398. English high tea amid holiday finery.

Other Recommended Restaurants and Lodgings

Bodega Bay

Bodega Coast Inn, 521 Highway 1; (707) 875–2217. Forty-four simple, contemporary rooms, each with ocean view and balcony, some with fireplaces and spas.

Chanslor Guest Ranch, 2660 Highway 1; (707) 875–2721. A historic 700-acre working ranch with a ranch house where guests relax and watch the sea, the wetlands, and the horses in the pasture; sunsets are memorable. Three rooms in the ranch house, a guest house with living room and three bedrooms, and a two-room loft suite with private balcony, fireplace, and whirlpool tub.

Inn at the Tides, 800 Highway 1; (707) 875–2751; www.innatthetides. com. On a hillside overlooking the town and the harbor, two-story inn buildings on landscaped grounds. Rooms have quite comfortable amenities, like fireplaces, sitting areas, sea views. Completely protected indoor/outdoor pool, spa, sauna. The restaurant here is casual in feel, top-notch in quality, and a place to linger when the sun is on the terrace.

Pomo/Miwok Campground, where the Russian River meets the sea at Bridgehaven, ten minutes off Highway 1; (800) 444–7275. Forty walk-in tent sites in a dense redwood forest at the end of the paved road (great for biking).

Sonoma Coast Villa, 16702 Highway 1; (707) 876–9818; www.scvilla. com. Five miles east of Bodega Bay, a small, luxurious, Mediterranean-style garden inn with romantic rooms, each with fireplace, beautiful furnishings, privacy, and pampering. Includes full breakfast; Jacuzzi spa; swimming pool; nine-hole putting green. The full-service beauty and health spa offers a variety of massage and body treatments, including salt scrubs, seaweed mud wraps, and the one-hundred-minute "Net Release," designed to alleviate repetitive-use syndrome and other workplace maladies, including footbath, heated neck wrap, aromatherapy massage, acupressure, and a personalized consultation—aaahhh.

Starfish, 1400 Highway 1, in the little shopping center across from the kite shop on the north end of town; (707) 875–2513. Great view from a sunny deck and killer breakfasts, fresh seafood, pasta, homemade pies, soups.

Freestone

Osmosis Enzyme Bath and Massage, 209 Bohemian Highway; (707) 823–8231; www.osmosis.com. In a stunning country garden retreat, enjoy Japanese-style massage, heat treatments, wraps, and tension-taming experiences. You haven't lived until you've been covered in warm, aromatic cedar shavings. If you can't move after this bliss, stay at the nearby Green Apple Inn, 520 Bohemian Highway (707–874–2526).

Occidental

Union Hotel (707–874–3555) and Negri's (707–823–5301), two Italian restaurants in an old mountain village, famous for decades for their super-colossal, multicourse, family-style dinners, on the main street of a one-street town. Take the Bohemian Highway through Freestone, about twenty minutes on the winding, scenic mountain road, to Occidental. The restaurants, along with a few galleries and shops, are on the highway, which runs through town.

For More Information

Bodega Bay Chamber of Commerce, 850 Highway 1, Bodega Bay, CA 94923; (707) 875–3422; www.bodegabay.com.

Department of Parks and Recreation, Russian River District, P.O. Box 123, Duncans Mills, CA 95430; (707) 865–2391. Information on private campgrounds.

Petaluma Chamber of Commerce, 215 Howard Street, Petaluma, CA 94952; (707) 762–2785.

Vacation Homes; (707) 875–4000. From cabins to spacious homes, a variety of rentals are available in the Bodega Bay area.

North Central Coastline on Highway 1

1 Night

The north Sonoma/south Mendocino coast is a stretch of wild, rocky shoreline with jewel-like beaches, a few resorts, a harbor or two, and a handful of seagoing towns where fishermen and loggers have lived since before the turn of the twentieth century. When San Francisco exploded with growth during the California gold rush of the mid-1800s, the demand for lumber from the great coastal redwood forests resulted in the establishment of the communities of Anchor Bay, Point Arena, Manchester, Elk, and Albion.

☐ Rugged coastline

☐ Rocky beaches

☐ Russian history

☐ Whale-watching

☐ Fishing harbors

☐ Seacoast villages

Tourism, some agriculture, and the products of resident artists and craftspeople are what fuel the present economy in this idyllic region, a magical kingdom between the misty seas and the dark forests.

Spring, with its breezes and clear days, brings wildflowers and baby lambs in the roadside meadows and the migration of the great gray whale, easily seen from the entire coastline. Summer, a time of warm weather with some foggy days, is busy with visitors, fairs, and festivals. The spectacular, warm fall is the perfect time to come, when most tourists have gone home and the weather is perfect, each beach looking like a postcard view. Winter is for lovers, when magnificent storms turn every beach into a treasure chest of driftwood, shells, and discoveries washed up by the crashing surf, while cozy fireplaces beckon from bed-and-breakfast inns.

Day 1 / Morning

From the Golden Gate Bridge, drive north on Highway 101 to the Guerneville Road exit on the north end of Santa Rosa, an hour's drive. Go west on Guerneville Road to Highway 116, proceeding west to Guerneville along the lush riparian corridor of the **Russian River.**

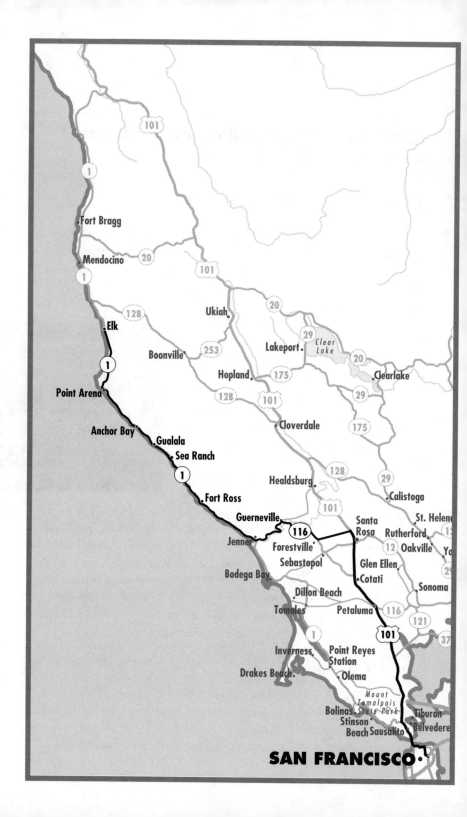

BREAKFAST: Sweet's Cafe and Bakery, 16251 Main, Guerneville; (707) 869–3383. Belgian waffles, omelettes, homemade croissants, espresso. Proceed to the Highway 1 junction, turning north toward Jenner. Here the mild, meadowy headlands of the southern Sonoma coastline abruptly turn steep. The 11-mile stretch of road between Jenner and Fort Ross winds cruelly along a narrow marine terrace with precipitous bluffs on one side—some 900 feet above the shore—and high cliffs on the other side. This is a challenging, spectacular drive; take your time, and take advantage of pullovers and vista points.

About 4.8 miles north of Jenner off Highway 1, the **Vista Trail** is a wheelchair-accessible, 1-mile loop in a meadow on a bluff with wide ocean views and picnic tables.

From the west end of the parking lot at **Fort Ross State Park,** 19005 Highway 1 (707–847–3286), walk down to the small, protected beach below the fort. As you breathe in fresh sea air before starting your explorations of the fort, think about the Russians who arrived in 1812, accompanied by Aleut fur hunters. They came to harvest otter and seal pelts and to grow produce for their northern outposts. Their small settlement of hand-hewn log barracks, blockhouses, and homes, together with a jewel of a Russian Orthodox church, was protected with high bastions and a bristling line of cannons, just in case the Spanish decided to pay a call. At the visitors center are exhibits, films, and guidebooks. Inside the restored buildings are perfectly preserved rifles, pistols, tools, furniture, and old photos. The "crib-style" architecture uses hand-adzed logs notched together and fastened with oakum, a jute-rope-and-tar combination. Several times a day costumed docents put on a demonstration of domestic activities.

Back on the highway, if you're ready for a snack, stop at the **Fort Ross Store and Deli** (707–847–3333) for an ice-cream cone. Then go on to **Salt Point State Park** (707–847–3221), 6,000 acres of sandy beaches, tidepools, high cliffs, sunny meadows, and hiking and biking trails: a good place to beachcomb, scuba dive, or get a little exercise. Campground sites on both sides of the road are private and protected. The dense forestlands of Salt Point are inhabited by gnarly pygmy pines and cypress, their ghostly gray, mossy trunks tickled by maidenhair ferns. Seven miles of coastline are characterized by long, sandy beaches; rocky coves with tidepools rich in wildlife; and many breeding and nesting locations for birds, such as at **Stump Beach,** where a large number of cormorants reside. On both sides of the highway, a wide variety of weather-protected campsites are available:

developed and primitive tent sites and biker/hiker sites, RV sites for up to 31-foot vehicles, and walk-in sites (800–444–7275).

Near the park, **Salt Point Lodge Bar and Grill** (23255 Highway 1; 707–847–3234) is a wonderful spot for casual dining, indoors or outdoors, with an ocean view. It specializes in mesquite-grilled fresh fish and a big salad bar. **Salt Point Lodge** here has comfortable rooms, a hot tub, and voluptuous gardens.

Just north of Salt Point, off Highway 1 at milepost 43, **Kruse Rhodod-endron State Park** (707–847–3221) should not be missed in the months of April, May, and June, when wild rhododendron glades up to 15 feet high are brilliant with bloom under redwood, oak, and madrone branches. There's a 1-mile dirt road into the park; a trail sign shows 5 miles of easy and challenging hikes through quiet forest and over picturesque bridges straddling fern canyons and streams.

LUNCH: Sea Ranch Lodge, 60 Sea Walk Drive, off Highway 1, Sea Ranch; (707) 785–2371 or (800) 732–7662; www.searanchlodge.com. All along the bluffs in this area and from the Sea Ranch restaurant, you can see whales in wintertime and a wide variety of other wildlife all year. Sandwiches, salads, homemade soups, fresh fish, lunch, and dinner.

Rooms at the rustic lodge are simple, each with a wide ocean view, within steps of sea-spray meadows and walking trails on the bluffs. The lounge bar has a big fireplace. Popular events at the lodge are the monthly gourmet wine dinners, featuring top Sonoma County wine makers.

Afternoon

The Sea Ranch Lodge is headquarters for a unique residential develop-ment that pioneered the use of extensive open space and architectural restraint. Widely scattered, naturally weathered wood houses on the head-lands and hillsides are barely visible; some have sod roofs. Cars are hidden, fences absent; grasses and trees are indigenous. Many of the homes are available to rent (Rams Head Realty; 800–785–3455).

There are great walking paths above the beaches and quiet, paved country roads on the highway side of the Sea Ranch in the redwood, madrone, fir, and pine forest. Wild azaleas, rhododendrons, and irises bloom in the spring; wild mushrooms are colorful most of winter and spring. A smashingly beautiful eighteen-hole, links-style golf course, laid out on the coastal bluffs and in the meadows and forestlands above the highway, makes this a weekend getaway destination. Designed by world-famous architect Robert Muir Graves more than two decades ago, the **Sea Ranch Golf Links,** in his words, "is the closest I've ever come to a true links course, and it reminds me of Scotland every time I look at it. Wild vegetation or a natural landscape hazard is allowed to cross or encroach upon the fairways. The rough is natural and is left unmowed, right up to the edge of the fairways. Depending on the growth each year, this does not always make me a popular person." Call for tee times: (707) 785–2468.

A string of quiet, sandy coves and rocky beaches are accessible for several miles along the Sea Ranch coast; **Shell Beach, Pebble Beach,** and **Black Point Beach** are the best.

When you see the lace curtains and wooden porches of the ninety-year-old Gualala Hotel, you've made it to the town of **Gualala,** your final destination for the day. At one time a logging center, Gualala is now an art colony and headquarters for steelhead and salmon fishing.

Several shops in the **Seacliff Center,** on the south end of town, are worth browsing. **Once Upon a Time** (707–884–4910) specializes in imported dolls, art glass, and "chain-saw sculpture," an art form unique to the redwood forest areas. A yarn and sweater store, **Marlene Designs** (707–884–4809), has contemporary hand-knit sweaters glowing with vivid colors, not the styles your grandmother used to knit. Prowl around town a bit to find art galleries and antiques shops.

DINNER: **Gualala Hotel,** 39301 Highway 1, Gualala; (707) 884–3441. Family-style Italian dinners, homemade cioppino on Friday nights, country fried chicken with biscuits and gravy, thirty-ounce steaks, fresh crab, and seafood galore, all in a lively, friendly atmosphere. Come in early for a tall one at the long bar, where local fishermen and tourists rub elbows beneath a museumlike array of photos of early days and fishing on the Gualala. Breakfast and lunch, too, and simple hotel rooms.

LODGING: **Whale Watch Inn by the Sea,** 35100 Highway 1, Anchor Bay (5 miles north of Gualala); (707) 884–3667; www.whalewatchinn. com. Five contemporary-design buildings on a cliff above the ocean, stained-glass windows, beautiful gardens. Eighteen luxurious guest rooms, whirlpool tubs, fireplaces, private decks with ocean views. Common lounge is comfy and lovely, with a coastal view, big fireplaces, leather couches, telescope. Full breakfast in your room. Private access to 0.5 mile of sandy beach with tidepools and a waterfall. No phones—bliss.

Day 2 / Morning

BREAKFAST: Sumptuous breakfast at the Whale Watch Inn.

Drive north to **Point Arena.** At the south end of the main street, turn west onto Port Road, following it to the **Point Arena Public Fishing Pier,** which thrusts 330 feet out into the water from the edge of a cove seemingly protected by high cliffs on either side. The original wooden pier was dramatically smashed to pieces in 1983, along with all of the buildings in the cove. In the **Galley at Point Arena** restaurant, Port Road, Point Arena (707–882–2189), are photos of the storm as it ripped and roared. The Galley serves chowder, snapper sandwiches, homemade pies, salads, and fresh crab in season. This is a good place to watch whales and crusty old salts. Fishing, crabbing, and whale-watching are good from the pier; tidepooling and abalone hunting, from the rocks.

Walk up to the **Wharf Master's Inn,** on the hill behind the pier. Built in the 1870s for wharf masters who watched over the port until the 1920s, this is the town's most elaborate building, a fantasy of turned posts, scroll brackets, and fancy window moldings. Prefabricated in San Francisco, the house was shipped here as a kit. Just below, the **Coast Guard House,** P.O. Box 117, Point Arena (707–882–2442), now a bed-and-breakfast inn, is a classic California Arts and Crafts–style house built in 1901 as a lifesaving station.

The Flag Room has a queen-size teak captain's bed built into a windowed alcove with views of the cove. Another room includes a Japanese bath and a woodstove and has beautiful ocean views.

Rollerville Junction, 3 miles north of Point Arena, is the westernmost point in the continental United States, the site of many a shipwreck; ten vessels went down on the night of November 20, 1865. The 115-foot **Point Arena Lighthouse** (707–882–2777) was erected here in 1870, then re-erected after the 1906 San Francisco earthquake. The lighthouse is the all-time best location for California gray whale-watching; December through April are the prime months. Scramble around in the lighthouse and visit the museum of maritime artifacts below.

Few people know that the three small homes at the **Point Arena Coast Guard** facility are available to rent; neat and clean, with kitchens, they're perfect for a family or several couples (707–882–2777).

Proceed north on the highway to **Elk,** a tiny community perched on cliffs above a spectacular bay. You'll recognize the **Greenwood Pier Inn** complex, 5928 Highway 1 in Elk, by the multitude of blooming flowers and trees. Take your time poking around in the gardens and in the **Country Store and Garden Shop,** 5928 Highway 1, Elk; (707) 877–9997. Owners Kendrick and Isabel Petty are artists, cooks, gardeners, and innkeepers, their works found throughout the store, the cafe, and the inn, which is a redwood castle with fabulous ocean views, with fireplaces, decks, and romantic privacy.

LUNCH: **Greenwood Pier Cafe,** (707) 877–9997. Fresh local seafood, greens and vegetables from the inn gardens, sandwiches, salads, breakfast.

Afternoon

You can drive back to the Bay Area by way of Highway 128 through Boonville and the beautiful Anderson Valley. If you retrace your Highway 1 route, stop in Sebastopol (south of Guerneville on Highway 116) at the first (hard) cider pub in the United States, the **Ace in the Hole,** where you can sample apple, berry, pear, or honey cider, and pub grub (3100 Gravenstein Highway; 707–829–1101; www.acecider.com).

There's More

Adventure Rents, at the Gualala Hotel Plaza, Gualala; (707) 884–4386. Rent canoes or kayaks to explore the Gualala River. Transportation to and from launch sites is included. In spring wild azaleas are rampant on the riverbanks. Bike rentals, too.

Gualala Point Regional Beach Park, 1 mile south of Gualala; (707) 785–2377. A mile-long, driftwood-strewn beach, with campground and picnic sites. Grasslands are habitats for a wide variety of bird life, including great blue herons, pygmy owls, hummingbirds, and seabirds. Coastside trails here connect to the Sea Ranch, and they are wildflowery all the way.

Stillwater Cove Regional Park, 16 miles north of Jenner on Highway 1; (707) 847–3245. A favorite surf-fishing spot, with boat access and picnic area. Five miles of hiking trails in the redwoods, a wheelchair-accessible trail, and a campground.

Special Events

February. Annual Red Wine and Chocolate Festival, Gualala; (707) 884–1138.

February–May. Gualala Arts Music Series; (707) 884–1138.

March. Gualala Whale Festival; (707) 884–3377.

July. California Wine Tasting Championships, Anderson Valley; (707) 877–3262.

Fort Ross Living History Day, Fort Ross State Park; (707) 847–3286.

August. Art-in-the-Redwoods Festival, Gualala; (707) 884–1138. Art, music, vintage car show.

Other Recommended Restaurants and Lodgings

Elk

Sandpiper House Inn, 5520 Highway 1; (707) 877–3587. A sweet old mansion in an English garden on a coastal bluff, white picket fences, path to private beach. Three rooms with ocean view, one with a fireplace and meadow view.

Gualala

Breakers Inn, 39350 Highway 1; (707) 884–3200. Decks overlooking the Pacific, nice rooms with fireplaces, and whirlpool spas.

Gualala Country Inn, P.O. Box 697, Gualala 95445; (800) 564–4466. Overlooking the Pacific and Gualala Beach, four rooms with traditional oak furnishings, comforters, with panoramic sea or river views, fireplaces, window seats, whirlpool spas.

Oceansong, 39350 Highway 1, at the south end of town; (707) 884–1041. With a bank of windows overlooking Gualala Beach and a sheltered dining deck, fresh fish tacos, salmon fish and chips, and blackened snapper; breakfast, lunch, and dinner.

Old Milano Hotel, 38300 Highway 1; (707) 884–3256. Romantic Victorian-inspired rooms in an inn established in 1905, on the National Register of

Historic Places. On three acres of gardens and cliff-top bluffs, a few rooms, a suite, and a cottage, with common outdoor spa with sea view. Big breakfast in your room, on the garden patio, or by the fire in the wine parlor. In a Victorian dining room with lace curtains and etched-glass lamps, guests dine by candlelight by the fire; renowned continental menu and top wine list.

Seacliff, P.O. Box 697, Gualala 95445; (707) 884–1213. Contemporary suites with fireplaces, spas, and private decks overlooking Gualala Beach; a prime whale-watching and fishing spot. The Top of the Cliff is the restaurant here, specializing in gourmet seafood, with a cocktail lounge warmed up nightly by the sunset over the Pacific.

Jenner

Fort Ross Lodge, 20705 Coast Highway 1; (707) 847–3333. Comfortable ocean-view rooms and suites, some with fireplaces, spas; reasonable. Barbecues on your private patio, store across the road.

Timber Cove Inn, 21780 Highway 1; (707) 847–3231. Eclectic rooms have fireplaces, decks, and hot tubs or Jacuzzis. On a whale-watching, ocean-viewing point; good restaurant; three-story stone fireplace in the lounge; romantic—a place for runaways.

Point Arena

Pangaea, 250 Main Street; (707) 882–3001. Located in a warm, terracotta–colored Mediterranean environment. Features baby beet salad with goat cheese, cassoulet of duck confit, quail with pine nut dressing, a changing daily menu including pizza from the brick oven, local fresh seafood. Surprising sophistication in a laid-back village.

Wharf Master's Inn, 785 Port Road, P.O. Box 674, Point Arena 95450; (800) 932–4031. New inn surrounding a landmark house from the mid-1800s; courtyards, private decks, fireplaces, spas, ocean views, upscale decor.

For More Information

California State Park Reservations: (800) 444–7275.

Gualala/Sea Ranch Coastal Chamber of Commerce, P.O. Box 338, Gualala, CA 95445; (800) 778–5252; www.gualala.com.

Sea Coast Hideaways, 21350 Highway 1, Jenner, CA 95450; (707) 847–3278. Vacation home rentals.

Sonoma County Tourism Program; (800) 380–5392; www.sonomacounty. com.

Mendocino and
Fort Bragg 8

Where the Forest Meets the Sea

3 Nights

Floating like a mirage on high bluffs above a rocky bay, Mendocino seems lost in another century. The entire town is a California Historical Preservation District of early Cape Cod and Victorian homes and steepled clapboard churches. Though thronged with tourists in summer, the town somehow retains the look and feel of a salty fisherman's and lumberman's village.

Old-fashioned gardens soften weather-worn mansions and cottages; picket fences need a coat of paint; dark cypress trees lean into the sea breezes. Boutique and art-gallery shopping is legendary, charming bed-and-breakfast inns abound; in fact, there are more B&Bs per capita in and around Mendocino than anywhere else in California.

And, this is a major cultural center with dozens of top art galleries, a large art center, and a busy annual schedule of festivals and exhibitions.

A few miles north of Mendocino, Fort Bragg has been a lumbering and commercial fishing town since 1857.

- ☐ Hidden coves
- ☐ Redwood groves
- ☐ Art galleries
- ☐ Harbor views
- ☐ Fishing, beachcombing, kayaking
- ☐ Whale-watching
- ☐ Bed-and-breakfasts

Restaurants and accommodations are more reasonably priced here than in Mendocino, and there are several magnificent coastal and forest state parks nearby, a picturesque fishing port at the mouth of the Noyo River, and the departure depot for the famous Skunk Train.

Day 1 / Morning

Head north from the Golden Gate Bridge on Highway 101 to Santa Rosa,

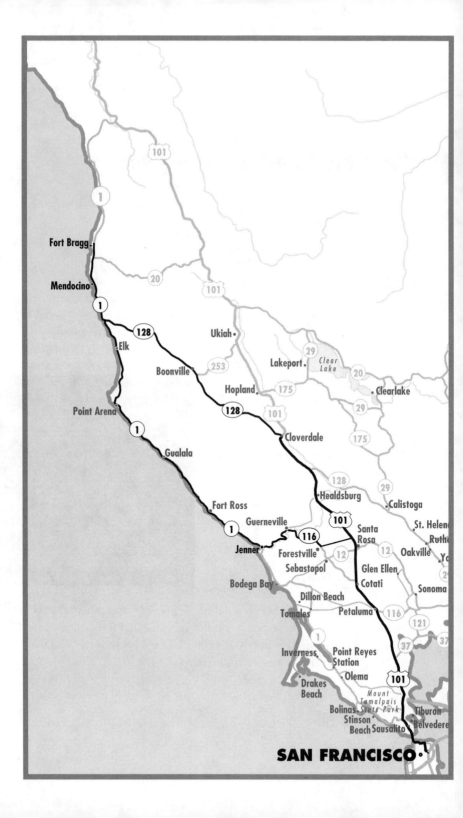

an hour's drive (it's about three and a half hours from the bridge to Mendocino).

Go west on Guerneville Road to Highway 116, heading west toward the coast, then north at the Highway 1 junction at Jenner. On the roller-coaster road from here to Mendocino, make frequent stops to enjoy cliff-hanging views of rocky coves, salt-spray meadows, redwood and pine forests, and a necklace of tiny fishing villages and loggers' towns. For a faster, less curvy route, take Highway 101 north to Highway 128, heading west to Mendocino.

LUNCH: Salt Point Lodge Bar and Grill, 23255 Highway 1, Jenner, just north of Timber Cove; (707) 847–3234. Solarium windows overlooking gardens and Ocean Cove; mesquite-grilled specialties, fresh fish, salad bar, barbecue.

Afternoon

After you arrive in Mendocino, revive yourself with a bracing walk along the bluffs, the grassy headlands that surround the town. From the bluffs are views of a deep river valley as it meets the sea at **Big River Beach,** and looking back at the town's skyline, you can imagine when horse-drawn carriages were parked in front of the Mendocino Hotel and ladies with parasols swept along the boardwalk in their long gowns. Rest rooms and a picnic area are found on the north end of the park along Heeser Drive.

Good old days in mind, now is the time to visit the **Kelley House Museum** on Albion Street (707–937–5791). A sunny yellow house built in 1852, it's set back from the street next to a huge water tower and a pond surrounded by an old garden. Among the historical photos are those of burly loggers hand-sawing ancient redwoods. Lumber for shipbuilding and for construction of the gold rush city of San Francisco brought Easterners here in the mid-1800s; it took them six months by ship from the East Coast to reach this wilderness of mighty river valleys and seacoast.

On Main Street's headlands is **Ford House** museum (707–937–5397), built in 1854. A scale model of Mendocino in the 1890s shows the dozens of tall water towers that existed at that time; more than thirty towers, some double- and triple-deckers, are distinctive features of today's skyline.

Step into **Out of This World** at the corner of Main and Kasten to get up-close views of the crashing surf through high-powered telescopes that are trained on the coastline. This unusual store specializes in premium optics, binoculars and scopes, and space and science kits (707–937–3324).

Have a sunset cocktail at the **Mendocino Hotel,** a gloriously overdecorated gathering place since 1878.

DINNER: MacCallum House Restaurant and **Grey Whale Bar,** 45020 Albion Street, Mendocino; (707) 937–5763; www.maccallumhouse dining.com. Haute cuisine in a rambling Victorian mansion: oysters, gnocchi, sesame-encrusted ahi tuna, duck in blackberry sauce, fresh salmon, and Meyers lemon curd Napoleons. Sophisticated wine list.

LODGING: Whitegate Inn, 499 Howard, Mendocino; (707) 937–4892; www. whitegateinn.com; e-mail: staff@whitegateinn.com. Julia Roberts and Mel Gibson (not together) adored the privacy at this dream of a Victorian mansion right in the heart of town. Behind a pristine white picket fence, a lush English garden and huge old cypress trees hint at the luxury within six inn rooms and a cottage. High-ceilinged and airy in their rococo finery, all rooms have European feather beds and down comforters, fireplaces, garden or sea views, gorgeous antique beds, and a romantic, but not fussy, aura. A full breakfast is served in the truly spectacular dining room, which looks onto the garden and the coastline 2 blocks away. Proprietors Carol and George Bechtloff, who live in the sweet cottage next door, manage to create a casual, friendly atmosphere in museumlike surroundings. Amenities are too numerous to mention; however, think about evening wine parties, a bottomless cookie jar, a concierge to make your local arrangements, sunny afternoons in a lounge chair on the garden terrace, carmel apple French toast, and a long soak in a claw-foot tub.

Day 2 / Morning

BREAKFAST: Whitegate Inn.

Set out from the inn to explore on foot. Browsing the boutiques and galleries in Mendocino village can take an hour or a week, depending on your love of discovery.

Many Mendocino artists are renowned not only throughout the state but internationally, and you will find galleries on every street of the town. At **Creative Hands of Mendocino,** 45170 Main (707–937–2914), look for handcrafted gifts for children and adults. The **Artists' Co-op,** upstairs at 45270 Main (707–937–2217), is operated by artists who show and sell primarily landscape works in a variety of media.

At Kasten and Ukiah Streets, in a glorious building from the 1870s, is the **William Zimmer Gallery,** an exceptional gallery of international stature, showing fine jewelry, handcrafted furniture, paintings, and more (707–937–5121). Some of the gallery's sculpture collection is displayed at Stevenswood Lodge, just south of Mendocino, in a gorgeous forest and garden setting. Look for miraculous wood sculptures of wheeled vehicles. Hub of the artistic community, the **Mendocino Art Center** offers classes, seminars, and special events related to countywide arts all year. **The Gallery** and **The Showcase** here exhibit and sell the fine work of member artists (45200 Little Lake Street between Williams and Kasten Streets; 707–937–5818).

When you see clouds of swirling birds, you're near **Papa Birds,** 45040 Albion Street (707–937–2730), a shop selling bird feeders, birdhouses, and bird paraphernalia. Their outdoor feeders attract feathered types. Free bird walks are conducted on Saturday mornings, starting at the shop.

Main Street shops of note are the **Highlight Gallery** (707–937–3132), for burlwood sculpture, and the **Irish Shop** (707–937–3133), for winter coats and sweaters. Farther down the street is a feminine fantasy, the **Golden Goose** (707–937–4655), two floors of European antiques, country-luxe bed and table linens, and a children's boutique for heirs and heiresses.

Overgrown country gardens will draw you up and down the side streets and alleys; look for the two old cemeteries, not in the least spooky, whose headstones are fascinating relics of the days when European sailors, Russian soldiers, and Chinese workers lived here.

Care for a taste of wine before lunch? Stop in at **Fetzer Vineyards' Mendocino Tasting Room** at 45070 Main, open 10:00 A.M. to 6:00 P.M. (707–937–6190). The organically grown Bonterra wines, and the limited-release reserves, are grown in the Anderson Valley nearby. The tasting room is a good place to shop for Wine Country souvenirs and gifts, too.

LUNCH: The Moosse Cafe, on the southwest corner of Kasten and Albion Streets, Mendocino; (707) 937–4323. This restaurant in the Blue Heron Inn features Asian-style gourmet fish and seafood dishes as well as pasta, pork, and fancy desserts. Open daily for lunch.

Afternoon

Three miles south of Mendocino on Highway 1, the beach, campground, and hiking trails at **Van Damme State Park** are popular weekend desti-nations (707–937–4016). This is the home of the uniquely beautiful **Pygmy Forest,** a Registered National Landmark. An easy 0.3-mile trail takes you through a lush fern canyon and spooky woods of dwarf cypress, rhododendrons, and other bonsai-like plants and trees. A fifty-year-old cypress, for instance, may be only 8 inches tall and have a trunk less than 1 inch in diameter. To reach the Discovery Trail and other trails, stop at the ranger station or take Little River Airport Road off Highway 1 and go 2.7 miles to the Pygmy Forest parking lot.

There are seventy-four developed campsites at Van Damme and sites for RVs up to 21 feet long. A few hike-in campsites are accessed by a 2-mile scenic trail.

A unique way to explore the coastline here is with **Lost Coast Kayaks,** whose experienced guides conduct sea kayak tours from Van Damme beach (707–937–2434). For both beginners and experienced kayakers, in boats that are easy to maneuver, the two-hour tours guide you in and out of sea caves and along the rocky edges of nearby coves. The guides identify shore- and seabirds and the denizens of tidepools, and you're likely to see harbor seals.

If you crave a little more strenuous outdoor adventure for the afternoon, call **Catch a Canoe and Bicycles, Too!** (707–937–0273) to ask about paddling the **Big River,** which runs into the sea below the high bluffs on the south side of Mendocino. Along banks lush with fir and redwood groves, wildflowers, and wild rhododendrons, you can paddle a canoe or a kayak from the mouth of the river 7 or 8 miles upstream on an estuary— the longest unchanged and undeveloped estuary in northern California— stopping at a tiny beach or a meadow for a picnic. You will undoubtedly see ospreys, wood ducks, and blue herons, probably harbor seals and deer, too.

Catch a Canoe and Bicycles, Too! is located at the wondrous **Stanford Inn by the Sea** complex on a hillside above the river across from Mendocino. The luxurious, twenty-six-room country inn is surrounded by spectacular gardens. Herds of llamas and horses graze in the meadows. Guests enjoy a spa, a sauna, and an Olympic-size swimming pool enclosed in a greenhouse crowded with tropical plants.

If you stay at the Stanford Inn (Highway 1 and Comptche-Ukiah Road, P.O. Box 487, Mendocino 95460; 800–331–8884; www.stanfordinn. com), you will enjoy a fireplace or wood-burning stove in your sitting area, a down comforter on your four-poster or sleigh bed, a private deck from which to watch the sun set over the sea, complimentary wine, and a bountiful buffet breakfast.

DINNER: **Cafe Beaujolais,** 961 Ukiah Street, Mendocino; (707) 937–5614; www.cafebeaujolais.com. Owner Margaret Fox and her classically French-trained chef are nationally known for their culinary creations. The

1910 Victorian house is surrounded by lush gardens, so exceptional they are toured at special events. Organically grown products from small farms and ranches in the area supply ingredients for the inventive menu of seasonal delights; save room for French bittersweet chocolate and sour cherry cake, and passion fruit crème brûlée. The wood-floored dining room is homey and relaxed, with flowery wallpaper and lace curtains; a sunny, glass-enclosed deck floats in the garden; and the wood-fired oven in The Brickery produces take-out breads to dream about. Reserve well ahead.

LODGING: Whitegate Inn.

Day 3 / Morning

BREAKFAST: Whitegate Inn.

On a drive north on Highway 1, on the way to the lumbering and fishing town of Fort Bragg, stop at a beach and forest parks and a botanical garden.

Two miles north of Mendocino on Highway 1, **Russian Gulch State Park** (707–937–5804) is known for sea caves, a waterfall, and a beach popular for rock fishing, scuba diving, and swimming in chilly waters. From the headlands in the park, you can see the Devil's Punch Bowl, a 200-foot-long tunnel with a blow hole. Inland, the park includes 3 miles of Russian Gulch Creek Canyon, with paved and unpaved trails in dense forest and stream canyons. A hiking trail leads to a 36-foot waterfall and to high ridges where views are breathtaking. A small campground here is particularly lovely, and there is a special equestrian campground with riding trails into **Jackson State Forest.** RVs up to 27 feet are allowed.

One mile north of Russian Gulch State Park, turn west into **Jug Handle State Reserve** (707–937–5804), a 700-acre park notable for an "ecological staircase" marine terrace rising from sea level to 500 feet. Each terrace is 100,000 years older than the one above, a unique opportunity to see geologic evolution. The plants and trees change from terrace to terrace, too, from wildflowers and grasses to wind-strafed spruce, redwood and pygmy forests of cypress and pine.

Save at least two hours for the **Mendocino Coast Botanical Gardens** (18220 Highway 1, 2 miles south of Fort Bragg; 707–964–4352; www.gardenbythesea.org), with forty-seven acres of plantings, forest, and fern canyons on a bluff overlooking the ocean. Two miles of easy paths lead through picture-perfect perennial and native-plant gardens, forests, a marsh, and organic vegetable gardens. From late April through early June, hundreds of rhododendrons, azaleas, and spring bulbs are in bloom. From November through January, Japanese maples and winter heathers are aflame. One of the loveliest walks is along a creek in a mossy fern canyon. On the coastal bluff are wildflower meadows above a dramatic, rocky shoreline with waves crashing in the coves below. On a windy day, the Cliff House shelter on the bluff is a warm, cozy spot from which to watch the waves and look through educational exhibits. You can see as many as eighty species of birds and many butterflies, squirrels, and, occasionally, deer and rabbits. The garden paths are primarily wheelchair accessible; two electric carts are available at no charge. You can buy superhealthy plants here at reasonable prices, as well as garden accessories and books. Bring a picnic lunch or snacks and enjoy the garden benches and picnic tables. Admission charge.

LUNCH: **The Wharf** bar and restaurant at 32260 North Harbor Drive, Fort Bragg (707–964–4283), overlooking the harbor, is a great place for lunch. Try the grilled fresh fish, grilled eggplant salad, mushroom crepe torte, or the apple-wood rotisseried game hen.

Just south of Fort Bragg, at the mouth of the **Noyo River, Noyo Harbor** is headquarters for a large fleet of fishing trawlers and canneries. Barking and posing, sea lions lounge on the wooden piers, waiting for the return of the boats at day's end.

Noyo Harbor is the best place on the coast to take a whale-watching cruise because the boats usually find the whales within fifteen or twenty minutes. The cost is about $25 per person for a two-hour trip. Whale-watching cruise companies include Anchor Charters (707–964–5440), All Aboard Adventures (707–964–1881), *Rumblefish* (707–964–3000), and Telstar Charters (707–964–8770). Companies that offer fishing trips include Anchor Charters on *Trek II* or *Irma II,* (707) 964–4550; Captain Tim on the *Sea Hawk,* (707) 964–1881; and Telstar Charters with Randy Thornton, (707) 964–8770.

Thousands of majestic gray whales parade off the North Coast each winter on their annual 12,000-mile, round-trip migration from the Arctic Circle to Baja California. On the 80-mile Mendocino coastline, they are spotted in late November through December, and they head north again in February and March. Some of the best whale-watching sites on the North Coast are MacKerricher State Park, Mendocino Headlands State Park, and Point Cabrillo Light Station.

DINNER: **Old Coast Hotel,** 101 North Franklin Street, Fort Bragg; (707) 961–4488. Red-checked tablecloths give no hint of the sophisticated menu and big wine list; oysters, jambalaya, twenty pastas, fresh fish in imaginative sauces, house smoked ribs. Warm and cozy on a cold night, live jazz on weekends.

LODGING: **The Lodge at Noyo River,** 500 Casa del Noyo Drive, off North Harbor Drive above Noyo Harbor, Fort Bragg; (707) 964–8045; www.noyolodge.com. On a forested bluff above Noyo Harbor, The Lodge at Noyo River is a California Craftsman mansion with warmly romantic inn rooms and a new annex with large suites. In 1868 Scandinavian boat builders handcrafted this unique home of prime redwood. It is furnished with comfortable antiques, oriental rugs, and vintage art and photos. Full breakfasts and evening wine are served in the sunny dining room over-looking the harbor or on the outdoor deck. Annex suites are spacious, with private decks, harbor views, fireplaces, huge soaking tubs, and sitting areas. With harbor or garden views, inn rooms vary in size and amenities; some have claw-foot or soaking tubs and sitting areas. If you are a light sleeper, ask for a room away from the barking sea lions.

Day 4 / Morning

BREAKFAST: The Lodge at Noyo River. Stroll the gardens and take the short path to the harbor to watch the fishing fleet head out into the morning mist.

Before heading back to the Bay Area, stop in at **For the Shell of It,** 344 North Main Street in Fort Bragg, to shop for shells and shell jewelry, shell posters, folk art, and all things shellish (707–961–0461). The **Wind and Weather** shop, 147 East Laurel (707–961–4153) is a fascinating place to see and buy weather instruments, vanes, and sundials. At the **Mendocino Chocolate Company** at 542 North Main, pick up hand-made truffles, chocolates, and edible seashells. Try these specialties: a dark, Rambo of a truffle—"Mendocino Macho"; "Mendocino Breakers," dark-dipped caramels rolled in almonds; and old-fashioned Convent Fudge (707–964–8800; www.mendocino-chocolate.com).

A beautiful, three-story, all-redwood home built before the turn of the twentieth century, the **Guest House** is a museum filled with photos and artifacts of local history and antique logging equipment, and it has a lovely garden (343 North Main Street; 707–964–4251). Check out the **U.L. Company Store** at Main and Redwood, an indoor shopping center con-taining several boutiques, the **Mendocino Cookie Company** (707–964–0282), and the **Mendo Bistro** (707–964–4974). At the Fort Bragg

Depot are a clutch of small shops, including **Fuchsiarama,** a gifts and fabulous fuchias store; the main Fuchsiarama location is 2 miles north, a lush and beautiful five-acre environment for fuchsias and fantasy gifts; you can also picnic here (23201 North Highway 1; 707–964–0429).

To stretch your legs before you head home, head for **Glass Beach** at the foot of Elm Street, where the sand is sprinkled with pebbles of glass and china that have been tumbled and smoothed in the sea. North of town past the first bridge, **Pudding Creek** has a beach play area and tidepools. Eight miles north of Fort Bragg, **Ten Mile River Beach** is acres of salt marsh and wetlands at the mouth of the Noyo River, inhabited by nesting birds and ducks; a 4.5-mile, duney stretch of sand extends south from the river.

Returning to San Francisco, head south on Highway 128 inland, connecting with Highway 101 South to the Golden Gate Bridge.

There's More

Coastwalk organizes camping and hiking trips along the coast. Schedule is available from Richard Nichols, 7207 Bodega Avenue, Sebastopol, CA 95472; (800) 550–6854; www.coastwalk.org.

Lost Coast Adventures, 19275 South Harbor Drive, Fort Bragg; (707) 961–1143. Kayak tours, mountain-bike and skin- and scuba-diving rentals, boat charters for fishing, diving, and whale-watching.

MacKerricher State Park, 3 miles north of Fort Bragg off Highway 1; (707) 927–5804. Eight miles of beach and dunes, with tidepools at the southern end of the park. Two freshwater lakes are stocked with trout. Horseback-riding, mountain-biking, and hiking trails are found throughout bluffs, headlands, dunes, forests, and wetlands. The headlands at Laguna Point are a prime spot for whale-watching, and harbor seals are seen here. The boardwalk affords wheelchair and stroller access, from the southwest corner of the parking lot. Developed campsites and RV sites for up to 35-foot vehicles, fire rings, rest rooms. Stretching the entire 8-mile length of the park, the paved Haul Road, a former logging road, is a fabulous jogging, biking, and walking route that crosses beautiful sand dunes and has ocean views.

Point Cabrillo Preserve, 2 miles north of Mendocino off Highway 1; (707) 937–0816. Three hundred acres of dramatic headlands and meadows on a rocky shore lined with sea caves, and the Point Cabrillo Lighthouse, built in 1908. Guided tours of the lighthouse are available on Sundays at 11:00 A.M. and at special events; dogs on leashes and children eight years and older are welcome; admission is free, and reservations are unnecessary. The 0.5-mile walk over unpaved grasslands is open daily.

Ricochet Ridge Ranch, 24201 North Highway 1, Fort Bragg; (707) 964–7669. Horseback riding on the beach.

Skunk Train, Laurel Street Depot at Main Street, Fort Bragg; (707) 964–6371 or (800) 77–SKUNK; www.skunktrain.com. Hauling logs to sawmills in the 1880s, the California and Western Railroad's historic diesel and steam Skunk Trains carry tourists on half-day or full-day trips to Willits and back. The trains rock alongside Pudding Creek and the Noyo River through redwood forests, crossing thirty bridges and trestles over river gulches, passing idyllic glades and meadows. You can sit inside or wander in and out, standing on open-air cars and enjoying the natural sights and the fresh air. At the halfway point, the train stops to fill up on water, and passengers can stretch their legs, have picnics, and buy souvenirs. On sale are freshly grilled hot dogs, homemade cookies, Pratt's wild organic apple juice, even cappuccino and Mendocino Sunrises—champagne and wild apple juice with fresh mint! It's wise to make reservations for summer weekends.

Special Events

January. Crab and Wine Days, Mendocino; (866)–goMendo (466–3636); www.goMendo.com. Crab cruises and whale-watching trips, cooking demonstrations, wine and crab tasting, carnival, wine-maker dinners, crab feed and crab cake cookoff, and more.

March. Fort Bragg Whale Festival; (800) 726–2780. Chowder and microbeer tasting, food and crafts booth, doll show, live music, classic car show.

Mendocino Whale Festival, Mendocino; (800) 726–2780. Chowder and wine tasting, wooden boat displays, food booths, street musicians, horse-drawn carriage rides, and live Saturday night concert.

April. Wild rhododendrons erupt into pink, white, and red blossoms April through June at Kruse Rhododendron State Reserve; (707) 847–3286.

May. Historic House and Building Tour, Mendocino; (707) 937–5791.

July. Mendocino Music Festival, P.O. Box 1808, Mendocino 95460; (707) 937–2044. Classical and jazz.

World's Largest Salmon Barbecue, Fort Bragg; (707) 964–6030.

August. Art in the Gardens, Fort Bragg; (707) 965–4352. Art, music, wine, and food at the Botanical Gardens.

September. Winesong! Buy your tickets early for this annual wine tasting and auction fund-raiser. California wineries and restaurants set up tasting booths throughout the beautiful Mendocino Coast Botanical Gardens in Fort Bragg, and live music is played throughout; (707) 961–4688.

Paul Bunyan Days, Fort Bragg; (707) 964–8687. Parade, arts and crafts, entertainment, games, food, wine, and beer.

November. Wine and Mushroom Festival. Known to chefs as porcini or cépe and to mushroom foragers as the king boletus, this popular wild mushroom thrives in the Mendocino woodlands. Join chefs on forest trails and learn how to spot and prepare wild edible mushrooms. Also mushroom hunts, classes, wild-mushroom dinners hosted by Mendocino wine makers; (866)–goMendo (466–3636); www.goMendo.com.

December. Candlelight Tours of Bed and Breakfast Inns, Fort Bragg, Little River, Albion, Mendocino; (800) 726–2780.

Other Recommended Restaurants and Lodgings

Albion

Albion River Inn, Highway 1, 6 miles south of Mendocino, P.O. Box 100, Albion 95410; (707) 937–1919. Overlooking the rugged coastline, ocean-front rooms with spectacular views, fireplaces, spas, contemporary decor; full breakfast, private headland path, lush gardens. The clifftop restaurant is one of the best on the coast, serving fresh seafood such as lime and ginger grilled prawns and Cajun oysters. More than one hundred top California labels are on the wine list.

Elk

Harbor House Inn, 5600 South Highway 1; (707) 877–3203. Classic Craftsman-style mansion, spectacular cliffside location, notable restaurant, lovely rooms.

Fort Bragg

Beach House Inn, 100 Pudding Creek; (707) 961–1700; www. beachinn. com. Overlooking the water, with spa tubs for two, fireplaces, private balconies; surrounded by lovely wetlands at the mouth of Pudding Creek. You can walk to the beach.

Fort Bragg Grille, 356 North Main Street; (707) 964–3663. A casual, fun place with unique specialties: chicken and andouille sausage gumbo, Greek salad sub sandwiches, jambalaya, grilled cod sandwiches, and always burgers and basic dishes for the less adventurous.

Grey Whale Inn, 615 North Main Street; (707) 964–0640 or (800) 382–7244; www.greywhaleinn.com. Built as a hospital in 1915, this three-story landmark has spacious rooms, with high windows looking to the sea or inward through the trees to town. You can walk right out the back door to take a long walk along the waterfront on the Old Coast Road. Rooms have sitting areas with armchairs, deep tubs, some fireplaces, and lots of books. Breakfast is a big buffet in the tiny dining room.

North Coast Brewing Company, 455 North Main Street; (707) 964–BREW. Exotic beers, ales, stouts, local fresh fish, ribs, Mendocino mud cake. If your innards are in good shape, try the Old Rasputin Russian Imperial Stout, the Route 66 chili, and the Cajun black beans and rice.

Pomo RV Park and Campground, 17999 Tregoning Lane off Highway 1, 1 mile south of Highway 20; (707) 964–3373. Secluded, spacious sites in a parklike setting.

Little River

Heritage House, 5200 North Highway 1; (707) 937–5885. Rooms and cottages on a bluff above a cove with sea views. Part of the lodge was built in the late 1800s, and the entire complex looks like New England. This is one of the most desired lodgings in the area, making it necessary to book weeks, and perhaps months, ahead. Rooms include full breakfast and dinner in a sedate and elegant atmosphere in three lovely dining rooms; almost every table has a view of the sea. Fresh local fish, Sonoma County poultry, lamb, and cheeses are put together for some of the best food you'll find in the region. Think about fresh Maine lobster bisque, Gewürztraminer-cured gravlax, apricot-stuffed pork chops with sour cherry sauce, pistachio cream cannoli with dark chocolate rum sauce. And for breakfast, brioche French toast and local Dungeness crab omelette.

Decor varies from old-fashioned comfortable to luxurious. Most rooms have fireplaces or wood-burning stoves; some have Jacuzzi tubs and ocean-view decks. Among the vast natural and introduced plantings, you will find Mediterranean, English country, and woodland gardens. Hire a limo here for guided tours of the coast and the Wine Country. Remember the film *Same Time Next Year,* with Alan Alda and Ellen Burstyn? The entire movie was written and filmed at Heritage House.

Little River Inn, 7751 Highway 1; (707) 937–5942. In the same family since it was built in the 1850s, a white wedding cake of a house that's expanded to become a sizable resort with one of the best restaurants in the area, a nine-hole golf course in the redwoods, and tennis. The bar is a favorite locals' meeting place. Rooms behind the inn have porches overlooking a beautiful beach and bay. On the menu may be rack of lamb marinated in Cabernet, polenta with porcini mushroom sauce, and warm ollalieberry cobbler.

Mendocino

Agate Cove Inn Bed and Breakfast, 11201 Lansing Street; (800) 527–3111. Right in town, garden cottages with fireplaces and private decks, ocean views. Breakfast by the fireplace in the dining room with a wonderful sea view.

Brewery Gulch Inn, 9401 Coast Highway 1 North; (800) 578–4454; www.brewerygulchinn.com. This newest inn on the coast is a grand lodge constructed with salvaged redwood. Grounds feature a heritage apple orchard, olive grove, trout pond, and mushroom forest. A pleasant trail winds through the property.

Glendeven Inn and Gallery, 1.5 miles south of Mendocino on Highway 1, P.O. Box 282, Mendocino 95460; (800) 822–4536. Antiques decorate rooms and suites in a gray and white farmhouse, big breakfasts. Walking path to the sea, gardens. Gallery of contemporary, handcrafted furniture, art, jewelry.

Hill House Inn, 10701 Palette Drive; (707) 937–0554 or (800) 422–0554; www.hillhouseinn.com. A New England–style, boutique hotel perched on a bluff above the sea, Hill House is recognized by those who watched *Murder She Wrote;* much of the TV program was filmed here. Most of the spacious, ultra-comfortable rooms and suites have patios or balconies with sea views, brass beds, cushy comforters, nice amenities, and some fireplaces. The Ocean View restaurant here features continental cuisine with lots of

The circa-1880 Joshua Grindle Inn is one of the oldest homes in Mendocino.

fresh seafood and a great wine list. A sunken fireplace and beautiful mahogany bar create coziness in the British-style pub.

Joshua Grindle Inn, 44800 Little Lake Road; (707) 937–4143 or (800) 474–6353; www.joshgrin.com. One of the oldest homes in town, a circa-1880 beauty on two cypress-bordered acres overlooking the town. Spacious New England–style rooms in the main house and very private accommodations in the water tower and the "chicken coop." Breakfast at the old harvest table may be baked pears, quiche, frittata, and fresh apple juice. A new guest house, just north of town, is a luxurious private home with two huge, ocean-view decks; a big fireplace; and a loft with separate bed and bath, perfect for two couples or a family.

Mendocino Hotel, 45080 Main Street; (707) 937–0511 or (800) 548–0513; www.mendocinohotel.com. On the National Register of Historic Places, this classic Victorian hotel built in 1878 is chock-full of period antiques, artifacts, and atmosphere. The smallish rooms in the hotel are charming, with ocean or town views. Some with fireplaces and four-posters, the luxurious cottage suites float in glorious gardens; all have down comforters and pampering amenities. The dinner restaurant serves top-notch California cuisine and American comfort food; think about grilled game hen, double-baked Brie with roasted garlic, and the hotel's signature French onion soup. The blooming Garden Room, brightened by skylights and ocean-view windows, is open for brunch and lunch at marble-topped tables, with a cafe bar menu in late afternoon. You can also get snacks. Notice the stunning stained-glass ceiling and the 200-year-old Dutch fireplace.

955 Ukiah Street Restaurant, 955 Ukiah Street; (707) 937–1955. In a rescued water tower, this is one of the best restaurants in town. Think about duck cannelloni, pork loin with port sauce, blackberry toasted-hazelnut ice cream, and strawberry-rhubarb pie. The upper dining area has an ocean view.

Sea Rock Inn, 11101 Lansing Street; (800) 906–0926; www.searock.com. One-half mile south of Mendocino in a wild garden, country cottages with kitchens, expanded continental breakfast.

Stevenswood Lodge, 8211 Highway 1, 2 miles south of Mendocino; (707) 937–1237 or (800) 421–2810; www.stevenswood.com. Surrounded by Van Damme State Park in a lovely forest setting with a sculpture garden and a dazzling collection of contemporary art. Suites are very nice, with hand-crafted furniture and some ocean views. Gourmet restaurant serves breakfast/brunch and dinner.

For More Information

Coastal Visitors Center, 990 Main Street, Mendocino, CA 95460; (707) 937–1938.

Fort Bragg–Mendocino Coast Chamber of Commerce, 332 North Main Street, Fort Bragg, CA 95437; (707) 961–6300 or (800) 726–2780; www.mendocinocoast.com.

Mendocino Area State Parks, (707) 937–5804; www.mcn.org/1/mendo parks/mendo. Information about camping, day use, and interpretive programs. For campsite reservations call (800) 444–PARK.

Mendocino Coast Accommodations (inns, hotels, bed-and-breakfast places, cottages, homes); (707) 937–5033.

Mendocino Coast Reservations, P.O. Box 1143, Mendocino, CA 95460; (800) 262–7801; www.mcmca.com. Vacation-home rentals, most with fireplaces, ocean views, and spas.

Advice: Driving can be hazardous on the twists and turns of Highway 1, and it's not recommended that you attempt it after dark or during storms. Farm animals and deer in the road can be a scary, and maybe deadly, surprise as you're coming around a blind curve.

Marin Waterfront

Sausalito and Tiburon

1 Night

On the north side of the Golden Gate, Marin County is a "banana belt," sunny and warm all summer when San Francisco is socked in with fog. It's nice to get away for a couple of quiet days in Marin's small, seaside towns.

- ☐ Sea views
- ☐ Waterfront cafes
- ☐ Hilltop walks
- ☐ Wildlife sanctuaries
- ☐ Island idyll
- ☐ Boutique shopping

Sausalito tumbles down steep, forested hillsides to the edge of the bay. Sophisticated shops, sea-view restaurants, and marinas lined with yachts and funky houseboats share postcard views of the San Francisco skyline.

A residential community of vintage mansions and luxury condos, Tiburon occupies a spectacular peninsula surrounded by the quiet waters of Richardson Bay, where kayakers paddle and sailboarders fly about. Raccoon Straits, a narrow, windswept channel carefully navigated by sailboats and ferries, runs between Tiburon and Angel Island, which is a state park.

Shopping, walks in the salty air, and fine dining are primary activities on this trip, with a Mount Tamalpais side trip on the way home.

Day 1 / Morning

Take a ferry to Sausalito, or, in your car, immediately to the north of the Golden Gate Bridge, take the Alexander Avenue exit, descending down into Sausalito; Alexander becomes Bridgeway, the main street.

BREAKFAST: Seven Seas, 682 Bridgeway, Sausalito; (415) 332–1304. From 8:00 A.M. every breakfast specialty you can think of is served, indoors or on the patio. Best breakfast in town.

Downtown Sausalito is a National Historic Landmark District and a long-established haven for artists, writers, and craftspeople. The annual **Sausalito Art Festival** attracts 50,000 people over Labor Day weekend.

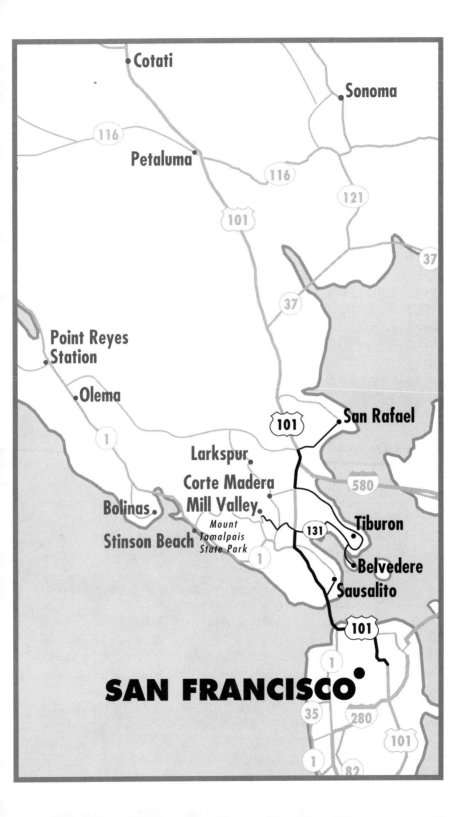

In midtown, where a hundred or so shops and restaurants are concentrated, is a small city park with palm trees and huge stone elephants with streetlights on their heads, leftovers from San Francisco's 1915 Exposition. Behind the park, ferries come and go to San Francisco and Tiburon.

Now, hit the Bridgeway shops and galleries! **Petri's** beautiful, big store holds a museumlike collection of art glass, the largest and most spectacular array I've ever seen (675 Bridgeway; 415–332–2225); look for the jellyfish. More art glass and crystals are on display at **Collector's Gallery** at 745 Bridgeway. Aloha-shirt collectors head for **Odyssey** at 673 Bridgeway (415–331–8677). A phenomenon in the art world in the last few years, sleek Zimbabwean Shona stone sculpture is featured at **Spirits in Stone** (585 Bridgeway; 415–332–2388).

Off Bridgeway, the **Armchair Sailor,** at 42 Caledonia (415–332–7505), has books, charts, games, and art for the nautically inspired. Just north of midtown, the **Heathware Ceramics Outlet,** 400 Gate 5 Road off Bridgeway (415–332–3732), is worth a stop for seconds from a major producer of stoneware. If you are interested in sports, entertainment, and historic figures, stop in at the **Mark Reuben Gallery** to see black-and-white photos of legendary stars and athletes (34 Princess Street, off Bridgeway; 415–332–8815). Explore the **Tapia Art Gallery** at 52 Princess Street (415–332–6177). Bob Tapia's local landscapes are luminescent, stormy skies and sunsets at the beach.

Heading north on Bridgeway, watch for the sign for **Bay Model,** 2100 Bridgeway at Spring Street (415–332–3871), a one-and-a-half-acre, hydraulic working scale model of the San Francisco Bay Delta, a fascinating research tool used by the U.S. Army Corps of Engineers; call ahead to find out when the tides in the model are scheduled for activity. The natural and cultural history of the bay are traced in exhibits—wetlands, wildlife, shipwrecks, antique equipment.

From the Bay Model, a 3.8-mile flat, paved path between Sausalito and Mill Valley, called the **Sausalito Bikeway,** makes a nice bike ride or walk (from Bridgeway and Wateree Street in Sausalito to Tennessee Avenue and Shoreline Highway in Mill Valley). You will pass the edge of Richardson Bay and Bothin Marsh Open Space Preserve, where shorebirds reside; a heliport; the famous Sausalito houseboats; and an old shipyard. Be warned that the bikeway is quite popular on weekends.

Nearby at **Open Water Rowing,** off Bridgeway at 85 Liberty Ship Way (415–332–1091), take a kayaking lesson on Richardson Bay between Sausalito and Tiburon; all ages find it easy to learn, and, a great way to get a gull's-eye view of wildlife on the bay. Along the Sausalito shoreline in this area is a series of yacht harbors, marinas, and houseboat moorings.

Sausalito Waterfront Activities offers bike and kayak rentals, tours, sunset cruises, and more outdoor recreation (803 Bridgeway; 415–331–4448).

Drive south out of town to Highway 101 to the Tiburon exit, taking Tiburon Boulevard south along Richardson's Bay to **Tiburon.**

LUNCH: Sam's Anchor Cafe, 27 Main, Tiburon; (415) 435–4527. One of several harborfront restaurants with views of the San Francisco skyline, Belvedere Island, and Angel Island. Ferries, yachts, and seagulls slide by; time slides by, too, as you sip a beer on the sunny deck and tuck into clam chowder, fresh crab, and fish of all kinds. Casual, with a frisky bar crowd. Weekend brunches are a reason to spend the day at Sam's.

If you plan to be here on the opening day of yacht season in April, arrive early for a good seat at Sam's or grab enough space for a picnic blanket on the lawns beside the bay. Decorated to the max, hundreds of pleasure craft are blessed; then they sail or motor back and forth while landlubbers engage in vernal behavior, like kite flying and boom-box playing.

Afternoon

From the waterfront on Main, you can walk up the wooded streets of **Belvedere**—covered with zillion-dollar mansions from several eras. It's an architectural sight-seeing adventure to drive or walk the steep, narrow lanes.

Prior to the 1920s, Tiburon was a lagoon lined with houseboats, called arks. When the lagoon was filled in 1940, the arks were placed on pilings. Today, curvy, tree-lined **Ark Row,** at the west end of Main, is a charming shopping street. Along with 1-block-long **Main Street,** Ark Row is also chockablock with art galleries. Between the two streets is the **Corinthian Yacht Club;** it's OK to walk in and look at the fancy yachts.

Windsor Vineyards, 72 Main (415–435–3113), will ship gift boxes of wine with your name on the bottles. **Westerley's,** 46 Main (415–435–4233), has old-fashioned penny candy, bubble gum cigars, chocolate sardines, and licorice pipes. The **Designer Watch Shop,** 28 Main (415–435–3732), sells cheapo copies of every name-brand watch; your friends will never know the difference. At **ForPaws** (90 Main Street; 415–435–9522), pick up a toy for your pet, a stuffed animal for your animal, gourmet dog treats, and glamour beds and bowls.

On the west side of Ark Row, at 52 Beach Road on an inlet of the bay, is the **China Cabin,** a delightful fragment from a sidewheel steamer that plied the trade routes between San Francisco and the Orient in the late 1800s. The saloon was salvaged when the ship burned and served as a home for decades before becoming a maritime museum furnished with period antiques and elaborate gold-leaf ornamentation. Call for a seasonal schedule (415–435–5633).

There are a number of historic buildings in Tiburon. You can get a walking-tour brochure from the Tiburon Peninsula Chamber of Commerce (415–435–5633).

From Main walk north on Tiburon Boulevard 3 blocks to the **Boardwalk** shopping center, where tucked into an alleyway are small shops, including **Shorebirds,** 1550 Tiburon Boulevard (415–435–0888), worth searching out for one-of-a-kind jewelry pieces, locally crafted ceramics and woodware, European toys, paintings, and nautical gifts.

From downtown Tiburon to the north end of Richardson Bay is a beautiful waterfront walk, 2 miles long, on a flat, paved path; there are benches along the way and a huge lawn for Frisbee tossing and sun-bathing. The path is popular with joggers, in-line skaters, bikers, and tykes on trikes. At the north end of the path is the **Richardson Bay Audubon Center and Wildlife Sanctuary,** 376 Greenwood Beach Road (415–388–2524; www.egret.org). Thousands of sea- and shorebirds, accompanied by harbor seals in wintertime, inhabit this 900-acre preserve. A self-guided nature trail and a bookstore are adjacent to **Lyford House,** a lemon-yellow landmark Victorian open to the public.

Reachable by a short ferry ride from Main Street (Red and White Fleet; 415–435–2131), **Angel Island State Park** (415–435–3522; www. angelisland.com) is just offshore. Popular activities here are walking and biking the breezy island paths and roads to get a gull's-eye view of three bridges and the bay. Once a Miwok hunting ground, then a cattle ranch, a U.S. Army base, and a prisoner of war camp, Angel Island has a unique past, and you will see several historical sites; take a narrated tour in an open-air tram. Historic buildings remain from World War II, when 5,000 soldiers a day were processed before leaving for the Pacific. Between 1910 and 1940 hundreds of thousands of Asians were detained on the island, awaiting admission into the United States.

Thirteen miles of hiking trails and 8 miles of mountain-biking roads crisscross the island. Mountain bikes are available to rent, or you can take sea kayaking tours—even moonlight paddle trips—that are conducted around the perimeter of the island with historical and ecological interpretation (415–332–4465). Less energetic visitors will enjoy sitting on the deck of the cafe with an espresso and a light lunch, watching sailboats and freighters glide by. A few environmental campsites are available (800–444–7275). No dogs, skateboards, or in-line skates are allowed on Angel Island.

The Angel Island–Tiburon Ferry offers a Sunset Cruise on weekends where you bring your own picnic dinner and enjoy cruising the bay in the early evening (415–388–6770). A popular new five-hour tour, called the **Island Hop,** combines visits to Angel Island State Park and Alcatraz; included are ferries, admission fee of about $30, audio tour of Alcatraz, and the motorized, narrated, open-air tram tour of Angel Island (Pier 41 at Fisherman's Wharf, San Francisco; 415–705–5555).

DINNER: Guaymas, 5 Main, Tiburon; (415) 435–6300. Spectacular waterfront location; nouvelle Southwest/Mexican food; lively bar and outdoor terrace.

LODGING: Panama Hotel, Restaurant, and Inn, 4 Bayview Street, San Rafael; (415) 457–3993 or (800) 899–3993; www.panamahotel.com. Unique in glitzy Marin, this European-style country garden inn is on a quiet street and has a quirky complex of reasonably priced cottages, suites, and rooms, some with balconies, claw-foot tubs, kitchenettes, ceiling fans, and a charming collection of furnishings and fun, arty decor. Guests return year after year for a certain special atmosphere and comfort. Hearty continental breakfast. Small, 1930s-decor restaurant serves excellent bistro food for lunch, dinner, and brunch, with live swing and jazz music several nights a week.

Day 2 / Morning

BREAKFAST: Sweden House, 35 Main, Tiburon; (415) 435–9767. Breakfast by the bay with the denizens of Tiburon. Swedish pastries, eggs, and everything else.

From the east end of Main Street, take Paradise Drive around the west side of the Tiburon Peninsula, a narrow, winding road through forestlands on the edge of the bay. After 1 mile, before Westward Drive, watch for the **Nature Conservancy Uplands Nature Preserve,** also known as the **Ring Mountain Preserve,** 3152 Paradise Drive (415–435–6465), a ridgetop, 377-acre piece of wilderness with walking trails and wonderful views. It's less than 1 mile's walk to the summit on a trail edged with knee-

A forest of masts at the Tiburon marina.

high native grasses dotted with wildflowers in spring. Bay trees, madrones, live oaks, and buckeyes provide shade in meadows inhabited by several endangered plant species, including the Tiburon mariposa lily, which exists nowhere else in the world. On the hilltop you'll have a 360-degree view of San Francisco Bay, Mount Tam, Marin County, and the East Bay hills.

LUNCH: Buckeye Roadhouse, 15 Shoreline Highway, adjacent to Highway 101 on the south end of Mill Valley; (415) 331–2600. A winding garden path lures you into a historic Bavarian-style lodge right off the freeway, warm and inviting with a fireplace, cushy booths, and big band–era music. The food is anything but Bavarian: California cuisine and American comfort food, light-hearted ethnic specialties. Open from lunch straight through the evening.

Afternoon

From the Buckeye take the Panoramic Highway north, winding several miles up on the east side of **Mount Tamalpais State Park** (415–388–2070). You can't miss Mount Tam—it's the 2,500-foot mountain peak that you can see from everywhere in Marin. Park at the Pan Toll Ranger Station and Visitors Center, get a trail map, and walk a bit on one of several hiking trails that start here; the shortest one is the **Twenty-Minute Verna Dunshea Trail,** which circles the peak. Views are beyond description, and it's often sunny up here when it's foggy everywhere below. Mount Tam's natural wonders are legion—canyons, forests, streams and meadows, waterfalls, and wildflowers—and offer opportunities for wild-and-woolly mountain biking or easy downhill walking.

Perhaps you'll want to stop for a sunset cocktail on the deck at **Mountain Home Inn,** 810 Panoramic Highway (415–381–9000), if you have a designated driver for the trip back to San Francisco.

There's More

Boating and Bay tours. Captain Case Powerboat and Waterbike Rental, Schoonmaker Point Marina off Bridgeway, Sausalito; (415) 331–0444. Boston whalers, tours on the bay, sunset cruises, water taxis, high-tech water bikes to play with on calm Richardson Bay. Water bikes are two-pontooned, one-person crafts with a seat in the center that you pedal with feet and hands, reaching a sizzling top speed of 10 miles per hour. It's so safe that you don't even need to wear a bathing suit.

Commodore Seaplanes, from the north end of Sausalito; (800) 973–2752; www.seaplane.com. San Francisco Bay tours, sunset champagne flights.

Hawaiian Chieftain; (415) 331–3214; www.hawaiianchieftain.com. One-hundred-three-foot replica of a 1790 square-rigged topsail ketch, romantic sunset sails, Sunday brunch, sail up the northern coast.

Sea Trek, Schoonmaker Point, Sausalito; (415) 488–1000; www. seatrekkayak. com. Guided kayak tours of the bay, classes, sunset and full moon paddles.

China Camp State Park, RR 1, P.O. Box 244, San Rafael 94901; (415) 456–0766. North of San Rafael, take the Civic Center exit off Highway 101 to North San Pedro Road, heading east. A 1,640-acre waterfront park on San Pablo Bay, with beach, hiking trails, a small museum, and primitive camping. Trails along the ridge offer views of the north Bay Area. Weather at the protected beach level is often warm when fog chills the rest of Marin. Sailboarding is a big deal from May through October.

Ferries. Tiburon, Sausalito, and Larkspur are accessible by ocean-going ferry: Angel Island Ferry, (415) 435–2131, www.angelislandferry.com; Blue and Gold Fleet, (415) 705–5555, www.blueandgoldfleet.com; Red and White Ferries, (800) 229–2784, www.redandwhite.com.

Marin Headlands, accessible from Bunker and Conzelman roads west of Highway 101, just north of the Golden Gate Bridge. Twelve thousand acres of wilderness with famous views of San Francisco, the bay, and the Pacific. Scattered throughout the headlands are old military tunnels and bunkers that guarded the Gate from the Spanish-American War through the Cold War. Remains of Forts Barry and Cronkhite, the Headlands Center for the Arts, the Marine Mammal Center, and more. A visitors center is located in Fort Barry. A trail map describing the historical and natural sites, wildlife, and suggested hikes is available by calling (415) 331–1540; www.nps.gov/goga.

Marine Mammal Center in the Marin Headlands; (415) 289–7325. A rare opportunity to see rescued marine mammals at this hospital for orphaned, sick, and injured seals, sea lions, dolphins, otters, and whales from California's 900-mile coast, from ten-pound newborn harbor seals to 600-pound sea lions. During some months, there are few animals on view; call ahead.

Muir Woods National Monument, 3 miles north of Highway 1 on Muir Woods Road; (415) 388–7059; www.nps.gov/muwo. The only remaining old-growth redwood forest in the Bay Area. It's a popular tourist destination frequented by tour buses, so arrive early in the day (opens at sunrise). Beside walking paths beneath towering redwoods are beautiful wildflowers and ferns. There is a visitors center, a gift shop featuring the works of more than 150 local artisans, and a snack bar.

The Point Bonita Lighthouse in the Marin Headlands is perched on a bit of rock at the entrance to the Golden Gate, with incredible views and a (slightly) swaying footbridge over crashing waves; walk down and back on your own and get the history from the ranger in the tiny visitors center, or take the guided walk, which takes (it seems) forever. Precipitous cliff-top trails near here are not for little kids.

Special Events

April. Opening Day of Yacht Season, Tiburon and Sausalito waterfront; (415) 435–5633. Pleasure craft decorated and blessed; a beautiful and exceedingly high-spirited day on the bay.

May. Tiburon Wine Festival, Tiburon; (415) 435–5623.

June. Humming Toadfish Festival, Bay Model, Sausalito; (415) 332–0505. Entertainment, games, food, in celebration of a famous fish.

Floating Homes Tour, Sausalito; (415) 332–1916. A chance to see surprising sophistication and inventive decor in Sausalito's famous houseboats.

Italian Street Painting Festival, San Rafael; (415) 457–4878. An Italian-style celebration of the arts with more than 400 professional and student *Madonnari* (street painters) covering the streets with their flamboyant, fabulous works. Strolling musicians, jazz, R&B, and swing on a main stage; dance performances; and more fun.

September. Sausalito Art Festival (415–332–3555), a gigantic event attracting top-notch artists and thousands of visitors, plus food and music.

October. Marin Center Fall Antiques and Art Show, San Rafael; (415) 662–9500.

Italian Film Festival, San Rafael; (415) 456–4056.

December. Lighted Yacht Parade, Sausalito; (415) 331–7262.

Other Recommended Restaurants and Lodgings

Corte Madera

Book Passage, 51 Tamal Vista; (800) 999–7909; www.bookpassage.com. One of the largest independent bookstores in the country. The in-store cafe has indoor and outdoor seating; opens early, closes late. Movie stars, literary lions, and the most interesting people in Marin County are seen at Book Passage.

Corte Madera Inn, 1815 Redwood Highway; (800) 777–9670; www.best western.com. Nice motel overlooking gardens and lawns, with swimming and wading pools, a laundry, playground, and a good coffee shop. Continental breakfast is free, and so is the shuttle to the San Francisco ferry. Can't beat this combo anywhere in Marin.

Embassy Suites Hotel, 101 McInnis Parkway; (800) EMBASSY; www. embassymarin.com. Upscale suites with two double beds, sofa bed, two TVs, microwave, and coffeemaker; guest laundry. Free shuttles to the Oakland and San Francisco airports and to the ferry. Room rate includes full breakfast and an early evening party of snacks, and cocktails.

Larkspur

The Lark Creek Inn, 234 Magnolia Avenue; (415) 924–7767. Internationally famous chef Bradley Ogden, American heartland and nouvelle cuisine, garden patio, vintage architecture.

Mill Valley

Gira Polli, 590 East Blithedale Avenue; (415) 383–6040. A hundred chickens at a time spin over a wood fire, emerging crisp and juicy, redolent of rosemary and sage, orange and lemon. Pasta, too, and risotto, antipasti, daily Italian specialties. Take-out and delivery.

Mill Valley Inn, 165 Throckmorton Avenue; (800) 595–2100. Sixteen inn rooms around an indoor/outdoor terrace where breakfast and afternoon refreshments are served. Contemporary European ambience, cottages and guest rooms, balconies or decks, fireplace or woodstove.

Pelican Inn, at Muir Beach (415–383–6000), is a coastal inn on the English channel: all brick and plaster walls with rough-hewn beams. Daily menu of prime rib, Yorkshire pudding, mixed English grill, and cottage pie. English hospitality, heavily draped canopy beds, and an English breakfast of grilled tomatoes and bangers, toast, and marmalade.

Tea Garden Springs, 38 Miller Avenue; (415) 389–7123. Asian-style spa for spending the day in heaven, therapeutic herbs, massage, aromatherapy, beauty treatments, teahouse, shiatsu, acupressure. A soothing environment of gurgling fountains, elegant treatment rooms, gardens, Jacuzzis, views of Mount Tam. If not now, when?

San Rafael

Gerstle Park Inn, 34 Grove Street; (415) 721–7611 or (800) 726–7611; www. gerstleparkinn.com. A luxuriously appointed, century-old country inn with ten gorgeous suites awash in Asian and Western art and antiques; private decks and patios, sumptuous robes and amenities, king Jacuzzis, some cottages with kitchens and sitting rooms; full breakfast and evening wine in the elegant main parlors or on the veranda.

Sausalito

Alta Mira Hotel and Restaurant, 125 Bulkley Avenue; (415) 332–1350. The breathtaking view from the terrace makes a sunset cocktail or Sunday brunch an event.

Caruso's Fish Market & Cafe, off Bridgeway Boulevard, at the foot of Harbor Drive; (415) 332–1015. Since 1957 Caruso's has been the place to come for Dungeness crab. Their soups, salads, and fish specials highlight the bounty of the deep blue sea. If they have the swordfish sandwich on the chalkboard you won't need to read further. The grill closes at 3:00 P.M.

Casa Madrona, 801 Bridgeway; (415) 331–5888. Dining terrace with retractable roof and sliding-glass walls, dramatic views of San Francisco Bay and Sausalito yacht harbor. Award-winning California-European cuisine and wine list, Sunday jazz brunch.

Casa Madrona Hotel, 801 Bridgeway; (415) 332–0502 or (800) 567–9524; www.casamadrona.com. Circa-1880 landmark inn, luxurious rooms, suites, and cottages with fireplaces, European antiques, garden and harbor views, outdoor Jacuzzi, in-room dining and massage, beautiful gardens; breakfast and evening refreshments.

Hotel Sausalito, 16 El Portal; (415) 332–0700; www.hotelsausalito.com. As if on the French Riviera, this small, charming boutique hotel is across from the waterfront park. Lovely pastel colors in rooms that vary in size and price, with armoires, wrought-iron beds, a small patio; some streetside rooms are noisy.

The Inn Above Tide, 30 El Portal; (800) 893–8433; e-mail: inntide@ix. netcom.com. Next to the ferry dock, luxurious suites with wide water views, fireplaces, private decks, breakfast, and wine hour.

Kitti's Place, 3001 Bridgeway; (415) 331–0390. In a homey atmosphere, comfort food extraordinaire, from homemade soup to Asian-inspired salads and entrees, and great sandwiches (try the portobello). Breakfast, lunch, and early dinner.

Ondine, 558 Bridgeway; (415) 331–1133. In a spectacular waterfront location with smashing views of the San Francisco skyline, Ondine has sleek, contemporary modern Japanese decor; a memorable wine list; and wonderful California cuisine with an Asian touch. Dinner and Sunday brunch.

Scoma's, 588 Bridgeway; (415) 332–9551. On the water at the south end of town, in a baby blue clapboard building. Dependably good seafood.

For More Information

Bed and Breakfast Exchange of Marin; (415) 485–1971.

Marin County Convention and Visitors Bureau, 1013 Larkspur Landing Circle, Larkspur, CA 94939; (415) 499–5000; www.visitormarin.org.

Sausalito Chamber of Commerce Visitors Center, 29 Caledonia Street, Sausalito, CA 94966; (415) 331–7262; www.sausalito.org.

Tiburon Peninsula Chamber of Commerce, 96 Main Street, Tiburon, CA 94920; (415) 435–5633; www.citysearch.com/sfo/tiburon.

Point Reyes
and Inverness 10

The National Seashore

2 Nights

More than a few weekends are needed to discover the many joys of the Point Reyes National Seashore, comprising 71,000 miraculous acres on the edge of the continent: two fingerlike peninsulas pointing jaggedly into the Pacific; the long, shallow biodiversity of Tomales Bay; the big curve of Drakes Bay, where the English explorer Sir Francis Drake set foot in 1579; and oyster farms, clamming beaches, tidepools, and wildlife sanctuaries.

- ☐ Natural seashore
- ☐ Beachcombing
- ☐ Bird-watching
- ☐ Wildflower walks
- ☐ Oyster farms ·
- ☐ Inns by the sea

Separated from the mainland by the San Andreas Fault, the unique location of the peninsula gives rise to several distinct habitats. More than 45 percent of the bird species in North America have been sighted here.

From February through early summer, the meadows and marine terraces of Point Reyes are blanketed with California poppies, dark blue lupine, pale baby-blue-eyes, Indian paintbrush, and a few varieties of wildflowers existing only here. Dominating the landscape is the green-black Douglas fir forest of Inverness Ridge, running northwest to southeast alongside the San Andreas earthquake fault. The summit of Mount Wittenberg, at 1,407 feet, is reachable in an afternoon's climb.

Subject to summer fogs and winter drizzles, Point Reyes is a favorite destination not only for those who love a sunny day at the beach but for intrepid outdoor types who follow cool-weather nature hikes with cozy evenings by a fireplace in a vintage bed-and-breakfast inn.

Day 1 / Morning

Take Highway 101 north to the Tamalpais-Paradise Drive exit, fifteen minutes north of the Golden Gate Bridge. Exit right and take the overpass to

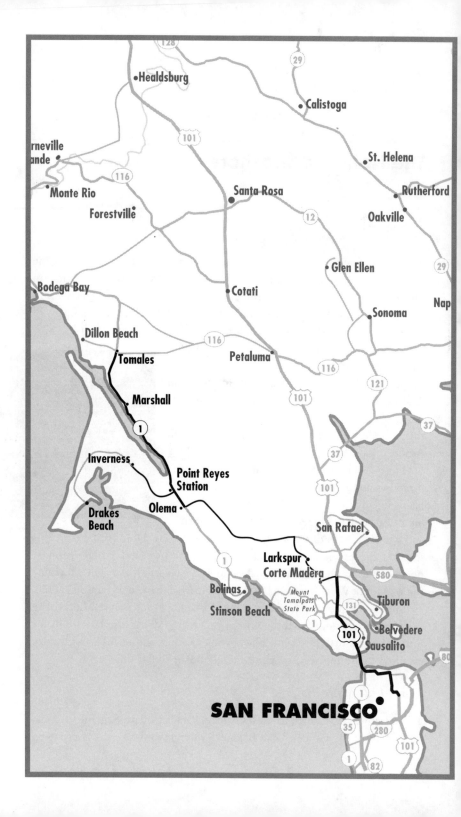

your left over the freeway. Turn left on Redwood Avenue then right on Corte Madera Boulevard, which becomes Magnolia Avenue.

BREAKFAST: Pull up to a pasticceria straight from San Marco Square with Italian mahogany, marble inlay, and a hand-painted mural. **Emporio Rulli** (464 Magnolia Avenue, Larkspur; 415–888–88RULLI; www.rulli. com) has traditional breads, pastries, hand-dipped chocolates, and more than nine house-roasted coffee blends. In short, the best breakfast stop in Marin. You can assemble an excellent picnic by choosing from the daily selection of panini (Italian sandwiches).

Continue driving north on Magnolia Avenue then turn left onto Sir Frances Drake Boulevard. Proceed west forty-five minutes on winding, two-lane Sir Francis Drake Boulevard to the **Point Reyes National Seashore Visitor Center** at **Olema** (415–663–1092; www.nps.gov/pore).

Exhibits, guidebooks, and trail maps at the Point Reyes Visitor Center will help orient you to the many destinations within the National Seashore. According to the day's weather, you may choose beachcombing and sunbathing (or fogbathing), backpacking to overnight sites, or easy walks or bike rides on meadowland paths, such as the 4.4-mile **Bear Valley Trail** to Arch Rock overlook at the beach—a sunny picnickers' meadow. Rest rooms are located halfway. This is the most popular and one of the most beautiful trails, leading through forest tunnels, along creeks and through meadows, ending on a bluff 50 feet above the sea.

At the end of Limantour Road, **Limantour Beach** is a long stretch of windswept sand that is good for surf fishing and sunbathing. Look for the Muddy Hollow Trail for an easy, 1-mile bird-watching and wildflower walk.

Bird-watching is excellent in the 500-acre **Limantour Estero Reserve,** west of Limantour Beach. You get to **Drakes Estero,** a much larger saltwater lagoon, from Sir Francis Drake Boulevard on the west side. This rocky intertidal area is a giant tidepool and bird sanctuary, rich with such wildlife as anemones, sea stars, crabs, and even rays and leopard sharks.

LUNCH: Picnic on the beach or in a trailside meadow.

Afternoon

Energetic hikers can make the steep but short ascent on Sky Trail to the summit of Mount Wittenberg, and beach bums will choose from many coastal access trails. The long sandy stretch of Point Reyes Beach is accessible in two places by car.

Short, easy walks near the visitors center include **Kule Loklo,** the Miwok Village, where an ancient Indian site has been re-created, and the **Woodpecker Trail,** a self-guided nature walk leading to the park rangers' Morgan horse ranch and a Morgan horse museum. Horses are bred and trained here on a hundred beautiful acres for the use of the National Park rangers in this park and in Zion and Hawaii Volcanoes National Parks. You can tour a blacksmith's shop, a museum, and the stables.

The **Earthquake Trail,** less than a mile in length, is where you'll see photos of the effects of the 1906 earthquake and signs explaining earth movement.

DINNER: Station House Cafe, Main Street, Point Reyes Station; (415) 663– 1515. Eclectic, hearty California food; pot roast, duck breast with cherry sauce, fresh fish, pecan pie; dinner served until 11:00 P.M. in the bar; live entertainment three nights a week. Kick up your heels to country music at the **Western Saloon** on Main Street (415–663–1661).

LODGING: Point Reyes Seashore Lodge, 10021 Highway 1, Olema; (415) 663–9000 or (800) 404–LODGE; www.ptreyesseashorelodge.com. Just south of Point Reyes. Reminiscent of national park lodges from a century ago, a castlelike re-creation of a large Victorian inn on the exterior, modern California Craftsman–style inside, sweeping lawns above a creek and woods, all bordering the National Seashore. Twenty-two rooms and suites with feather beds, down comforters, bay windows, fireplaces, and Jacuzzi tubs. Breakfast is generous, with bowls of fresh fruit, yogurt, granola, pastries, and breads. A large library of guidebooks and restaurant menus is a big help. The staff will arrange bike, kayak, and horse rentals for you.

Day 2 / Morning

BREAKFAST: At the Point Reyes Seashore Lodge.

Give your hiking legs a break and spend the morning shopping and cafe lounging in the town of **Point Reyes Station.** Many one-hundred-year-old buildings remain on the main street of this narrow-gauge railroad town founded in the 1800s. The train depot is now the post office, the Fire Engine House a community center. Dairy ranches and commercial oyster companies fuel the rural economy.

Black Mountain Weavers, on Main Street (415–663–9130), is a co-op gallery of fine woven rugs, sweaters, and tapestries, plus jewelry and art. At **Susan Hayes Handwovens,** slip into luscious silk and chenille jackets and vests (80 Fourth Street; 415–663–8057). Equestrians will go into **Cabaline Saddle Shop,** on Main Street (415–663–8303), for English and western saddlery and clothing. Also on Main is **Toby's Feed Barn** (415–663–1223)—fresh flowers, plants, produce, T-shirts, body and bath items, souvenirs, and hay for your horse.

Shakers Shops West is a unique resource for authentic Shaker-design furniture and furniture kits, tinware, baskets, and rag rugs (415–669–7256; www.shakershops.com). This and several other specialty stores are in the Livery Stable at Fourth and B Streets, next door to **Tomales Bay Foods,** which is owned by a graduate of the restaurant Chez Panisse, the birthplace of California cuisine. An airy emporium of luscious hot and cold take-out foods, organic produce, flowers, and homemade ice cream, the place features products from local farms, ranches, and wineries (415–663–9335). On weekends, there are often wine, cheese, and seafood tastings, and cooking demonstrations.

Marin County's only kite store is a great one, at Third and B Streets, **Into the Blue.** You will find dual-line, stunt, and acrobatic kites, as well as parafoils, boomerangs, and Frisbees (415–663–1147).

LUNCH: From Point Reyes drive north on Highway 1 along the shoreline of Tomales Bay a few miles to **Nick's Cove,** 23240 Highway 1, Marshall; (415) 663–1033. Rustic, aromatic, on the wetlands of the bay, barbecued oysters and seafood galore, a list of beers as long as your arm; lots of fun. Also in Marshall, **Hog Island Oyster Company** (20215 Highway 1; 415–663–9218) sells the succulent shellfish and provides shucking knives, tables, and BBQ kettles.

Afternoon

Five miles farther north, the minitown of **Tomales** is a 2-block-long headquarters for crabbing, clamming, and surf fishing. At low tide in winter, catch a clammer's barge from here out to the flatlands around Hog Island in the bay. Hog Island and nearby Duck Island are private wildlife sanctuaries frequented by harbor seals.

In a wooden, false-front, antiques-bedecked building, the **Old Town Cafe** in Tomales is a cozy spot for sandwiches, homemade soup, and fresh fish (707–878–2526).

On your way back from Tomales to Point Reyes, then around to Inverness, take a walk or swim in the quiet waters of **Heart's Desire**

Beach in **Tomales Bay State Park** off Sir Francis Drake Boulevard on Pierce Point Road; (415) 669–1140. Backed by a dramatic stand of first-growth Bishop pine, the wind-protected, easily accessible beach on the bay is the mildest environment in the area for swimming, sailboarding, kayaking, and clam digging. There are picnic tables, 6 miles of easy to moderate trails, and a few hike-in or bike-in campsites.

A resort village since 1889, **Inverness,** population 1,000, is a day-tripper's rest stop and a community of country cottages on steep wooded slopes at the northern end of **Inverness Ridge,** overlooking Tomales Bay. There are seafood cafes, bed-and-breakfast inns, a small marina, and not much else but eye-popping scenery.

Discovered by Spanish explorers in the 1600s, **Tomales Bay** is 13 miles long, 1 mile wide, and very shallow, with acres of mudflats and salt- and freshwater marshes. Commercial oyster farms line the western shore. More than one hundred species of resident and migrating waterbirds are the reason you'll see anorak-clad, binocular-braced bird-watchers at every pullout on Highway 1. Perch, flounder, sand dabs, and crabs are catchable by small boat.

Rent a kayak and paddle around Tomales Bay, a calm piece of water. You will likely see bat rays, jellyfish, and osprey and seal, among other wildlife. Rent kayaks and wet suits and get instructions at **Blue Waters Kayaking** (next to Barnaby's by the Bay restaurant, 12938 Sir Francis Drake Boulevard, Inverness; 415–669–2600; www.bwkayak.com).

DINNER: **Manka's Inverness Restaurant,** 30 Calendar Way, Inverness; (415) 669–1034. A 1917 fishing lodge nestled under the pines; game and fresh fish grilled in an open fireplace, house-cured meat and poultry, homegrown produce; comfortably cozy, candlelit atmosphere; notable chefs; reservations essential. Accommodations here are in a country-luxe lodge in Adirondack style with log beds, Arts and Crafts furnishings, fireplaces, and Ralph Lauren linens; plus, a rose-covered cottage.

LODGING: **Ten Inverness Way,** 10 Inverness Way, Inverness; (415) 669–1648; www.teninvernessway.com. Country-style inn with five rooms filled with quilts, lace curtains, comfort, and light. Common room with big stone fireplace; lovely gardens, hot tub, full breakfast, walk to hiking trails.

Day 3 / Morning

BREAKFAST: At Ten Inverness Way.

Drive north on Sir Francis Drake Boulevard to the Pierce Point Road;

McClure Beach is a great place to explore.

take a right and park in the upper parking lot at **McClure Beach.** It's a 9-mile round-trip around **Tomales Point** and along the coastline. Spring wildflowers float in the meadows; whales spout December through February. A herd of elk live in the grassy fields of **Pierce Ranch** on the tip of the peninsula. These windswept moors remind some visitors of Scotland.

McClure Beach is wide, sandy, backed by high cliffs, and dotted with rocks and great tidepools. Bluffs framed by groves of Bishop pine look like Japanese woodcut prints; these pines are found only in a few isolated locations on the California coast.

Point Reyes Lighthouse, at the end of Sir Francis Drake Boulevard, 15 miles south of Inverness, is reachable by 400 steps leading downhill from a high bluff. Many shipwrecks occurred off the **Point Reyes Headlands** until the lighthouse was built in 1870. Below the dramatic cliffs are miles of beaches accessible from Sir Francis Drake Boulevard. Exposed to the full force of storms and pounding surf, these beaches are unsafe for swimming or surfing. The headlands, tidepools, sea stacks, lagoons, wave-carved caves, and rocky promontories are alive with birds—endangered brown pelicans, cormorants, surf skooters, sandpipers, grebes, terns—and sea life such as giant anemones and sea palms, urchins, fish, and even the occasional great white shark offshore of Tomales Point.

From Sir Francis Drake Boulevard near the lighthouse, take the turnoff to Chimney Rock to the most spectacular wildflower walk in the park, an easy, 1.5-mile route.

At the 7-mile-long crescent of **Drakes Beach** are a visitors center and picnic tables. During whale-watching season, December through spring, a shuttle bus may be operating between the lighthouse and the beach. Some 20,000 California gray whales travel the Pacific coastline going south to breed in Mexican waters and then return with their babies to the Arctic.

LUNCH: Barnaby's by the Bay, 12938 Sir Francis Drake Boulevard, 1 mile north of Inverness at the Golden Hind Inn; (415) 669–1114. Two decks overlooking a marina; fresh fish, salads, barbecued oysters and chicken, and ribs from the applewood smoker; jazz on weekends; you'll be tempted to stay here for the rest of the day.

Head back to the Bay Area.

There's More

Bolinas. Just north of Stinson Beach off Highway 1, Olema-Bolinas Road; (415) 499–6387. A rustic, nineteenth-century village near beautiful **Bolinas Lagoon,** where salt marsh, mudflats, and calm sea waters harbor thousands of birds and ducks, and a mile of shallow tidepools (415–868–9244; www.egret.org). Agate Beach is a small county park. Four miles northwest of Bolinas on Mesa Road, a short nature trail leads to the **Point Reyes Bird Observatory,** where you can observe bird banding (415-868-1221). This is the Palomarin Trailhead which leads to four freshwater lakes and to Double Point Bay; 3 miles from the trailhead, watch for Bass Lake, a secret swimming spot. Have breakfast, lunch, and yummy snacks at the **Bolinas Bay Bakery and Cafe,** 20 Wharf Road, Bolinas (415–868–0211); organic-ingredient pastries, breads and pies, pizza, soups, sandwiches. Stop in at the tiny **Bolinas Museum** (48–50 Wharf Road; 415–868–0330) and prowl the interesting old cemetery off Olema-Bolinas Road.

Dillon Beach, 4 miles west of Tomales on Highway 1; (707) 878–2442. Not really a town, just a collection of Craftsman-style beach cottages from the 1930s and a few nineteenth-century buildings near the intersection of Main Street and Dillon Beach Road. The Church of the Assumption, just south of town, was built in 1860. Often very windy, the wide, duney beach has some of the richest tidepools on the entire coastline. There is a $4.00 admission charge to the beach, which is privately owned. A mile south at Lawson's Landing, hang gliders often ride the winds. There is a large campground and an RV park at Lawson's Landing.

Horseback riding. Bear Valley Stables; (415) 663–1570.

Five Brooks Trailhead; (415) 663–8287. Three miles south of Olema.

Samuel P. Taylor State Park, off Sir Francis Drake Boulevard, 14 miles from Highway 101, 5 miles east of Olema; (415) 488–9897. The park comprises 2,600 acres of cool and shady redwood and Douglas fir forest, with beautiful biking, horseback-riding, and hiking trails. The Paper Mill Creek trail is a moderately easy, 4-mile loop. Rest rooms and picnic areas are located throughout the park.

Special Events

July. Coastal Native American Summer Big Time, Point Reyes National Seashore; (415) 663–1092. Demonstrations of crafts, skills, music, dancing.

Other Recommended Restaurants and Lodgings

Inverness

Blackthorne Inn, 266 Vallejo; (415) 663–8621. Five charming rooms in a wooded canyon, a treehouse with decks, hot tub, fireman's pole, spiral staircase, and glass-sided "eagle's nest." Includes buffet breakfast.

Dancing Coyote Beach bed-and-breakfast, P.O. Box 98, Inverness 94937; (415) 669–7200. Four Southwest-style cottages with decks, views, fireplaces, kitchens.

Golden Hind Inn, 12938 Sir Francis Drake Boulevard; (415) 669–1389. Bay view and poolside rooms, some fireplaces, kitchens, fishing pier, swimming pool.

Sandy Cove Inn, 12990 Sir Francis Drake Boulevard; (415) 669–2683. Three suites with fireplaces, sitting areas with garden views, hammocks, path to a cove on Tomales Bay, full breakfast.

Olema

Olema Ranch Campground, 0.25 mile north of Highway 1 and Sir Francis Drake Boulevard, 10155 Highway 1, Olema 94950; (415) 663-8001 or (800) 655–2267; www.campgrounds.com/olemaranch. RV facilities, tent sites, forest and meadow setting, gas, store. Campfires allowed.

Point Reyes Station

Holly Tree Inn and Cottages, 3 Silverhills Road; (415) 663–1554. On nineteen acres of lawns, gardens, and wooded hillsides; French provincial decor, antiques, fireplaces; French doors open to the meadows. Four guest rooms. Cottages have hot tubs and fireplaces.

Pine Cone Diner, 60 Fourth Street; (415) 663–1536. Stick-to-your-ribs breakfasts and lunches of buttermilk pancakes, brioche French toast, boysenberry pie, chowder, salads, burgers.

Taqueria La Quinta, Third Street and Highway 1; (415) 663–8868. In a very casual setting, fresh Mexican food (made without lard), homemade tortillas, fruit smoothies.

Thirty-nine Cypress, 39 Cypress Road; (415) 663–1709. With wonderful views of the Point Reyes Peninsula, a redwood country inn with three guest rooms. Private patio, hot tub, antiques, fireplace; breakfast with stay.

For More Information

Coastal Traveler; www.coastaltraveler.com. Information and Web pages for artisans, lodgings and restaurants, events and town histories.

Inns of Point Reyes, P.O. Box 145, Iverness, CA 94956; (415) 485–2649. Referral service for several inns.

Point Reyes Lodging Association, P.O. Box 878, Point Reyes, CA 94956; (415) 663–1872 or (800) 539–1872; www.ptreyes.com. Inns, small hotels, cottages.

West Marin Chamber of Commerce, P.O. Box 1045, Point Reyes Station, CA 94956; (415) 663–9232; www.pointreyes.org.

SOUTHBOUND

ESCAPES

Old California in the Central Valley 1

San Juan Bautista and the Pinnacles

1 Night

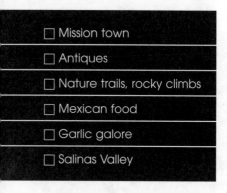

☐ Mission town

☐ Antiques

☐ Nature trails, rocky climbs

☐ Mexican food

☐ Garlic galore

☐ Salinas Valley

Between the tawny Gabilan Mountains on the east and the coastal range of the Santa Lucias on the west, vegetable fields surround a handful of small farming towns in the Salinas Valley. The Salinas River curls and twists around the valley, finally relaxing into Monterey Bay. Meadows and foothills are carpeted with lupines and poppies in spring, turning to knee-high yellow mustard, then to golden grasses all summer.

Here John Steinbeck lived and wrote about the struggles and romances of early farm families. Father Junípero Serra founded his largest mission here, around which grew a town that's not much changed in a hundred years. Thrusting dramatically up in rocky spires, Pinnacles National Monument goes lush and green when winter rains fill the waterfalls and rushing streams.

Day 1 / Morning

From the Oakland Bay Bridge, drive south on Highway 880 to Highway 101, for about ninety minutes, to Gilroy, edging out of the smog into the oak-studded, rolling hills of San Benito County.

The scent of fresh garlic announces **Gilroy,** home of the **Gilroy Garlic Festival,** attended each July by 150,000 lovers of the stinking rose. About 10 miles south of the Highway 152 junction, watch for a huge red barn on the left. On weekends here there's a big flea market and farmer's market, a barbecue, and an antiques fair.

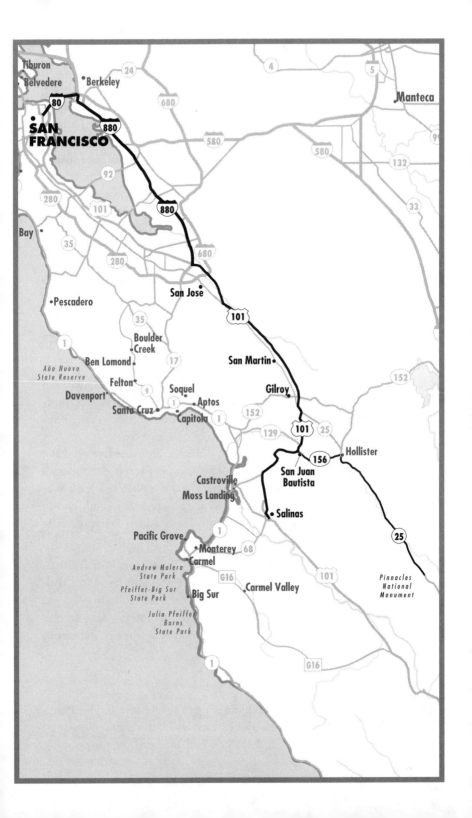

Take the Highway 156 exit to **San Juan Bautista,** often called San Juan, a Spanish village since the late 1700s, in the arms of the Gabilan Range. Park at the first available space. The little town consists of a large state historic park, one of the most beautiful of California's missions, and a few charming streets of antiques shops and Mexican restaurants shaded with pepper trees, mimosa, and black walnuts. Everything is within walking distance. Go to the grassy plaza on the north side of town and start at the heart and soul of San Juan, the magnificent **Mission San Juan Bautista,** at Second and Mariposa Streets (831–623–2127). Founded in 1787, it's the largest of all California mission churches, with three aisles and a glorious 40-foot-high ceiling of grayed beams in traditional viga-latilla formation. Light floods the cathedral, making vibrant the rust-and-blue painted decoration. It's OK to stand at the back, near the giant entry doors, before and during the masses, when local families mingle and chat, little girls flit about in their ruffled best dresses, and their brothers jet up and down the aisles.

Surrounding the cathedral are a series of rooms, once living quarters for the padres, housing a museum of early Indian, Spanish Colonial, and Victorian artifacts, including one of the best collections of Mission furniture in the world. You'll see a small kitchen with iron pots in an open fireplace, from which 1,200 people were fed three times a day.

The mission gardens are dense with old cacti, aromatic lavender, and climbing roses. Behind the church under ancient olive trees, 4,300 Indians and early pioneers are buried. The cemetery and the plaza overlook vast, flat fields and the San Andreas earthquake fault, here at the south end of the Santa Cruz Mountains. A seismograph sits in a glass box, recording every tremor.

LUNCH: Jardines de San Juan, 115 Third Street, San Juan Bautista; (831) 623–4466; www.jardinesrestaurant.com. A Mexican restaurant with a big, popular garden patio. Guitarists strum, breezes ruffle the fig and maple trees, people-watching is excellent; it's tempting to stay for a second margarita. Lunches and dinners are served at umbrella tables or indoors in art-filled dining rooms.

Afternoon

The plaza is circled by historic buildings open to inspection. The **Plaza Stable,** a barn museum of horse-drawn carriages and wagons, dispatched coaches for seven stage lines in the 1860s. San Juan was on a main route

The Mission San Juan Bautista, the largest of all California mission churches.

between San Francisco and Los Angeles, with silver and gold miners trading, resupplying, and traveling through town; as many as eleven coaches a day arrived, with about seventeen passengers each.

Restored and completely furnished, the **Plaza Hotel** was the first place the dusty travelers headed, to get a beer or something stronger in the bar and to book a room for the night. The owner of the hotel, Angelo Zanetta, built himself a magnificent dwelling on the plaza; the structure—the **Zanetta House**—now houses an outstanding collection of early California furnishings and personal items.

The red-tile–roofed **Castro House** was owned by a family from the Donner party who struck it rich in the gold rush; behind the house is a 150-year-old pepper tree shading lovely gardens. Fat-trunked pepper trees, mimosa, and black walnuts shade the few streets of San Juan.

Twelve antiques stores await discovery, plus small shops of every description, delightfully untrendy. **Tops,** 5 Second Street (831–623–4441), offers semiprecious stones and rare rocks in a museumlike store.

Within a small circle of shops graced by a magnificent, ancient pepper tree, **Mission Gallery** is the finest gallery in town for prints and paintings of the valley, plus opulent Asian accessories for the home (106 Third Street; 831–623–2960). **Reyna's Galleries and American Indian Museum** is a fascinating shop that sells Native American–inspired clothing, artifacts and crafts, an eclectic array of books and cards, and monthly exhibits of local artisans' works (311 Third Street; 831–623–2379). Ask here about the annual American Indian and World Cultures Festival.

DINNER: Mariposa House, 37 Mariposa Street, San Juan Bautista; (831) 623–4666. Wonderful Mediterranean cuisine in a Victorian house, noted for its filet mignon, salmon with wine sauce, and homemade mushroom soup.

LODGING: Posada de San Juan Hotel/Inn, 310 Fourth Street, San Juan Bautista; (831) 623–4030. Spacious, attractive rooms with fireplaces, balconies, and whirlpool tubs.

Day 2 / Morning

BREAKFAST: Joan and Peter's German Restaurant, 322 Third Street, San Juan Bautista (831–623–4521), serves cappuccino and homemade Danish on the garden patio. Breakfast buffet features German specialties, including apple strudel.

It's an hour's drive from here—through Hollister on Highway 25—to **Pinnacles National Monument,** Paicines (831–389–4485). Spires and crags rising dramatically out of the valley are what's left of an ancient volcano; the other half of the volcano lies 195 miles to the southeast, thanks to the San Andreas Rift Zone. All through winter and spring, and in fall after the rains have come, the 1,600-acre wilderness park attracts rock climbers, hikers, cave explorers, and picnickers. Short, easy paths make ferny creeks and mountain views accessible. At the visitors center, a jewel of a stone building constructed in the 1930s by the Civilian Conservation Corps, pick up trail maps and chat with the rangers. They'll head you toward the Bear Gulch waterfalls, a swimming hole, and a short trail to spooky caves. Midsummer can be extremely hot and dry, with temperatures in the hundreds. Spring is spectacular with riots of wildflowers, which bloom here earlier than in most parts of the state. Winters are mild, fresh, and green. A nice private campground at the entrance to the park has a swimming pool: **Pinnacles Campground** (831–389–4462).

LUNCH: **La Casa Rosa,** 106 Third Street, San Juan Bautista; (831) 623–2960. A taste of old Spanish days in San Juan; hearty American food in an antiques-filled, pink clapboard house built in 1858. Try the Old California Casserole and the chicken soufflé. Famous treats to take home—chutney, preserves, pickles.

Don't leave town without a loaf of Portuguese bread, panetone, brownies, and a pie from **San Juan Bakery,** 319 Third Street (831–623–4570).

Afternoon

Before heading back to the Bay Area, take the short trip to a major new museum, the **National Steinbeck Center** (One Main Street, Salinas; 831–796–3833; www.steinbeck.org). If you've read John Steinbeck's *East of Eden, Of Mice and Men,* or *The Grapes of Wrath,* this is a must. The spectacular 37,000-square-foot museum houses unique interactive displays of Steinbeck's books and the time and places he lived. You can open a drawer to see his childhood treasures; feel the chill of an "ice-packed" boxcar filled with lettuce; experience the smells and the sounds of "Doc" Rickett's science lab on Cannery Row; and learn of migrant life in the Salinas Valley. There are vintage photos, ongoing videos and movies, doors and windows that open into historic vignettes, and Steinbeck's charming camper truck, in which he motored with his dog and wrote *Travels with Charley.* The cafe here is light and airy, with a sunny patio and reasonably priced snacks and lunches. A few blocks away, Steinbeck's boyhood home is a beautifully restored, elaborately decorated Victorian loaded with memorabilia (132 Central Avenue; 831–424–2745).

On the way north again, consider a stop at the **California Antique Aircraft Museum,** 6 miles north of Gilroy in San Martin, to see planes from 1928 to the 1950s—a Sopwith Pup, a Bowlus Albatross, a Benson Gyrocopter, and more rare aircraft (12777 Murphy Avenue, across the street from the airport; 831–683–2290).

Take home some wine from **Mirassou Vineyards,** 3000 Aborn Road, San Jose (408–274–4000), owned by America's oldest wine-making family. Dozens of wineries are located in the Salinas, Gonzales, and Soledad areas. A directory and map of the Salinas Valley/Monterey Wine Country is available by calling (408) 375–9400.

There's More

Casa de Fruta, 9840 Pacheco Pass Road, Gilroy; (831) 637–7775. You've never seen a place like this: neon-neato RV park, swimming pool, carousel, miniature train, country store, fruit stand, bakery, candy factory, souvenir shop, seasonal events.

Christopher Ranch, 305 Bloomfield Avenue, Gilroy; (408) 847–1100. The ultimate source for garlic.

Fremont Peak State Park, 11 miles south on San Juan Canyon Road; (831) 623–4255. On rolling hills and wildflowery meadows, hiking trails are best in spring. On the peak a 30-inch telescope is open to the public several times a month (831–623–2454).

Golf. Ridgemark Golf and Country Club, 3800 Airline Highway, Hollister; (831) 637–8151. Golf, tennnis, lodging, restaurant.

Special Events

May. American Indian Spring Market, San Juan Bautista; (831) 623–2379.

June. Early Days in San Juan; (831) 623–2454. Celebration of the founding of the State Historic Park. Horse-drawn carriage, period dress, music, food, fandango.

Peddler's Faire, San Juan Bautista; (831) 623–2454. Held on the historic streets of San Juan, this fair features more than 200 vendors.

July. Gilroy Garlic Festival, Gilroy; (831) 842–1625. Huge food fair featuring garlic dishes—even garlic ice cream—entertainment, arts and crafts.

August. Annual Flea Market and Antiques and Collectible Show, on the streets of San Juan; (831) 623–2454.

September. All-Indian Market, San Juan Bautista; (831) 623–2379.

Fine Arts and Crafts Show, San Juan Bautista; (831) 623–2454. Some 300 artisans and crafters.

December. Christmas festival; (831) 623–2454. Merchants' holiday open house, Christmas scavenger hunt, and visit from Santa to light tree at dusk.

Other Recommended Restaurants and Lodgings

San Juan Bautista

Betabel RV Resort, 9664 Betabel Road; (831) 623–2202. Nicely landscaped, full hookups, heated pool, minimart.

Cutting Horse, 301 Third Street; (831) 623–4549. Steak and hearty, traditional American fare in a new, comfortable, attractive dinner house.

Dona Esther Restaurant, 25 Franklin Street; (831) 623–2518. Authentic Mexican food, bar, live entertainment on weekends.

Felipe's Restaurant and Bar, 313 Third Street; (831) 623–2161. Where the locals go for the best Mexican and Salvadoran food in town. Salvadoran dishes are not complete without the zippy pickled cabbage, *curtido*. Try the specialties of the house, fried plantains and fried ice cream. Live music on weekends.

Orient Express, 35 Washington Street; (831) 623–2978. The owner-chef was trained in France and brings a delicate touch to traditional Chinese cuisine in this casual, bright, and pretty place. Lunch specials and "Family Dinners" are inexpensive. Try the calamari in garlic ginger sauce, and mu shu shrimp.

Mission Farm RV Park, 400 San Juan–Hollister Road, on the southeast corner of town; (831) 623–4456. Old barns, a store, all facilities, simple surroundings in a walnut orchard.

San Juan Inn, 410 Alameda Street; (831) 623–4380. A forty-two-unit motel. Local art and photos decorate the walls, outdoor patio; all-you-can-eat buffet on weekends.

For More Information

San Juan Bautista Chamber of Commerce, 402A Third Street, P.O. Box 1037, San Juan Bautista, CA 95045; (831) 623–2454; www.san-juan-bautista.ca.us.

Advice: Midsummer temperatures in San Juan can reach a hundred degrees or more, so bring a hat. Evenings are cool, as sea breezes rise and fog creeps in from the coast.

Santa Cruz 2

A California Beach Town

1 Night

The resort town of Santa Cruz is famous for more than 20 miles of wide, sandy, warm-water beaches and an old-fashioned waterfront boardwalk with rides and concessions. Here at the top end of Monterey Bay, the climate is mild, surf's up every month of the year, and the attitude is young and healthy, due to a large population of university students and residents who love outdoor recreation.

☐ Beaches

☐ Bikes

☐ Butterflies

☐ The Boardwalk

☐ Wineries

☐ Redwoods

☐ Shopping

The town has many fanciful Victorian homes and a variety of architectural styles, such as Queen Anne, Gothic Revival, Mission Revival, and California bungalow. Pacific Avenue, the main street, is a tree-shaded boulevard with outdoor cafes and dozens of shops. The University of California at Santa Cruz and Cabrillo College are located here, and the community is culturally oriented, with a large contingent of artists and musicians in residence and a lively annual schedule of arts events and music festivals.

Even if you are not a beach person, there is much in the way of outdoor recreation and sight-seeing to enjoy, and not just in summer. Near the city of Santa Cruz and in the **Santa Cruz Mountains** are country roads that meander through ancient redwood groves and along the banks of the San Lorenzo and Santa Cruz Rivers. Walking and biking trails and campgrounds are liberally scattered throughout the region.

Day 1 / Morning

Drive south from San Francisco on Highway 280, south on Highway 85 to Highway 17 to **Santa Cruz,** about a one-and-a-half-hour drive, unless it's late Friday afternoon, when it will be a longer trip. As an alternative to the Bay Area's congested highways, the coast route is longer but far more scenic.

A good way to orient yourself in Santa Cruz and get right to the ocean views is to continue on Highway 17 northwest when you reach the junction with Highway 1 at Santa Cruz. Highway 1 along this stretch is a four-lane street (Mission Street). For the easiest route to Natural Bridges, turn south onto Swift Street, right on Delaware, and left on Swanton. Drive south along West Cliff Drive to **Mark Abbott Memorial Lighthouse,** at Lighthouse Point Park overlooking Monterey Bay and the city. Walkers, bikers, joggers, and passengers in baby strollers love the city, sea, and sea-lion views from West Cliff Drive. Go into the lighthouse to see a small surfing museum (831–420–6289).

Almost every day there are surfers in "Steamers Lane" below. In May the **Longboard Invitational** is held here, and hundreds of surfers from all over the world compete (831–684–1551). The major surf competition, the **O'Neill Coldwater Classic,** is held in the fall (831–479–5648). If there is a surfer in your family, he or she will be blown away by the great surfing in the Santa Cruz area. **Club Ed** at **Cowell Beach** is the place for lessons and board rentals (831–464–0177). **Richard Schmidt School of Surfing** at 849 Almar Avenue is also well-regarded (831–423–0928; www. richardschmidt.com). A service of the Santa Cruz City Beach Lifeguards, the Surf Report gives weather and water conditions from Memorial Day through Labor Day (831–429–3460).

Twin Lakes State Beach below East Cliff Drive is where the sailboarders go. There are fire rings here, outdoor showers, and, nearby, wild-bird sanctuaries (831–429–2850) at **Schwan Lake.** Prowl around (watching out for poison oak) to see Virginia rail, chickadees, swallows, and belted kingfishers, among dozens more species of birds and waterfowl. You can kayak and canoe on the lake.

The main Santa Cruz beach at the boardwalk and the pier, **Cowell Beach** (831–420–6014) is the most popular piece of sand on the central coastline for sunning, swimming, and volleyball. A special beach-going wheelchair is available from the lifeguards. The relatively tame waves here are perfect for beginning surfers.

Proceed on West Cliff Drive to Pacific Avenue and downtown Santa Cruz with two blocks of boutiques, sidewalk cafes, coffeehouses, and galleries—more than 200 stores in all. In this artists' town, notice the many sidewalk sculptures, and watch for building-size murals on side streets. The tree-lined, flower-bedecked boulevard is loved by the browser. Book lovers make a beeline to the restored St. George Hotel building at Pacific and Front to **Bookshop Santa Cruz** (831–423–0900), one of the largest independent bookstores in northern California. Scattered throughout are benches, stools, and armchairs, comfortable spots to peruse the books and the huge variety of domestic and international magazines and newspapers. There is a cafe in the store, and they serve fresh, organic salads, sandwiches, pastas, and chocolate (831–427–9900).

At the corner of Pacific and Cooper, **Pacific Wave** is headquarters for surfboards, skateboards, and all the cool accessories and clothing to go with them (831–458–9283). At **Pacific Edge Indoor Climbing Facility,** try the newest California craze. With the use of safety harnesses, the climbing wall is safe and fun, and you can cool off at the juice bar (104 Bronson; 831–454–9254). River and sea kayaking for all ability levels are also offered by **Adventure Sports** (303 Potrero #15, in the Old Sash Mill; 831–458–3648; www.asudoit.com).

Shen's Gallery (2404 Mission Street; 831–457–4422) is seductive with exotic scents, flute sounds, and Asian antiques and art. It has a large collection of one-of-a-kind tiny ceramic teapots from mainland China, "shard" boxes, and very beautiful tea chests. Notice the storefront of **Bead It** (1325 Pacific; 831–426–0779)—bead appetizers, bead entrees, bead desserts. Look for fine, locally produced crafts and art at **Annieglass** (110 Cooper Street, 831–427–4260).

In the oldest building downtown, circa 1850, **LuLu Carpenter's Cafe** has divine pies and other treats, and a nice courtyard (1545 Pacific; 831–429–9804).

The **Santa Cruz Art League,** nearby at 526 Broadway (831–426–5787), has three galleries and a shop selling fine arts and crafts.

The **Museum of Art and History at the McPherson Center** is a cultural ghetto, encompassing the Art Museum and the History Museum of Santa Cruz County and shops (705 Front Street; 831–429–1964).

LUNCH: Browse the downtown area's lunch spots, checking out menus and ambience. Here are my favorites: **Pearl Alley Bistro** (831–429–8070), **Gabriella Cafe** (831–457–1677), and **El Palomar** (831–425–7575).

Afternoon

Proceed to the foot of Beach Street for a beach ramble, or go to the **Santa Cruz Beach Boardwalk,** the only beachside amusement park on the West Coast, to indulge in some of the twenty-five rides, the old-time arcade, the shops, and restaurants (831–423–5590). The classic 1911 carousel and the Giant Dipper roller coaster are National Historic Landmarks. At

Neptune's Kingdom, an indoor miniature golf course, volcanos erupt, pirates threaten, cannons fire. If you hear screaming, it's probably coming from the roller coaster, the Hurricane, guaranteed to make you forget your name. Get rid of your spare cash in the Casino Arcade, or just sit on the boardwalk and watch the bikinis and the sailboats glide by.

Within sight of the boardwalk, **Santa Cruz Municipal Wharf** (831–420–6025) is all about fishing off the pier, shopping in tourist traps, browsing the fresh-fish markets, eating chowder and shrimp cocktail in waterside cafes, and watching the sea lions, the pelicans, and the passing boats. Deep-sea fishing trips and bay cruises depart from the harbor.

On the south side of Santa Cruz, **Santa Cruz Yacht Harbor** (831–475–6161) and its beach are where the locals go to escape the tourists. You can kayak and sail and have a sandwich or a seafood plate at the **Crow's Nest** (2218 East Cliff Drive; 831–476–4560; www.crowsnest-santacruz. com). The casual, multilevel restaurant has a heated, glassed-in deck overlooking the busy harbor; locals crowd the bar at night.

Drive south 4 miles from the Santa Cruz Wharf on East Cliff Drive to **Capitola Village** (or take the quicker, less-winding route, Highway 1). An oceanside resort since 1861, Capitola remains a quaint artists' colony, one-tenth the size of Santa Cruz. Swimmers, waders, and sunbathers flock to **Capitola Beach,** sheltered by two high cliffs. A riparian shelter for birds and ducks, Soquel Creek meanders right through town into the sea. Restaurants with outdoor patios are lined up at beachfront on the Esplanade, and there are a few blocks of boutiques, art galleries, and beachwear shops.

DINNER: Shadowbrook Restaurant, 1750 Wharf Road, Capitola; (831) 475–1511; www.shadowbrook-capitola.com. On the banks of Soquel Creek, Shadowbrook is reached by a self-operated cable car down a flower-bedecked hillside or by a winding pathway. Romantic; live music; outdoor terrace; reservations absolutely necessary. Winner of many awards for continental and California cuisine. Sunday brunch, too.

LODGING: Inn at Depot Hill, 250 Monterey Avenue, Capitola; (831) 462–3376; www.innatdepothill.com. Eight suites with fireplaces, feather beds, marble bathrooms, private garden patios, hot tubs, European traditional furnishings, and antiques. Award-winning luxury and service. Wonderful breakfasts; walking distance to Capitola Beach.

Up for some nightlife in Santa Cruz? Head for **Palookaville,** a smoke-free nightclub and juice bar featuring big-name performers, big band swing, and jazz (1133 Pacific Avenue; 831–454–0600). **Moe's Alley** is the number one blues club in the area, with live blues nightly and an outdoor patio with barbecue (1535 Commercial Way; 831–479–1854). **Kuumbwa Jazz Center** presents major jazz artists on Monday and Friday, with dinner (320 Cedar Street; 831–427–2227).

Day 2 / Morning

BREAKFAST: Zelda's, #203 on the Esplanade at the beach, Capitola; (831) 475–4900. Sit by the window or on the deck while the early morning sea turns from rosy to silver-blue as it laps Capitola's scruffy old fishing pier. Home-fry scramble, blackened snapper with eggs. Zelda's is a fun hangout any time of day. Live jazz on the weekends.

Capitola Beach and most public beaches in the area are cleaned nightly; even in summer they start out trash-free and pearly white every day.

The shops and galleries near the beach are touristy but fun. **Dragginwood** (216 Capitola Avenue; 831–475–0915) sells crystals and magical chotchkes. **Capitola Dreams** (118 Stockton Avenue; 831–476–5379) has an eye-popping collection of bikinis and wild beachwear. Painted wood gewgaws and jewelry from Thailand are featured at **Oceania** (204 Capitola Avenue; 831–476–6644). For a hundred stores in an indoor mall, go up the hill to the **Capitola Mall** on Forty-first Avenue (831–476–9749).

Capitola Beach sports a small fishing pier; licenses are not required. Join in a volleyball game on the beach. At **New Brighton Beach** (831–464–6330) there is a nice campground, where cypress and pines provide a sense of privacy between campsites. Surf fishing and clamming are good, and a continuous stretch of sandy beach runs 15 miles.

The next beach south of New Brighton, **Seacliff State Beach** at **Del Mar** has almost 2 miles of shoreline backed by steep sandstone cliffs. A 500-foot wooden pier and the wreck of a concrete ship are roosting spots for birds, and you can fish off the pier. There is a campground and a small visitors center where you can sign up for walking tours to see the fossilized remains of multimillion-year-old sea creatures lodged in the cliffsides (831–685–6442). The paved path here is popular for strollers, wheelchairs, and in-line skates.

Just south of Capitola at **Aptos, Rio Del Mar Beach** is a wide stretch of sand with a jetty and lifeguards. Shopping and restaurants are within walking distance (831–685–6500).

Surf fishing at Seacliff State Beach.

On the north side of Highway 1, just south of Capitola, the village of Aptos is where you'll find **Village Fair Antiques,** behind the Bay View Hotel on Soquel Road (831–688–9883). This is a big antiques collection in a huge old barn, a place for losing track of time. The next village north, **Soquel** is a one-horse town with more than twenty antiques shops on Soquel Drive.

LUNCH: Cafe Sparrow, 8040 Soquel Drive, Aptos; (831) 688–6238; www.cafesparrow.com. Across the street from the Bay View Hotel is this charming dining room serving chicken and fresh fish entrees plus seasonal specialties.

Afternoon

A cool, green place to take a walk in the highlands near Santa Cruz is the

Forest of Nisene Marks State Park, a densely forested 10,000-acre wilderness on Aptos Creek (831–763–7063). Popular with runners, bikers, horseback riders, hikers, and picnickers, the park ranges in elevation from 100 to 2,600 feet. Unpaved roads and trails lead to a wide variety of mixed evergreen woods and creekside willows and ferns. Walk-in camping is permitted, as are horseback riding and steelhead fishing in certain areas.

Near the entrance to the park, **Mangels House** bed-and-breakfast is in a wedding-cake-white, circa-1880 mansion, with six rooms (831– 688– 7982).

A beautiful beach that makes a nice stop on the way home from Santa Cruz is **Natural Bridges State Beach,** whose entrance is at 2531 West Cliff Drive at the intersection of West Cliff Drive and Swanton Boulevard (831–423–4609). Named for dramatic sandstone arches, Natural Bridges has tidepools rich with sea life; guided tidepool tours are often conducted. A short boardwalk from the beach parking lot leads through a eucalyptus forest to the **California Monarch Butterfly Preserve.** Depending on the time of year—early October through March is best—you'll see hundreds of thousands of butterflies hanging in the trees and moving about in great golden clouds. A 0.75-mile self-guided nature walk begins at the Monarch trail and heads for Secret Lagoon, where blue herons, mallard ducks, and more freshwater and seagoing birds live.

Seymour Marine Discovery Center, at Long Marine Lab, a University of Santa Cruz research facility near Natural Bridges, is at 100 Shafer Road (831–459–3800). On a bluff with spectacular ocean views, the facility focuses on marine research and shows how scientists study, care for, and explore ocean life. Features include interactive exhibits, aquaria, touch tanks, an 85-foot blue whale skeleton, and more, plus a gift shop and bookstore.

If you have time to spare on your way back to San Francisco, dawdle in the Santa Cruz Mountains among ancient redwood groves, on sunny river banks, and in quiet little resort towns affording peaceful getaway days. Discover rustic boutique wineries, known for their dark Pinots and German varietals. Take a ride on a rollicking steam train, chugging up into redwood country or all the way down to the beach (more on the mountains follows).

Retrace your route back to San Francisco.

There's More

Big Basin Redwoods State Park, off Highway 236 near Boulder Creek in the Santa Cruz Mountains; (831) 338–8860. Thousand-year-old redwoods, fern canyons, the Bay Area's most wonderful waterfalls; a round-trip hike to the falls takes four to five hours. There are 80 miles of skyline to sea trails. The Sea Trail drops from mountain ridges to Waddell State Beach through dense woodlands, along Waddell and Berry Creeks; waterfalls, sea and mountain views; 11 miles one-way. Bike, horse rentals; campground, store.

Boating. Chardonnay Sailing Charters, at the harbor, Santa Cruz; (831) 423–1213; www.chardonnay.com. Whale-watching, wine-maker, brewmaster, ecology, and brunch cruises, and sunset sails.

Pacific Yachting, 790 Mariner Park Way, Santa Cruz; (831) 423–7245. Day tours.

Felton Covered Bridge, on Highway 9 near Highway 236. Built in 1892, this is the tallest bridge of its kind in the country and one of the few left in the state.

Golf. Aptos Seascape Golf Course, 610 Clubhouse Drive, Aptos; (831) 688–3213. Eighteen holes by the sea.

Boulder Creek Golf and Country Club, 16901 Big Basin Highway, Boulder Creek; (831) 338–2111. Eighteen beautiful holes in the redwoods, restaurant, tennis.

DeLaveaga Golf Course, 401 Upper Park Road at DeLaveaga Drive, Santa Cruz; (831) 423–7212. Eighteen holes.

Pasatiempo Golf Club, 20 Clubhouse Road, off Highway 17 near Santa Cruz; (831) 459–9169; www.pasatiempo.com. One of the top one hundred courses in the United States. Top-notch restaurant. Adjacent to the course, the Inn at Pasatiempo has very nice rooms (800–834–2546; www.innatpasatiempo.com).

Henry Cowell State Park, 101 North Big Trees Park Road, Felton; (831) 335–4598. Eighteen hundred acres of stream canyons, meadows, forests, and chaparral-covered ridges along the meandering San Lorenzo River and Eagle Creek. Short, easy trails, such as **Redwood Grove Nature Trail** to the **Big Trees Grove,** offer a rare opportunity to see first-growth redwoods. Besides big redwoods and pines, you'll see sycamore, elders, madrone, manzanita, California poppies, doves, quail, waterfowl, deer, and maybe poison oak. The redwood-dotted campground in the park has more than a hundred tent and RV sites, for vehicles up to 24 feet, with no hookups (800–444–7275).

Roaring Camp and Big Trees, just south of Felton on Graham Hill Road in the Santa Cruz Mountains; (831) 335–4484; www.roaringcamp. com. A re-creation of an 1880s logging town, complete with covered bridge, general store, and a wonderful narrow-gauge steam train that you can ride up through forests of giant redwoods to the summit of Bear Mountain on the steepest railroad grade in North America. A second route runs along the San Lorenzo River down to Santa Cruz Beach. A chuck-wagon barbecue serves charcoal-broiled steak and chicken burgers in a forest glade.

Santa Cruz County Cycling Club, 224 Walnut Street, Santa Cruz; (831) 438–0706. Day trips, map of area bikeways.

Wilder Ranch State Park, 1401 Coast Road, 2 miles north of Santa Cruz; (831) 426–0505. A 7,000-acre working ranch since the 1800s. Stroll in and out of the old barns, homes, and gardens. A fern grotto is chiseled into the beachfront cliffs, and there are miles of hiking and mountain-biking trails. Just north of the ranch, Four Mile Beach is reachable by a hike down a bluff—a nice spot to lie on the sand.

Wineries in the Santa Cruz Mountains. Bonny Doon Vineyard, 10 Pine Flat Road, 3 miles northeast of Highway 1 and Davenport via Bonny Doon Road; (831) 425–4518. The wine maker has made his wines famous with crazy labels like Clos de Gilroy, Le Cigare Volant, Big House Red, and Old Telegram. Hang out in the redwood grove on Soquel Creek and try his European "ice wines," produced in just a handful of American wineries.

Byington Winery and Vineyard is on Bear Creek Road, with dizzying views of Monterey Bay from the picnic grounds (408–354–1111).

David Bruce Winery, Bear Creek Road east of Boulder Creek; (408) 354–4214. A gold-medal maker of Pinot Noir and Chardonnay. Open for tasting on the weekends, by appointment during the week.

Hallcrest Vineyards, Felton-Empire Road; (831) 335–4441. Specializing in organic Gewürztraminers, Rieslings, and grape juices.

Wineries near Santa Cruz. Bargetto Winery, 3535 North Main Street, Soquel; (831) 475–2258. Overlooking Soquel Creek, the winery is at a scenic spot where you can buy homemade fruit wines and vinegars—raspberry, olallieberry, and apricot.

Storrs Winery, 303 Potrero Street, No. 35, Soquel; (831) 458–5030. Sample great Santa Cruz Chardonnay and Pinot Noir in the Old Sash Mill tasting room.

Special Events

February. Migration Festival, Natural Bridges State Beach, Santa Cruz; (831) 423–4609. The monarchs are celebrated at the largest butterfly colony in the west.

March. Jazz on the Wharf, Municipal Wharf, Santa Cruz; (831) 420–5273. Kayak Surf Festival, Steamer Lane, Santa Cruz; (831) 458–3648; www.asu doit.com. Hundreds of kayak surfers from all over the world compete at the national championships; free kayak clinics.

April. Wineries Passport Program, Santa Cruz County; (831) 479–9463. Open house at wineries, meet wine makers, tours, special tastings, music, food.

May. Art and Wine Festival, Boulder Creek; (831) 338–7099.

Civil War Battles and Encampment, Roaring Camp; (831) 335–4484. Reenactment of Civil War battles and camp life; the largest encampment in the United States.

Longboard Invitational, Steamers Lane, Santa Cruz; (831) 684–1551. Hundreds of surfers compete. Watch from Cliff Drive.

June. Art on the Wharf, Santa Cruz Municipal Wharf; (831) 420–5273. Art show and live jazz.

Japanese Cultural Fair, Mission Plaza, Santa Cruz; (831) 462–4589. Celebration of Japanese-American culture, arts, foods, and entertainment.

July. Summertime Free Concerts, Santa Cruz Boardwalk; (831) 423–5590. Free Friday night concerts, hits of the '60s, '70s, and '80s.

Summer Fat Fry, Aptos Village Park; (831) 420–2800. Headliners at a two-day music festival in a park near the sea.

August. Cabrillo Music Festival, held at various locations on the Cabrillo College campus; (831) 426–6966. An internationally acclaimed two-week musical extravaganza.

September. National Begonia Festival, Capitola; (831–476–3566). Residents vie for awards for their spectacular waterborne floats that are maneuvered perilously down Soquel Creek into town; you've never seen a watery parade like this one.

December. First Night Santa Cruz, downtown Santa Cruz; (831) 425–7277. New Year's Eve party with a grand procession, live entertainment all afternoon and evening, alcohol-free party.

Lighted Boat Parade, Santa Cruz Yacht Harbor; (831) 457–6161.

Other Recommended Restaurants and Lodgings

Aptos

Seascape Resort, 1 Seascape Resort Drive off San Andreas, south of Santa Cruz; (800) 929–7727. On a bluff overlooking miles of beach, upscale, comfortable studio, and one- and two-bedroom condos for up to eight people, with balconies or patios, sofa sleepers, fully equipped kitchens. This is a full-service resort with a nice sea-view restaurant, supervised activities for kids, golf packages, and extras like in-suite massage, "Beach Fires to Go"—you are driven down to the beach, where a fire is built for you, "s'mores" are provided, and you are picked up later, after a romantic evening on the beach—and "Feast in a Suite" Thanksgiving dinners. The resort offers access to an adjacent golf course and sports club with lighted tennis courts, an Olympic-size pool, and fitness center.

Capitola

Capitola Venetian Hotel, 1500 Wharf Road; (800) 332–2780; www.capitolavenetian.com. On the beach, a 1920s Mediterranean pink stucco motel, unassuming eclectic/eccentric decor, kitchens. Reasonable rates for families and groups.

Gayle's Bakery and Rosticceria, 504 Bay Avenue, on the corner of Bay and Capitola Avenues; (831) 462–1127. Homemade pasta, salad, pizza, sandwiches, spit-roasted meats. The bakery is famous for pies, cheesecake, breads, and pastries.

Monarch Cove Inn, 620 El Salto Drive; (831) 464–1295. In a luxurious garden overlooking Monterey Bay, beautifully furnished Victorian guest rooms, cottages, and apartments. Continental breakfast.

Paradise Beach Grille, 215 Esplanade; (831) 476–4900. A casual cafe with a jukebox and charcoal grill. The menu, printed every day, includes a huge variety of fresh seafood.

Felton

Fern River Resort, 5250 Highway 9; (831) 335–4412. Nice little red house-keeping cabins; some fireplaces; on four acres of lawns, trees, and fern gardens; private sandy river beach; adjacent to Cowell Park and Roaring Camp.

Santa Cruz

Babbling Brook Inn, 1025 Laurel Street; (831) 458–9166. Country French bed-and-breakfast inn, lovely gardens, full breakfast. Ask for a room near the creek.

Beach Street Cafe, on the corner of Beach and Cliff Streets across from the boardwalk; (831) 476–0636. The walls are literally covered with prints by Maxwell Parrish, a famous pre–art deco artist. Bistro food, espresso.

Best Inn and Suites, 600 Riverside Avenue; (800) 527–3833. A nice chain motel 4 blocks from the beach with pool, continental breakfast.

Casablanca, 101 Main Street; (831) 426–9063. Overlooking beach and boardwalk, elegant, candlelit, fresh seafood, notable wine list, wine-tasting dinners. Some of the very nice thirty-three ocean-view rooms here have fireplaces, kitchens, balconies, or terraces.

Chaminade at Santa Cruz, 1 Chaminade Lane; (800) 283–6569. An executive retreat, resort, and a restaurant in a eucalyptus forest on a hill overlooking Monterey Bay on the south side of Santa Cruz. Fitness center, lighted tennis courts, pool. Suites are often available, and this is a good place for families to stay. Sunday brunch here is legendary.

Cliff Crest, 407 Cliff Street; (831) 427–2609. A Queen Anne mansion built in 1887 with five guest rooms, antiques throughout, four-poster beds, claw-foot tubs. On a quiet street 2 blocks from the sea and the boardwalk.

Villa Vista, 2-2800 East Cliff Drive, ten minutes from downtown; (408) 866–2626; www.villavista.com. Two perfectly wonderful condo units with living rooms, each with three master bedrooms with baths, gourmet kitchen, sea-view patio, home entertainment center, and laundry facilities. Great for several couples or a large family.

Zachary's, 849 Pacific Avenue; (831) 427–0646. Voted "Best Breakfast in Santa Cruz"; sourdough pancakes, scones, corn bread, and more. Breakfast, lunch, brunch.

For More Information

Santa Cruz Mountains Winegrowers, 7605 Old Dominion Court, Suite A, Santa Cruz, CA 95063; (831) 479–WINE. Free brochure and map describing nineteen wineries.

Santa Cruz Visitor Information Center, 1211 Ocean Street 3 blocks from Highways 1 and 17, Santa Cruz, CA 95060; (831) 425–1234 or (800) 833–3494; www.santacruzca.org.

State campground reservations: (800) 444–7275.

Half Moon Bay 3

Harbor Lights, Tidepool Treasure

2 Nights

The small Victorian town of Half Moon Bay and the beaches and harbors nearby hold several days' worth of discoveries. Accessibility to the San Francisco Bay Area, good weather, sea air, and the outdoor fun to be had here are what create bumper-to-bumper traffic at times on summer weekends. Weekdays and off-season are the times to come, although you can get pleasantly lost and alone in the redwoods or on the beach any day of the year.

Besides commercial ocean fishing, the important endeavor in Half Moon Bay is flower and vegetable growing. The annual Pumpkin and Art Festival and Great Pumpkin Parade in October draw hundreds of thousands of revelers and their children.

☐ Beaches, bikes, hikes, fishing

☐ Wellness retreat

☐ Art and antiques

☐ Flower marts, veggie farms

Within huge greenhouses and in the fields around them, flowers are grown for shipment all over the world, and you can buy plants and flowers—and Christmas trees—at several places along the highways.

A stroll through the town of Half Moon Bay turns up Western saloons, country stores, fancy boutiques, galleries, and hundred-year-old hotels and homes, many on the National Register of Historic Places.

At the north end of the big curve of the bay, Pillar Point Harbor is a good place to escape the tourist mania. You can watch fishing boats and yachts go in and out of the marina, fish for flounder and rockfish from the wharf, or go shelling on the little beach west of the jetty. South along the coast, within an hour of Half Moon Bay, beaches, nature preserves and two tiny old villages await the visitor.

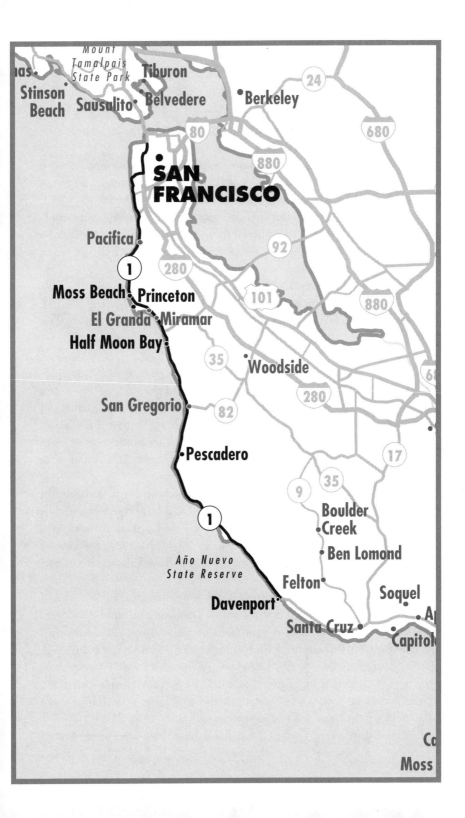

Day 1 / Morning

Drive south from San Francisco on Highway 1, along the Pacific Coast through Pacifica to **Moss Beach,** an hour's drive. This estimated time does not account for heavy weekend and holiday traffic.

The **Fitzgerald Marine Reserve** in Moss Beach (650–728–3584) is a good place to stretch your legs. A walking trail loops through meadows and along a bluff above some of the richest tidepools on the Pacific Coast. At low tide, a kaleidoscope of sponges, sea anemones, starfish, crabs, mollusks, and fish emerges. With a special fishing license, you can take abalone and some rockfish. For the best tidepooling, call ahead to find out when the low tides are scheduled.

The best place to stay in Moss Beach is the **Seal Cove Inn,** a big yellow mansion in an English garden on the edge of the Marine Reserve (650–728–4114). The inn is a classic, with spacious, luxurious public rooms and guest rooms, all with garden views, wood-burning fireplaces, and traditional furnishings.

Drive south to **Pillar Point Harbor** at Princeton-by-the-Sea, a picturesque harbor busy with a fleet of more than 200 fishing boats and yachts. Park in the harbor parking lot and walk on trails to beaches and marshlands on both the north and south sides of the harbor. Pillar Point Marsh is a favorite bird-watching site. Due to the confluence of both fresh- and saltwater, and a protected environment, nearly 20 percent of all North American bird species have been sighted here.

From December through April, whale-watching boats depart from the wharf. You are almost guaranteed to see California gray whales on their 4,000-mile migration from the Arctic to Baja. **Captain John's** (800–391–8787) and **Huck Finn Sportfishing** (800–572–2934) are charter companies based at the harbor that offer regular whale-watching and fishing expeditions.

Just south of the harbor, Surfer's Beach is popular not only for surfing but for ocean kayaking, boogieboarding, sailboarding, and jet skiing. (When the waves begin to call your name, order a custom-made surfboard at **Cowboy Surf Shop** from veteran surfer Craig MacArthur at his shop, 2830 Cabrillo Highway; (650) 726–6968. Call (650) 726–0654 for the daily surf report. Surfers from around the world come to Maverick's off Pillar Point, where 30-foot waves breaking over a rocky reef up the ante; some say these are the biggest waves in the world.

Two fish markets at the harbor sell a huge variety of fresh, locally caught seafood, and there are several small cafes and bars frequented by locals who wouldn't be caught dead in the trendy downtown establishments of nearby Half Moon Bay.

LUNCH: Ketch Joanne and the Harbor Bar, 25 Johnson Pier, Pillar Point Harbor, Princeton; (650) 728–3747. A bowl of clam chowder in a booth next to the woodstove can be a warm experience.

Afternoon

Save at least a half day for browsing Main Street in Half Moon Bay, a few blocks of buildings built early in the twentieth century that are now inhabited by upscale, country-chic shops, cafes, and galleries. On the south end of the street, at 604 Main in a terra-cotta–colored enclave called **La Piazza,** are several shops of note and a popular bakery that serves coffee drinks and pastries in a streetside cafe (**Moonside Bakery;** 650–726–9070).

Other shops on Main include **Quail Run** (412 Main; 650–726–0312), a nature-oriented emporium with elaborate bird mansions for the feathered few and butterfly gardens for kids; and the **Coastal Gallery** (424 Main in a garden alley; 650–726–3859), with rooms full of prints, oil paintings, and watercolors by regional artists, including the regionally famous Thomas Kinkade. If you have time to visit only one shop on Main Street, go to **Cedanna,** a gallery store loaded with one-of-a-kind avant garde artisans' inventions such as iron furniture, mirrors, handmade cards, jewelry, photo frames, prints, and painted fantasies (400 Main at Mill; 650–726–6776). A marine and wildlife shop, the **Harbor Seal Company,** sells unusual sea- and bird-life toys, puzzles, soft animals, educational toys, books, and games (406 Main Street; 650–726–7418).

One of the oldest established businesses in town, **Cunha's** (448 Main; 650–726–4071) is a grocery with a large deli, its own line of homemade packaged gourmet foods, and, upstairs, Western boots, hats, souvenirs, hardware, and T-shirts. On the corner across from Cunha's, the city has set up a nice picnic table area.

At the north end of Main, **The Tinnery** is another indoor mall crammed with small shops and cafes, including a sushi bar, a coffee cafe, a card shop, and a gallery.

DINNER: San Benito House, 356 Main Street, Half Moon Bay; (650) 726–3425. A renowned European country–style place serving Mediterranean cuisine, named by *National Geographic Traveler* as the finest restaurant on the coast between San Francisco and Monterey. Garden patio.

Waterfront at Pillar Point in Half Moon Bay.

LODGING: Half Moon Bay Lodge, 2400 South Cabrillo Highway (Highway 1) Half Moon Bay; (650) 726–9000 or (800) 368–2468; www. woodsidehotels.com. Eighty spacious rooms with small patios or balconies overlooking lovely gardens and lawns; traditional furnishings, comforters, some fireplaces; swimming pool; large, enclosed spa; fitness center; sauna. Continental breakfast. Many extras such as borrowable best-sellers, down pillows, beach blankets. The unassuming exterior belies the comfort, attractiveness, and amenities within the nice rooms; ask for a room overlooking the golf course.

Less than five minutes from here, you can walk or bike a coastal trail that runs along the bluffs above the beaches several miles to Princeton-by-the-Sea. The easiest part of the trail is a 3-mile path between Kelly Avenue at Half Moon Bay and Mirada Road in Miramar. Beaches are accessible all along the way.

Day 2 / Morning

BREAKFAST: Main Street Grill, 435 Main at Kelly, Half Moon Bay; (650) 726–5300. Cajun sausage, artichoke omelettes, and homemade waffles and muffins. Also good for lunch: grilled sandwiches, thick milk shakes, microbrewed beers, and a jukebox.

South from Half Moon Bay along Highway 1 are a string of beaches, wildlife preserves, and two tiny historic towns. It's 15 miles to the **Pescadero State Beach,** one of the prettiest, duniest, tidepooliest places you could spend an afternoon (650–726–6238). On the inland side of Highway 1, **Pescadero Marsh** is 588 acres of uplands and wetlands, an important stop on the Pacific Flyway. More than 200 species of waterfowl and shorebirds make this a must-see for avid birders or for anyone wishing to walk the trails through the marsh. Great blue herons nest in the blue gum eucalyptus trees, egrets walk stiffly in the shallow waters, northern harriers glide above, and marsh wrens follow you around.

It's 2 miles from Highway 1 on Pescadero Road to **Pescadero,** a block or so of clapboard buildings and steepled churches, circa 1850. Peek into the few antiques boutiques and stop at **Norm's Market,** where the irresistible aroma of warm artichoke and garlic/cheese bread wafts out the door; some of the twenty-four kinds of bread are "halfbaked"—to take home, stow in the freezer, and bake later.

A half-mile beyond the town on Pescadero Creek Road, park under the giant oak and get out your camera at **Phipps Ranch** (650–879–0787), a combination produce market, farm, plant nursery, and menagerie of exotic birds and farm animals. There are fancy chickens, big fat pigs, a variety of bunnies, and antique farm equipment. You can pick your own berries or buy them at the produce stand.

A real sleeper of a park and campground, **Butano State Park** off Pescadero Road is a lush piece of the earth, with magnificent redwood groves freshened by creeks and ferny glades (2 miles past Pescadero, turn right onto Cloverdale Road; travel 5 miles to park entrance; 800–444–7275). From small, pretty campsites, you can walk streamside paths or take a challenging mountain hike on an 11-mile loop to the **Año Nuevo Island** lookout.

Back on the highway, proceed south; it's 22 miles to **Davenport,** where you'll have lunch. On the way is the circa-1870, ten-story-tall **Pigeon Point Lighthouse,** open for tours on weekends (650–879–2120). The hostel here offers inexpensive private and shared rooms and marvelous views (www.norcalhostels.org). Just north of the lighthouse are beautiful beaches, tidepools, and wildflower meadows.

Proceed to the village of Davenport for lunch (36 miles south of Half Moon Bay).

LUNCH: **New Davenport Cash Store Restaurant and Inn,** on Highway 1, Davenport; (408) 425–1818; www.davenportinn.com. Tuck into grilled chicken sandwiches, homemade soup, omelettes with home-made chorizo, big killer brownies, and fresh fruit from nearby farms. The gift shop sells guidebooks and a top-notch array of African masks, Turkish jewelry, Mexican crafts, and Santa Fe jewelry. Breakfast and brunch are very popular here on weekends and are definitely worth the wait. Upstairs is a casually comfy bed-and-breakfast. Across Highway 1 from the restau-rant are a short walking path on the bluffs and a nice beach.

Afternoon

If art glass is one of your interests, don't miss the **Lundberg Studios,** a mecca for aficionados of Tiffany-style lamps and art deco paperweights (131 Old Coast Road; 831–423–2532). At 111 Old Coast Road, **David Boyce Knives Gallery** is a showplace of unique handcrafted cutlery (408–426–6046).

Returning north 9 miles, stop at **Año Nuevo State Reserve,** which may turn out to be the highlight of your trip on the Central coast (650–879–0227 or 800–444–4445; www.anonuevo.org). On 1,200 acres of dunes and beaches, the largest groups of elephant seals in the world come to breed from December through April. A 0.5-mile walk through grassy dunes brings you to an unforgettable sight: dozens of two-ton animals lounging, arguing, maybe mating, cavorting in the sea, and wiggling around on the beach. As many as 2,500 seals spend their honeymoons here, and there's lots of other wildlife to see, too. During the mating season it is necessary to reserve spaces in guided interpretive tours (800–444–7275). At other times you can wander around on your own but are not allowed to come too close to the animals. No pets.

DINNER: **Duarte's Tavern,** 202 Stage Road, Pescadero; (650) 879–0464. Crowded on sunny weekends but worth the wait, Duarte's has for more than fifty years been a family restaurant serving cioppino, seafood specialties with a Portuguese accent, artichoke soup and fresh artichokes with garlic aioli, deep-fried calamari, cracked crab, abalone sandwiches, shrimp cakes, and olallieberry pie. Local ranchers belly up to the Old West–style bar. Daily breakfast, lunch, and dinner.

LODGING: Half Moon Bay Lodge.

Day 3 / Morning

BREAKFAST: Half Moon Bay Coffee Company, 20A Stone Pine Road at the north end of Main Street, Half Moon Bay; (650) 726–1994. A casual place busy with locals and tourists digging into homemade pies and pastries, pancakes, burgers, sandwiches, and simple, hearty entrees. Breakfast, lunch, and dinner.

Buy a kite at **Lunar Wind Inventions** in town, and head for 3 miles of sand at **Half Moon Bay State Beach** just south of town; to get there, go west on Kelly Avenue (650–726–8820). At Francis Beach, the most popular of the three beaches here, are developed RV and tent campsites, cold showers, BBQs, picnic sites, and the ranger station. (If the campground is full, try the nice Pelican Point RV Park on Miramontes Point Road, 650–726–9100.) Water temperature is chilly, even in summer, and the surf can be treacherous, so plan to dip your toes and play on the sand.

On Kelly Avenue, the **Andreotti Family Farm** sells fresh-picked fruits and veggies, juices, eggs, garlic, and vinegars, as it has since 1926 (650–726–9151).

Before you leave town, drive 3 miles east on Highway 92 and keep a sharp eye out for the right turn into **Half Moon Bay Nursery** (11691 San Mateo Road; 650–726–5392). This is a rambling, gorgeous kingdom of blooming garden and house plants, from orchids and ferns to thousands of geraniums, herbs, azaleas, camellias, climbing vines, hanging baskets, and seasonal bulbs—a veritable flower show. In wintertime, it's cozy in the main greenhouse by the woodstove.

LUNCH: On your way back to San Francisco on Highway 1, have lunch at the **Moss Beach Distillery** (Beach and Ocean, Moss Beach; 650–728–5595), said to be haunted by the Blue Lady, who wanders the nearby cliffs where she died mysteriously in the 1930s. On a spectacular hilltop overlooking a cove, with an outdoor patio and indoor dining room and bar with sea views, Moss Beach Distillery serves luscious fresh local seafood for lunch, dinner, and weekend brunch.

There's More

Bach Dancing and Dynamite Society, P.O. Box 302, El Granada 94018, at Miramar Beach, 2.5 miles north of Half Moon Bay; (650) 726–4143. Begun in a private home years ago, Sunday-afternoon jam sessions evolved into big-name jazz and classical concerts with catered lunches and dinners; purchase tickets in advance.

Bean Hollow Trail, 18 miles south of Half Moon Bay on Highway 1 (park at Pebble Beach or Bean Hollow State Beach); (650) 879–0832. A 2-mile bluff trail crossing six bridges. You'll see the legendary gemlike pebbles at Pebble Beach (it's forbidden to gather them), harbor seals on the offshore rocks, unique limestone formations, and sheets of blooming seaside plants such as lupines and primroses. Rest rooms.

Bicyclery, 432 Main Street, Half Moon Bay; (650) 726–6000. Rentals, accessories, service.

Burleigh Murray State Park, Mills Creek Ranch Road off Higgins Purissima Road, a mile south of Half Moon Bay; (650) 726–8820. Century-old dairy barn, said to be the only one of its kind remaining in the state. Past the barn, a pretty creekside trail ambles for about a mile.

Coastside Trail. From the coastal/west end of Poplar Avenue, drive 4.2 miles north to Pillar Point; (650) 726–8297. A flat, easy, paved biking and walking trail along the coastline—beautiful. There is a parking lot here, a picnic area, and a bridge to the southern coastal trail.

Half Moon Bay Golf Links, 2000 Fairway Drive off Highway 1, Half Moon Bay; (650) 726–4438. Rated number four in the state by the PGA, the Links Course, designed by Arnold Palmer, has typical links breezes, coastal weather, barrancas, and bluffs, as does the new Ocean Course, with tight fairways and knolls, a challenging layout. Architect Arthur Hills kept turf to a minimum, uniting each hole with the original native grasses; only eleven cypress trees grace the course, where constant sea breezes, and sometimes gales, call for the irons (*Golf Magazine* calls the Ocean Course a "rip-roaring experience"). Be happy with your bogies and head for a window table at Caddy's restaurant here. Just beyond the eighteenth hole, perched 100 feet above the Pacific, is the 261-room Ritz-Carlton Hotel.

Point Montara Lighthouse, Highway 1 at Sixteenth Street, Montara; (650) 728–7177. A short, chunky lighthouse on a high bluff, the 1875 Point Montara Fog Signal and Light Station is open to the public.

Purissima Creek Redwoods, Higgins Purissima Road, a mile south of Half Moon Bay; (650) 691–1200. On the western slope of the Santa Cruz Mountains, a redwood preserve with hiking, biking, and equestrian trails, some handicapped-accessible trails. Wildflowers, ferny creeks, giant redwoods, maples, and alders.

Sea Horse and Friendly Acres Horse Ranches, Highway 1 at Half Moon Bay; (650) 726–2362. Ride on your own or guided rides on the beach and trails; hayrides; picnic area.

Special Events

July. Tours des Fleurs, tours of coastside nurseries and flower farms; (650) 726–8380.

August. Pescadero Arts and Fun Festival, Pescadero; (650) 879–0848.

September. Harbor Day at Pillar Point Harbor; (650) 726–5202. Crafts booths, music, fantastic seafood barbecue.

October. Pumpkin and Art Festival, Half Moon Bay; (650) 726–9652. Great Pumpkin Parade, entertainment, contests—carving, pie-eating, biggest pumpkin. The town is mobbed.

November. California Coast Air Show, Half Moon Bay Airport; (650) 726–3417. Antique and modern aircrafts displayed, stunning air show.

December. Harbor Lighting Ceremony, Pillar Point Harbor; (650) 726–5202. Boat owners compete with lighted and decorated boats.

Other Recommended Restaurants and Lodgings

El Granda

Harbor View Inn, at Pillar Point Wharf; (650) 726–2329. A contemporary Cape Cod–style motel, large rooms with bay windows.

Half Moon Bay

Beach House Inn, 4100 North Cabrillo Highway; (800) 315–9366; www.
beach-house.com. Luxurious loft suites right on the seaside with private
patios or balconies, sleeper sofas, kitchenettes, fireplaces, soaking tubs, luxurious bath amenities, and cozy flannel robes. Heated lap pool, Jacuzzi
overlooking the ocean, lavish continental breakfast, and evening wine; full-
service beauty and health spa.

Old Thyme Inn, 779 Main Street; (650) 726–1616; www.inntraveler.com/
oldthyme. A Queen Anne Victorian in an English garden on the quiet end
of Main. Four-posters, fireplaces, whirlpool tubs, full breakfast.

The Ritz-Carlton, One Miramontes Point Road; (650) 712–7000 or (800)
241–3333. Resembling a grand nineteenth-century seaside lodge, the
Ritz-Carlton, Half Moon Bay is a 261-room oceanfront golf and spa resort
on a scenic bluff. The resort features a spa, two golf courses, traditional
English tea, and romantic sunset dining. Two-thirds of the guest rooms
have panoramic ocean views and include either a fireplace, built-in window seat, or outdoor terrace. Guests on the fifth floor enjoy a private
lounge where complimentary breakfast, light lunch, afternoon tea and
hors d'oeuvres, and desserts are available daily. The attentive staff also serves
cocktails throughout the evening.

San Benito House, 356 Main Street; (650) 726–3425. English garden bed-
and-breakfast inn built at the turn of the twentieth century. Fresh flowers
throughout, twelve rooms with antiques and brass beds. European country–
style restaurant with garden patio, the most celebrated in the region.

Miramar

Cafe Classique, corner of Granada and Seville, across the highway from
Pillar Point Harbor at the stoplight; (415) 726–9775. Cappuccinos, fresh
juices and monster muffins, hearty sandwiches, soups; very casual. Open
early for breakfast, lunch.

Cypress Inn, 407 Mirada Road; (650) 726–6002. On 5 miles of beach,
eight contemporary-design, luxury rooms and suites; sumptuous breakfasts
and afternoon wine; a few steps from the beach. Fireplaces, private decks,
sea views, skylights, in-house massage therapist!

Miramar Restaurant and Bar, 131 Mirada Road, 2.5 miles north of Half
Moon Bay; (650) 726–9053. Lunch, dinner, and weekend brunch across

the street from Miramar Beach, fresh seafood specialties, lively bar crowd, sometimes live music.

Pescadero

Costanoa Lodge and Camp, P.O. Box 842, 2001 Rossi Road, Pescadero 94060; (650) 879–2600 or (877) 262–7848; www.costanoa.com. Surrounded by beautiful parklands, Costanoa is a new idea in upscale camping—luxury tents, cabins and lodge rooms, RV and tent sites. Light breakfast, spa and sauna, bikes to rent, well-stocked general store with gourmet and deli foods to take out or eat at picnic tables. You can hike into pristine wilderness, right from the camp.

Princeton

Barbara's Fish Trap, 281 Capistrano Road; (650) 728–7049. Perched right on the bay, big plates of fresh seafood.

Pillar Point Inn, 380 Capistrano Road at Pillar Point Harbor; (800) 400–8281. Small, romantic, New England–style inn with sea views, overlooking the harbor. Fireplaces, feather beds, steam baths, great breakfast.

San Gregorio

Rancho San Gregorio, 5086 San Gregorio Road (near Pescadero); (650) 747–0810; www.sangregorio-lodging.com. A Spanish Mission-style mansion with four delightful bed-and-breakfast rooms, some with woodstoves. Sumptuous breakfasts include fruit from the orchard, homemade crepes, scones, and muffins.

Woodside

Lodge at Skylonda, 16350 Skyline Boulevard; (800) 851–2222. If you travel south on Highway 280, exit at 92 West to Half Moon Bay and turn left at Highway 35, which is Skyline Boulevard. It's 10.5 miles on your right. Skylonda's wellness classes focus on health and fitness, beginning with yoga at 6:30 A.M., followed by a morning hike, then, in the late afternoon, Pilates, aqua-aerobics, tai chi. Spa treatments incorporate techniques from Thailand, India, Japan, and China. The two-night getaway package includes gourmet meals prepared by chef Sue Chapman, daily classes, use of the facilities, and a one-hour spa service.

For More Information

Half Moon Bay Coastside Chamber of Commerce, P.O. Box 188, 520 Kelly Avenue, Half Moon Bay, CA 94019; (650) 726–5202; www.half moonbaychamber.org.

State campground reservations, Año Nuevo tour reservations: (800) 444–7275.

Monterey and Big Sur 4

Spanish History, Wild Coastline

3 Nights

In the late 1700s Spanish explorers arrived in force on the Monterey Peninsula, making it headquarters for their huge Baja and Alta California domains, and Father Junípero Serra built one of his largest and most beautiful missions. Then Mexico took a turn as occupier of Monterey for more than twenty years.

This rich Hispanic heritage remains in the thick-walled adobes and Spanish Colonial haciendas of Monterey. Beneath the gnarled old olive trees, in courtyard gardens planted by the early conquistadors, and beside spectacular Monterey Bay are the upscale shops, world-class restau-

- ☐ Museums, mansions, mountains
- ☐ Beachcombing
- ☐ A golfer's dream
- ☐ Shopping, biking, hiking
- ☐ Chowder and cioppino

rants, and museums that draw visitors today. Add eighteen championship golf courses within 12 miles, and more than a weekend is called for on the Monterey Peninsula.

In stark contrast to the historic neighborhoods and sophisticated atmosphere of present-day Monterey, Big Sur is a sparsely developed stretch of wilderness running 90 miles south to San Simeon, a series of cliffs and river valleys hemmed in by a high mountain range on one side and a largely inaccessible seacoast. A longtime resident of Big Sur, author Henry Miller, said of the area, "It is a region where extremes meet, a region where one is always conscious of weather, of space, of grandeur, and of eloquent silence."

Day 1 / *Morning*

Drive south from San Francisco on Highway 101, south on Highway 156 to Highway 1 south to Monterey, about two hours. Pick up a walking-tour map at the **Monterey County Visitors Bureau,** Camino El Estero at the foot of Franklin Street, between Fremont and Del Monte Avenues.

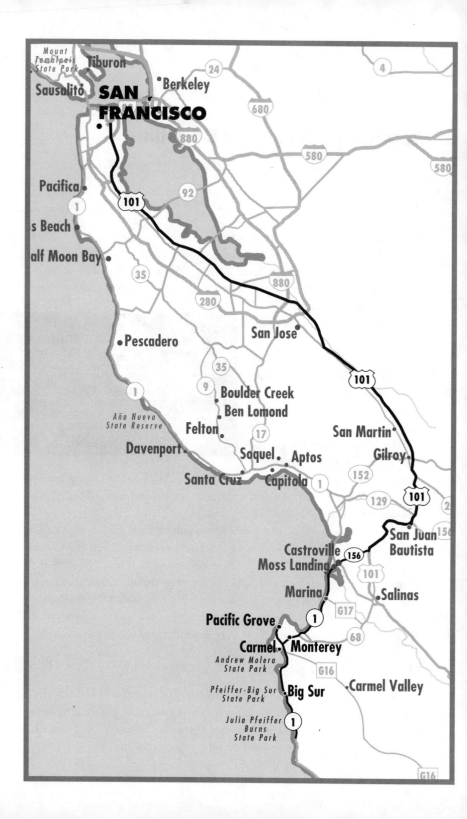

Between Memorial Day and Labor Day, ride the **WAVE** shuttle buses that run around downtown Monterey, Pacific Grove and popular tourist destinations, parking garages, hotels, and motels. Stops are marked with blue banners.

Spend a couple of hours strolling in and out of the historic buildings and garden courtyards on the Monterey State Park **"Path of History,"** a 2-mile walk that includes the grassy knolls of **Colton Hall,** at Pacific and Jefferson, a museum in an old school. Notice the small plastered-adobe homes in back of Colton Hall, some of the first built in California.

Part of the park complex, **Cooper Store,** on Polk Street, sells antique toys, postcards, and souvenirs. Go through the store to the museums and gardens behind; a spectacular cypress towers overhead. In the heart of the Historic District is the **Monterey Peninsula Museum of Art,** 559 Pacific Street (831–372–5477), with a fine collection of Western and Asian art and photography.

The **Maritime Museum of Monterey** at the waterfront focuses on the Monterey Peninsula's long seagoing history (831–373–2608). Priceless marine artifacts include the 16-foot-tall, 10,000-pound lens that once operated atop the Point Sur Lighthouse. When you are ready to get off your feet for twenty minutes, take in the historical film here—it's free.

LUNCH: Abalonetti's, 57 Fisherman's Wharf, Monterey; (831) 373–1851. Sit indoors or on the wharf; calamari, Italian antipasto, pizza, seafood pasta; for forty years one of the best fish cafes on the wharf.

Afternoon

Somehow avoiding the architectural upgrade and commercial development that destroyed an "Old Town" ambience once found on Cannery Row, **Fisherman's Wharf** (831–649–6544; www.montereywharf.com) still smells of salt spray and caramel corn. Fishing boats bob in the harbor, seagulls squawk and wheel overhead, and sea breezes blow between slightly seedy boardwalk cafes and tourist shops.

Walk along the waterfront **Monterey Peninsula Recreational Trail** that runs from the wharf all the way along Cannery Row and around Pacific Grove, a distance of 5 miles, if you care to walk that far. It's fun to dodge brown pelicans and watch sea lions barking to get your attention. You can even rent a pedaling vehicle, powered by two adults in back, with room for two little kids in front.

Along the way are drinking fountains, benches, picnic sites, and bike racks.

DINNER: Fishwife, 1996½ Sunset Drive, Pacific Grove; (831) 375–7107. Casual, popular, reasonably priced cafe at Asilomar Beach with sunset views. Wide variety of fresh fish, Cajun blackened snapper, salmon Alfredo, Key lime pie; reservations a must. Lunch, dinner, Sunday brunch.

LODGING: Green Gables Inn, 104 Fifth Street, Pacific Grove; (800) 722–1774. Regal above the bay, an 1888 Queen Anne Victorian with stunning views from every room; one of the most exquisite inns in the state, with luxurious interiors, fireplaces, bicycles, extraordinary service; full, elaborate breakfasts and luscious afternoon teas. Walk to the aquarium, Cannery Row, and the bayside path.

Day 2 / Morning

BREAKFAST: Green Gables Inn.

Don't miss a visit to the **Monterey Bay Aquarium,** 886 Cannery Row (831–648–4800; www.mbayaq.org). In summer and on weekends and holidays, it's important to arrive here at Monterey's most popular attraction when it opens at 10:00 A.M. (an alternative is after 3:00 P.M.). In an architectural masterpiece, some 6,000 sea creatures reside here in giant tanks. The three-story Kelp Forest is the world's tallest aquarium exhibit, so huge that it feels as if you're swimming around in there with the sharks and the schools of silvery fish. The Monterey Bay Habitats exhibit is 90 feet long, full of fascinating reef life. Playful sea otters and bat rays have their own watery homes, and it's fun to watch them during feeding time. There are frequent live videos from a research submarine prowling Monterey Bay, as deep as 3,000 feet.

A million gallons of seawater behind the largest window on the planet, the Outer Bay exhibit contains species that the world's aquariums have not dared to exhibit, such as 10-foot-tall, 1.5-ton sunfish; pelagic stingrays; green sea turtles as big as dining room tables; vast schools of yellowfin tuna; and species of sharks too big for other aquariums.

The Drifters gallery contains the largest-scale jellies exhibit in the world. Otherworldly music and a dreamlike design for the jellies venue transfix viewers before the pulsing, drifting, rainbow-hued beings. The new Splash Zone is an interactive, simulated marine-environment venue for kids and toddlers. Allow at least three hours to tour the aquarium.

Light lunches are available in the cafe. The aquarium is fully accessible to the disabled, and wheelchairs are available. Many hotels and motels in the area offer packages that include lodgings and aquarium tickets (800–756–3737).

One of the most biodiverse marine environments in the world, Monterey Peninsula waters attract divers from all over the world to the **Monterey Bay National Marine Sanctuary,** encompassing 4,000 nautical square miles of kelp forests and rocky reefs inhabited by a miraculous variety of creatures such as leopard shark, bright nudibranchs, and hundreds more species, plus the ever-present otters, dolphins, and whales. *Scuba Diving* magazine chose Monterey Bay as the "Favorite Shore Dive in the U.S.," and the bay has also been in the top five "Favorite Beginner's Dive Destinations."

The **Monterey Bay Dive Center,** 225 Cannery Row (831–656–0454 or 800–GO–SCUBA), is a PADI dive center where you can rent complete diving equipment, take a guided dive tour, and arrange to get certified as a diver.

LUNCH: Montrio, 414 Calle Principal, Monterey; (831) 648–8880. Euro-American urban bistro in a 1910 landmark firehouse. From the display kitchen come Dungeness crab cakes, grilled salmon with fennel ratatouille, and homemade pasta; from the wood-burning rotisserie come rosemary and garlic chicken, plus Black Angus ribeye. The wine list received an award of excellence by *Wine Spectator.* If you can't get a reservation, you can eat in the pleasant cocktail lounge.

Afternoon

Stroll about and shop on **Cannery Row.** At one time just a few blocks of weathered cannery buildings with funky shops and cafes, the waterfront promenade is now rampant with elegance and élan. Steinbeck and sardines were replaced by upscale boutiques and fancy hotels. The seals, otters, and sailing yachts of Monterey Bay remain.

Shopping is primo on Cannery Row and on a few adjacent streets. **Cannery Row Antique Mall,** at 471 Wave Street (831–655–0264), is more than 20,000 square feet housing the antiques and collectibles of a hundred dealers. At 700 Cannery Row is a complex of almost three dozen shops and galleries plus a wax museum, a winery, and cafes. Located here is **A Taste of Monterey,** where you can enjoy a panoramic view of

Monterey Bay, wine and food tasting, exhibits, and a multimedia show about the region (831– 646–5446).

Shoppers and cafe-sitters are drawn to the sophisticated eateries and boutiques on 2 blocks of old Alvarado Street, downtown between Del Monte Avenue and Jefferson Street. Serious cigar smokers stop at **Hellam's,** which also holds an astonishing array of chotchkes, unique metal dolls, and arguably the world's largest collection of Zippo lighters (831–373–2816). Locals head for **Rosine's** for home-style breakfasts, lunches, and dinners, six-layer cakes, pasta, and burgers (434 Alvarado; 831–375–1400). It's **Supremos** for artichoke enchiladas and lobster burritos, in an 1850 adobe house (500 Hartnell Street behind the Cooper adobe at the end of Alvarado; 831–373–3737), and contemporary Italian food at the bistro, **Tutto Buono** at 469 Alvarado (831–372–1880).

Drive to the Spanish Bay entrance to the **17-Mile Drive,** at Asilomar near the Fishwife restaurant; you'll pay a $7.00-per-car entry fee that's well worth it, even on a foggy day. Ghostly cypress forests and red lichen-painted rocks frame the many vista points. Stop and explore the beautiful beaches and many tidepools; walk or jog on the winding waterfront path. If you're a golfer, this is a chance to see three of the most famous and most difficult courses in the world.

DINNER: **Fandango,** 223 Seventeenth Street, Pacific Grove; (831) 372–3456. By the fire in the dining room, on the glass-domed terrace, or on the garden patio, European country–style cuisine in a Mediterranean setting. Wood-burning grill, pasta, paella, seafood, cassoulet. Signature dishes are rack of lamb Provençal and Velouté Bongo Bongo Soup. Full bar, exceptional wine list; lunch, brunch, and dinner.

LODGING: Green Gables Inn.

Day 3 / Morning

BREAKFAST: Green Gables Inn.

Drive south on Highway 1 to Big Sur, about 30 miles on a two-lane, winding mountain road. The brooding mountain shoulders of the **Santa Lucia Mountains** loom to the left, and to the right it's a sheer 1,000-foot drop to a rocky, mostly inaccessible coastline pierced by the small valleys of the Big and Little Sur Rivers. Several river and forest parks are here in the **Los Padres National Forest** (831–385–5434), where you'll also find good campgrounds and walking and hiking trails. Big Sur is a banana belt, with higher temperatures than Carmel and Monterey, getting more inches of rain but more sunny days. In wintertime you'll often find clear blue skies here when it's drippy just a few miles north.

You'll cross the **Bixby Creek Bridge,** also known as the Rainbow Bridge, a 260-foot-high single-spanner constructed in 1932. At **Andrew Molera State Park** (831–667–2315), the **Big Sur River** flows down from the Santa Lucias through this 4,700-acre park, falling into the sea at a long sandy beach. One of many hiking trails runs along the river, through a eucalyptus grove where monarch butterflies spend the winter, to the river's mouth, where you can see a great variety of sea- and shorebirds. For trail maps and information, write in advance to the USDA Forest Service, 406 South Mildred, King City 93930 (831–385–5434).

One of the most unforgettable ways to see Big Sur is on horseback. **Molera Horseback Tours** offers daily two-hour rides, each featuring a different perspective, such as the beach, redwood groves, mountain ridges, and sunset excursions (800–942–5486).

LUNCH: Nepenthe, Highway 1 just south of Ventana Inn, Big Sur; (831) 628–6500. The stone patios of the restaurant are perched on a magical promontory at the edge of the continent, with a bird's-eye view of a long shoreline. Just offshore are natural arches and seastacks, rocky remnants of an ancient coastline. Try the ambrosia burger or the fresh fish.

Afternoon

Drive through **Big Sur Valley,** not a town, really, but a handful of river resorts and campgrounds on both sides of the highway. **Pfeiffer Big Sur State Park** (831–667–2315) is another place to hike, picnic, and fish in the Big Sur River. Docent-led nature walks are given in summer; one trail leads to **Pfeiffer Falls,** in a fern canyon.

Just inside the entrance to the park, the casual restaurant at **Big Sur Lodge** overlooks the river (831–667–2315). Cottage-style lodge rooms are in big demand during vacation season. The nearby **Post Ranch Inn** (P.O. Box 219, Big Sur 93920; 831–667–2200; www.postranchinn.com) is a luxurious, visually stunning inn with fireplaces, spa tubs, a renowned restaurant, and complete privacy for guests.

Ten miles farther down the coast, **Julia Pfeiffer Burns State Park** is 2,400 acres of undeveloped wilderness. Trails along McWay Creek lead to a waterfall that plunges into the ocean (831–667–2315). The Partington Creek trail goes through a canyon and a 100-foot-long rock tunnel to

Partington Cove beach, where sea otters play in the kelp beds. A popular walk in the woods is the **Pine Ridge Trail,** right off Highway 1 at Big Sur Station visitors center, just south of Julia Pfeiffer Burns State Park. Wild iris and columbine bloom in shady redwood glens and fern grottoes, and if you can make it 7 miles, there are swimming holes at the Big Sur River and a hot springs another 3 miles farther on. Get a topographical map and check trail conditions at the visitors center.

(If you decide to continue to southern California, take note that the two-lane Big Sur highway south from here to San Simeon is crossed by thirty bridges over deep canyons and stream-cut valleys—breathtaking scenery—and is unrelentingly curvy. About halfway to San Simeon, **Jade Cove** is actually a string of coves, where Monterey jade is found at low tide and following storms. It's a 0.25-mile walk down to the cove from the highway, where you are allowed to collect what will fit into your pockets.)

DINNER: Ventana Inn and Spa (Cielo), 30 miles south of Carmel on Highway 1, Big Sur; (800) 678–6500. After dark, the walk up lighted outdoor stairs through a forest is a romantic beginning to a romantic evening in the four-star restaurant, which serves lunch and dinner. Indoors, a warm, woodsy atmosphere; outdoors, a stone patio floating high above the sea.

LODGING: Ventana Inn and Spa. Rustic country-luxe, a private, quiet resort on a hillside between the sea and mountain ridges, the resort has a compound of several pine buildings, each with canyon or ocean views. High-ceilinged, wood-paneled luxury suites with fireplaces and a feeling of isolation. Decor is of stone, wood, soft earth-toned fabrics.

There are two lap pools, Japanese hot baths, sauna, and massages on your own completely private deck. Indulge yourself in the full-service spa with wraps, scrubs, massages, and exotic, soothing therapies in a glorious natural setting. The elaborate afternoon wine and cheese buffet is in the main lounge. Wild gardens abloom with native flowers and vines; oceans of clematis and jasmine pour over balconies; tree ferns create shady glades. Call ahead for a monthly listing of scheduled special events, from guided naturalist hikes to history, literary, and gardening lectures and musical performances.

Day 4 / *Morning*

BREAKFAST: At the Ventana Inn. Enjoy the big breakfast buffet in the sunny dining lounge, outside on a choice of several garden patios, or in your room. Fresh berries, melons, tropical fruits; homemade coffee cakes, croissants, muffins, yogurt, granola.

After a morning exploring the meadow and mountainside trails that start at Ventana Inn, head back to the Bay Area.

There's More

Culinary Center of Monterey, 625 Cannery Row, Monterey; (831) 333–2133; www.culinarycenterofmonterey.com. Gourmet food takeout; beer, wine, and hors d'oeuvres bar; cooking classes and demonstrations with celebrity chefs; retail outlet featuring cookbooks and kitchen items—a food and wine mecca with a bay view.

Golf. Bayonet & Black Horse, 1 McClure Way, Seaside; (831) 899–7271. The Bayonet and Black Horse courses here on Monterey Bay host PGA qualifying tournaments and are tough, beautiful, established layouts made playable for the average golfer by several sets of tees.

Del Monte Golf Course, 1300 Sylvan Road, Monterey; (831) 373–2700. Eighteen holes, public, oldest course west of the Mississippi.

Laguna Seca Golf Course, 10520 York Road off Highway 68, Monterey; (831) 373–3701. Eighteen holes, public.

The Links at Spanish Bay, 17-Mile Drive, Pebble Beach; (800) 654–9300. One of the "Greatest Resort Courses" and "Best Golf Resorts in America." All but four of the holes flank the sea, and, in true Scottish fashion, the course is marked by waves of low, sandy mounds; fescue grass fairways; pot bunkers; and few trees.

Pacific Grove Links, 77 Asilomar Boulevard, Pacific Grove; (831) 648–5777. Eighteen holes, public, links-style.

Pebble Beach Golf Links, 17-Mile Drive, Pebble Beach; (800) 654–9300. Legendary site of U.S. Opens, PGA Championships, and the Crosby Clambake (now the AT&T Pro-Am). Pebble rides the headlands over Stillwater Cove, as it has since 1919. The notorious combination of swirling winds and misty hazes, long tee shots over gaping crevasses, and tiny greens remains a golfing challenge equaled by few courses in the world.

Poppy Hills Golf Course, 3200 Lopez Road, 17-Mile Drive, Pebble Beach; (831) 625–2035. Eighteen holes, public.

Spyglass Hill Golf Course, Stevenson Drive and Spyglass Hill, Pebble Beach; (800) 654–9300. Semiprivate, eighteen holes.

Monterey Bay Whale Watch, P.O. Box 52001, Pacific Grove 93950; (831) 375–4658. Three-hour winter and spring cruises to see gray whales and dolphins.

Monterey State Historic Park, from Fisherman's Wharf south to Pacific and Madison and east to Camino El Estero, 20 Custom House Plaza; (831) 649–7118; www.mbay.net/~mshp. Self-guided tour with entrance to many historic buildings is free. A two-hour guided tour is $5.00 per person.

Mopeds, bikes, kayaks. Adventures by the Sea, 299 Cannery Row, Monterey; (831) 372–1807; www.adventuresbythesea.com.

Bay Bikes, 640 Wave Street, Monterey; (831) 646–9090.

Monterey Bay Kayaks, 693 Del Monte Avenue, Monterey; (831) 373–KELP; www.montereybaykayaks.com.

Monterey Moped, 1250 Del Monte, Monterey; (831) 373–2696.

Point Lobos State Reserve, 2.5 miles south of Carmel on Highway 1; (831) 624–4909. A rocky point surrounded by a protected marine environment; otters, whales, harbor seals, sea lions; scuba diving; spectacular landscape; picnicking, walking, photo snapping.

Special Events

January. AT&T Pebble Beach National Pro-Am; (800) 541–9091.

Whalefest, Monterey; (831) 784–6464. Located on Old Fisherman's Wharf, this festival highlights information and fun with whale exhibits, whale-watching, museum tours, and food.

January–February. Monterey Whalefest, Monterey; (831) 644–7588. One of the largest whale celebrations in the country, with whale-watching expeditions, museum tours, kids' storytelling, living-history performances, special exhibitions, music, special events at the aquarium, and more.

March. Dixieland Monterey. Three days of Dixieland and Swing feature top national jazz bands and local groups. Hotline: (888) 349–6879; www.dixieland-monterey.com.

Hot Air Affair, Monterey; (831) 649–6544. Four hundred balloons compete in events, many in the early morning. Public rides in tethered balloons and helicopters. Skydiving exhibition.

April. Adobe Tour, Monterey; (831) 372–2608. Twenty-five adobes and gardens, period costumes.

Monterey Wine Festival, the oldest and largest California wine fest. Auction, food, special tastings, live entertainment.

May. Great Monterey Squid Festival. The incredible, edible squid is grilled, sautéed, tossed, and tasted, along with beers and wines; entertainment.

June. Monterey Bay Blues Festival, Monterey. The best of the best regional and national blues artists.

July. Living History Day in Old Monterey; (831) 647–6204. Travel back in time and find out what life was like in the 1840s.

California Rodeo Salinas; (831) 775–3100. Professional competition in steer wrestling, bull riding, calf roping, and bareback bronco riding; www.carodeo.com.

August. Winemakers' Celebration; (831) 375–9400; www.wines.com/ monterey. Special tastings, food and live entertainment, auction, open houses.

September. Monterey Jazz Festival; (831) 373–3366. The oldest continuous jazz fest in the world; internationally known performers.

October. Butterfly Parade and Bazaar, Pacific Grove. School bands and children in butterfly costumes welcome the Monarchs' return to their winter home in Pacific Grove, a charming hometown event. The Pacific Grove Museum of Natural History shows a short film and diorama of the famous butterfly trees of Monterey County (Forest and Central Avenues; 831–648–3116; free admission).

November. Great Wine Escape Weekend; (831) 375–9400; www.monterey wines.org. Special winery tours and open houses, wine-maker dinners, discounts. Transportation provided.

December. Christmas at the Inns, Pacific Grove; (831) 373–3304; www. pacificgrove.org. A self-guided tour of B&Bs decked in holiday splendor.

La Posada, Monterey; (831) 646–3866. A Christmas candlelight parade led by Joseph and Mary with participants singing Spanish and English Christmas carols. Followed by a piñata party and refreshments.

First Night Monterey, downtown Monterey; (831) 373–4778; www.first nightmonterey.org. Celebrate New Year's Eve through the arts with music, dance, poetry, art installations, and exhibits throughout historic downtown Monterey.

Other Recommended Restaurants and Lodgings

Big Sur

Big Sur Lodge, just inside the entrance to Pfeiffer Big Sur State Park; (800) 424–4787; www.bigsurlodge.com. Casual lodge dining room with patio overlooking the river; California cuisine, pasta, local seafood. Cozy, simple cottages in a forest; kitchens; fireplaces; lovely views; pool.

River Inn, Pheneger Creek; (800) 548–3610. Eighteen rooms and family suites with balconies overlooking the river; simple, rustic accommodations. Restaurant and bar, swimming pool, general store, near state parks.

Rocky Point, 10 miles south of Carmel on Highway 1; (831) 624–2933; www.rocky-point.com. Spectacular views of the coast from the dining room and the terrace make breakfast, lunch, and dinner memorable experiences. Try the enchiladas, the crab salad, or one of the fabulous steaks.

Marina

Marina Dunes Resort, 3295 Dunes Drive, 10 miles north of Monterey; (831) 883–9478; www.coastalhotel.com. Brand new and stunning, a sixty-unit luxury resort right on the dunes of Monterey Bay. Rooms and ranch-style bungalows, steps from the beach, are sleek and luxurious with outdoor spa tubs, fireplaces, Ralph Lauren–style decor, and gorgeous bathrooms. In the main lodge is a beauty and health spa, a workout facility, and A. J. Spurs, an Old West theme restaurant serving hearty beef, chicken, and seafood, and an open tapas bar. One of the two swimming pools is designed especially for kids.

Monterey

Hotel Pacific, 300 Pacific Street; (831) 373–5700 or (800) 554–5542; www.coastalhotel.com. Contemporary Spanish-hacienda suites with fireplaces, down comforters, private patio or balcony; continental breakfast, afternoon tea, fountains, hot tubs, and gardens.

Lone Oak Lodge, 2221 North Fremont; (831) 372–4924. Best-kept secret for inexpensive lodgings.

Monterey Bay Inn, 242 Cannery Row; (831) 372–8057 or (800) 558–1900; www.montereybayinn.com. A small, upscale, seaside hotel; each room has a king-size bed, sofa bed, and a pair of binoculars to watch the sea from the private balcony. Complimentary continental breakfast on the sunny garden patio; private path to a small beach; walk to the aquarium.

Monterey Plaza Hotel and Spa, 400 Cannery Row; (800) 334–3999. A four-star, luxury hotel with top-notch restaurants, in a bayside setting with sea views from nearly every public space and from more than half of the 285 rooms. Open to the public, big-name summer jazz concerts are held on the outdoor decks of the hotel.

Old Monterey Cafe, 489 Alvarado Street; (831) 646–1021; www.cafe monterey.com. Voted "Best Breakfast" in the county. Try the buckwheat pancakes, huge omelettes, and great salads and soups for lunch.

Old Monterey Inn, 500 Martin Street; (831) 375–8284; www.oldmonterey inn.com. A vine-covered, 1929 Tudor mansion with patios abloom with wisteria, aromatic jasmine, and hundreds of hanging baskets and pots. Understated European country-house decor, fireplaces, elegant extras, extraordinary service. Two honeymoon cottages. Full breakfast by the fire in the elegant dining room.

Spindrift Inn, 652 Cannery Row; (800) 841–1879. On the water, forty-one luxury rooms, half with ocean views, all with fireplaces, down comforters, marble baths, window seats or private balconies.

Tarpy's Roadhouse, Highway 68 and Canyon Del Rey, near the Monterey airport; (831) 647–1444. Originally a ranch house built in the 1920s; stone walls trailing with vines on the outside, covered with art on the inside; large wine cave; garden courtyard dining; updated versions of old-fashioned comfort foods such as polenta with wild mushrooms, Cajun prawns, fresh local seafood, grilled meats, honey mustard rabbit with apples and thyme.

Victorian Inn, 487 Foam Street; (800) 232–4141. Sixty-eight charming rooms and suites, marble fireplaces, private balconies or patios, some with living rooms and kitchenettes, hot tub; breakfast buffet and afternoon refreshments; walking distance to Cannery Row and the Wharf.

Pacific Grove

Asilomar Conference Center, 800 Asilomar Avenue; (831) 642–4222 or (888) 733–9005; www.asilomarcenter.com. Unknown to most tourists, this secluded, rustic, historic conference resort hides in a pine and oak forest above beautiful Asilomar State Beach. When space is available, individuals and families rent rooms and suites here at very reasonable rates that include a bountiful breakfast buffet in a bright, pleasant dining room (dinner available, too). There is a heated pool, volleyball, a game room, some fireplaces, some kitchens, and easy accessibility to the wonderful tidepools and the wide, sandy beach; unsuitable for swimming. Sixty acres of dunes are traversed by a mile-long boardwalk, and a trail leads to wildflowery clifftops and stunning sea views.

Centrella, 612 Central Avenue; (831) 372–3372. Three-story, elegant Victorian bed-and-breakfast establishment; romantic; quiet.

Lighthouse Lodge and Suites, 1150 Lighthouse Avenue; (831) 655–2111; www.lhls.com. In a seacoast environment of its own on Point Pinos; heated pool; thirty-one suites with ocean views, fireplaces, Jacuzzi tubs; full breakfast, afternoon refreshments. All lodge rooms include complimentary poolside barbecue each evening. Casual and quite reasonably priced.

Passionfish Grill, 701 Lighthouse Avenue; (831) 655–3311; www.passion fish.net. Line-caught local fish, slow-roasted meats, organic vegetables and salad greens from local farmers.

For More Information

Big Sur Chamber of Commerce, P.O. Box 87, Big Sur, CA 93920; (831) 667–2100; www.bigsurcalifornia.org.

Maritime Museum Visitors Center, Maritime Museum at Fisherman's Wharf, P.O. Box 1770, Monterey, CA 93942; (831) 649–1770 or (800) 555–WAVE; www.monterey.com.

Monterey County Convention & Visitors Bureau, P.O. Box 1770, Monterey, CA 93942; (888) 221–1010; www.montereyinfo.org.

Monterey County Visitors Center, Lake El Estero at Franklin and Camino El Estero, Monterey, CA 93940; (831) 649–1770.

Monterey Peninsula Reservations; (888) 655–3424; www.monterey reservations.com.

Pacific Grove Chamber of Commerce, P.O. Box 167, Pacific Grove, CA 93950; (831) 373–3304.

Resort 2 Me, 2600 Garden Road, #111, Monterey, CA 93940; (800) 757–5646; www.resort2me.com.

Home on the Ranch, Shopping Mecca

2 Nights

The Carmel River ambles over the valley floor between two mountain ranges through horse farms, ranch resorts, and meadows liberally sprinkled with spreading oaks. Just a few miles from the Pacific coast, but a world away, the tawny climate of Carmel Valley is warm and dry. Except for a big shopping and restaurant complex at Highway 1 and Carmel Valley Road, the valley has little commercial development. Your choices are golf, horseback riding, hiking, biking, tennis, or lying in the sun by a swimming pool.

□ Cowboy days

□ Tennis, golf, horseback rides

□ Beach walks

□ Serra's mission

□ Boutique binge

□ Art galleries

Once settled in the peace and quiet and sunshine of the valley, you may find it difficult to leave, but you will enjoy forays to the ocean beaches and to the artists' colony and shopping mecca of Carmel, a square-mile village of rustic country cottages and shingled beach houses in an idyllic forest setting. Carmel's winding lanes are shaded with ancient oaks and cypress, and everyone in town, it seems, is an avid gardener. Hanging baskets and blooming window boxes are everywhere.

Shopping at the literally hundreds of boutiques and art galleries is the main activity of visitors to Carmel. Originally a Bohemian artists' and writers' colony, the town has more than one hundred art and photography galleries.

Day 1 / *Morning*

Drive south from San Francisco on Highway 280, south on Highway 17 to Santa Cruz and Highway 1, then south to **Moss Landing,** about 1.75 hours from San Francisco. You can't miss Moss Landing. Just look for the twin 500-foot boiler stacks of the second largest fossil-fuel thermal electric

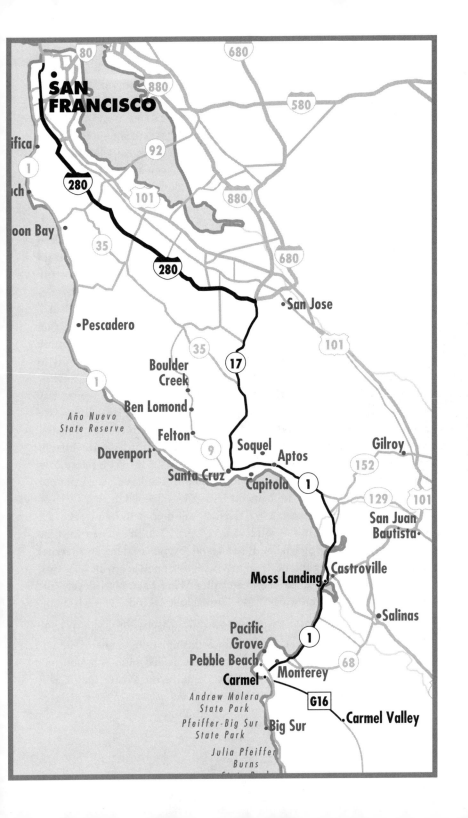

plant in the world. When you see a bright pink building with blue awnings, that's the **Whole Enchilada** (Highway 1 and Moss Landing Road, Moss Landing; 831–633–3038), an excellent Mexican restaurant. Nearby is **Phil's Fish Market and Eatery,** on the waterfront off Moss Landing Road in a wood warehouse with green awnings (7600 Sandholdt Road, Moss Landing; 831–633–2152; www.philsfishmarket.com). Turn west at the restaurant into the community of Moss Landing on Elkhorn Slough, where you will find twenty-five antiques shops in Western false-front buildings, a marina of fishing boats, and a boat graveyard. Elkhorn Slough is home to thousands of sea- and shorebirds and animals. You can walk on 4 miles of easy trails in the mudflats and salt marshes of the **Elkhorn Slough National Estuarine Research Reserve** and visit the **Moss Landing Marine Laboratory,** which is operated by nine California state universities (831–728–2822). A vast stretch of tidal wetlands, extending more than 7 miles inland, the slough shelters more than 260 species of birds, including thousands of migrating ducks and geese in winter and spring. Guided kayak and pontoon–boat tours with natural history narration are the best way to see wildlife (Slough Safari, 831–424–3939; Venture Quest, 831–427–2267; Kayak Connections, 831–724–5692, www.cruzio. com; Monterey Bay Kayaks, 800–649–5357, www.kayakelkhornslough.com). Boat tours take advantage of the tides, and the guides know where to find leopard sharks, bat rays, seals, otters, and other creatures. At **Moss Landing State Beach,** you can fish, surf, and horseback ride (831–649–2836). **Moss Landing Oyster Bar,** at the south end of Moss Landing Road, is a casual, popular cafe serving fresh fish and homemade pasta (831–633–5302).

Continue on Highway 1 to Carmel, another half hour. Take the **Carmel Valley** exit on the south end of Carmel and head east into the valley. Drive out Carmel Valley Road about twenty minutes to **Carmel Valley Village.** Along the way, you may wish to stop in at a winery or two; four are right on the roadside. **Château Julien Wine Estate** has a lovely tasting room and top-notch wines (8940 Carmel Valley Road; 831–624–2600).

LUNCH: Bon Appetit, 7 Delfino Place, Carmel Valley Village; (831) 659–3559. Sit outdoors under an umbrella, watch the passing scene of the village, and enjoy bouillabaisse, paella, mesquite-grilled fresh fish, gourmet pizzas, and a notable wine list. Another top choice, the **White Oak Grill,** is famous for hearty pork-loin sandwiches and *pommes frites* with gorgonzola (19 East Carmel Valley; 831–659–1525).

Afternoon

Stretch your legs on some of the 5,000 acres at **Garland Ranch Regional Park** with a hike, stroll, or bike ride along the **Carmel River,** across the forested hillsides and up on the high ridges overlooking the valley (831–659–4488). An easy, flat 1-mile walk is the Lupine Loop in the lower meadow, a pleasant, wildflowery route in winter and spring, but hot and dry in summertime and fall, unless it has recently rained. The Waterfall Trail is lush with ferns, rushing streams, and beautiful falls that run winter through spring. Other trails take you to breezy hilltop meadows and ponds where birds and ducks reside.

Just a few steps from the parking lot, picnic sites beside the river are pleasant. John Steinbeck wrote in *Cannery Row,* "The Carmel [River] crackles among round boulders, wanders lazily under sycamores, spills into pools, drops in against banks where crayfish live . . . frogs blink from its banks and the deep ferns grow beside it. . . . It's everything a river should be."

Plan to arrive at your valley lodgings early enough to enjoy a late afternoon swim or a game of tennis or perhaps golf.

DINNER: Marinus at Bernardus Lodge, 415 Carmel Valley Road, Carmel Valley; (831) 658–3500 or (888) 648–9463. Amble by the jazz combo in the lobby, settle into a gold velvet banquette by the 12-foot-wide stone fireplace, and sip a glass of smoky-cherry Bernardus Cabernet while contemplating the menu. Signature dishes include portobello soup, yellowfin tuna tartare, and lobsterlike, local "spot" prawns.

LODGING: Bernardus Lodge, 415 Carmel Valley Road, Carmel Valley; (831) 658–3400; www.bernardus.com. You are greeted with—what else?—a glass of Bernardus wine at this posh Mediterranean-style retreat in a stunning mountain setting. The lodge feels like a big villa, with shady arbors and gardens, thick walls and stone terraces, a big swimming pool, tennis, bocce, and a croquet lawn. Exceptionally spacious, cozy rooms have fireplaces, overstuffed sofas and chairs, two-person tubs, and feather beds with silky, imported linens. French doors open onto sunny balconies with mountain views—aaahhhh. Special services are many, including twice-daily room freshening and nightly wine and cheese in your room. A glamorous full-service beauty and health spa offers head-to-toe pampering; workout rooms; eucalyptus steam, sauna, and vichy showers; an array of exotic massages and treatments; and healthy drinks. Couples like the Vineyard

Romance Experience for two, one hundred minutes of pampered privacy including crushed grape seed and red wine scrub, massage, aromatherapy, and more.

Day 2 / Morning

BREAKFAST: Bernardus Lodge.

Head back on Carmel Valley Road to the shopping complex near Highway 1, turn left into the complex on Carmel Rancho, then right onto Rio Road and across Highway 1 to the **Mission San Carlos Borromeo del Rio Carmel,** one of the most impressive in California's chain of missions (831–624–1271). Star-shaped stained-glass windows, cool colonnades, and beautiful courtyard gardens and fountains make this a good place to linger. A warren of thick-walled rooms, restored from original mission buildings, holds a magnificent museum collection of early Indian, religious, and historical California artifacts. Inside, the cathedral, cool and silent even on the hottest days, is sienna, burnt umber, and gold, with soaring ceilings and heavy wooden pews.

Continue on Rio Road 2 blocks to Santa Lucia, turning left and following this street to the waterfront, bearing left to the north end of **Carmel River State Beach** (831–624–4909), adjacent to **Monastery Beach** and the **Carmel River Bird Sanctuary.** Frequented by a wide variety of waterfowl and shorebirds, these two beaches are visited by fewer people than Carmel Beach. Wander over the dunes that form a "plug" for the Carmel River most of the year. Pick up driftwood and shells or make a 4-mile round-trip run or walk. You may see scuba divers getting ready to descend into the kelp forests of the **Carmel Bay Ecological Reserve** offshore.

Monastery Beach is fine for picnicking, but heavy surf can make it unsafe for swimmers.

Four miles south of Carmel on Highway 1 is **Point Lobos State Reserve,** named for the offshore rocks called Punta de los Lobos Marinos (Point of the Sea Wolves), where sea lions lie about (831–624–4909). A rocky, forested point surrounded by a protected marine environment, the park's spectacular landscape includes several miles of trails, pebbled beaches, and one of only two naturally occurring stands of Monterey cypress (the other is at Pebble Beach). In the late 1800s, Robert Louis Stevenson called it the "most beautiful meeting of land and sea on earth."

From 6 miles of coastline, whales, harbor seals, and otters are often seen, as well as storms of pelicans, gulls, and cormorants. In the meadows mule deer tiptoe through purple needlegrass and wild lilac. Point Lobos is completely protected—the land, the marine life on the beach and in the tidepools, and the flora and fauna underwater. Not a thing may be removed or disturbed, dogs are not allowed, and visitors are required to stay on hiking trails or beaches. Sea Lion Point is accessed by an easy half-hour walk to Headland Cove, where sea lions bark and you can see the otters. Come early on weekends; guided interpretive walks are conducted by park rangers.

LUNCH: Thunderbird Bookshop and Restaurant, at the Barnyard, Highway 1 and Carmel Valley Road, Carmel Valley; (831) 624–1803. Indoor or outdoor dining at a big, bountiful bookstore, a fixture in the valley for decades. Healthy salads, grilled sandwiches, homemade soups, monster desserts. Cozy by the fireplace in wintertime.

If you are in the mood for Southwestern-style food, look for the **Rio Grill** in the adjacent Crossroads shopping center (831–625–5436). Southwestern-style decor and award-winning food, voted "Best Restaurant in Monterey County," make this a top choice. A wood-burning grill and an oak-wood smoker produce fresh fish, meat, and poultry specialties.

Afternoon

The Barnyard (831–624–8886) is a rambling complex of fifty shops and restaurants in barnlike buildings. If you're a garden fancier, this could be a highlight of your trip. In every nook and cranny are riots of blooming native perennials; thousands of flowers, shrubs, and trees; and oceans of bougainvillea, rivers of begonias, and streams of California poppies. A horticulturalist leads a guided tour of the gardens on Friday (831–624–8886). There is a **Monterey County Visitors Center** here, too (831–626–1424).

Among the Barnyard shops, in a storybook forest at **Twiggs** (831–622–9802), are gnomes, trolls, raccoons, bunnies, twittering birds, and fantastical creatures. The fanciest store for dogs and cats you're ever likely to encounter, **Enchanted Tails** has decorated collars, stuffed animals for animals, cushy mats and sleeping baskets, and an array of dog biscuits and treats, such as veggie hearts, liver unicorns, and banana bears (831–625–9648). Bubbling water and ringing chimes sound nice in another unique shop, **Succulent Gardens and Gifts,** which specializes in "water features"—indoor waterfalls, fountains and pools, plus wind chimes, bonsai, and garden statuary (831–624–0426).

What is a crumpet? Find out at the **Carmel Crumpet Company,** where scrumptious scones, sandwiches, and coffee drinks are also sold

(831–625–8165). From a glassed-in, heated outdoor deck overlooking the mountains and the Barnyard gardens, the **Sherlock Holmes Pub and Restaurant** holds forth with a British and American pub menu and exotic ales and beers (831–625–0340). Several more restaurants in the Barnyard include a Japanese open-hearth grill, a Chinese place, and a pizzeria.

In the adjacent shopping center, the Crossroads, look for **The Jazz Store** if you are a jazz fan (236 Crossroads Boulevard; 831–624–6432). Touted as the "world's only all-jazz store," it's the offical Monterey Jazz Festival merchandise headquarters, selling an amazing array of new and vintage records and CDs, art, apparel, books, memorabilia, instruments, and more.

DINNER: Mission Ranch Restaurant, 26270 Dolores Street on the south end of Carmel; (831) 625–9040. Overlooking the Carmel River with views of the bay and Point Lobos, Mission Ranch is a place where cowboys and cowgirls kick back and eat steak, local fresh fish, and California cuisine in upscale, casual surroundings.

LODGING: Carmel Mission Ranch, 26270 Dolores Street, Carmel; (831) 624–6436. Plush, pricey rooms here are in charming former ranch buildings; some have fireplaces, living rooms, and memorabilia from Clint Eastwood's movies (he owns the place).

Day 3 / Morning

BREAKFAST: Rub elbows with the locals at **Katy's Place** (downtown Carmel, Mission Street between Fifth and Sixth; 831–624–0199), and dig into platters of French toast, eggs, and cottage fries like Grandma used to make.

Lace up your walking shoes, warm up your credit cards, and set off for a day of shopping and gallery hopping.

On San Carlos between Fifth and Sixth is the visitors bureau, upstairs in the Eastwood Building, where you can pick up a walking-tour map and schedule of events (831–624–2522).

If time is short, stroll down one side of Ocean Avenue and up the other. With time on your hands, wander the side streets, the courtyards, and alleyways. Even those allergic to shopping will enjoy the mix of architecture, everything from English country cottage to California Mission style.

A few notable places to visit: the **Carmel Art Association** at Dolores between Fifth and Sixth (831–624–6276), a cooperative with a wideranging collection of the works of top artists; the **Weston Galleries** at

Sixth and Dolores (831–624–4453), where three generations of famous photographers are represented; the **Mischievous Rabbit** (Lincoln between Ocean and Seventh; 831–624–6854), a warren of Peter Rabbit–inspired treasures—hand-painted baby clothing, rabbit videos and books, carrot surprises. You will often find internationally renowned artist **Howard Lamar** painting in his studio on Dolores between Ocean and Seventh (831–626–6725).

Careful browsers discover gardens and shops in more than sixty courtyards; a short courtyard-tour map is available at the visitors bureau. Look for the winding path to the **Secret Garden,** on Dolores between Fifth and Sixth, to see unique statuary, a bevy of blooming baskets, and wind chimes (831–625–1131). Garden sculpture and fanciful topiaries are the specialties of **The Dovecote,** in a landmark Carmel cottage at Ocean and Dolores (831–626–3161).

Gardeners like **Devonshire,** the English garden shop at Ocean and Monte Verde (831–626–4601). Francophiles go to nearby **Pierre Deux** for fantasies created with famous French country fabrics (831–624–8185).

LUNCH: Porta Bella, Ocean between Lincoln and Monte Verde, Carmel; (831) 624–4395. Inventive Mediterranean cuisine in the flowerbedecked Court of the Golden Bough, in the charming cottage, or on the year-round heated garden patio. Lunch, afternoon tea, and dinner.

Afternoon

Aviation is the theme at **Wings America,** on the corner of Dolores and Seventh (831–626–WINGS). The collection of aircraft model sculptures and specialty authentic aviation apparel is astonishing; also books, videos, and jewelry. New and antique art, decoys, and gifts with waterfowl, wildlife, and sporting dog motifs are on display at **The Decoy,** on Sixth between Dolores and Lincoln (831–625–1881).

Golf is on stage at **Golf Arts and Imports** (Dolores and Sixth; 831–625–4488)—part shop, part museum and gallery—in photos and paintings of legendary courses and collectibles and antiques. Look for a second shop at the Lodge at Pebble Beach.

Many of the inns and hotels in Carmel are historic landmarks, such as **La Playa Hotel** at Eighth and Camino Real, a pink Mediterranean mansion built in 1904 (831–624–6476). Take a peek at the luscious gardens blooming beneath a canopy of Angel's Trumpet trees. The lobby is a museumlike world of heirloom furnishings and contemporary art. Rooms are upscale traditional, with views of the sea, the gardens, or the village. Cottages are hidden in a pine and cypress grove; each has a kitchen, a fireplace, and a private terrace. With a lovely ocean-view terrace, the **Terrace Grill** here is one of the best restaurants in town for breakfast, lunch, dinner, and brunch (831–624–4010); you can dine until 11:00 P.M. in the lounge.

Before leaving town, take a late-afternoon walk on **Carmel Beach** at the foot of Ocean Avenue—truly white, powdery sand; truly memorable sunsets.

Drive north on Highway 1 to Highway 156, connecting with Highway 101 north to San Francisco.

There's More

Golf. Golf Club at Quail Lodge, 8000 Valley Greens Drive, Carmel Valley; (831) 624–2770. Eighteen stunning holes for lodge guests or members of other private clubs. Luckily, you are not required to take a cart, all the better to enjoy the 840 acres of wild countryside and elaborate landscaping.

Rancho Canada Golf Course, Carmel Valley Road, 1 mile from Highway 1; (831) 624–0111. Two eighteen-hole public courses with mountain backdrop and valley views.

Jacks Peak County Park, Jacks Peak Road, Carmel Valley; (888) 588–2267. Hike in an enchanted pine forest, up the trail to valley views, or take a short trek to a picnic spot.

Mission Trail Park, Carmel. Thirty-five acres of native vegetation, 5 miles of trails. Enter at Mountain View and Crespi, at Eleventh Street and Junípero, or on Rio Road across from the Mission.

Tor House and Hawk Tower, 26304 Ocean View Avenue, Carmel; (831) 624–1813. Medieval-style stone house and tower, the former home of poet Robinson Jeffers. Tours Friday and Saturday.

Special Events

May. Carmel Art Festival, Carmel; (831) 659–4000. Gallery Walk open house and entertainment; meet the artists at dozens of Carmel galleries; gala party and auction, sculpture in the park, four days of numerous events.

June–August. Outdoor Forest Theatre Season, Carmel; (831) 626–1681.

July. Carmel Bach Festival; (831) 624–1521; www.bachfestival.com. Internationally acclaimed; two weeks of concerts and classes.

Annual Antique and Flea Market, Moss Landing; (831) 633–5202.

August. Carmel Valley Ranchers' Days, Carmel Valley Trail and Saddle Club; (831) 659–4000. Horned steers herded through town, rodeo, 300 roping teams.

Carmel Valley Fiesta, Carmel Valley Village; (831) 659–2038. Wild-boar barbecue, street dance, arts and food booths, entertainment on outdoor stages.

September. Carmel Shakespeare Festival; (831) 649–0340.

Sand Castle Building Contest, Carmel Beach; (831) 624–2522. Architects and amateurs vie for biggest, best, most outrageous sand structure.

Other Recommended Restaurants and Lodgings

Carmel

Bruno's Market and Deli, Sixth and Junipero; (831) 624–3821. Voted "Best Grocery Store" in the county. Wonderful gourmet sandwiches and salads, ready-made entrees, sushi, barbecued chicken and meats, beautiful produce.

The Cottage, Lincoln between Ocean and Seventh; (831) 625–6260. Panettone French toast for breakfast, artichoke soup and chicken stew in a sourdough basket for lunch, lemon chicken for dinner.

Highlands Inn, 4 miles south of Carmel on Highway 1; (831) 624–3801. Since 1917, wonderful accommodations at a full-service, five-star resort with glorious ocean views. The renowned restaurant, Pacific's Edge, has spectacular sea views from big windows and a California/French menu to match. *Gourmet* magazine calls it the most satisfying place to dine on the *entire* California coast. Twenty-seven thousand bottles of wine in the cellar. The casual California Market cafe here is a fun place to have lunch on the way to Big Sur—a table on the deck overlooking the coast or indoors by the pot-bellied stove; pasta, salads, sandwiches. Luxurious rooms have wood-burning fireplaces, outdoor decks, or balconies. Suites have Jacuzzi tubs, kitchens, and special amenities like terry robes and large dressing areas. Heated pool, spa.

Lincoln Green Inn, Carmelo between Fifteenth and Sixteenth; (831) 624–1880. In the true spirit of Carmel-quaint, sweet one- and two-bedroom garden cottages have fireplaces and kitchens.

Vagabond House Inn, Fourth and Dolores; (831) 624–7738. Half-timbered English Tudor country inn; blooming courtyard gardens; elegant, traditional decor; continental breakfast.

Village Corner, Dolores and Sixth; (831) 624–3588. For more than fifty years, inside and on the patio, locals have been meeting here to complain about how Carmel isn't like it used to be. Breakfast, good sandwiches, salads; less expensive than most.

Carmel Valley

Carmel Valley Ranch Resort, 1 Old Ranch Road; (831) 625–9500. Newly renovated, a sprawling luxury resort on an oak-studded hillside overlooking a beautiful golf course and the valley. An outdoor dining and cocktail terrace overlooks a spectacular pool and gardens. Huge suites are private and quiet, secluded in the trees. Twelve tennis courts come with a full-time pro, and the Pete Dye championship golf course is one of the most challenging on the peninsula; with a clubhouse restaurant.

Cobblestone Inn, Junipero between Seventh and Eighth; (800) 833–8836. A real Carmel charmer in the English style, with stone fireplaces in each room, antiques, four-posters, and privacy. Full breakfast on the garden patio and afternoon tea by the fire. Bicycles; warm, special attention.

Los Laureles Lodge, 313 West Carmel Valley Road; (831) 659–2233. Behind white picket fences, a ten-acre horse ranch from the 1930s transformed into a country inn and restaurant with a pool, gardens, bar with live music. Ask for a unit away from the road. Special events include BBQs and country music.

Quail Lodge Resort and Golf Club, 8205 Valley Greens Drive; (831) 624–1581. Upscale, full-service resort with a spectacular golf course at the foot of the mountains. Rooms, suites, and villas open into lush gardens; some have fireplaces. Special services at this four-diamond, four-star hostelry include an introduction to local wineries, scenic excursions, spa treatments, and golf packages. *Travel and Leisure* calls it one of the "Best Small Hotels in the World." The Covey Restaurant here is one of the best on the peninsula, a casually elegant place with views of a lake, gardens, and the hills. Swimming pool, tennis, nearby walks, and a certain relaxed luxury make this a place to hide away for a long weekend.

Riverside RV Park and Saddle Mountain RV Park, a mile off Carmel Valley Road on Schulte Road; (831) 624–9329. Tree-shaded RV sites, with valley or river views, hot showers, games, and barbecues. An attractive swimming-pool terrace has picnic tables under the oak trees.

Stonepine, 150 East Carmel Valley Road; (831) 659–2245. Old-world elegance at a circa-1920 country estate, with tennis, horseback riding, sumptuous accommodations in the château or in a guest house. Impeccable service, privacy, and unparalleled natural surroundings.

Pebble Beach

Casa Palmero, 17-Mile Drive; (800) 654–9300; www.pebblebeach.com. Swanky and brand new, a former mansion is now a small, very private, very elegant Mediterranean-style resort adjacent to the Lodge at Pebble Beach. You might catch a glimpse of a movie star or a golf hero in the billiards room or by the pool. Rooms have fireplaces, oversize tubs, some private garden spas. Advantages of staying here or at the Lodge are access to tee times at the golf course and use of the beach and tennis club.

Inn at Spanish Bay, 2700 17-Mile Drive; (800) 654–9300. In the lee of the dark, brooding Del Monte cypress forest, the luxurious resort hotel lies a few hundred feet from the shoreline. Contemporary-design rooms and suites, each with private patio or balcony, marble bathrooms, some fireplaces, sitting rooms. One of the top tennis complexes in the country, fitness club, complete spa facilities and beauty treatments, restaurants, and upscale shops. Surrounded by the Links at Spanish Bay, the inn is a mecca for golfers who play here and at nearby Pebble Beach.

Fabulous sea views, glamorous blond art deco decor, and world-class Euro-Asian cuisine make **Roy's at Pebble Beach,** at the inn, a special occasion restaurant (831–647–7423).

Located at the inn, the **Ansel Adams Gallery** (831–375–7215) shows a huge collection of Adams's photos and the works of other well-known nature photographers, plus Native American jewelry and fine crafts. Camera Walks are conducted from the gallery for small groups.

The Lodge at Pebble Beach, 17-Mile Drive; (800) 654–9300. One of the world's great hostelries, Pebble feels like a private club. Luxury rooms and suites, all quite spacious, most with private balcony, sea or garden views, large dressing and sitting areas, some with fireplace. Guests may play golf not only at Pebble Beach Golf Links—California's most famous course—but at nearby Links at Spanish Bay, Spyglass Hill, and Old Del Monte. Pool with sea view, fourteen tennis courts, fitness club, equestrian center, several outstanding restaurants and cafes. *Spectacular* is too small a word to describe Pebble Beach.

Stillwater Bar and Grill, 17-Mile Drive; (831) 625–8524. At one of the world's great hostelries—the Lodge at Pebble Beach—within view of crashing waves of the Pacific and the notorious eighteenth hole of the Pebble Beach Golf Links. Fresh seafood is superb in a fresh, contemporary, casual setting; don't miss the grilled abalone appetizer.

For More Information

Carmel Business Association (visitors bureau), San Carlos between Fifth and Sixth, P.O. Box 4444, Carmel, CA 93921; (831) 624–2522; www. chamber.carmel.ca.us.

Carmel Valley Chamber of Commerce, Oak Building, P.O. Box 288, Carmel Valley Road, Carmel Valley, CA 93924; (831) 659–4000.

Inns by the Sea; (800) 433–4732. Reservation services for several inns.

Monterey Peninsula Golf Packages, P.O. Box 504, Carmel Valley, CA 93924; (831) 659–5361.

Resort Time Roomfinders; (831) 646–9250.

EASTBOUND
ESCAPES

Sacramento Delta Loop 1

Levee Towns and Old Sacramento

1 Night

Wide, cool, and green, fringed with overhanging trees and alive with fishing boats and water-skiers, the mighty **Sacramento River** slides through the metropolitan capital of Sacramento and heads south, spreading out into a vast delta scattered with ramshackle river towns, where life remains slow and sweet. Boats and ferries, sailboards and houseboats ply miles of meandering waterways. Blue herons silently stalk the lagoons and sloughs, home to thousands of birds and ducks, a bird-watcher's mecca. Small towns were abandoned by the Chinese workers who built the levees a hundred years ago, but crawfish cafes, scruffy saloons, and a few inns remain for weekenders seeking quiet getaways.

☐ Exploring the delta

☐ Old Town shopping

☐ Railroad museum

☐ The capitol

☐ Crawdads and
   California history

☐ Cruising the river

You'll hang out on the boardwalks of the old port of Sacramento, where ships sailed in for supplies and refreshment in the wild days of the gold rush—as many as 800 vessels in 1849. The look and feel of Forty-niner days has been re-created by the miraculous refurbishment of original hotels, saloons, restaurants, firehouses, and establishments of questionable reputation. There are upscale and down-home restaurants, paddle wheelers for river cruises, dozens of shops, and several museums highlighted by the largest railroad museum in the United States.

Topping off your Sacramento delta weekend is a tour of the magnificent state capitol building and grounds.

Day 1 / Morning

Drive north on Highway 80 from the Oakland Bay Bridge for about an hour. Two miles south of Fairfield, turn east on Highway 12, past the Jelly

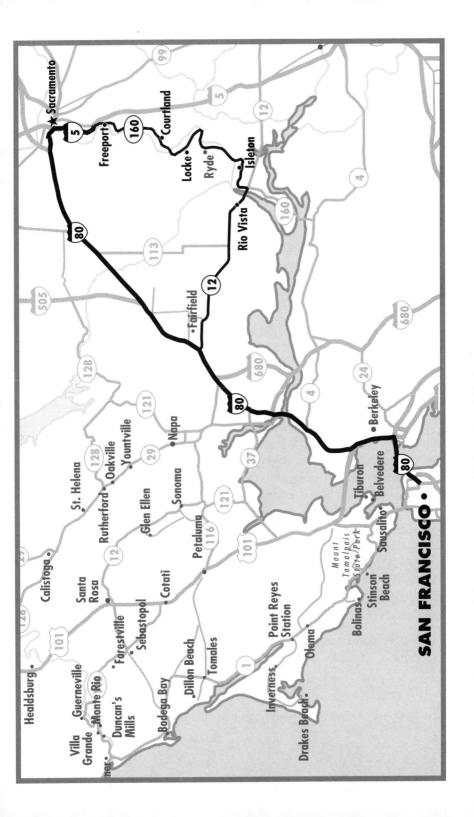

Belly factory, through the flat cattle country of Solano County, to **Rio Vista** on the Sacramento River, a 25-mile trip.

Before crossing the Rio Vista bridge, go north along the river 2 miles to the ferry to **Ryer Island,** one of the last remaining ferries in the delta; it's free. Prowl around the island a little and take a walk or bike ride on the winding levee road to where the *J-Mack,* a cable-guided ferry, will give you a free ride across Steamboat Slough to shady Hogback Park, where you can launch a boat and picnic. For information on fishing-boat and houseboat rentals and delta tours, go to www.californiadelta.org. Return to the bridge and take Highway 160 north, the levee road.

On the east side of the river is the **Brannan Island State Recreation Area** (916–777–6671), where campers and boaters enjoy fishing and swimming in the Sacramento and a couple of sloughs. There are tent and RV camps, boat-in campsites, a public beach, and picnic sites. Windy Cove at Brannan Island is one of the prime sailboarding spots in the state.

BREAKFAST: At **Isleton,** bear right at the Y to **Ernie's,** 212 Second Street (916–777–6510). Seems as though Ernie's restaurant and bar has been here forever, serving crawfish for breakfast, lunch, and dinner.

Isleton consists of a down-at-the-heels collection of tin-front and false-front Western buildings. Antiques shops nearby are worth a browse.

You'll drive through **Walnut Grove,** a quiet community on both sides of the river, with a ghostly, empty Chinatown. At **Locke** turn right, leaving the highway, at Yuen Chong grocery; go 1 block down the hill and park. Just 1 block long, Locke is the only surviving rural community built and lived in by Chinese early in the twentieth century. Now it's a maze of creaky wooden buildings connected by a boardwalk. The **Dai Loy Museum,** open on weekends, is a spooky former gambling hall and opium den. **Al the Wop's** (916–776–1800) bar and cafe is dustily atmospheric and frequented by farmhands and fishermen. Thousands of dollar bills are tacked to the ceiling, jars of peanut butter and jelly sit on the tables, and the steak sandwiches and burgers are legendary. **Locke Ness** buys "junque" and sells antiques.

LUNCH: Courtland Docks at the Courtland Marina, Highway 160 at Courtland; (916) 775–1172. Burgers, salads, homemade soup, and apple pie.

Afternoon

At Freeport are several seafood restaurants and bars attracting day-trippers

A historic paddle wheeler, Old Town Sacramento.

from Sacramento. It's just 9 miles farther to **Sacramento,** where you'll connect with I–5 north, proceeding for a few minutes to the J Street/Old Sacramento exit; there are parking garages on the east side of Old Town.

Top off the day with a late-afternoon cruise on the river. The *Spirit of Sacramento* paddle wheeler departs from the L Street landing in Old Sacramento for one-hour sight-seeing trips (916–552–2933).

Sacramento became a boomtown during the gold rush in the mid-1800s and was the first link in the transcontinental railroad. At the confluence of the American and Sacramento Rivers, with a deepwater connection to San Francisco Bay and the world, the fortune-seeker's town of the 1800s is now a modern metropolis and a gathering place for state representatives. Summer days average in the nineties, with many days more than a hundred degrees, but this is a city of more than a million trees and ready access to the water, so relief is never far away.

DINNER: Crawdad's River Cantina, 1375 Garden Highway, Sacramento; (916) 929–2268. On the levee near I–5; Cajun popcorn, fresh fish, steaks, salads, lively atmosphere. Several excellent marinas with restaurants and boat tie-ups are found along the Garden Highway on the north edge of the city. Closed in winter.

LODGING: Radisson Hotel Sacramento, 500 Leisure Lane, Sacramento; (916) 922–2020 or (800) 333–3333. Five minutes from Old Town, a comfortable oasis of a resort hotel with swimming pools, fitness center, access to the 35-mile-long biking and walking trail along the American River (bike rentals here), gardens surrounding a small lake, and several restaurants with garden patio seating. Each room or suite has a balcony or patio, most overlooking the gardens. The nightclub is a popular spot for night owls who like to dance.

Day 2 / Morning

BREAKFAST: Fox and Goose Public House, 1001 R Street, Sacramento; (916) 443–8825. Belgian waffles, homemade cinnamon rolls, steak and eggs.

Take 16th Street into **Old Town Sacramento.** (916–264–7777; www.oldsacramento.com). Cool early morning is the best time to prowl the boardwalks, taking photos of the wooden falsefronts and climbing around on antique railcars.

The **California State Railroad Museum** (916-445-6645; www. californiastaterailroadmuseum.org), on the north end of Old Sacramento, comprises 100,000 square feet housing three dozen locomotives and railcars in pristine condition. One of the engines weighs a mere million pounds. The Canadian National sleeping car rocks back and forth as if on its way down the track. Sound effects, snoozing passengers, and compartments that look as if they're occupied give you a taste of vintage train travel. Retired conductors in their dark blue uniforms are available to answer questions and pose for photos. On the second level is a dream of a toy train running through tiny towns and over bridges. The **Railroad Museum Gift Shop** next door has fabulous train-related toys, books, and souvenirs.

Nearby, the **Discovery Museum & History Center** (916–264–7057) features artifacts of Sacramento's historical and cultural heritage, including the 1849 gold rush.

Explore the **Delta King,** 1000 Front Street (916–444–KING [5464]), a huge Mississippi riverboat permanently moored here at the waterfront.

Now a forty-four-stateroom hotel and restaurant, the *Delta King* has small but comfortable cabins with windows overlooking the river; the bars and restaurant have fine river views and are popular, although somewhat touristy, for brunch, lunch, and dinner. The **Visitor Information Center** is located at 1101 Second Street (916–442–7644).

From spring to fall, a bright yellow water taxi runs from the L Street landing to three marinas along the river, where you can stop and dine at waterfront restaurants.

LUNCH: California Fats, 1015 Front Street, Old Sacramento; (916) 441–7966. A New Age offshoot of the famous Victorian-style Fat City establishment next door. A contemporary jade, fuchsia, and royal blue cafe decor seems aquariumlike as you step downstairs into the narrow dining room; subtle sounds of a 30-foot waterfall mask everyone's conversation but your own. On the menu are nouvelle Chinese specialties and fresh fish, Peking duck pizzas, grilled crab sandwiches, salads, and banana cream pie; exotic drinks include a Sacramento Slammer and Electric Lemonade.

Afternoon

A hundred or so shops await your discovery in Old Sacramento. The **Artists' Collaborative Gallery,** 1007 Second Street (916–444–3764), the best gallery in Old Sacramento, is a large space displaying paintings, ceramics, weavings, and jewelry by local artists. Navajo rugs and Native American turquoise and silver jewelry are the specialty of **Gallery of the American West,** at 121 K Street (916–446–6662).

Brooks Novelty Antiques, Firehouse Alley (916–443–0783), is a delightfully musty, crowded place, filled with old records, jukeboxes, weird TVs, radios, vintage bikes, magazines, and posters. **Visions of Eden,** 126 J Street; (916) 448–1499. The store embraces the art of graceful living; gifts for the home, garden, and bath.

Decorated to the max for every holiday and smelling like chocolate heaven, the **Rocky Mountain Chocolate Factory,** 1039 Second Street (916–448–8801), lures you in with hand-dipped ice-cream bars, caramel apples, chocolate-covered strawberries, and freshly made candy. **Fanny Ann's,** 1023 Second Street (916–441–0505), is five floors of crazily antiques-crammed restaurant and bar; it's a fun place to take the kids during the day, while an adult crowd gathers here at night.

Walk or drive the few blocks to the **California State Capitol,** Tenth and Capitol Mall (916–324–0333), for a tour of the remarkable double-domed building and surrounding grounds.

A guided tour provides background on the magnificently carved stair-cases, elaborate crystal chandeliers, marble inlay floors, historic artwork, and zillions of columns, cornices, and friezes decorated in gold. You'll learn about California lawmaking, and you may even be able to sit in on a leg-islative session.

Take a tour of the grounds, or stroll around on your own through forty acres of specimen plants and trees, many planted in the 1870s. Springtime in Capitol Park brings waves of blooming camellias, azaleas, and dogwood, and rivers of tulips and daffodils. Walk between twenty-four gigantic magnolias that are more than 60 feet tall, seek out the Vietnam Memorial, and gaze up at the towering hardwoods that were planted here as saplings from Civil War battlefields.

From the capitol it is just a couple of blocks to shopping malls down-town and a twenty-minute walk to Old Sacramento. A free shuttle links the K Street Mall and the Downtown Plaza with Old Sacramento. Thousands of magnificent old trees and glorious Victorian mansions line the downtown streets. Beautiful homes are found from 7th to 16th Streets, and from E to I Streets; don't miss the Heilbron home at 740 O Street and the Stanford home at 800 N Street.

It's 90 miles from Sacramento to San Francisco on Highway 80.

There's More

Antiques. Several large shops at Del Paso Boulevard and Arden Way and a dozen in the 800 block of 57th Street, Sacramento. Pick up a booklet here to locate other shops in Sacramento.

Ten minutes east of Sacramento in Rancho Cordova is California's largest antiques mall, the Antique Plaza, with more than 250 dealers (off Highway 50 between Sunrise and Hazel; 916–852–8517).

Bike and Surrey Rentals of Old Sacramento, 1050 Front Street; (916) 441–0200. Get around Old Sacramento or ride 26 miles of paved bike paths on the Jedediah Smith Memorial Bicycle Trail, which follows the American River Parkway, or 23 miles of scenic pathway from Old Sacramento to Folsom Lake.

Crocker Art Museum, Third and O Streets, Sacramento; (916) 264–5423. A gigantic restored Victorian sheltering the oldest public art museum in the West, European paintings and drawings, nineteenth-century art.

Grizzly Island, south of Highway 12 between Fairfield and Rio Vista (go south on Grizzly Island Road at the Sunset Shopping Center, then 9 miles to the wildlife preserve); (707) 425–3828. A relaxing place to take an outdoor break between Sacramento and the Bay Area, Grizzly Island is best in winter, when thousands of migratory waterfowl stop to feed and rest in the Suisun Marsh surrounding the island (avoid October through mid-January, which is duck-hunting season). River otters, turtles, tule elk, egrets, herons, coots, wigeons, grebes, and many more are the birds and animals you'll see in this 8,600-acre wildlife preserve in the Sacramento Delta. When paying your entrance fees of $2.50 per adult at the ranger station, ask where to see the most wildlife.

Old Sacramento Public Market, Front Street across from the *Delta King;* (916) 264–7031. It's great fun to browse more than twenty open-air food and produce shops, flower stands, and bakeries selling Asian specialties, spices, cheese, wine, meat, poultry, and fish, plus an Italian deli and places to get walk-around snacks.

Southern Railroad Excursions, Front Street in Old Sacramento at the railroad depot; (916) 445–6645; www.csrmf.org. Forty-minute, 6-mile ride along the river in vintage passenger coaches or an open-air gondola pulled by a steam locomotive.

Towe Auto Museum, 2200 Front Street, Sacramento; (916) 442–6802. Travel on a sentimental journey to see more than 150 vintage vehicles.

Special Events

February. Chinese New Year and the Great Asian March and Delta Parade, in Isleton, Highway 160 south of Sacramento; (916) 777–5880. Live Chinese music, ceremonial drummers, food, lion dancers, rickshaw rides, demonstrations.

April. Festival de la Familia, Old Sacramento; (916) 264–7777. Hundreds of art, souvenir, food and drink vendors, and free live Latin, Caribbean, and Native American music.

May. Sacramento Jazz Jubilee, Old Sacramento and other town venues; (916) 372–5277. Largest traditional jazz festival in the world; more than one hundred bands from around the world and more than 100,000 jazz lovers dancing their feet off.

Pacific Rim Street Fest, Old Sacramento; (916) 264–7777. Asian and Pacific Islands cultures are presented in song, dance, exhibitions, and food: Lion dancers prance in the street, Japanese taiko drummers rattle your brain, and local ethnic dance and music clubs put on shows.

June. Crawdad Festival, in a small town on the delta near Sacramento, Isleton; (916) 777–5880. World's largest celebration of the crawdad, with Cajun food and cook-off, parade, arts and crafts, carnival, live entertainment, and dancing in the streets.

August–September. California State Fair, Sacramento; (916) 924–2032. One of the biggest state fairs in the country, top-name entertainment, traditional livestock and agricultural exhibits, a carnival, rodeo, nightly fireworks, big crowds, hot summer nights.

Other Recommended Restaurants and Lodgings

Old Sacramento

Fat City Bar and Cafe, 1001 Front; (916) 446–6768. Hundred-year-old bar, bistro-style cafe.

The Firehouse, 1112 Second Street; (916) 442–4772. In an 1853 firehouse; eat indoors in romantic surroundings and on the garden patio; continental cuisine voted "Best in Sacramento" and "Most Romantic."

Ryde

Ryde Hotel, 14340 Highway 160; (916) 776–1318; www.rydehotel.com. Art-deco riverfront resort with thirty-two rooms. Dining room open all day.

Sacramento

Amber House Bed and Breakfast Inn, 1315 22nd Street; (916) 444–8085; www.amberhouse.com. In two restored mansions are opulent, luxurious, romantic inn rooms; Jacuzzi tubs, fireplaces; gourmet breakfast in the dining room, on the veranda, or in guest rooms; evening refreshments; bikes available. One room has a heart-shaped Jacuzzi and a waterfall!

Ernesto's Mexican Food, 1901 16th Street; (916) 441–5850. *Chile verde* and luscious *carnitas* bring folks from miles around to one of the best Mexican cafes in a town with a large Mexican population.

Hawthorn Suites, 321 Bercut Drive; (916) 441–1444. Contemporary suites with separate living rooms, some with microwaves and refrigerators; continental breakfast. Jacuzzi, swimming pool; complimentary shuttle to airport, downtown, Old Sacramento, and the capitol.

Lemon Grass, 601 Munroe Street; (916) 486–4891. Wonderful Vietnamese and Thai food in a serene, contemporary atmosphere; luscious rack of lamb with hoisin-cabernet glaze, catfish in a clay pot, award-winning traditional dishes.

Max's Opera Cafe, 1725 Arden Way at Arden Fair Mall; (916) 927–6297. This New York–style upscale deli cafe serves fabulous sandwiches, burgers, pasta, and salads, with legendary mile-high pieces of pie and cake. At night, the staff sings opera and show tunes.

Ristorante Piatti, 571 Pavilions Lane; (916) 649–8885. Upscale, lively Italian country atmosphere; rotisserie-roasted meats, fish and poultry, homemade pasta. This is one in a small, successful chain of restaurants in northern California, including locations in Palo Alto, Sonoma, and Yountville.

Sacramento Brewing Company, Fulton and Marconi Avenues in the Town and Country Village; (916) 485–HOPS. One of the best of the many new brewpubs, with great, hearty food and a delightful European bistro atmosphere.

Silva's Sheldon Inn, 900 Grant Line Road, south of Sacramento near Elk Grove; (916) 686–8330. Cowboys and CEOs, tourists and locals flock here for hearty American-style steak dinners, Italian- and Asian-influenced pasta and fish dishes, fine food in a nice roadhouse. Dinners, Sunday brunch, and family-style Sunday dinner.

Sterling Hotel, 1300 H Street; (916) 448–1300. In a landmark Victorian mansion, a small, luxury hotel; stunning rooms with spa tubs, room service; fine restaurant.

For More Information

California Division of Tourism, 801 K Street, Sacramento, CA 95814; (800) 462–2543; www.visitcalifornia.com. Information, brochures for travel statewide.

Sacramento Convention and Visitors Bureau, 1303 J Street, Suite 600, Sacramento, CA 95814; (916) 264–7777; www.sacramentocvb.org.

Gold Rush North 2

Forty-Niner Towns in the Sierra Foothills

2 Nights

The foothills of the California Gold Country stretch more than 300 miles along the western slopes of the Sierra Nevadas all the way to the southern gate of Yosemite National Park. In several river corridors—the Yuba, the American, the Mokelumne, the Stanislaus, the Tuolumne, and the Merced—dozens of boomtowns exploded in population in the mid-1800s, when gold was discovered, only to be abandoned by the miners and adventure seekers when the lodes were exhausted.

Of the remaining communities still thriving today, Nevada City is the most completely original gold rush town in the state, having somehow escaped the devastating fires that plagued most of the rest of the Gold Country. More than a hundred Victorian mansions and Western false-front saloons and hotels cluster cozily together here on a radiating wheel of tree-lined streets on small hills. At an elevation of about 3,000 feet, the whole place becomes red and gold in fall, when hundreds of maples, aspens, and oaks turn blazing bright.

- [ ] Gold mines and museums
- [ ] River rambles
- [ ] Victoriana antiques
- [ ] Old West
- [ ] Nuggets and gems

Inhabited during the gold rush by thousands of English and Irish miners who worked five major mines in the area, the town of Grass Valley is honeycombed with underground tunnels and shafts. On Mill and Main Streets remain dozens of buildings built in the mid-1800s, when this was the richest mining town in the state. A block off Main, take a stroll on Neal and Church Streets to see rows of magnificent Victorian mansions and churches.

Just a few miles to the east, 1.2 million acres of wilderness in the Tahoe National Forest afford endless hiking, camping, fishing, and cross-country skiing opportunities.

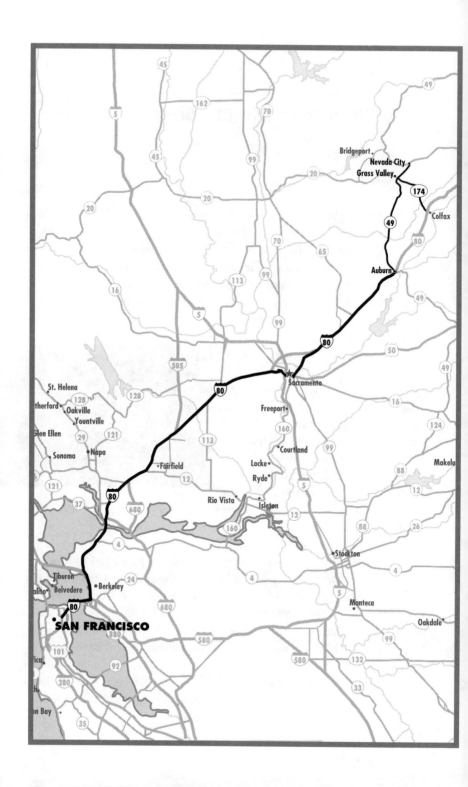

Day 1 / Morning

From the Oakland Bay Bridge, drive north on Highway 80 beyond Sacramento to **Auburn**—about two and a half hours—and take the Maple Street exit, parking on or near Maple. On a ridge overlooking the north fork of the **American River,** where gold was discovered in 1848, Auburn has a compact, charming Old Town of antiques shops and restaurants, worth an hour or so of investigation. For breakfast or a snack on the deck above Old Town, go to **Awful Annie's,** at 160 Sacramento Street (530–888–9857).

Leaving Auburn, take Lincoln Way, off Maple, north past the 1894 courthouse, a domed dazzler still in use today; continue north on Highway 49 for about thirty minutes to **Nevada City.**

Take the Sacramento Street exit into town, parking in the lot at Sacramento and Broad. Put on your walking shoes and head across the bridge into town on Broad, the main street. Take a right down to the stone-and-brick **Yuba Canal Building,** at 132 Main, built in 1850 on the banks of Wolfe Creek, where you can pick up tour maps at the **Chamber of Commerce.** Since early in the twentieth century, the downtown has remained lost in time, architecturally speaking, and there is much to discover within 3 or 4 blocks.

Next door, at 214 Main, the **Firehouse Museum** has two floors of gold rush and Indian artifacts.

LUNCH: Posh Nosh, 318 Broad, Nevada City; (530) 265–6064. Eat on the tree-shaded patio. Sandwiches, pasta, salads, homemade desserts.

Afternoon

The National Hotel, 211 Broad (530–265–4551), is the oldest continuously operating hotel west of the Rockies; take a look at the long bar, shipped around the Horn more than a hundred years ago. Rooms here are small and sweet, with Victorian furnishings and gimcracks: Some have balconies overlooking the street. Keep your credit cards handy. Yesterday's dusty, quaint shops on Broad Street are now upscale boutiques.

Tanglewood Forest, 311 Commercial Street (530–478–1223), is a fantasyland of wizards, fairies, and strange dolls. Next to the **Nevada Theatre,** the oldest theater in California, at 401 Broad, is **Utopian-Stone,** at 212 Main (530–265–6209), which specializes in gold quartz jewelry.

Mountain Pastimes Fun and Games, 320 Spring Street (530–265–6692), has toys and games for grown-ups. Across the street you can

A parade in the Gold Country, Nevada City.

taste Nevada County wines made right here at the **Nevada City Winery,** 321 Spring (530–265–9463). In the past couple of decades, vineyards and wineries have popped up all over the county; they celebrate in September with a Wine Fest and Grape Stomp at the Miners Foundry Cultural Center up the street.

When you reach the top of Broad Street, sink into a chair at **Broad Street Books and Espresso Bar** (426 Broad; 530-265-4204) and have a sweet treat and a cup of tea while browsing the best-sellers.

The **Deer Creek Miners Trail,** perpendicular to Broad Street near the highway, is a short, easy walk along Deer Creek. Six interpretive stations describe gold prospecting in the early days, when the creek yielded a pound of gold a day.

DINNER: New Moon Cafe, 203 York Street, Nevada City; (530) 265–6399. In a sleek, contemporary cafe, seasonal California cuisine—chicken in vermouth with sun-dried cherry balsamic honey sauce, pork chop stuffed with peaches in Marsala sauce, a fabulous rib-eye steak, and house-made pastas, with some Asian-inspired inventions. Reservations are a must.

LODGING: Red Castle Inn, 109 Prospect, Nevada City; (800) 761–4766. In a cedar forest, a spectacular four-story 1860 Victorian Gothic mansion overlooking the town, one of only two genuine Gothic Revival brick houses on the West Coast. Seven romantically decorated rooms and suites with private verandas and sitting rooms are chock-full of extraordinary and valuable antiques and art. *Sunset Magazine* calls it "a uniquely American architectural treasure," and so it is, ensconced on a magical hillside with views of the town, surrounded by an opulent, old-fashioned garden with private nooks and crannies under the trees. Innkeepers Mary Louise and Conley Weaver are both learned history buffs; she an expert on antiques and vintage art, he a prominent architect with tales to tell about famous Bay Area buildings. Book early for this B&B, one of the most unique and spectacular in the West. And do arrive in time for the late-afternoon sweets and spiced tea.

Day 2 / Morning

BREAKFAST: At the Red Castle Inn. Choose from the elaborate, gourmet breakfast buffet and retire to the porch, to a garden glade, or to your room. Take a stroll around the neighborhood to see pretty gardens and country homes; it's a short walk into town.

Drive south on Highway 49 to the south end of Grass Valley to the Empire Mine exit, going east on Empire Street for five minutes to reach **Empire Mine State Park** (530-273-8522), a 784-acre mining estate. The largest, deepest, and richest hard-rock gold mine in California operated here for more than a hundred years, producing $100 million in gold from 360 miles of underground channels, some 11,000 feet deep. On a tour or on your own, see an extensive complex of buildings and equipment, including part of the main shaft. A visitors center recounts the history of the mine in photos, exhibits, and films.

Sweeping lawns beneath 100-foot sugar pines surround the mine owner's home, **Bourne Cottage,** an outstanding example of a Willis Polk–designed English country manor with lovely gardens. An annual old-fashioned **Miners' Picnic** takes place in June in the park, with food, contests, gold panning, and entertainment (530-273-4667). Ten miles of trails crisscross the park. The 2.5-mile Hardrock Trail loop, which begins and ends at the park entrance, meanders beneath tall pines along Little Wolf Creek, passing mining ruins.

LUNCH: Drive back on Empire Street, across the freeway, to the first right, Mill Street, following Mill down and under the freeway to the **North Star Mining Museum** and powerhouse (530–273–4255), where a shady lawn over Wolf Creek makes a delightful picnic spot. Among antique equipment here is the largest Pelton wheel in the world, a water-wheel that produced power from the creek for the North Star Mine. A large collection of photos traces mining history; admission is free.

Marshall's Pasties is a good place to take out fresh Cornish pasties and English sausage rolls and other picnic fare. At 203 Mill Street in Grass Valley (530–272–2844), Marshall's is on the main street of town, five min-utes from Wolf Creek.

Afternoon

Follow Mill Street north into downtown Grass Valley, parking near the center of town.

Step into **The Holbrooke Hotel,** 212 West Main (530–273–1353), the grand dame of Grass Valley since 1862. A glance in the hotel register turns up such famous guests as Presidents Cleveland and Garfield. At 114 Mill are three antiques shops. At Church and Chapel Streets, the **Grass Valley Museum** (530–273–5509) is a restored school and orphanage exhibiting gold rush artifacts, clothing, paintings, and domestic items. The **Nevada County Chamber of Commerce,** 248 Mill (530–273–4667), is in the reconstructed home of Lola Montez, a notorious dance-hall entertainer of the 1800s. One block off Main, Neal and Church Streets are ideal to stroll and see several magnificent Victorian mansions and churches.

If you plan to spend time hiking, camping, fishing, or panning for gold on the nearby South Yuba River and environs, stop in at **Swenson's Surplus** for equipment, clothing, and supplies, including fanny packs, water bottles, hunting clothing, winter boots, rain gear, auto gear, and all the basics for gold panning (105 West Main Street; 530–273–7315).

On the **Yuba River,** a few miles southwest of Grass Valley in **Bridgeport,** is one of only a dozen covered bridges still standing in the state. At 256 feet, the **Bridgeport Covered Bridge** is possibly the longest single-span covered bridge in the world. Mellowed sugar-pine shingles and massive, old-growth Douglas fir beams are warm reminders that buggies and mule teams once clattered across the wooden floorboards. There are nice pic-nic spots near the bridge, walking trails along the river, and shallow wading pools among the rocks. During much of the year, docents and rangers teach gold panning and conduct interpretive tours of the bridge (530–432–2546).

Not far from Bridgeport, **Englebright Lake** on the Yuba River is a slender piece of water with nice camping and fishing spots accessible only by boat (530–639–2342). Pleasant boat-in campgrounds have sandy beaches and trees. The shore is steep and rocky except at the campgrounds. Fishing for trout, bass, and catfish is good in quiet, narrow coves. All kinds of boats and houseboats are for rent at **Skipper's Cove Marina** on the lake (530–639–2272).

D I N N E R : **Kirby's Creekside Restaurant,** 101 Broad Street, Nevada City; (530) 265–3445. Above the rushing waters of Deer Creek, the outdoor deck is the place to be on a warm summer night. Inside are candlelit tables before a fireplace. Fresh fish, poultry, and meats in exotic sauces; homemade pumpkin ravioli in Chardonnay cream sauce; smoked stuffed pork chops; and more creative fare. The wine list is top-notch; live music on weekends.

L O D G I N G : Red Castle Inn.

Day 3 / Morning

B R E A K F A S T : Another extravaganza of a breakfast at the inn. (If you can squeeze in a piece of pie, stop in at the **Apple Fare,** 307 Broad Street, Nevada City, 530–234–2555, and sit at a big round table with the locals.)

For a fascinating trip along the south fork of the Yuba River, take Highway 49 north from Nevada City to Tyler Foote Crossing Road, turn right, and continue to where Tyler splits to the left to Alleghany; then turn right onto Cruzon Grade Road, proceeding to **Malakoff Diggins State Historic Park** (530–265–2740), the largest hydraulic mine site in the world, a rather shocking and strangely beautiful remnant of gold mining in the 1800s, when giant waterjets, called monitors, destroyed entire mountains. Weird and colorful pinnacles, domes, and spirals, as well as a milky lake, are fringed with pines. There are reconstructed buildings and hiking trails in the park, swimming at Blair Lake, and a campground. Swimming and fishing holes on the South Yuba River and a 21-mile river corridor park are accessible near the Diggins.

Eight miles north of Nevada City on Highway 49, just before the arched Yuba River Bridge, watch carefully for the **Independence Trail** sign (530–474–4788). Easy for all ages and abilities, the trail meanders 7 miles through forests and, in some places, is dramatically suspended over the Yuba River Canyon on boardwalk bridges and flumes. You get into eye-popping scenery within a minute. The packed-dirt paths and boardwalks make it wheelchair- and stroller-accessible. There are picnic platforms along the way and ramps leading to fishing holes. Take the trail on the west side of the highway to see Rush Creek Falls and a fabulous suspended flume over a waterfall, 1 mile from the start.

On your way back to the Bay Area, take Highway 174 south from Grass Valley to Colfax, on the oldest, the twistiest, and one of the prettiest roads in the county, past horse ranches and small farms. Another pie emporium is on this road—the **Happy Apple Kitchen,** 18352 Colfax Highway, Chicago Park (530–273–2822).

There's More

Hiking. The Tahoe National Forest is 5 miles west of Nevada City. Obtain maps and information on hiking and camping at the forest headquarters office at 631 Coyote Street in Nevada City; (530) 265–4531.

Lake Spaulding, 30 miles from Nevada City off Highway 20; (916) 923–7142. A glacier-carved bowl of granite at 5,000 feet surrounded by huge boulders and a forest. Good fishing for trout, small lakeside beaches, power boating and sailing, and a small, developed campground for tents and RVs. Nearby **Fuller Lake** has just a handful of drive-in campsites but is quite a lovely, quiet, small lake for fishing and boating.

Scotts Flat Lake, 20 minutes from Grass Valley off Highway 20; (530) 265–5302. A nice day trip for swimming, fishing, hiking, or for camping lakeside in the national forest. The campground has developed tent and RV sites, sandy beaches, a store, and picnic areas.

Sierra Discovery Trail; (530) 265–4531. From Highway 20 take Bowman Lake Road .06 mile to the parking lot. Along the Bear River, a 1-mile, easy trail, partly paved, part gravel, part boardwalk, and accessible to wheelchairs and strollers, winding through a pine and cedar forest. Meadows are awash with wildflowers, and a small waterfall rushes year-round. Watch for water ouzels at the waterfall—they are the only American songbirds that dive into the water.

Special Events

June. Tour of Nevada City Bicycle Classic, Nevada City; (530) 265–2692.

June–July. Music in the Mountains, Nevada City; (530) 265–6124. Classical music in glorious outdoor settings.

July. Summer Nights in Nevada City; (530) 265–2692. Everyone comes in costume; fine art, classic cars, food and drink, entertainment.

August. Nevada County Fair, Grass Valley; (530) 273–6217.

September. Nevada County Wine Fest and Grape Stomp, Nevada City; (530) 272–8315.

October. Gold Rush Jubilee Crafts Fair, Auburn; (530) 887–2111.

December. Cornish Christmas Celebration, Grass Valley; (530) 272–8315. Victorian Christmas, Nevada City; (530) 265–2692.

Other Recommended Restaurants and Lodgings

Auburn

Madame Rouge in the Auburn Promenade, 853 Lincoln Way; (530) 888–7766. A talented singing wait staff breaks into song from time to time while you enjoy dinners of salmon moutarde and steak Diane; Sunday brunch.

Grass Valley

Alta Sierra Village, 11858 Tammy Way; (530) 273–9102 or (800) 992–5300. A little-known lodging choice: unassuming, clean, reasonably priced motel-style rooms on the golf course; there is a clubhouse restaurant and a small deli-grocery.

Holbrooke Hotel, 212 West Main Street; (530) 273–1353. Twenty-eight restored rooms, beautiful dining room and saloon.

Swiss House Restaurant, 535 Mill; (530) 273–8272. Swiss, German, and American cuisine; lunch and dinner.

Tofanelli's, 302 West Main Street; (530) 272–1468. Hearty American menu with huge plates of food, breakfast burritos, raspberry chicken. Breakfast, lunch, dinner, and Sunday brunch.

Nevada City

Kendall House, 534 Spring Street; (530) 254–0405. With a beautiful garden and swimming pool, a bed-and-breakfast inn on a quiet street within a few blocks of downtown. Large, comfortable, very private rooms with baths, plus a two-room cottage with living/dining room, fireplace, private deck, and kitchen. Full breakfast in the solarium or on the garden terrace.

Northern Queen Inn, 400 Railroad Avenue; (530) 265–5824; www. northernqueeninn.com. On the south end of town; spacious, comfortable motel rooms; pool; cottages with kitchenettes; chalets on the creek; family-oriented restaurant; restored train cars and a nineteenth-century narrow-gauge engine.

For More Information

Auburn Chamber of Commerce, in the old railway depot, 601 Lincoln Way, Auburn, CA 95603; (530) 885–5616.

Grass Valley/Nevada County Chamber of Commerce, 248 Mill Street, Grass Valley, CA 95945; (530) 273–4667; www.gvncchamber.org.

Historic Bed and Breakfast Inns of Grass Valley/Nevada City, P.O. Box 2060, Nevada City, CA 93959; (530) 477–6634 or (800) 250–5808; www. innsofthegoldcountry.com.

Nevada City Chamber of Commerce, 132 Main, Nevada City, CA 95959; (530) 265–2692 or (800) 655–6569; www.ncgold.com. In the stone-and-brick Yuba Canal Building, built in 1850 on the banks of Deer Creek.

Placer County Visitor Information, 13411 Lincoln Way, Auburn, CA 95603; (530) 887–2111 or (800) 427–6463.

Columbia, Bear Valley, and Jamestown

2 Nights

From the charming village of Murphys to the wide-open meadows of Bear Valley, then to old Columbia and rough-and-ready Jamestown, you get a lot of Gold Country in this quick escape.

Wine lovers linger around Murphys, where seven top-notch wineries welcome visitors for tours, tastings, picnics, and annual events.

The most perfectly re-created gold rush town in the United States, Columbia is a living museum, with costumed performers, horse-drawn vehicles, and sights and sounds of the past that make you feel as if you've traveled back in time. Pines and maples shade the boardwalks in the hot sum-mer months, when the place is packed with families; spring and fall are the best times to visit.

- ☐ Big trees, big valley
- ☐ Wineries
- ☐ Rail town
- ☐ Historic park
- ☐ Caverns
- ☐ Gold rush village

This brief warm-weather introduction to Bear Valley may encourage a return visit when the snow flies. The ski resort appeals to Bay Area residents who prefer a casual country atmosphere for their cross-country and downhill skiing.

On the way home you'll spend a morning in the rowdy little burg of Jamestown, with perhaps a ride on a steam train.

Day 1 / Morning

Drive from the Oakland Bay Bridge east on Highway 580, connect with 205 east to 5 north, then 120 east to Highway 49. Turn north to the Highway 4 junction, stopping in the town of **Murphys**—all told, about two and a half hours from the Bay Area.

Ulysses S. Grant and Mark Twain sat a spell on the veranda of the **Murphys Hotel and Historic Lodge,** before the locust trees became

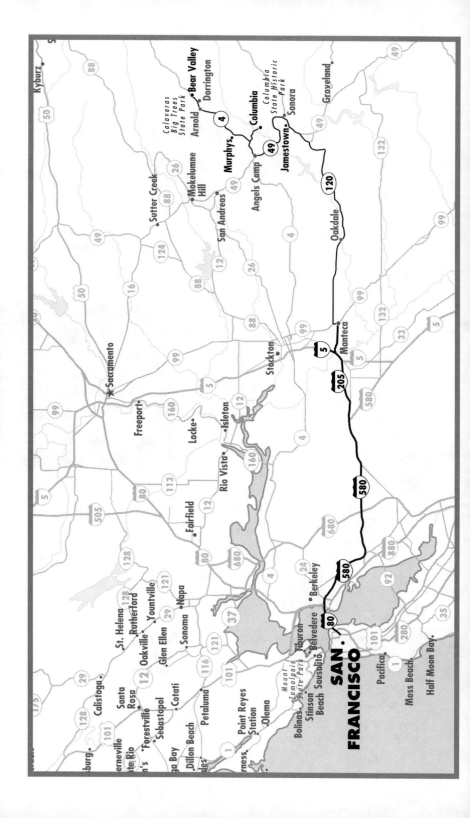

the tall umbrellas we see today. More than a dozen centuries-old buildings line the main drag, while narrow side streets are a kaleidoscope of wild country gardens, white picket fences, and ancient walnut trees shading cottages and mansions.

Murphys Creek runs cheerily through town, and there is a small park on its banks that's perfect for a picnic. "A Taste of Murphys" is a narrated horse-drawn wagon tour that you can take around town, on scenic back roads, and to nearby wineries (209–728–2602). The trip includes a gourmet picnic lunch creekside in Murphys Park.

LUNCH: The Peppermint Stick, 454 Main, Murphys; (209) 728–3570. Soup, salad; Miner's Bread Bowl filled with soup, chili, or beef stew; espresso, ice-cream sodas, sundaes.

Afternoon

Strolling Main Street, you'll come to **Bella Murphys Store** (209–728–2700), where you can get a Western outfit or a Victorian dress.

Bullet holes in the front door of **Murphys Hotel,** 457 Main Street (209–728–3444), remain from the good old days when Black Bart trod the floorboards; step in for a look at the great, old, long bar, where Saturday nights can be quite lively. Rooms and suites here are reasonably priced and include a substantial continental breakfast; rooms near the street can be noisy.

One mile north of Murphys, on Sheepranch Road, **Mercer Caverns** (209–728–2101) are irresistibly spooky, cool, and fascinating limestone chambers of crystalline formations.

Seven small wineries are located within 5 miles of Murphys, including ivy-covered **Black Sheep Winery** (209–728–2157; www.blacksheep winery.com), on the west end of town. In an old carriage house at 276 Main Street beside Murphys Creek, **Millaire Winery** (209–728–1658) is a tourist attraction in fall, when crushing and pressing take place for all to see.

Just off Sheepranch Road, at 2690 San Domingo Road, is the **Stevenot Winery** (209–728–3436), in a lovely valley at 1,900 feet. In the sod-roofed miner's cabin that is the tasting room, try medal-winning Zinfandel, Chardonnay, and Cabernet.

At the end of a winding, vineyard-lined road near Murphys, thousand-acre **Kautz Ironstone Vineyards** offers a multifaceted experience to wine lovers and sightseers (1 mile south of the Murphys Hotel on Six Mile Road; 209–728–1251). In the seven-story main building, a 40-foot-tall limestone fireplace anchors the tasting room, gourmet deli, and gift shop. Daily tours include a demonstration kitchen, a Western art gallery, a music room with the majestic restored Alhambra Theater pipe organ, and cool caves where the Chardonnay and Merlot are stored. Among the annual events at Kautz is the **Civil War Reenactment** in October. You can buy a picnic here and lounge by a landscaped lake.

The lovely gardens and picnic tables at **Chatom Vineyards** make this a nice place to stop at midday. The winery is built of thick rammed-earth walls (1969 Highway 4, just south of Murphys; 209–736–6500; www.chatomvineyards.com).

Take Highway 4 for about forty-five minutes through the Stanislaus National Forest to **Bear Valley,** in a spectacular, high mountain meadow at 7,200 feet, surrounded by dramatic granite peaks, snowcapped in wintertime and early spring. What can you do here? Just mountain bike, walk in the pines, fish in seven nearby lakes, climb a rock, play tennis, or hike to scenic ridgetops in the **Calaveras Ranger District** (209–795–1381). Camping and fishing are popular on the **Stanislaus River** and at Alpine lakes sprinkled about the nearby **Ebbetts Pass** area. More than 100 miles of off-road trails make this a prime area for bike nuts. On free Sunday Fun Rides in July and August, you can choose from beginner or intermediate guided trail rides. Maps, rentals, and tours are available at **Bear Valley Mountain Bike and Kayak Center** (209–753–2834).

Music from Bear Valley is a big annual summer festival that brings hundreds of people to hear big-name classical, opera, jazz, and theatrical performers (209–753–BEAR).

Winter fun includes skiing on one of the most extensive networks of cross-country trails in the country: 65 miles of groomed trails and endless acres of unmarked meadows. Or you can ski downhill from 8,500 feet on **Mount Reba** or skate on an acre of ice. The **Bear Valley Mountain Resort,** on Highway 4, 28 miles east of Arnold, is one of the last family-built and -operated ski resorts in the West (P.O. Box 5038, Bear Valley 95223; 209–753–2301). With 450 inches of snow annually and an emphasis on beginner and intermediate skiing, this is a good place to learn to ski. Lift tickets and lodging costs are lower here than at Lake Tahoe ski resorts.

Ice skating is popular on a frozen lake near the lodge. On weekend nights, lights, music, and a bonfire make skating fun to try or to watch. You can take skating lessons here, too.

Except for the highway, most roads remain unplowed in the valley in wintertime, giving Bear Valley a unique Alpine atmosphere.

Between Calaveras Big Trees State Park and Bear Valley, **Cottage**

Mountain biking in Bear Valley.

Springs is a small resort that offers a snow play area, a tubing hill, and downhill skiing for beginners and intermediates. This is a good, inexpensive place to take younger children for ski lessons (209–795–1401). Along Highway 4 are several snow play areas and cross-country ski trailheads, including Forest Service roads used by both skiers and snowmobilers. Two miles west of Bear Valley, **Tamarack Pines Lodge and Cross-Country Ski Center**, in the **Stanislaus National Forest** at 7,000 feet, grooms miles of trails (209–753–2080). You can rent equipment here, take lessons, and enjoy hearty meals in the lodge. Ski/lodging packages are available for simple lodge rooms.

Within walking and skiing distance of the village, **Bear Valley Cross-Country Ski Area** (209–753–2834) is the largest track system in the central Sierras, with three dozen trails dotted with warming huts.

A couple of miles from Bear Valley, **Lake Alpine Snow-Park** (209–795–1381) is where snowmobilers and cross-country skiers head into the backcountry on the road to Mosquito Lake. Snow-Park permits are necessary in order to park here, and you can snow camp in this area

(916–322–8993). To make year-round campsite reservations at Lake Alpine and at other USDA Forest Service sites, call (209) 795–1381.

DINNER AND LODGING: Bear Valley Lodge, P.O. Box 5038, Bear Valley 95223; (209) 753–2327. Rooms in the five-story lodge are simple and comfortable, with a pool, tennis courts, and an inviting atrium lounge with a giant fireplace made of king-size boulders. If you decide to stay more than a day or two, condominiums and cabin rentals may be the way to go (800–794–3866). Camping is also available.

Day 2 / Morning

BREAKFAST: European breakfast buffet and cappuccinos at Bear Valley Lodge.

Heading back west on Highway 4, if you've a mind to see some *big* sequoias and take a walk or a hike, stop at **Calaveras Big Trees State Park** (209–795–2334). Short nature trails are accessible near the visitors center, but the biggest trees—1,300 of them—are found in the South Grove, 1 mile from the parking lot up the **Big Trees Creek Trail.** One giant stands 320 feet high, and another measures 27 feet around. Hike a network of trails leading to high ridgetops above the 4,800-foot elevation.

Winding throughout the park, the **Stanislaus River** has sandy and pebbly beaches for swimming and wading. Developed campsites are set up for RVs to 27 feet, and there are environmental campsites for backpackers. The park is open all year and is a popular cross-country ski area. A 1-mile loop near the main parking area and an outer 3-mile loop are groomed; snowmobiles are not allowed.

Continue on Highway 4, connecting with 49 and Parrotts Ferry Road to **Columbia State Historic Park** (209–532–0150). When gold was discovered here in 1850, the population boomed within a month from fewer than one hundred to six thousand people, and 150 saloons, gambling halls, and stores opened up. Many Western falsefronts and two-story brick buildings with iron shutters remain, inhabited by costumed proprietors who contribute to the living-history atmosphere. The state began to accumulate artifacts and restore the buildings in the 1940s. Musicians and performers are encountered on the street corners and in the restaurants and the theater; horse-drawn stages clip-clop up and down the streets; artisans demonstrate horseshoeing, woodcarving, and other vintage crafts; and you can pan for gold or take a horseback ride.

A few of the many shops and restaurants: **Fallon Ice Cream Parlor** (209–533–2355), for floats, shakes, and sodas at an authentic soda fountain counter; **Matelot Gulch Mine Supply Store** has gold nuggets, rocks, guidebooks, and history books; **Columbia Candy Kitchen** (209–532–7886), where a four-generation family makes fresh taffy, brittles, fudge, and penny candy; and **De Cosmos Daguerrean** (209–532–0815), to get your tintype taken.

Columbia Candle and Soap Works in the old feed store sells freshly milled soaps in clove, oatmeal honey, rosemary, chocolate, and lavender scents, plus millions of beautiful handmade candles (209–536–9047).

LUNCH: **Columbia House Restaurant,** Main Street, Columbia; (209) 532–5134. Traditional American fare in a 150-year-old house.

Afternoon

The Columbia experience is enriched by "talking buttons" outside several storefronts; push these buttons to hear about the museum displays in the windows. Trodding the creaky floorboards of the **Columbia Museum,** at Main and State Streets, you'll see photos of the people who lived here during the gold rush, as well as huge chunks of ore, quartz, and semiprecious stones. More than $1.5 billion in gold was weighed on the Wells Fargo Express scales in this town.

On the north end of town, the **Columbia Grammar School,** in use from 1860 to 1937, is outfitted with an endearing collection of antique desks, inkwells, old books, and kids' stuff.

Snacks, sodas, and sarsaparillas are easy to find in one of the several saloons (kids OK). Take a ride through the woods nearby on the **Columbia Stage** (209–588–0805).

Farther along on Parrotts Ferry Road is **Natural Bridges,** where Coyote Creek has created a colorful limestone cave. Walk on the streamside nature trail and consider swimming or rafting through the cave—not as scary as it looks.

No trip to the Sierra foothills is complete without a tour of **Moaning Caverns** (5350 Moaning Cave Road, Vallecito; 209–736–2708; www.caverntours.com). The Adventure Trip is as close as you can get to full-fledged spelunking. If you love heights and tight spaces you'll be delighted with the 165-foot rappel. Otherwise stick to the walking tour. Both operate daily year-round.

DINNER: City Hotel, Washington Street, Columbia; (209) 532–1479. Big-city cuisine in elegant gold rush–era surroundings; superb continental menu and good wine list; dinner daily, weekend lunch and brunch. You'll be surprised to find out who the chefs and wait staff are, and you will love the marinated veal chops with roast garlic risotto and shiitake Marsala sauce, the rack of lamb with garlic pine-nut crust, and the mango tart with ginger cream!

The **What Cheer Saloon** in the hotel still has the original cherry-wood bar shipped round the Horn from New England. Special vintner dinners hosted by renowned California wine makers are offered several times a year.

The hotel has ten charming, small rooms with many of the original antiques. Popular mystery weekends, with professional actors and hotel guests playing their parts all over town, are often featured.

LODGING: Fallon Hotel, on Washington Street on the south end of town, next door to the City Hotel and the Fallon Theatre, Columbia; (209) 532–1470. A Victorian extravaganza of rococo wallpaper, antique furniture, and oriental rugs.

Day 3 / Morning

BREAKFAST: Expanded continental breakfast at the Fallon Hotel.

Continue on Highway 49 through Sonora to Jamestown. (**Sonora** is the county seat and a highway junction; traffic somewhat spoils the old-town atmosphere here, although side streets, antiques shops, and historic buildings make this worth a stop if you have the time.)

Boomed and busted several times in the past 150 years, **Jamestown** retains an anything-can-happen, Wild West atmosphere, from the days when it was just a bawdy cluster of tents on a dusty road. When the gold began to rush, saloons and dance halls were erected, then hotels and homes. Dozens of antiques and curio shops line the streets, and almost as many saloons and restaurants. If the town seems familiar to you, it may be because much of the movie *Butch Cassidy and the Sundance Kid* was filmed here. As in most of the Gold Country, summer temperatures are usually in the nineties. And, if you have any doubt about whether there is still gold in them thar hills—a sixty-pound slab of pure gold was discovered in the Jamestown Mine in 1993 and is currently displayed at the Kautz Winery.

Attractions include the **Railtown 1897 State Historic Park** on Fifth

Avenue (209–984–3953; www.csrmf.org/railtown), a twenty-six-acre exhibit of vintage steam locomotives and passenger cars, a roundhouse, and a grassy picnic area in an oak grove. You can take a forty-minute train ride through the foothills.

A stroll up and down Main Street will turn up the **Saunders Gallery of Fine Art,** at 18190 Main, in the historic 1877 **Carboni House** (209–984–4421), which shows carvings, photos, and paintings by local artists, and **Jamestown Mercantile I** and **II** (209–984–6550), two large antiques co-ops. Behind the Jamestown Hotel in the Marengo Courtyard, check out Native American art, jewelry, and baskets at **Alta California Traders** (209–984–1025).

The **Jamestown Hotel,** circa 1920, at 18153 Main (800–205–4901; www.JamestownHotel.com), is an old beauty restored to its former elegance, with a long bar and a restaurant famous throughout the region for prime rib, pepper steak, and seasonal specialties made with fresh local poultry and fresh produce. Eight rooms re-create the gold rush era, with antiques and Victorian baths. The Lotta Crabtree suite has a pink claw-foot tub, the Jenny Lind a king-size brass-and-iron bed.

When you see people panning for gold in a wooden trough on the main street (18170 Main), you are at the headquarters for **Gold Prospecting Expeditions,** where you can find out about gold panning and prospecting day trips and rafting trips on nearby creeks and rivers (209–984–4653 or 800–596–0009; www.goldprospecting.com).

LUNCH: The **Willow Steakhouse,** 18273 Main, Jamestown; (209) 984–4388. In a roadhouse built in 1862, Willow serves platters of steak of every description from filet mignon to pepper steak to London broil, plus hot and cold sandwiches. For Tex-Mex, go to the **Smoke Cafe** (18191 Main Street; 209–984–3733), in a building that is a good example of the Pueblo Revival architecture popular in the 1920s.

Afternoon

Retrace your route back to the Bay Area.

There's More

Bear Valley side trips. A few miles east of Bear Valley off Highway 4, **Utica, Union,** and **Spicer Meadows Reservoirs** are undeveloped and great for launching your small boat and fishing for trout, bass, and catfish. Near here, the **Stanislaus River Campground** (209–795–1381) is an eight-site spot nicely located on the river, but with no running water. Up the highway on the way to **Ebbetts Pass, Highlands Lakes** has a small developed campground (209–795–1381).

From Ebbetts Pass, twisty, two-lane Highway 4 runs through some of the most dramatic Alpine-like landscape you will ever see. It is a good idea to bring picnic fare along and take advantage of the many beautiful turnouts and rest stops along the way. You can connect to Highway 89, over **Monitor Pass,** to drop south to the east gate of Yosemite National Park or head north on 89 to Lake Tahoe or into Nevada. The Ebbetts Pass and Monitor Pass roads are closed in wintertime and are not recommended for larger RVs at any time of year.

Biking. Bear Valley Mountain Bike Center, Bear Valley; (209) 753–2834. Rentals, trail maps, guides.

Golf. Forest Meadows Golf Course, 14 miles east of Angels Camp on Highway 4, Murphys; (209) 728–3439. Eighteen holes in a pine forest.

Phoenix Lake Golf Course, 21448 Paseo De Los Portales, Sonora; (209) 532–0111. Ten minutes from Sonora; nine beautiful holes under oak trees beside a lake.

Special Events

February. President's Wine Weekend, Murphys; (209) 223–0350. Wine releases and library tastings, special discounts, food, and music.

April. Gunfighters Rendezvous at Railtown, 1897 State Park, Jamestown; (209) 984–3953. Gold panning, old-fashioned BBQ, musical hoedown, surprise train robberies, historical costumes.

May. Snyder's Pow Wow, Angels Camp; (209) 772–1265; www.valleysprings powwow.com. On a working cattle ranch, more than 200 booths with arts, crafts, gems, minerals, food and drink; also games, camping, and entertainment.

June. Dixieland Jamboree, Sonora; (209) 984–4616.

July. Wine, Art and Beer Festival, Bear Valley; (209) 753–BEAR.

July–August. Music from Bear Valley; (209) 753–BEAR. Big-name classical, opera, jazz, and theatrical performers.

September. Gold Fest, Angels Camp; (209) 728–1251. Gold-panning instruction and competition, Forty-niner camp, Native American dance. Acorn Festival, Tuolumne Rancheria; (209) 928–3475. Indian crafts, food, dances

October. Harvest Festival, Columbia State Historic Park; (209) 532–0150.

December. Christmas Lamplight Tour, Miner's Christmas, and Las Posadas, Columbia State Historic Park; (209) 532–0150.

Other Recommended Restaurants and Lodgings

Arnold

Lodge at Manuel Mill, White Pines Road; (209) 795–2622. Bed-and-breakfast inn, totally secluded on forty-three acres of woods; five rooms with private baths and woodstoves; full breakfast.

Bear Valley

Bear Valley condominiums and cabin rentals, P.O. Box 5038, Bear Valley 95223; (800) 794–3866.

Red Dog Lodge, P.O. Box 5034, Bear Valley 95223; (209) 753–2344. Simple accommodations for persons on a budget, fourteen rooms and dorm-style bathrooms, sauna. Ski out the door on cross-country trails, shuttlebus to chairlifts. Informal dining (burgers, ribs, steak), saloon.

Columbia

Harlan House, 22890 School House; (209) 533–4862. Victorian mansion renovated in 1992; three rooms with baths; full breakfast.

Trails End RV Park, 21770 Parrotts Ferry Road; (209) 533–2395. Shady spots near the state park.

Dorrington

Dorrington Hotel and Restaurant, P.O. Box 4307, Dorrington 95223; (209) 795–5800. Historic, small, cozy bed-and-breakfast, 20 miles south of Bear Valley on Highway 4, near Calaveras Big Trees State Park. Since 1859, small rooms nicely decorated with antiques, patchwork quilts, and brass beds, including expanded continental breakfast. The nineteenth-century redwood bar, charming dining room, and vine arbor terrace are popular for lunch, brunch, and dinner; reasonably priced, hearty, family-style Italian dinners are on the menu.

The Palm Hotel Bed and Breakfast, 10382 Willow Street; (209) 984–3429; www.palmhotel.com. Eight beautiful rooms in a Victorian. Get a brochure in advance to peruse the descriptions—one room has twin claw-foot tubs, one a double-headed shower, one stained glass, and the Grand Suite has a private balcony with wicker furniture, a large sitting area, and can accommodate five people. Full breakfast is included. Innkeepers Rich and Sandy Allen are experts on the local sights and history.

Jamestown

Michelangelo's, 18228 Main Street; (209) 984–4830. Contemporary cafe and bar; nouvelle Italian menu, pizza, pasta.

National Hotel, 77 Main Street; (209) 984–3446; www.national-hotel. com. Since 1859, small and simple rooms, some with small baths, and a popular restaurant.

Murphys

Dunbar House, 271 Jones Street; (209) 728–2897. Luxurious, historic bed-and-breakfast inn near Main Street; private baths; gardens; bountiful breakfast and wine buffet.

Redbud Inn, 402 Main Street; (800) 827–8533. The first inn built in this town in more than a century. Eleven luxurious rooms, Jacuzzis, fireplaces, balconies, bay windows, big breakfasts.

For More Information

Bear Valley Ski Company, P.O. Box 5038, Bear Valley, CA 95223; (209) 753–2301; snow phone: (209) 753–2308.

Calaveras County Visitors Bureau, P.O. Box 637, Angels Camp, CA 95222; (209) 736–0049 or (800) 225–3764; www.visitcalaveras.org.

Calaveras Lodging and Visitors Association, 1301 South Main, Angels Camp, CA 95222; (209) 736–0049.

Calaveras Wine Association, P.O. Box 2492, Murphys, CA 95247; (800) 225–3764, ext. 25; www.calaveraswines.org. Maps and events information for Calaveras County wineries.

Caltrans Highway 4 Hotline: (209) 948–7858. Updated highway conditions.

Jamestown Visitors Information Center, 18239 Main Street, P.O. Box 699, Jamestown, CA 95327; (209) 984–4616.

Tuolumne County Visitors Bureau, 542 West Stockton Street, P.O. Box 4020, Sonora, CA 95370; (800) 446–1333; www.thegreatunfenced.com.

Old Tahoe on the West Shore 4

Mansions in the Mountains

2 Nights

The 1920s were the halcyon days of Lake Tahoe's west shore, when wealthy nabobs from San Francisco built mansions and zipped about in sleek varnished speedboats, and when wooden steamers still cruised the lake, revelers aboard. Much of this area is still privately owned; restaurants and beaches are frequented by people who've spent their vacations here for decades. The pace is slow, except in the nightspots and shops of Tahoe City. Even in the high summer season, you can doze on a quiet beach, walk and bike on silent forest trails, and poke around contentedly in a rented boat. And the rowdy, rushing Truckee River is always there for fishing, rafting, and strolling along beside.

- ☐ Vintage mansions
- ☐ River rambling
- ☐ Mountain hikes
- ☐ Beaches, bikes, hikes
- ☐ Boating on quiet bays
- ☐ Winter fun

The sun shines an average of 274 days a year at Tahoe. Soft spring days are clear and wildflowery; fall is brisk, with aspen color glittering through the pines. Winter is lively at several small, inexpensive downhill and cross-country resorts and positively posh at the big ski resorts: Squaw Valley, Northstar, and Alpine Meadows.

Day 1 / Morning

From the Golden Gate Bridge, drive north on Highway 101, turning east onto Highway 37 to Vallejo, where you'll catch Highway 80 northeast; it's a four-hour drive to the west shore of Lake Tahoe.

A lovely place to take a break is the highway rest stop at Donner Summit, at 7,227 feet, and a few miles farther you'll turn right onto Highway 89, driving 13 miles south to Tahoe City, past Squaw Valley, through the **Truckee River Canyon.** Here you get a first view of Tahoe, North America's largest Alpine lake, 22 miles long and 12 miles wide.

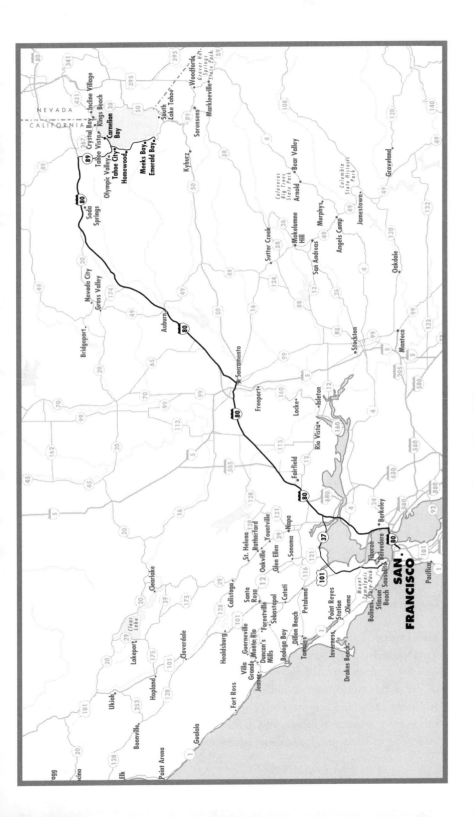

The paved **Truckee River Bike Path** starts at Alpine Meadows, winds along the Truckee 4 miles to Tahoe City, then takes a 9-mile route south along the lake. At some point during your west shore sojourn, you'll want to rent bikes at Tahoe City, or just walk, jog, or push a baby carriage on the path. In the low-water days of late summer and fall, the river slides quietly along. In winter and spring it boils and crashes past ice-decorated trees and snowy islands.

Arriving in Tahoe City, turn right at the junction with Highway 89, which turns sharply south along the western lakeshore. Cross **Fanny Bridge**—where people are always lined up, leaning over to see the trout ladder where the Truckee joins the lake—and stop at the **Gatekeeper's Cabin Museum** and lakeside park, 130 West Lake Boulevard, Tahoe City (530–583–1762), to see an exceptional collection of Washoe and Paiute Indian baskets, artifacts, and historical memorabilia.

LUNCH: Fire Sign Cafe, 1785 West Lake Boulevard, Tahoe City; (530) 583–0871. Home-style cooking, cozy country atmosphere. Try the Gouda scrambled (eggs, gouda, hash browns, biscuits).

Afternoon

Drive 9.5 miles south on Highway 89 to **Sugar Pine Point State Park** (530–525–7982) to visit one of the grand dames of Tahoe, a spectacular three-story, 12,000-square-foot Queen Anne–style summer home, the **Ehrman Mansion.** Built at the turn of the twentieth century by a San Francisco banker, the mansion still looks like the privately owned lakeside estate it once was, surrounded by sweeping lawns shaded by tall pines. Rangers give daily tours of the mansion and boathouse, imparting stories of old days on the lake. After the tour, wander around the grounds, spread a blanket on the beach, or take a walk on trails along the lakeshore. A longer hike is accessible from the large campground across the road; rangers have maps for you.

In the late afternoon, drive north on 89 to **Sunnyside Restaurant and Lodge,** 1850 West Lake Boulevard, 2 miles south of the Tahoe City Y (530–583–7200). Sunnyside has one of the best blue water and high mountain views on the lake. People-viewing is excellent here, too. Boats of every description come and go in the marina; French-fried zucchini and onion rings are tops; and once you get settled outside on the deck or inside by a lakeside window, you'll find it hard to move from the spot. Here you can rent jet skis, sail- and powerboats, and take a sailing lesson.

Winter evenings are warm and friendly in the lounge in front of a giant river-rock fireplace. Casually elegant, small, lakefront lodge rooms and suites here have tiny balconies, some fireplaces, and include breakfast buffet.

DINNER: Chambers Landing, 1 mile south of Homewood; (530) 525–7672. Overlooking the lake on a glass-enclosed and heated terrace. Try the Moroccan lamb or fresh fish, and you owe it to yourself to have a Chambers Punch. A small bar on the Chambers pier is popular with locals. On one side of the pier is a private beach for people staying in the Chambers Landing condos (see Other Recommended Restaurants and Lodgings), and on the other side is a public beach, one of the nicest on the west shore.

LODGING: The Rockwood Lodge, 5295 West Lake, Homewood; (530) 525–5273. A stone mansion, circa 1930, with a knotty-pine interior emboldened by hand-hewn beams, the Rockwood is only 100 feet from the lake but seems a million miles away. The four rooms are cozy and comfortable, with European-style down beds, in-suite basins, robes, and views of the trees or the lake. The main lounge has a huge stone fireplace and a bottle of wine waiting for you.

Day 2 / Morning

BREAKFAST: The Rockwood Lodge. Belgian waffles and fruit crepes are part of a robust selection of goodies. The dining room looks onto a grassy meadow shaded by tall pines. An expert on local wildlife, proprietor Connie Stevens runs a wildlife reserve on the property, taking in injured animals and birds until they are well enough to be returned to the wild.

With Rockwood beach chairs and towels, step across the road to the public beach at **Obexer's Marina** (530–525–7962) and swim, if you dare; at 6,229 feet, the miraculous sapphire-blue, clear water of the lake is always chilly. Surface temperatures in August allegedly reach the low seventies. Get a few rays on the beach, or rent a boat here and motor along the shoreline.

Now pick up picnic supplies in Homewood and head south toward Emerald Bay. On the way, check out **Meeks Bay Resort and Marina** (530–525–7242), owned by the USDA Forest Service, a popular jet- and water-ski beach with an unparalleled view of the lake. This is a good place for beachy activities like rowing, canoeing, and paddleboating (all rentable), or just hanging out in the sun, though all the motors create plenty of noise during summer. A little cafe serves snacks and burgers, and there are a few cottages and a 150-unit campground.

The transparent waters of Lake Tahoe are always chilly.

About 5.5 miles from Meeks Bay, **Emerald Bay** appears in its glittering glory far below. One of the most photographed pieces of scenery in California, the bay can be seen from several vista points along Highway 89, but you must trundle down a steep 1-mile trail (or take a tour boat) to reach the real treasure of the bay—the Scandinavian **Vikingsholm Castle** (530–525–7232), built in 1928. A cross between an eleventh-century castle and an ancient church, the mansion is considered the finest example of Scandinavian architecture in North America. Take a ranger's tour to see the extensively decorated and furnished estate home.

In the clear blue depth of Emerald Bay is California's first underwater shipwreck park. Two wooden barges from the 1930s were originally pulled by steamers, the most common form of transportation before the highway was completed. The barges were intentionally scuttled in Emerald Bay for scuba divers to explore. There are a permanent dive buoy and underwater interpretive panels at the site (530–525–7232).

At the **Emerald Bay State Park Campground** are one hundred tent and RV sites and boat-in campsites (503–525–7232). The campground is closed from mid-September until mid-June.

LUNCH: Have a picnic at Vikingsholm.

Afternoon

From Highway 89 at Emerald Bay, there is an easy 2-mile loop hike to **Eagle Falls** and beautiful **Eagle Lake,** surrounded by the sheer walls of Desolation Wilderness, where many trailheads lead into the southern part of the Tahoe National Forest.

One of the most accessible but least known wilderness areas at Tahoe is **Blackwood Canyon,** off Highway 89 just north of Tahoe Pines. Perfect for easy walks, in-line skating and biking, the paved road is the only development and has almost no traffic; this road is a good add-on to the shoreline bike path. Forests, meadows, and the banks of Blackwood Creek make good picnic spots. You can hike on the flat valley floor or drive up the road to the steep trails of 8,000-foot **Barker Pass,** hooking up with the **Pacific Crest Trail.** An off-road-vehicle camp and trails area are also here in the canyon (530–573–2600). A new 150-mile trail circles the lake, running along ridges and mountain tops. Access the **Tahoe Rim Trail** (775–588–0661) south of Fanny Bridge in Tahoe City: ample parking lot and well-marked trailhead.

DINNER: Gar Woods Grill and Pier, 5000 North Lake Boulevard, Carnelian Bay; (530) 546–3366. On the lake, with a zinger of a view, the glassed-in deck with heaters is a place to take your time enjoying pasta and fresh seafood. The bar is popular and lively, a good place to have an appetizer and people-watch. Sunday brunches are legendary. Try the White Chocolate Snickers Cheesecake.

LODGING: Rockwood Lodge.

Day 3 / Morning

BREAKFAST: Rockwood's.

Explore the small town of **Tahoe City,** the action and shopping headquarters of the west shore. Boutiques are found in the **Cobblestone, Boatworks,** and **Roundhouse** malls; pine-scented breezes and lake views make shopping at the Boatworks particularly pleasant. **Sports Tahoe** in the marina mall (530–583–1990) is jammed with fabulous clothes for every season at the lake.

Tahoe City is the hub of the annual winter festival in March, **SNOWFEST,** the largest winter carnival in the western states (800–TAHOE–4–U). Fireworks at Squaw Valley start off a weekend of parades, ice carving, ice cream eating, live entertainment, and the Polar Bear Swim. More than one hundred events include the Great Ski Race—a 30K Nordic event between Tahoe City and Truckee—and the Snowboard Spectacular. It's wall-to-wall people and lots of fun.

Just north of Tahoe City is the **Watson Cabin Museum,** 560 North Lake Boulevard (530–583–8717), one of the oldest structures on the lake. Docent guides in period costumes will point out the interesting original furnishings.

LUNCH: River Ranch, Highway 89 and Alpine Meadows Road, Tahoe City; (530) 583–4264. On your way out of Tahoe City to head home, stop here for lunch and a last look at the Truckee. A small, charming hotel on the river, River Ranch offers a popular indoor/outdoor restaurant and bar, located at the south end of the Truckee bike path.

Highway 89 takes you to Highway 80 south and the Bay Area.

There's More

Alpine Meadows Ski Area, P.O. Box 5279, Tahoe City 96145; (530) 583–6914. A major ski area for all abilities, priding itself on the longest season and a casual, family-oriented atmosphere. Ski runs have scary names like Chute That Seldom Slides, Promised Land, and Our Father. Kids are VIPs at Kids School and Ski Camp. On the new Sun Kid beginner surface lift, children just step onto a slow conveyor belt with their equipment on, avoiding the sometimes intimidating chairlift until they are ready for it. Programs for all ages are offered for racing, snowboarding, telemark, freestyle, and just plain skiing; and there is ski instruction for people with mental and physical disabilities. Sled-dog tours from here are an exciting way to get out into the beautiful forest and snow-covered meadows.

B. L. Bliss State Park, 3.6 miles south of Meeks Bay. Mistix reservations: (800) 444–7275. One hundred sixty-eight campground sites, beautiful white-sand beach, picnics, good swimming, and a lovely 4-mile trail that leads to Emerald Bay.

Golf. Northstar, Basque Drive, Truckee; (530) 562–2490. Eighteen holes; one of the prettiest and most challenging courses at Tahoe.

Resort at Squaw Creek, Squaw Valley; (530) 581–6637. Eighteen-hole Robert Trent Jones course, surrounded by the glory of the valley. Tahoe City Golf Course; (530) 583–1516. Nine holes.

Granlibakken Ski Area, 667 Lakeshore Drive, Tahoe City; (530) 525–2992 or (800) 543–3221; www.granlibakken.com. A perfect headquarters for summer or winter, this 160-unit condominium resort has a beginner ski and snowboard hill, Nordic skiing, developed snow play area (all for day use, too), and a big swimming pool. Some units have fireplaces, kitchens, lofts, and decks or patios. The complimentary hot breakfast is huge!

Hiking. Donner Lake to the Pacific Crest Trail. Drive 4 miles west on Old Highway 40 from the lake's west end; watch for the trailhead on the left. A 15-mile, strenuous hike along the ridge of the Sierra crest that descends down Squaw Valley's Shirley Canyon. Park one car at Squaw Valley's Olympic Village Inn.

Mount Tallac; (916) 573–2600. A four-hour loop to the 9,700-foot summit; trailheads at Baldwin Beach and Fallen Leaf Lake.

Shirley Lakes Trail. Starts behind the Olympic Village Inn. A nice 4-mile hike from the Squaw Valley; do all or part of a four-hour round-trip, stopping to wade or swim in the creek or the lake, gambol in wildflower-strewn meadows, and nap under the pines.

Tahoe Rim Trail. For maps and information, call (916) 577–0676. From Fairway Drive in Tahoe City, you can connect with the 150-mile hiking and equestrian path that follows the ridgetops of the Lake Tahoe Basin, passes through six counties in Nevada and California, and incorporates about 50 miles of the Pacific Crest National Scenic Trail. The Tahoe Rim Trail is also accessible from several other trailheads around the lake.

Homewood Mountain Resort, 5145 West Lake Boulevard, 6 miles south of Tahoe City; (530) 525–2992; www.skihomewood. One of the most easily accessible and reasonably priced ski mountains, with big views of Lake Tahoe. On "Wild Wednesdays" (every Wednesday during ski season, from January 1 on), adult lift tickets are two for one. Call ahead to book the Homewood shuttle from sites on the west shore.

Kayak Cafe, in Carnelian Bay next to Gar Woods; (530) 546–9337. Cafe and kayak rentals.

Public beaches. Chambers Landing, Obexer's, Sugar Pine Point, Meeks Bay, Homewood. Just north of Tahoe City is the uncrowded beach and pier at Lake Forest; boats can be launched, and camping is available.

River rafting. Fanny Bridge Raft Rentals, Tahoe City; (530) 583–3021. Truckee River Rafting Center, 205 River Road, Tahoe City; (530) 583–RAFT.

Squaw Valley USA, P.O. Box 2007, Olympic Valley 96146; (800) 545–4350; snow phone: (530) 583–6955; www.squaw.com. One of the world's largest and best ski mountains, actually five peaks with thirty lifts and more than 8,300 acres of skiable terrain. The ski school is the best, too, for all ages, from toddlers on up, with lessons, supervised skiing, and snow play. The Fun in the Sun program introduces skiing to first-timers, including a free cable-car ride, free rentals, and demonstrations.

The Squaw Valley Nordic Center consists of 20 miles of groomed track and wilderness trails, plus a telemark downhill area accessed by lifts. The valley is spectacular in every season. You can stay here in a luxury hotel, a reasonable lodge, a bed-and-breakfast inn, a rented condo, or a house. A 150-passenger aerial cable car accesses the High Camp complex, where you can ice skate, hike, mountain bike, swim, picnic, play volleyball and tennis, bungee jump, or just blink in amazement at the mountain surroundings. It's fun to try scrambling up the Headwall Climbing Wall, a popular facility inside the High Camp tram building. The deli in the tram building serves good, simple food at reasonable prices. At High Camp, Alexander's is a good place to eat while enjoying the view. Ride the heated cable car to the restaurant and have dinner before you ride back down or ski down the illuminated, 3.5-mile Mountain Run.

Sugar Bowl Ski Area, 3 miles southeast of Norden exit off Highway 80; (530) 426–9000; www.sugarbowl.com. Snow phone: (530) 426–3847. New express lifts, more trails, and a new lodge make this one of the best medium-size ski resorts at the lake, and it's closer to the Bay Area by as much as an hour than most ski areas. A new beginning quad chair and learning area are located right next to the lodge. Ask about winter and summer accommodations packages. Almost half of the ski runs are intermediate, about 40 percent are advanced.

Tour boat. Departing from behind the Lighthouse Shopping Center in Tahoe City, the *Tahoe Gal* (850 Noth Lake Boulevard, Lighthouse Mall, Tahoe City; 530–583–0141 or 800–218–2464; www.tahoegal.com) is a historic Mississippi stern-wheeler that goes to Emerald Bay and along the shoreline past Fleur du Lac and other magnificent old Tahoe estates. Breakfast, lunch, shoreline, and evening cruises.

Special Events

March. Snowfest, Tahoe City and at several ski resorts; (530) 583–7625. Largest winter carnival in the western United States.

August. Tahoe Yacht Club Concours D'Elegance, Boatworks Mall, Tahoe City; (530) 583–8022. Classic wooden boats.

Squaw Valley Festival of Fine Arts and Crafts; (530) 583–6985.

Truckee Championship Rodeo; (530) 587–6462.

September. Splendor of the Sierra Fine Art Show, Northstar-at-Tahoe; (530) 587–0288.

Antique and Classic Car Show, Tahoe City; (530) 525–4429.

October. Oktoberfest, Alpine Meadows Ski Resort; (530) 583–2371. Dining, dancing, and Bavarian festivities.

Other Recommended Restaurants and Lodgings

Homewood

Chambers Landing, P.O. Box 537, Homewood 95718; (530) 525–7202. On West Lake Boulevard near Sugar Pine Point. Some forty-three privately owned condos; a quiet, private hideaway in an aspen grove; lawns, views; private beach and pool. One of the nicest condo complexes at Tahoe, offering three- and four-bedroom luxury.

Meeks Bay

Sugar Pine Point State Park Campground reservations, Meeks Bay; (800) 444–7275. Offers 175 sites.

Olympic Valley

Olympic Village Inn, 1909 Chamonix Place; (530) 581–6000. Suites with kitchenettes; pool and five Jacuzzis.

Plump Jack Squaw Valley Inn, 1920 Squaw Valley Road; (530) 583–1576 or (800) 323–7666; www.plumpjack.com. In a charming shingle-and-stone complex near the ski tram, sixty delicious contempo rooms with cushy comforters and more comforting amenities; some suites with oversize tubs. A circular fireplace warms up the popular cocktail lounge. Pretty garden terrace with swimming pool and Jacuzzis. Ski lifts within walking distance. The Tatler calls it one of the top 101 best hotels in the world. Even if you don't stay here, stop in to see some stunning contemporary interior design. The upscale restaurant, with eye-popping mountain views, has one of the most exotic menus at the lake, as well as a legendary wine list.

Resort at Squaw Creek, 400 Squaw Creek Road; (800) 3CREEK3; www.squawcreek.com. A 400-room luxury destination resort with a championship Robert Trent Jones golf course, shops, a tennis complex, and a chairlift to ski runs and to High Camp. The terraces of three outdoor pools (and a 120-foot water slide) overlook waves of wildflowers in summer and snowy meadows in winter. Mountain Buddies is the daytime camp for ages three to thirteen, and there are special excursions for teens. Golf and ski packages. Cross-country ski from the hotel. A glamorous, state-of-the-art spa opened in 2000. Without using your car at all, you can have a fabulous vacation in this multifaceted resort, with plenty of outdoor recreation, on-site and nearby.

Squaw Valley Lodge, 201 Squaw Peak Road; (530) 583–5500 or (800) 922–9970; www.squawvalleylodge.com. A sprawling, all-suite lodge with one or two bedrooms and lofts, equipped kitchens, and luxurious amenities like down comforters. Park your car here and get to outdoor recreation, restaurants, and sights on foot, by cable car to High Camp, and valley shuttles. Enjoy the tennis courts and big pool, and unlimited use of a nearby health club with Nautilus. Ski right out the door to the lifts!

Tavern Inn, 203 Squaw Valley Road; (800) 435–9467. Luxury condos sleep four to ten, all with fireplaces. All of the Squaw Valley inns and condos are convenient to a ski shuttle and hiking and biking trails.

Soda Springs

Rainbow Tavern Lodge, P.O. Box 1100, Soda Springs 95728; 677 Highway 80 at Rainbow Road exit; (530) 426–3871. Old Tahoe–style lodge, circa 1925; small, comfortable hotel rooms; good restaurant and bar. On the Yuba River near cross-country and downhill skiing, hiking, fishing.

Tahoe City

Chinquapin Resort, 3600 North Lake Boulevard; (800) 732–6721. Three miles north of town. Spacious one- to four-bedroom condos with lake views, fireplaces, fully equipped kitchens; pool, tennis courts.

Cottage Inn, 1690 West Lake Boulevard; (530) 581–4073. Two miles south of Tahoe City on Highway 89. Fifteen mountain-style cottages with Scandinavian decor, fireplaces; hearty breakfasts, sauna, private beach. Ask for a unit away from the road.

Fast Eddie's Texas BBQ, 690 North Lake Boulevard; (530) 583–0950. The best barbecue in the Tahoe Basin; lunch and dinner.

Jake's on the Lake, 780 North Lake Boulevard, Boatworks Mall; (530) 583–0188. Groovy, popular, lots of fun, right on the lake. Seafood bar and backgammon in the lounge; continental cuisine and hearty mountain food.

Rubicon Deli, in the Tahoe Tree Nursery, 401 West Lake Boulevard; (530) 583–0577. Two miles north of Tahoe City. Super-yummy sandwiches to eat on-site or take out; within a beautiful plant nursery and gift shop.

Tahoe Tavern, 300 West Lake Boulevard; (530) 583–4349. Near Fanny Bridge. Large complex of casual condos in a pine grove, right on the water; pool, lawns; quiet, pretty location on the edge of town.

Truffula, 550 North Lake Boulevard; (530) 581–3362. New and noteworthy, unassumingly hidden in a mini-mall, a small, pretty dining room where miracles occur: hearty California cuisine from scallops with foie gras to wild game and heavenly gnocchi, plus great service from an experienced staff.

Wolfdales, 640 North Lake Boulevard; (530) 583-5700. California cuisine with a unique Japanese flair in a century-old house by the lake; reservations essential.

Tahoe Vista

Captain Jon's, 7220 North Lake Boulevard; (530) 546–4819. French country cuisine, fresh seafood, casual elegance, one of the best restaurants at Tahoe. Cocktail lounge and lunch cafe on the lake; the dinner house has a partial view.

For More Information

Caltrans Road Conditions. San Francisco: (800) 427–7623; Sacramento: (916) 653–7623.

North Lake Tahoe Resort Association, P.O. Box 1757, Tahoe City, CA 96145; (530) 583–3494 or (888) 434–1262; www.tahoe-4-u.com.

Advice: In summer and on snowy weekends, avoid driving to Tahoe on Friday afternoons or returning on Sunday afternoons, unless you've got hours to waste. Every month of the year, check the weather and road conditions. Snow can fall even in June.

Tahoe South 5

Blue Waters and Silver Dollars

2 Nights

From the neon lights and casinos of South Lake Tahoe to lakeside beaches, boating, hiking, and historical sights, here is a nice combination of nighttime fun and days in the pure mountain air on the south side of the Tahoe Basin.

Sandwiched between Lake Tahoe and a magnificent wall of Sierra Nevada peaks, the city of South Lake Tahoe has undergone major redevelopment on the main street and the lakefront to include two large resort hotels, an outdoor ice rink, a movieplex, new shops, restaurants, and a gondola that zips passengers from town to the mountaintop. And not only that: There is now nonstop airline service from Los Angeles, Las Vegas, San José, Fresno, and San Diego; you can also fly into Reno and take a seventy-five-minute luxury motorcoach shuttle to South Shore (800–446–6128), Tahoe Casino Express.

☐ High mountain views

☐ Hiking, biking

☐ Casino night

☐ Old Tahoe estates

☐ Beachtime

Beautiful beaches and resorts are located all along the lakeshore, from one end of town to the other. From here, it's a short drive to a tremendous variety of outdoor recreation and sight-seeing destinations.

Highlights of your visit might be a winter sleigh ride behind a team of beautiful blond Belgian draft horses, or a summer sail across the lake on a huge catamaran. Watch for road signs announcing snow play and ski areas, public beaches, and trailheads.

You'll get your first glimpse of Lake Tahoe, the largest Alpine lake on the continent, at Echo Summit on Highway 50.

Day 1 / Morning

Take Highway 80 to Sacramento, then Highway 50 to Kyburz, a three-and-a-half-hour trip from San Francisco or the East Bay.

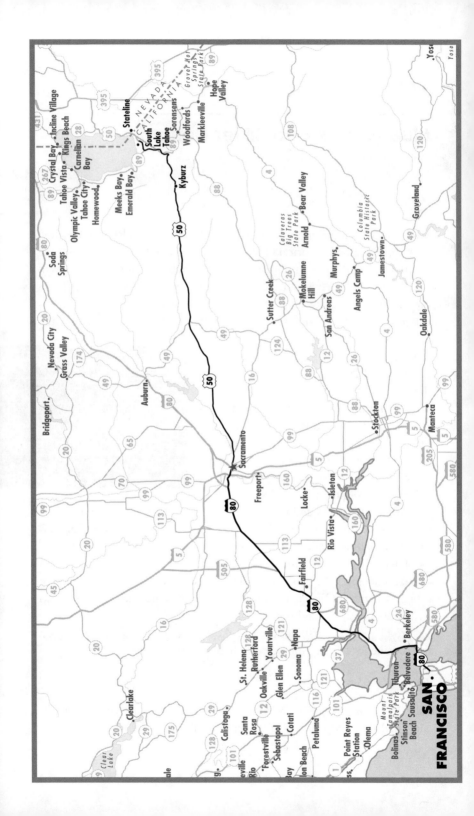

LUNCH: Strawberry Lodge, Highway 50, Kyburz; (530) 659–7200. Good American food and soda-fountain specialties in a restored 1940s lodge; walking trails nearby. Small lodge rooms here are quiet and comfortable. You can hike, fish, swim, and cross-country ski near here in the national forest.

Afternoon

Continue to South Lake Tahoe. An exciting twelve-minute ride into the sky on the **Heavenly Gondola,** right in the middle of town, is the best way to get a bird's-eye view of Lake Tahoe on one side and Nevada's Carson Valley on the other, and hundreds of miles of high desert stretching out into the distance (between Stateline and Park Avenue; 775–586–7000). On the 10,100-foot summit, an easy 2-mile trail loops the mountaintop; you can also take a guided nature hike, a sunset hike, an early evening birding hike, or a full-moon or stargazing hike. There is a restaurant that serves good, but pricey, lunches, brunches, and dinners.

For a never-to-be-forgotten introduction to Lake Tahoe, take one of the big tour boats across the lake. Beautiful stern-wheelers and a catamaran cross the lake to Emerald Bay and cruise along the lakeshore (see There's More, Cruises on the Lake).

Three public beaches in town have extensive recreational facilities including playing fields and swimming pools: **El Dorado Beach, Regan Beach,** and **Connelly Beach.** At **Nevada Beach** and **Zephyr Cove** you can rent every imaginable type of watersports equipment and take lessons, take a boat tour of the lake, try parasailing, go fishing, or just lie in the sun.

A nice shopping area, the **Ski Run Marina Village,** at Lake Tahoe and Ski Run Boulevards, has specialty shops, a cafe, and an upscale lakeside restaurant.

DINNER: Llewellyn's, Highway 50, Stateline; (775) 588–2411. In the nineteenth story of **Harveys Resort Casino,** an elegant room with stunning views of the lake and mountains. Choose from a creative mix of French, Asian, and California cuisine. Can't get reservations here? Try **The Summit,** on top of Harrah's, a similar experience, continental dining at tables on terraced levels with breathtaking views (north end of South Lake Tahoe; 775–588–6611).

Polish up your silver-tipped cowboy boots and hit the casinos—they are open twenty-four hours. Several multistory casinos are within a coin flip of one another, some connected by an underground walkway. Big names put on big shows at **Caesars Tahoe** (like Chaka Khan, Wynonna, and David Copperfield). You can see old favorites at **Harrah's** (like Tower of Power and the Everly Brothers) and sizzling stage shows at Harveys and the Horizon.

Take a late-night break with a burger by the huge stone fireplace at the **Hard Rock Cafe** in Harveys, or dance all night at **Nero's 2000** in Caesars Tahoe.

LODGING: Lakeland Village, 3535 Lake Tahoe Boulevard, South Lake Tahoe; (703) 234–3340 or (800) 822–5969. One of the largest and nicest resorts in town is spread out along the lake on nineteen acres of pines, with a private, sandy beach; two heated swimming pools; and tennis courts. The choices here are condo or lodge units, some with fireplaces and kitchens. Shuttle buses connect with nearby ski areas and downtown.

Day 2 / Morning

BREAKFAST: The Red Hut Waffle Shop, 2723 Highway 50, 3.5 miles south of Stateline; (530) 541–9024. A popular retro cafe with comfy booths, a big counter, and an American comfort-food menu.

Toss your last few quarters into a slot machine and head south, following Highway 89, also called **Emerald Bay Road,** out of town to the south end of the lake. At 9,735 feet, **Mount Tallac** towers over a plethora of sights and things to do on the south shore. Relive the 1920s heyday of the rich and famous at the **Tallac Historic Site** (530–541–4975). Restored and open to tour are several formerly private estates, an old casino, and a hotel. Many musical and art events are held at Tallac, from jazz to bluegrass, from craft demonstrations to photo exhibits. In August the **Great Gatsby Festival** looks like the good old days, with antique boats and merrymakers in period costume.

Baldwin, Pope, and **Kiva beaches** are accessible by bus (530–542–6077) from South Lake Tahoe; a network of hiking trails connects the beaches, and the Tallac Historic Site. The popular **Emerald Bay State Park** campground has one hundred tent and RV sites and boat-in campsites. It is closed from mid-September until mid-June (530–525–7232).

At Baldwin Beach is the **USDA Forest Service Lake Tahoe Visitors Center,** where you can see exhibits of geology, animal habitat, and history; get maps and advice on trail conditions and campground availability and sign up for ranger-led interpretive walks (530–573–2600). Stroller- and handicap-friendly, the **Rainbow Trail** is a paved path that wanders past signs that explain the natural habitat; more than one hundred species of wildflowers bloom alongside the trail. The "Stream Profile Chamber" is a cross-section of a real stream filled with rushing water, fish, plants, and other wildlife. In the fall, thousands of visitors come to watch brilliant red spawning salmon wriggle their way from Lake Tahoe up Taylor Creek. A four-hour, 5-mile, rather strenuous loop hike from here to the summit of Mount Tallac rewards trekkers with magnificent views at 9,700 feet. Trailheads are across from the road at Baldwin Beach.

LUNCH: The Beacon, east of Emerald Bay on Highway 89 at Camp Richardson; (530) 541–0630. The place to see and be seen at the beach. Watch the boats arrive and have a Rum Runner while waiting for your blackened salmon or burger to arrive. Live music in the summertime. Lunch, dinner, weekend brunch.

Afternoon

Go on an afternoon sail with **Woodwind Sailing Cruises** (see There's More, Cruises on the Lake) from Camp Richardson. Or take a guided horseback ride from here to Fallen Leaf Lake, about three hours. This is very popular, so reserve ahead. Fallen Leaf Lake is accessible by road off Highway 89 and makes a wonderful day trip. With Camp Richardson as headquarters, you can hike around the lake, swim, and picnic, barbecue, or launch a boat (see Other Recommended Restaurants and Lodgings).

DINNER: Riva Grill, 900 Ski Run Boulevard at Ski Run Marina Village, South Lake Tahoe; (530) 542–2600. Overlooking the lake, Riva serves California cuisine in a vintage wooden boat interior with outdoor deck. Steaks, seafood, Mediterranean food.

LODGING: Lakeland Village.

Day 3 / Morning

BREAKFAST: Ernie's, near the Y, 1146 Emerald Bay Road, Stateline; (530) 541–2161. Down-home American food for breakfast, lunch, and dinner; where the locals go.

Drive north from South Lake Tahoe to near the junction of Highways 28 and 30, about twenty minutes, to **Spooner Lake.** You can take a short hike around a small lake and enjoy the mountain meadows, fish for trout, picnic, and, in the wintertime, cross-country ski (rentals available); this is a great place for beginning skiers. The trailhead for the moderately strenuous, uphill,

10-mile hiking and mountain biking Flume Trail to Marlette Lake is here. Spectacular views of the lake and surrounding mountains are the reward at the top, especially in the fall when the aspens are blazing yellow. You can see vestiges of a huge system of wooden flumes, which were built in the mid-1800s to move water from the lake to the booming silver mining towns of Virginia City and Carson City, on the east side of the mountains.

Mountain bikers ride up the trail to the lake, then down the mountain on the other side to Incline Village, a 14-mile ride. To obtain a Tahoe area mountain-biking brochure, call the Tahoe Douglas Chamber of Commerce, (775) 588–4591, or the South Lake Tahoe Chamber, (530) 541–5255.

Another place to mountain bike, right above South Lake Tahoe, is on Heavenly's bike trail network; new bikes and equipment can be rented (877–243–0003).

LUNCH: Sprouts Natural Foods Cafe, 3123 Harrison Street at Highway 50 and Alameda, South Lake Tahoe; (530) 541–6969. Grab a luscious Tahoe Turkey sandwich to go or sit at the counter or outside to enjoy a veggie burrito, a fruit smoothie, and some homemade soup. A very, very popular place.

Heading home, retrace your route on Highway 50.

There's More

Casinos. Caesars Tahoe, Highway 50, Stateline; (775) 588–3515 or (800) 648–3353; www.caesars.com. Four hundred forty rooms, most with whirlpool tubs.

Harrah's Lake Tahoe, Highway 50, Stateline; (775) 588–6611 or (800) 427–7247; www.harrahstahoe.com. Five hundred suite-style rooms, each with two bathrooms; a four-star, four-diamond hotel.

Harveys Resort Hotel, Highway 50, Stateline; (775) 588–2411 or (800) 427–8397; www.harveystahoe.com. Seven hundred rooms, each with lake or mountain view.

Horizon Casino Resort, Highway 50, Stateline; (775) 588–6211 or (800) 648–3322; www.horizoncasino.com. Five hundred rooms and suites, Olympic pool.

Cruises on the Lake. MS *Dixie II,* 5 miles north of South Lake Tahoe on Highway 50, Zephyr Cove; (775) 588–3508. This beautiful paddle wheeler was once a cotton barge on the Mississippi in 1927, then a floating casino at Tahoe, when it sank and was raised and converted into a tour boat.

Tahoe Queen, 9090 Ski Run Boulevard, South Lake Tahoe; (530) 541–3364; www.hornblower.com. Huge, beautiful paddle wheeler; day and evening trips to Emerald Bay. Ski cruises to Tahoe City, too.

Woodwind Sailing Cruises, Zephyr Cove Marina, South Lake Tahoe; (775) 588–3000; www.sailwoodwind.com. A fifty-passenger, 41-foot trimaran with a glass bottom, indoor/outdoor seating. Also a catamaran that sails out of Camp Richardson.

Golf. Edgewood Tahoe Golf Course, Highway 50 at Stateline; (775) 588–3566. Eighteen holes; the site of major tournaments; the most challenging course at the lake. Located behind the Horizon Casino.

Tahoe Paradise Golf Course, on Highway 50 in Meyers; (530) 577–2121. Eighteen-hole course.

Grover's Hot Springs. Four miles west of Markleeville, a unique state park with natural hot pools (530–694–2248). The water, at 148 degrees, flows out of underground springs into swimming and soaking pools. It's fun to float in the warm, steamy water, especially in the wintertime when snow is on the ground. There are campgrounds here and walking trails, but the hot pools are the main attraction.

Heavenly Ski Resort, 4004 Ski Run Boulevard, South Lake Tahoe; (775) 586–7000 or (800) 243–2836; www.skiheavenly.com. One of the biggest ski resorts in the world with one of the highest skiable summits in the United States. Nearly eighty runs get an average of 360 inches of the white stuff a year. On the Nevada side, hundreds of miles of high desert stretch out into the distance, and on the California side you have the phenomenal experience of feeling as though you are skiing right into the lake. If your legs can take it, start from the top of Sky Express and ski nonstop 5.5 miles.

Hiking. Desolation Wilderness. Hundreds of lakes, thousands of acres of outback, many trails. Easy accessibility makes it extremely popular; best off-season. For an 11.4-mile loop day trip, take the Glen Alpine trailhead at the end of Fallen Leaf Lake Road, hiking to Lake Aloha.

Round Lake, 6.4-mile loop to a neato swimming hole. Take Highway 89 south out of Meyers; 3.6 miles before Luther Pass is roadside parking on the north, trailhead on the south.

Tahoe Rim Trail. Trailhead information: (775) 588–0686. A 150-mile trail around the lake.

Hope Valley. A half hour east of South Lake Tahoe on Highway 88, in an aspen-studded high-mountain meadow above 7,000 feet, the mile-wide Hope Valley cradles the Carson River, a ribbon of water beloved by trout anglers. Fall colors are spectacular, wildflowers are knee deep in the spring. The fishing is great on the Carson. Buy guidebooks and fishing licenses at Sorensen's Resort (530–694–2203 or 800–423–9949) and get advice on where to catch the big ones; fishing and cross-country ski instruction and rentals are available, too.

Kirkwood Meadows, P.O. Box 1, Kirkwood, CA 95646; (209) 258– 6000; www.kirkwood.com. Thirty-five miles east of South Lake Tahoe; at 7,800 feet, highest base elevation in the Tahoe area. Extraordinarily long ski season and dependably top snow conditions. On hundreds of acres of Alpine meadows, Nordic skiing is perfection. Condos, lodge rooms, and rental houses make Kirkwood a major vacation destination in summertime, when the meadows turn to rippling waves of wildflowers. Biking and hiking trails and lake and stream fishing are popular. New in 2000 were the Mountain Club, a deluxe condo hotel with one- and two-bedroom units with lofts, and Snowcrest, a condo complex at the base of the lifts. Snazzy boutique shops and restaurants are new additions, too, transforming Kirkwood into a major destination resort, adding glamour to a formerly backcountry atmosphere—the surrounding wilderness setting remains as glorious as ever. Among the unique adventures to be had here are horse-drawn sleigh rides, outdoor ice skating, and snowshoeing after dark with headlamps. Nearby at the summit of Carson Pass, Caples Lake attracts trout anglers, canoers, sailboarders, and swimmers. Trails lead into the Mokelumne Wilderness.

Lake Tahoe Historical Society Museum, 3458 Lake Tahoe Boulevard, South Lake Tahoe; (530) 541–5458.

Special Events

March. Kirkwood Cross Country Race, Kirkwood; (209) 258–7248.
Torchlight Parade and Fireworks, Kirkwood; (209) 258–6000.

June. Train Parade, South Lake Tahoe; (530) 644–3761. Annual mile-long historic wagon train brings the Old West to life. Hundreds of people dressed in period costume in wagons, stagecoaches, or on horseback—mountain men, scouts tracing the original route of the Pony Express.

Valhalla Renaissance Festival, Tallac Historic Site; (530) 542–4166. An old English country "faire" with knights in combat, archery contests, jugglers, magicians, dancers, plays, period music, food vendors, crafts, psychic readings, and more. Wear costumes to the festival!

June–July. Lake Tahoe Sailweek, Tahoe Keys Marina; (800) AT–TAHOE. Sailboats from across the country converge for a weeklong series of races.

June–September. Valhalla Summer Festival of Art and Music, South Lake Tahoe; (530) 542–4166. Concerts and exhibits in and around historical mansions.

July. Rhythm and Brews Festival, Tallac Historic Site; (530) 541–4975. Live bands and the beers of forty Western breweries.

July–August. Shakespeare Festival, Sand Harbor; (530) 583–9048.

August. Hot August Nights in Reno; (775) 829–1955. Fifties and sixties cars, rock 'n' roll.

Great Gatsby Festival, Tahoe Keys Marina, Tallac Historic Site; (530) 546–2768. Antique and classic wooden boat show, Roaring Twenties living history.

September. Reno National Championship Air Races, Reno; (775) 972–6663.

Other Recommended Restaurants and Lodgings

Hope Valley

Sorensen's Resort, 14255 Highway 89; (530) 694–2203 or (800) 423–9949. In a pine and aspen grove on the west fork of the Carson River; cabins; a rustic cafe with great food; fishing, hiking and cross-country skiing. Cabins have home-spun country decor, brass beds, woodstoves, some kitchens. A popular place for families; reservations are necessary weeks and sometimes even months in advance. Kids fish in the small stocked pond for trout. An old logging road leads from here into the Toiyabe National Forest, with views of a jagged range of mountains. Ask about the guided hike on the Emigrant Trail.

South Lake Tahoe

Black Bear Inn, 1202 Ski Run Boulevard; (800) AT–TAHOE or (877) 232–7466; www.tahoeblackbear.com. Lodge and cabins in a wooded acre, luxurious interiors with fireplaces, full breakfast.

Camp Richardson, P.O. Box 9028, South Lake Tahoe 96158; (530) 541–1801. Just east of Emerald Bay on Highway 89. A favorite family summer-vacation resort for decades; rooms in the cavernous main lodge are small and simple. There are a marina, a sandy beach, riding stables, restaurants, cottages to rent, a 230-unit campground, and a general store. A convenient headquarters from which to set off on horseback or on foot into Desolation Wilderness. Paddleboats, jet skis, and other water toys are rentable. Kayak Tahoe here rents boats for self-guided and guided lake tours (530–544–2011).

The historic post office is now restored and open as a 1920s-style trading post, with locally crafted toys, art and souvenirs, Native American art and scenic paintings of the lake, and logo items. A new children's activity camp offers supervised winter and summer play for guests of the camp and of Harrah's Casino Hotel.

Breakfast and steak-dinner guided horseback rides from Camp Richardson to Fallen Leaf Lake are fun for families; they take about three hours and are very popular, so reserve ahead.

Embassy Suites Resort, 4130 Lake Tahoe Boulevard; (800) 924–9245; www.embassytahoe.com. Luxury suites; Old Tahoe–style architecture; full breakfast and cocktail hour free. Indoor pool and spa, sun deck, workout room, seasonal packages; shuttle to airport, Heavenly Ski Resort, and casinos.

Forest Inn Suites, 1 Lake Parkway; (530) 541–6655 or (800) 822–5950. One- and two-bedroom suites with equipped kitchens on five acres of forest with pools, spas, and health club, shuttle to Heavenly Valley Resort.

Scusa! on Ski Run, 1142 Ski Run Boulevard; (530) 542–0100. Load up on fresh pasta with seafood, hearty calzones, or pizza. A casual, popular place.

Tahoe Keys Resort, 599 Tahoe Keys Boulevard; (530) 544–5397; www.caltahoe.com. Homes and condos for rent. You can fly into the international airport and be there in ten minutes. Some of the amenities: indoor and outdoor swimming pools, a health club, bicycles, outdoor games, a playground, a private beach, ski shuttles, powerboat rentals, parasailing, jet skis, boat launching—in other words, vacation central. Sailboats from across the country converge at Tahoe Keys for a weeklong series of races in June, the Lake Tahoe Sailweek.

For More Information

California State Campgrounds, P.O. Box 942896, Sacramento, CA 94296-0001; (916) 653–6995 or (800) 777–0369; www.cal-parks.ca.gov. Call or write for the *Camping Reservation Guide,* a complete explanation of how to make campsite reservations, and a complete directory of campgrounds, facilities, and costs.

Lake Tahoe Accommodations, 2048 Dunlap Drive, #4, South Lake Tahoe, CA 96150; (530) 544–3234 or (800) 544–3234. Condo and home rentals.

Lake Tahoe Visitors Authority, 1156 Ski Run Boulevard, South Lake Tahoe, CA 96151; (800) AT–TAHOE; www.virtualtahoe.com. Use this number to book reservations, get tickets to events and casino shows, buy airline tickets, and hear about weather and road conditions.

Road conditions and ski reports: (415) 864–6440 or (800) 427–7623.

Tahoe North 6

Peaceful Pines and a Western Town

2 Nights

The Washoe Indians called it *Tahoe,* or "Big Water." Twenty-two miles long and 12 miles wide, Lake Tahoe is 1,600 feet deep and "clear enough to see the scales on a cutthroat trout at 80 feet," according to Mark Twain. Surrounded by snow-frosted mountains and dense evergreen forests, the translucent blue water is hypnotic and cold, very cold. Legends tell of Indian chiefs in full regalia and women in Victorian garb floating motionless and frozen at the bottom of the lake.

- ☐ Mountain meadows
- ☐ Lakeside walks
- ☐ Old railroad town
- ☐ Beachtime
- ☐ Winter resorts

On the north shore are less traffic, less honky-tonk, and a more residential atmosphere. Fewer beaches and restaurants, too, but some of the best. A handful of small casinos add spice.

The old miners' and loggers' town of Truckee, still rough-and-tumble after all these years, makes a fun stop on your way to the lake.

Day 1 / Morning

From the Oakland Bay Bridge, drive north on Highway 80 to Sacramento; it's a four-hour drive to the north shore.

At Donner Summit, just past Baxter, stop at the **Emigrant Gap Viewpoint** on the west side of Highway 80. Looking out over hundreds of miles of high country, you see the tremendous tilted block of the Sierras, sloping shallowly toward the west. Glacial canyons are gouged out of the granite, and the Yuba and Bear Rivers have cut their own valleys. Pioneers winched their wagons down into the Bear Valley from here at 4,000 feet, then dragged themselves back up to Washington Ridge on the opposite side of the valley, the most difficult section of their journey to a new life in the West.

Beyond the summit of Donner Pass, take a rest stop at **Donner Memorial State Park** (530–544–3053), a camping and picnic area at

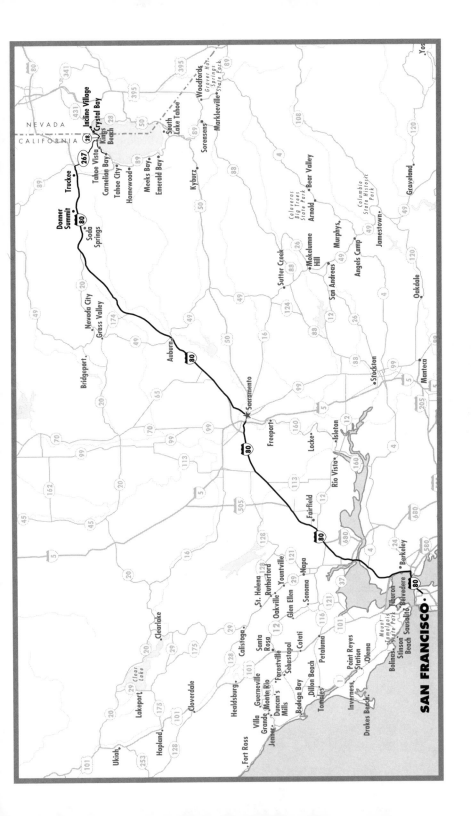

5,950 feet, with a short, pleasant walking trail. The **Emigrant Trail Museum,** located within the park, depicts stories of the Donner party tragedy and the building of the railroad through the Sierras in the 1800s. You'll see train tracks, mostly covered with snow, running along rugged mountainsides above Donner Lake. Taking the Amtrak train from Oakland to Truckee is a relaxing way to get to Tahoe; parties of skiers have fun doing this in wintertime, and the scenery—wow!

Donner Lake, 3 miles long, is a smaller, quieter, less developed version of Tahoe, and many vacationers prefer it. You can camp, launch a boat, rent a cabin, fish, hike, ski, and enjoy the crystal blue waters. **Donner Lake Village Resort** rents lodgettes, studios, and one- and two-bedroom condos (916–587–6081). There are nearly thirty public piers on the north side for fishing and boating. Shoreline Park offers bank fishing and a pier, boat launching, picnic sites, and swimming. On the west end, a swimming area is supervised by lifeguards.

Below the lake, in Coldstream Canyon, is an easy mountain-bike trail. On the west end of Donner Lake is a trailhead for the **Pacific Crest Trail.** From here you can take a strenuous, 15-mile hike along the ridge of the Sierra crest, descending down into Squaw Valley's **Shirley Canyon.** On the opposite side of Highway 80 is a leg of the **Donner Lake Rim Trail,** a route that now encircles the lake.

Continuing on Highway 80, take the Central Truckee exit into Truckee.

A popular stop on the way to the west shore, the tiny town of Truckee was a rollicking railroading, logging, and ice-harvesting headquarters in the 1800s. The picturesque main street is lined with Western wear and outdoor-equipment stores, restaurants and saloons in brick and stone falsefront buildings facing the railroad tracks, and the 1869 depot where Amtrak trains blast into town daily. In May, Truckee steps back in time with a weekend of gunslinger reenactments, gold panning, strolling musicians, and storytelling (www.truckee.com).

LUNCH: Andy's Truckee Diner, next to the railroad tracks and Highway 267, Truckee; (530) 582–6925. An authentic 1940s diner moved from Pennsylvania, open twenty-four hours with a huge all-American menu. Got an appetite? Try the chicken-fried steak, a juicy burger, a hot turkey sandwich, or a Philly cheese steak, with a thick shake followed by a banana split.

Afternoon

Proceed east out of Truckee on Highway 267 through the **Martis Valley,** passing **Northstar** (see page 260) as you climb up Brockway Summit—a short but icy ascent in the winter—on your way to the stoplight at Kings Beach. Stop here and jump in the lake, then take a left onto Highway 28, crossing into Nevada at Crystal Bay; it's five minutes to **Incline Village.**

If there is a secret hideaway at Tahoe, it's Incline Village, a small community of gorgeous homes and condos sprinkled on the shores of the lake and across steep mountainsides, with breathtaking views. Traffic-free and quiet, Incline has many virtues, such as the small, excellent ski resort of Diamond Peak; two Robert Trent Jones golf courses; two of Tahoe's loveliest beaches; and one elegant casino hotel.

Incline's private beaches, and a beautiful recreation center with a pool, playground, and tennis courts, are available only to those who rent, own, or stay at selected hotel and motel accommodations in Incline. Renting a condo or house is the way to go here, and it can be as cost-effective as a resort or a motel. When you make your arrangements for accommodations, be sure to ask about getting an "IVGID" card from the Incline Village General Improvement District, which will admit you and the family to the beaches and the rec center.

A small, exquisite beach park, **Burnt Cedar Beach,** has a big heated pool, a lifeguard, a snack bar, a kids' playground, shady lawns for lounging, picnic tables, barbecues, shallow water for wading, deep water for swimming, and a killer view.

Ski Beach, in front of the Hyatt Regency Lake Tahoe, has many amenities, and it's long enough for a morning walk.

Park at the east end of Lakeshore Drive at the Hyatt and walk back along the lake. The paved sidewalk runs for several miles, past the beaches and lovely homes—perfect for jogging, baby carriage–pushing, walking, and biking. Giant sugar pine cones are scattered liberally about, free for the taking. The gardens and the architecture are interesting sights in themselves.

Have a sundown cocktail at the **Lone Eagle Grill** (775–832–1234), a stunning wood-and-granite bar with a massive river-rock fireplace, a floor-to-ceiling view of the lake, and an elegant restaurant. You may find it difficult to leave here.

DINNER: Cafe 333, 333 Village Boulevard, Incline Village; (775) 832–7333. On the patio or indoors; a casual, upscale place with a creative menu: walnut-crusted chicken with Gorgonzola pesto sauce, seared fresh salmon with sun-dried tomato coulis, and heartier dishes, plus a great wine list. Breakfast, brunch, lunch, and dinner.

LODGING: Hyatt Regency Resort Casino Lake Tahoe, 111 Country Club Drive at Lakeshore Drive, Incline Village; (775) 832–1234. A 460-room, full-service hotel and casino. European-style mountain lodge room interiors, lakeside cottages, health club, pool, tennis, and shuttles to major ski resorts. Among the several upscale eating places are the indoor/outdoor restaurant on the beach with a lively bar, a twenty-four-hour-a-day cafe, and an Italian/Asian fine restaurant. You can walk or bike to all beaches and most restaurants in Incline from the Hyatt.

This evening, lurk around the Hyatt, even if you're not a gambler. The "Fantasy Forest" in the casino is something to see: full-size pine trees studded with a zillion tiny lights and huge chandeliers reflected in a mirrored ceiling—even lights in the carpet. You can lounge in front of the big fireplace and people-watch, or you can plunge in and throw some money away. Tip: Play the slot machines at the ends of the aisles, near the center of the room; payoffs occur on the most visible machines.

Day 2 / Morning

BREAKFAST: Wildflower Cafe, 869 Tahoe Boulevard, Incline Village; (775) 831–8072. Rub shoulders with skiers (snow or water) and construction workers at the counter or at a wooden table and have a Paul Bunyan–size breakfast of waffles or eggs and potatoes. Next, stop at **Grog & Grist Market and Deli,** located at Highway 28 at Northwood, (775) 831–1123, and pick up some picnic fare to enjoy later.

If tennis is your game, you will be glad to know that Incline has the largest concentration of top-quality tennis facilities at the lake, with twelve professional courts at the **Lakeside Tennis Club,** Highway 28 at Ski Run Boulevard (775–832–4860), and seven courts at the **Incline Village Recreation Center,** 980 Incline Way (775–832–1310). As an "IVGID" guest at the rec center, you can come in for the day and use the indoor Olympic pool and fitness facilities, as well as the child care.

You can launch a boat at Incline Beach (775–831–1310) or at Sand Harbor (775–831–0494). Rentals of ski boats, paddleboats, canoes, and kayaks are available at **Action Water Sports** on the beach in Incline (775–831–4386).

For a day of hiking and exploring in the mountains, drive east on Tahoe

Hiking near Incline Village, Lake Tahoe.

Boulevard to Country Club Drive and turn left, then right at the top of the hill onto Highway 431, also known as the Mount Rose Highway.

Dominating the mountain skyline on the north shore is Mount Rose, above Incline. From the scenic overlook on 431, almost the entire 22-mile-long lake gleams below, rimmed by the Sierras on the west and the Carson Range on the east. Seven miles beyond the lookout point is **Tahoe Meadows,** at 8,600 feet, a series of huge meadows where you can enjoy miles of cross-country skiing and summertime hiking, easy or strenuous. The meadows are crisscrossed with small streams and crowded with wild-flowers most of the year. Tahoe Meadows Whole Access Trail is a wide, 1.3-mile loop designed for persons in wheelchairs and baby strollers.

Just beyond Tahoe Meadows, **Mount Rose Campground** is nice and cool in midsummer and often has tent and RV sites available when campgrounds near the lake are full (775–882–2766). Stop here for fresh water and rest rooms. You can walk from the campground to the top of the mountain and the Tahoe Meadows trail system.

The 12-mile-loop hike to the summit of Mount Rose, at 10,776 feet, is a half-day trip that starts on an old jeep road near the cinderblock building. Even if you can't make it to the top for the view that awaits, you may wish to start up this trail; there are a pond with a frog chorus in residence and wildflowers galore. At the top you'll see the whole lake basin and the Carson Valley sweeping away into the distance, and even Lassen Peak on a very clear day.

LUNCH: Have a picnic here or take it back down the mountain to Tahoe Boulevard, going east out of Incline on Highway 28 a few miles to **Sand Harbor State Park** (702–831–0494), which is picturesque, with two white-sand beaches, tree-shaded picnic spots, and lake and mountain views—the most beautiful beach park at the lake.

Afternoon

The annual Music and Shakespeare Festival is held here at Sand Harbor on July and August evenings. On a clear summer night, you'll watch the sun go down over the lake while you sit on a blanket sipping wine and the kids play on the sand nearby. The lights go down, the stars come out, and magic begins on stage.

After an afternoon dip in the lake or a dip in the Burnt Cedar pool, or perhaps a nap, drive to **Crystal Bay,** at Stateline (five minutes west of Incline on Highway 28), and go into **Cal-Neva Lodge** (800–225–6382), the high-rise hotel casino at Stateline. It's one of the oldest casinos on the lake, made famous by a former owner, Frank Sinatra. Off the lobby, the Indian Room is a vast, beam-ceilinged lounge with a big boulder fireplace and a fascinating collection of early Tahoe artifacts, bearskins, and bobcats. If you're in the mood to tie the knot, step into one of three wedding chapels on the grounds.

As the sun starts to set, continue on Highway 28 to **Gar Woods,** 5000 North Lake Boulevard, Carnelian Bay (916–546–3366), for cocktails or tea; this is one of a handful of restaurants located right on the lake.

DINNER: **Big Water Grille,** 341 Ski Way, at the top of Incline Village; (775) 833–0606. With views of the world from 7,000 feet; California cuisine in an elegant setting. Lunch, dinner, weekend brunch.

LODGING: Hyatt Regency Lake Tahoe.

Day 3 / Morning

BREAKFAST: The Original Old Post Office, 5245 North Lake Boulevard, Carnelian Bay; (530) 546–3205. Down-home cooking, with monster-size breakfasts starting at 6:00 A.M. every day.

Before heading back to the Bay Area, play a round of golf on one of Incline's falling-off-the-mountain golf courses; play tennis on one of the town's twenty-six courts; or take the kids to the Ponderosa Ranch (see There's More).

On Highway 28, within a few minutes' drive of Incline, is a string of small villages attuned to the tourist trade, including **Crystal Bay, Kings Beach, Tahoe Vista,** and **Carnelian Bay.** At Crystal Bay a few casinos are clustered. Kings Beach has huge arts and crafts fairs on summer weekends near the beach and a golf course that turns into a snowmobile park when the snow flies. At Tahoe Vista, **North Tahoe Regional Park,** at the end of National Avenue off Highway 28, is a great place for beginning cross-country skiers, on nearly 7 flat miles of groomed tracks, plus a snow play hill. When the snow melts, stop off here to take a short walk on the tree-lined trails or have a picnic or a barbecue (775–546–7248).

There's More

Boreal Ski Area, Highway 80 at Donner Summit; (530) 426–3666. A reasonably priced, non-intimidating choice for new skiers. The Nugget chairlift for beginners is free, and there is a snowplay area with rental saucers, or you can bring your own. Night skiing is popular at Boreal, especially with teenagers, who like the illuminated terrain park with huge half-pipe, tabletop jumps and rolls. The view from the top of the Sunset Boulevard run is dazzling; all-day lift tickets are valid for night skiing. Admission is free at Boreal's Western American Ski Sport Museum, where ski history from the 1850s to the present is depicted in photos, displays, and vintage movies.

Diamond Peak Ski Area at Mount Rose, 1210 Ski Way, on Highway 431 above Incline Village; (775) 832–1177; www.diamondpeak.com. A medium-size ski resort with spectacular lake and mountain views from downhill and cross-country trails. Intermediates and beginners are happy here; expert skiers will head for larger resorts. Snow conditions are less dependable than at higher-elevation resorts, but the snow can be primo, the runs uncrowded, and the atmosphere casual. Ski, snowboard, and cross-country lessons and clinics. During the Northern Lights Celebration in December, skiing is free with a local lodging reservation. The snowshoe and cross-country center offers 40 kilometers of lakeview and forest track for touring, skating, and snowshoeing at a higher altitude than at most other Nordic centers at the lake.

Fishing. Giant Kokanee salmon, released into the lake by accident in 1940, lurk below rocky ledges on the north shore, along with several species of trout. Crystal Bay is the best spot to catch them.

Golf. Incline Championship and Executive Courses, Incline Village; (775) 832–1144. Two beautiful mountainside courses. The lower course doubles as a cross-country ski area used primarily by residents, but you can rent skis in town and ski here, too.

Old Brockway Golf Course, North Lake Boulevard at Kings Beach; (530) 546–9909. Nine holes; inexpensive and easy.

Tahoe Donner Golf Course, Truckee; (530) 587–9440. Eighteen holes.

Northstar-at-Tahoe, between Truckee and Lake Tahoe on Highway 267; (800) 466–6784; snow phone: (530) 562–1330; www.skinorthstar.com; e-mail: nstar@sierra.net. In a glorious mountain and forest setting, one of the largest all-year vacation resorts at the lake, the Northstar complex includes a golf course; equestrian, mountain-biking, and hiking trails; shops, a deli, and a grocery; several bars and restaurants; beautiful pool and tennis complexes; and many condos, lodge rooms, and houses to rent. You can settle in here for a vacation and never need a car, getting around on the forest paths and the resort shuttles. In summer, chairlifts take hikers and bikers up to 100 miles of marked, mountaintop trails. There is a busy schedule of activities and events all year, including guided nature hikes, orienteering, and sports and fishing classes. From mountain bikes to the latest ski designs, rental equipment is state-of-the-art. Licensed child care is available. The Adventure Park includes a ropes course and outdoor climbing walls.

One of the largest in the Western states, Northstar's ski mountain is about equally beginning, intermediate, and advanced, and free ski clinics are offered to all ages. Ask about the special First Tracks program, which gives early risers a head start before the lifts open to the public, and includes breakfast. Snow play is state-of-the-art here, with snowscoots, snowbikes, and snowsliding toys; tubing; and the Zorb, a 9.5-foot clear plastic sphere that rolls downhill with a passenger inside. At night, on weekends, and on holidays, Polaris Park is an illuminated snow playground with music. The sunny Summit Deck on the top of Mount Pluto is lively and fun for casual lunches and snacks.

Ponderosa Ranch, on the east end of Incline Village on Highway 28; (775) 831–0691. The original set used to film the TV show Bonanza. An elaborate Western town and theme park, with haywagon breakfasts, shooting gallery, museum, gold panning, Hossburgers, ice cream parlor. If the kids are younger than twelve or so, this is a must.

Royal Gorge, near Donner Summit, off Highway 80 and Old Highway 40; (800) 500–3817; www.royalgorge.com. In the Sierra National Forest, the largest Nordic ski area in the nation, voted the best in North America. Spend the day on the trails, or ski to the lodge and stay overnight. Wrapped in fur robes, you can also be ferried in a horse-drawn sleigh to the European-style wilderness lodge, built in the 1930s. Thirty-five private rooms, hearty meals, gourmet dinner by candlelight, ski clinics. Warming huts with snacks available are scattered generously throughout the trail network.

Tahoe Donner Ski Area, 897 Donner Pass Road, Truckee; (530) 587–9484. A small, friendly, reasonably priced Nordic ski resort with a day lodge, restaurant, and lots of flat meadow trails for beginners.

Special Events

June. Gigantic Arts and Crafts Fair at Kings Beach; (530) 546–2935. Truckee Tahoe Air Show; (530) 587–1119.

July. North Lake Tahoe Symphony Association Summer Music Series; (775) 832–1606. Sunday-afternoon concerts.

July–August. Music and Shakespeare at Sand Harbor; (530) 583–9048. Beautiful outdoor amphitheater.

October. Pray for Snow Party (Tahoe Biltmore) and Native American Snow Dance (Incline Village); (800) GO–TAHOE. One hundred performances by four tribes of traditional, jingle, and snowshoe dances; drums, food, crafts.

Other Recommended Restaurants and Lodgings

Incline Village

Club Tahoe Resort, 914 Northwood Boulevard; (800) 527–5154. Two-bedroom town houses sleeping six; simple decor, fireplaces, fully equipped kitchens, laundry, linens, tennis, racquetball, pool, sauna, ski shuttles.

Inn at Incline, 1003 Tahoe Boulevard; (775) 444–6758. Motel units in a forest setting; indoor pool, sauna, spa. Continental breakfast, some kitchens.

Lone Eagle Grille, 111 Country Club Drive; (775) 832–3250. The flagship restaurant at the Hyatt Regency, right on the beach with stunning lake views; warm and cozy in the lounge in the wintertime, sunny and breezy outdoors on the terrace, fresh and beautiful in the dining room.

Kings Beach

Steamer's Beachside Bar and Oven, 8290 North Lake Boulevard; (530) 546–2218. One of the most popular pizza restaurants on the north shore, with an outdoor patio on the beach. Try the calzone!

Soda Springs

Rainbow Lodge, P.O. Box 1100, Soda Springs 95728, off Highway 80 at Rainbow Road exit; (530) 426–3661. Historic thirty-room hotel, restaurant, bar. Like an old chalet in the Alps, beside a rushing bend in the Truckee River. Small, country-style inn rooms are fresh with comforters and brass beds. Cross-country ski from here right onto Royal Gorge trails.

Tahoe Vista

Le Petit Pier, 7238 North Lake Boulevard; (530) 546–4464. In the French country tradition; a small, elegant place on the lake with a world-class wine list and nouvelle cuisine. Sundown cocktails in the lakeside bar.

Truckee

Donner Lake Village Resort, 15695 Donner Pass Road, #101; (800) 621–6664. Lodgettes, studios, and one- and two-bedroom condos on the lake; private beach, water-toy rental.

Truckee Tahoe Inn, 11331 Highway 267 between Truckee and Northstar; (530) 587–4525; www.bestwesterntahoe.com. Reasonably priced, newish motel with simple, fresh rooms and suites with sofa beds; complimentary continental breakfast, sauna, and spa. Ask about ski packages and off-season rates.

For More Information

BRAT Resort Properties, 120 Country Club Drive, Incline Village, NV 89452; (888) 266–3612; www.bratresort.com. Rental condos and houses, with ski and vacation packages.

Incline Village Visitors Bureau, 969 Tahoe Boulevard, Incline Village, NV 89451; (775) 832–1606; www.gotahoe.com.

Tahoe North Visitors and Convention Bureau, P. O. Box 1757, Tahoe City, CA 96145; (530) 583–3494 or (888) 434–1262; www.tahoe-4-u.com.

Truckee Donner Chamber of Commerce, 12036 Donner Pass Road, Truckee, CA 96161; (530) 584–2757; www.truckee.com.

Vacation Station, P.O. Box 7180, Incline Village, NV 89452; (775) 831–3664. Homes and condos to rent.

ESCAPES
FARTHER AFIELD

Mountain Majesty, Rivers, Lakes, Timberlands

2 Nights

One in a chain of Cascade Range volcanoes stretching from northern California to southwestern Canada, Mount Shasta is a frosty, 14,162-foot presence that seems to take up half the sky in Siskiyou County. Mist-shrouded glacial peaks and white rivers of ice are visible for hundreds of miles. Mount Shasta presides over vast timberlands and wilderness areas freshened with lakes, rivers, and streams, offering a paradise for hikers, anglers, summer- and winter-sports enthusiasts, and just plain lovers of high country scenery.

☐ Lakeside walks

☐ High country views

☐ Waterfowl, waterfalls, wilderness

☐ Houseboating and fishing

☐ Cavernous pursuits

On a weekend in the Shasta area, you may fall under the magic spell of the mountain and return again to see it streaked with lightning in a summer thunderstorm or transformed into a frozen white wave in winter.

Your route along Highway 5 follows the mighty Sacramento River—wide, cool, and green; fringed with overhanging trees; plied by fishing boats and water-skiers.

Day 1 / Morning

From San Francisco it's 325 miles to Redding. Take Highway 80, connecting with Highway 505 above Vacaville; then take Highway 5 north to Redding. Bordering the valley are the crumpled eastern foothills of the Coast Range and the distant peaks of the Sierra Nevada. Defunct volcanoes called the **Sutter Buttes** rise dramatically above the valley floor. Near Redding the valley begins to roll, and the peaks of the Klamath Mountains and the Cascades emerge in the distant north and east. The Sierra Nevada ends; the Cascades begin.

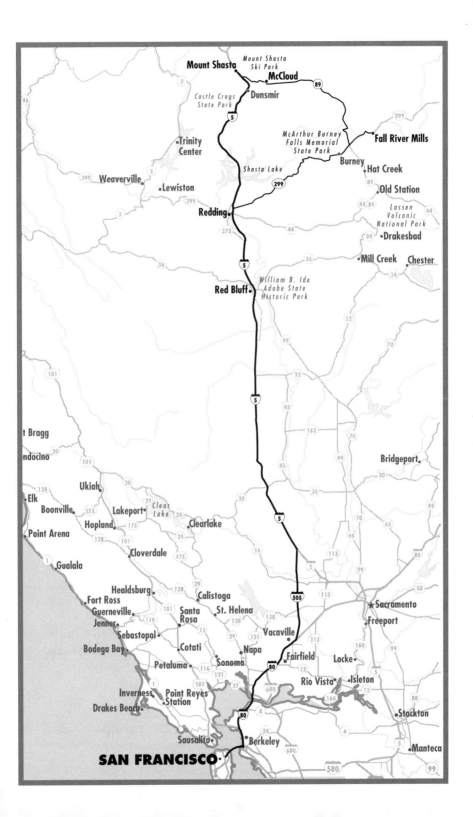

LUNCH: Take the Central Redding/Highway 99 exit into town, turning left on Market for half a block to **Cheesecakes Unlimited,** 1334 Market Street, Redding (530–244–6670). Super croissant sandwiches, pita bread concoctions, and that *cheesecake.*

For a refreshing, easy walk in Redding, drive north on Market Street to Riverside Drive on the south side of the Sacramento River, then go west to the parking lot, where the **Sacramento River Trail** begins; (800) 874–7562. A tree-shaded, 7.7-mile path along the riverbanks and through a residential area, the trail continues to Caldwell Park, with interpretive signs and benches along the way.

In three or four hours, rafters and canoers float south on the Sacramento River from Redding to Anderson River Park. Beneath overhanging sycamores, cottonwoods, oaks, and willows, you slide quietly along or stop to fish. Raft-rental companies pick you up at the park and shuttle you back to Redding.

Afternoon

It's 23 miles beyond Redding on Highway 5 north to **Shasta Lake,** one of the best fishing lakes in California, fed by the Sacramento, McCloud, Pit, and Squaw Rivers. At an elevation of 1,000 feet, surface water reaches eighty degrees in the summer, perfect for houseboating and waterskiing.

Take the Shasta Caverns Road exit, driving 2 miles to **Lake Shasta Caverns** (530–238–2341), a dramatic natural wonder. The tour includes a fifteen-minute boat ride across the lake to a wooded island, where groups of about twenty people are guided into a series of giant chambers, up and down hundreds of stone steps. The atmosphere is delightfully spooky, damp, and drippy—a constant fifty-eight degrees, refreshing in summer, when outside temperatures can reach more than one hundred degrees. Multicolored columns, 20-foot-high stone draperies, stalactites and stalagmites, brilliant crystals, and unusual limestone and marble formations are subtly lighted and fascinating.

It's 38 miles from the caverns to the town of **Mount Shasta,** in the shadow of the mountain and almost completely surrounded by the **Shasta National Forest.** Motels line the road into the town, an overnight stopping point for travelers on their way to the Northwest.

DINNER: Mount Shasta Resort, 1000 Siskiyou Lake Boulevard, Mount Shasta; (530) 926–3030 or (800) 958–3363; www.mountshasta resort.com. A popular, comfortable restaurant with great views of Mount

Shasta. Wide variety of hearty American fare, steaks, pasta, grilled chicken, and fish. Book ahead for weekends and holidays.

LODGING: Mount Shasta Resort. In a pretty wooded setting near walking trails and lakes. Settle into a beautiful one- or two-bedroom chalet with fireplace, sofa bed, fully equipped kitchen, spacious living room, and deck. The golf course here is spectacular and challenging; it's popular, so call ahead for a tee time. There are tennis courts, an outdoor dining deck at the clubhouse, and a comfortable restaurant with views of the mountains, plus a snack bar with outdoor tables. Ask about ski and golf packages.

Day 2 / Morning

BREAKFAST: Lily's, 1013 South Mount Shasta Boulevard, Mount Shasta; (530) 926–3372. Hearty all-American breakfasts and gourmet specialties like polenta fritters and giant omelettes. At lunch and dinner, California cuisine, Asian specialties, and even enchiladas.

Off Siskiyou Lake Boulevard are the **Sisson Museum** and **Mount Shasta Fish Hatchery,** 1 North Old Stage Road (530–926–5508), with displays of the history, geology, and climate of the mountain. Walk around to see the hatching and rearing ponds.

Drive 3 miles south on Stage Road to **Lake Siskiyou,** surrounded by dazzling mountainscapes and a tree-lined shore. **Lake Siskiyou Camp-Resort,** 4239 West Barr Road, Mount Shasta (530–926–2618 or 888–926–2618; www.lakesis.com), is one of the prettiest multiuse camping and RV facilities in California. You can even rent a fully equipped trailer for use on-site. Walk around the 430-acre lake, lounge on the beach and swim, launch a boat, or rent water toys, kayaks, canoes, pedalboats, sailboats, and fishing equipment. A store, snack bar, outdoor movies, and playground are also found here.

To see one of the clearest, prettiest lakes in the Sierras and take an easy walk or a strenuous hike, continue on West Barr Road, and go left on Castle Lake Road to the parking area for **Castle Lake;** (530) 926–4511. This is one of the most easily accessible alpine lakes in northern California. The parking lot is within a few yards of the lakeshore, and within a few minutes' easy stroll you can be in an idyllic, seemingly isolated wilderness setting. Walk in either direction along the lakeshore through the forest, putter around in the creek, fish in the lake, launch your skiff or kayaks, have a picnic, or set up your tent. The water here is pure and clear, and the fishing and (chilly) swimming are great. For a 3-mile, round-trip, moderately strenuous hike, take the trail to the left of the lake near the stream, along the lakeside, and up to 5,900 feet. Bear to the right up another 100 feet to **Heart Lake,** a small gem that warms up in summer. One of the best photo ops of Mount Shasta is on Castle Lake Road, about 0.5 mile before the parking lot. The road is plowed all winter for ice fishing. For maps and information on area trails and hiking Mount Shasta, go to **Fifth Season,** North Mount Shasta Boulevard (530–926–3606), or **Shasta Mountain Guides,** 1938 Hill Road (530–926–3117).

LUNCH: Michael's, 313 North Mount Shasta Boulevard, Mount Shasta; (530) 926–5288. Italian specialties and Continental dishes, homemade pasta, soups, sandwiches, burgers. Try the deep-fried zucchini or the teriyaki turkey sandwich. Lunch and dinner.

Afternoon

From Mount Shasta take Highway 89 east around the base of the mountain into the **Shasta National Forest** and **McCloud River Valley.** Two miles south at the first exit is **Mount Shasta Board and Ski Park** (530–926–8610), with ski runs at 5,000 feet. Here you'll find downhill and cross-country skiing; a day lodge, restaurant, and ski school; and equipment rental and night skiing. Among the advantages of skiing here are the reasonable cost, the lack of lift lines and crowds, and a carefree drive up on Highway 5, which is seldom encumbered with enough snow to require chains. In summer, take the lift up to the mountaintop, hike around, picnic, and take the lift back down, or bring your mountain bikes up on the lift (you can rent them here) and pedal the excellent trails, ending up back at the lodge. Wildflowers in the spring and summer and fall colors are truly spectacular. There are frequent concerts and festivals in the beautiful outdoor amphitheater, and you can buy hot food to eat here on the sunny deck, or cold picnic fare to carry away. A 24-foot, man-made climbing tower is safe for all ages and abilities, and there is also a free multimedia exhibit about the formation of Mount Shasta.

For more cross-country ski trails, watch for **Bunny Flat, Sand Flat,** and **Panther Meadows** off Highway 89. Marked trails for beginners and intermediates are maintained by the USDA Forest Service (530–926–4511 or 530–926–3781). Rest rooms and parking are available only at Bunny Flat, which is also a snow-play area.

Seventeen miles farther on Highway 89, at Fowlers Campground, the

McCloud River Falls is a side trip well worth taking. Accessible by car, the three falls on a 2-mile stretch of river plunge into deep pools perfect for swimming. The third cascade has picnic tables above and a ladder that divers use to jump into the pool.

It's about an hour's drive over 4,000-foot Dead Horse Summit to **McArthur-Burney Falls State Park** and **Lake Britton** (530–335–2777). The big attraction here is two million gallons of water a day tumbling over a misty, fern-draped, 129-foot cliff. Take the 1.5-mile hike down into a forest fairyland gorge where wild tiger lily, maple, dogwood, black oak, and pine decorate the streamside; the loud rush of the falls and the stream intensifies the experience. It takes about a half hour for the fit and fast, an hour for amblers and photographers, and two hours for waders, anglers, and walkers who take offshoot trails. Good trout fishing can be had in the deep pool at the foot of the falls and in the 2-mile stream above and below.

Fund 9-mile-long Lake Britton are camping and RV sites, not too private. Accessible by boat (rentals here), with a terrific swimming hole at its foot, **Clark Creek Falls** is a jet of frigid water crashing into the lake. Crappie, bass, and catfish bite all season; some of the best fishing is downstream from the lake at the outlet of Pit River.

Head back to McCloud, on Highway 89.

DINNER: McCloud Guest House, 606 West Colombero Drive, McCloud; (530) 964–3160. In the old-fashioned dining room of a glorious 1907 Victorian mansion, yummy dinners of steak, chicken, fresh fish, and homemade pasta in the American tradition are served. Upstairs, five nice guest rooms with antiques and four-poster beds.

LODGING: McCloud Hotel, 408 Main Street, McCloud 96057; (530) 964–2822 or (800) 964–2823. Fourteen spacious rooms and suites, some with Jacuzzi tubs and four-poster beds, all delightfully decorated with antiques; queen or twin beds. A place to linger by the fireplace in a big armchair, the lobby is cozy and outfitted with comfy furnishings, games, and books. Arrive in a pre–World War II car, and you get a discount! Expanded continental breakfast and afternoon tea.

For dinner, amble over to one of two dance halls in town to join in the square dancing; open May to September.

Day 3 / Morning

BREAKFAST: At the McCloud Hotel.

Just north of Highway 89 on Highway 299, Fall River Mills is head-quarters for fishing and hiking in the northern Lassen River valleys. There is golf to be had at the **Fall River Valley Golf Course,** west of town on Highway 299 (530–336–5555). Open May through October, the **Fort Crook Museum,** in town (530–336–5110), has exhibits of pioneer history, Indian artifacts, and several historical buildings.

Take Highway 299 west to Highway 5 and south to Red Bluff.

LUNCH: **Raging Fork Riverfront Grille,** 500 Riverside Way near Highway 5, Red Bluff; (530) 529–9453. A casual place with a deck on the river; steaks, chicken, pasta, fish, sandwiches, burgers, soups, and daily specials.

Afternoon

Just north of Red Bluff is a lovely spot on the river, **Ide Adobe State Park,** 3040 Adobe Road (530–527–5927), cool and shady, with giant oaks, lawns, picnic tables, and historical displays. You can fish here, but swimming in the fast current is not advisable.

Head south to the Bay Area.

There's More

Backpacking. The Shasta-Trinity National Forest offers exceptional back-packing. The Pacific Crest Trail can be accessed west of Mount Shasta at Parks Creek, South Fork Road, Whalen Road, and at Castle Crags State Park. Trailheads up the east side of Mount Shasta offer challenging hikes. Wilderness permits and maps are available at Mount Shasta Ranger District, 204 West Alma Street, Mount Shasta; (530) 926–3606.

Castle Crags State Park, 6 miles south of Dunsmuir off I–5; (530) 235–2684. A 6,000-foot granite fortress of giant pillars and monster boulders; good trout fishing in several streams; 2 miles of the Sacramento River; swimming, hiking, rock climbing. Get maps at the park office and amble up the sun-dappled Indian Creek Nature Trail, a 1-mile loop. The Vista Point loop is 5 view-filled miles. The Crags Trail to Castle Dome is 5.5 strenuous miles up and into the Castle Crags Wilderness; the Pacific Crest Trail is accessible from here.

Golf. Lake Shastina Golf Resort, 5925 Country Club Drive, Weed; (916) 938–3201.

Mount Shasta Resort Golf Course, 1000 Siskiyou Lake Boulevard, Mount Shasta; (530) 926–3052. Eighteen spectacular holes with mountain views.

Houseboats. With a shoreline of 365 miles, Shasta is very popular for houseboating. Boats range from 15 to 56 feet long and sleep four to twelve people; they're easy to navigate and may include air-conditioning, TV, and washers and dryers. Rentals at twelve houseboat marinas cost $1,000 per week and up.

Antlers Resort and Marina, P.O. Box 140, Lakehead 96051; (916) 238–2553. Houseboat rentals, cabins, and water-sports equipment.

Bridge Bay Resort, 12 miles north of Redding, Bridge Bay exit off Highway 5, 10300 Bridge Bay Road, Redding; (530) 275–3021 or (800) 752–9669; www.sevencrown.com. Under a big bridge over the lake, a full-service marina with houseboat rentals, cabins, ski boats, patio boats, personal watercraft, and a clean, simple motel with a swimming pool and some kitchens—a great headquarters for plying the lake or trying out a houseboat. The houseboat rental company, Seven Crown Resorts, is one of the largest and oldest of its kind. They have rental operations also at Digger Bay on Shasta, and in the California Delta and other states.

Jones Valley Resort, 22300 Jones Valley Marina Drive, on the Pit River arm of Lake Shasta; (916) 275–7950; www.houseboats.com. Specializes in luxury houseboats with gourmet galleys, fancy entertainment systems, and flying bridges.

Lassen Volcanic National Park. A half hour east of Redding and Red Bluff, Lasser has three park entrances (main park headquarters at 38050 Highway 36, just east of Mineral; 530–595–4444). On a 35-mile drive over the 8,000-foot summit, you can see snow-covered peaks and crystalline lakes, woodlands, meadows, streams, and the largest "plug dome" volcano in the world. Short walks to hot springs, boiling mudpots, ancient lava flows, and sulfury steam vents; camping, hiking on 17 miles of the Pacific Crest Trail, nonpowered boating, cross-country skiing, and snowshoeing. Near the north entrance, Manzanita Lake is a postcard-perfect, evergreen-surrounded lake with dazzling views of the mountain. Easy 1.5-mile hike around the lake; campsites are pretty and private. Near the southwest park entrance, Bumpass Hell is the most active thermal area.

Living Memorial Sculpture Garden, between the towns of Mount Shasta and McCloud on Highway 97, 0.25 mile north of County Road A12. Vietnam vet and local artist Dennis Smith honors veterans with a dramatic and touching bronze tableau.

McCloud Railway Shasta Sunset Dinner Train; (800) 733–2141; www. mctrain.com. Excellent, elegant dinners in restored vintage dining cars pulled by a 2,000-horsepower locomotive through spectacular scenery below Mount Shasta, Castle Crags, and the Trinity Alps.

Mossbrae Falls, off Highway 5. Take the Dunsmuir Avenue exit; go to Scarlett Way down the hill and over the river and the railroad tracks. A forty-minute easy walk along the river brings you to magical 70-foot-high falls.

Railroading. The Blue Goose, P.O. Box 660, Yreka 96097; (916) 842–4146. A circa-1910 train hauling lumber and freight daily between Yreka and Montague, a 7-mile trip. Climbing on board the steamer at 10:00 A.M., you'll cruise past cattle ranches, sawmills, and lovely landscape. The train may be attacked by "bandits" as it approaches the historic town of Montague. There's an hour or so to picnic on the village green or take a horse-drawn tour; then it's back to Yreka.

Shasta Dam, off Highway 5 just north of Redding, on Shasta Dam Boulevard (a half-hour drive on summer weekdays, longer on weekends); (530) 275–4463. Walk out on the rim of the second-tallest concrete dam in the United States. Take a look at historic photos and watch a short film in the visitors center. The guided tour into the dam involves an elevator ride that kids younger than about age eight may find scary.

Sweetbriar Falls, 8 miles south of Dunsmuir. Take the Sweetbriar exit off Highway 5. Park on the west side of the railroad tracks and walk across the bridge to see feathery falls surrounded by ferns and trees. Photos are best in late morning.

Special Events

May. Old Time Fiddler's Jamboree and Art Fair, Mount Shasta; (800) 874–7582.

June. Heritage Days at McArthur-Burney Falls State Park; (530) 335–

2777. Large crowds turn out for Native American dancers, musicians, pioneer crafts, square dancing, fiddlers.

Dunsmuir Railroad Days; (530) 235–2177. Since 1940 a celebration of historic railroad days; parade, barbecue, jazz festival.

Sacramento River Jazz Festival, Dunsmuir; (530) 235–2721. Great day on the green in Dunsmuir City Park.

July. McCloud Lumberjack Fiesta; (530) 964–2520. Fishing tournaments, parade, barbecue, entertainment, lumberjack show.

Redding Air Show; (530) 222–1610.

Other Recommended Restaurants and Lodgings

Dunsmuir

Railroad Park Resort, 100 Railroad Park Road; (530) 235–4440. Restaurant and motel in antique railroad cars; pool, spa. Good jumping-off point for exploring and hiking in Castle Crags. Also, RV park, campground, cabins.

Mount Shasta

Edson House, 203 Birch Street; (530) 926–1754. On a secluded knoll with panoramas of the mountain and Castle Crags, a large 1904 farm home. Some rooms have fireplaces, Jacuzzis, kitchenettes, sitting areas.

Mount Shasta KOA Campground, 900 North Mount Shasta Boulevard; (530) 926–4029. A grassy, gardeny place for RVs and tents; animal corrals, camping cabins, store, pool, playground.

Mount Shasta Ranch, 1008 W. A. Barr Road, five minutes from Lake Siskiyou; (530) 926–3870; www.travelassist.com/reg/ca121s.html. In a beautiful country setting, a B&B with spacious rooms and suites in a circa-1920 ranch house, cottages, and a carriage house; gigantic common living room and game room, full breakfast. Children are quite welcome in the carriage house.

Strawberry Valley Inn, 1142 South Mount Shasta Boulevard; (530) 926–2052. Lovely landscaped grounds and shade trees make this reasonably priced motel a winner; some rooms have two beds, and there are two-room suites. A huge breakfast buffet is served on a sunny patio or by the fireplace.

Tree House Best Western, 111 Morgan Way, at Highway 5 and Lake Street; (530) 926–3101. Large, nicely landscaped motel; large heated indoor pool; casual restaurant.

Redding

Hilltop Inn, 2300 Hilltop Drive; (800) 221–6100. A very nice motel with spacious rooms, swimming and wading pools, complimentary continental breakfast, and two reasonably priced restaurants.

Jack's Grill, 1743 California Street; (530) 241–9705. In a casual, noisy, hometown atmosphere. Sixteen-ounce steaks, deep-fried prawns, big plates of good old American food; dinner only.

Lava Creek Lodge, 1 Island Road, 12 miles north of Highway 299, east of Redding; (530) 336–6288. Small, rustic lodge with cabins in a wooded setting on a lovely piece of the Fall River, adjacent to Ahjumawi Lava Springs State Park. The lodge will arrange fly-fishing instruction for you and/or rent boats and gear; or bring your own. Hearty American fare in the dining room.

For More Information

Fall River Valley Chamber of Commerce, P.O. Box 475, Fall River Mills, CA 96056; (530) 336–5840.

Mount Shasta Visitors Pavilion, 2 blocks east of the Highway 5 central exit at Lake and Pine Streets; (800) 926–4865.

Redding Convention and Visitors Bureau, 7777 Auditorium Drive, Redding, CA 96001; (800) 874–7562.

Shasta Cascade Wonderland Association, 1619 Highway 273, Anderson, CA 96007; (530) 365–7500 or (800) 474–2782, www.shastacascade.org.

State park camping and RV site reservations: (800) 444–7275.

Mammoth Lakes 2

Multisports Mecca in the High Eastern Sierra

3 Nights

Owing its existence to the pristine beauty of the Eastern Sierra, Mammoth Lakes found its niche over the years, in catering to the comforts of the outdoor-sports set. After the boom-and-bust mining days, people exploring Mammoth found a haven for fishing, camping, hiking, mountaineering, and horseback riding. By the 1920s and 1930s, skiers were pulling off Highway 395 and being propelled up McGee Mountain, Deadman Summit, and Conway Summit, powered by Ford Model A truck motors. These rope tows gave skiers the adrenaline rush of alpine skiing.

☐ Winter skiing and snowshoeing

☐ High-country lodge

☐ Wilderness hiking

☐ Alpine lakes

☐ Fishing

☐ Golfing

One of these dedicated rope-tow operators was Dave McCoy, who obtained the rights from the Forest Service to build a permanent rope tow on Mammoth Mountain. In 1955, he opened Chair 1 with 250 skiers. Now Mammoth Mountain has twenty-nine lifts and a gondola that whisks skiers to the 11,053-foot summit. After the snow melts, lifts and gondola reopen for mountain bikers, hikers, and sightseers.

Enjoy a different sport every day at Mammoth. After a day of hiking, biking, fishing, rock climbing and golfing, rest up at a high-country lodge, modeled after the stone-and-timber park lodges of the early 1900s. The shortest route to the action at Mammoth Lakes is through Yosemite National Park via Highway 120.

Day 1 / Morning

Begin the five-and-half-hour trip in the early morning to avoid commuter

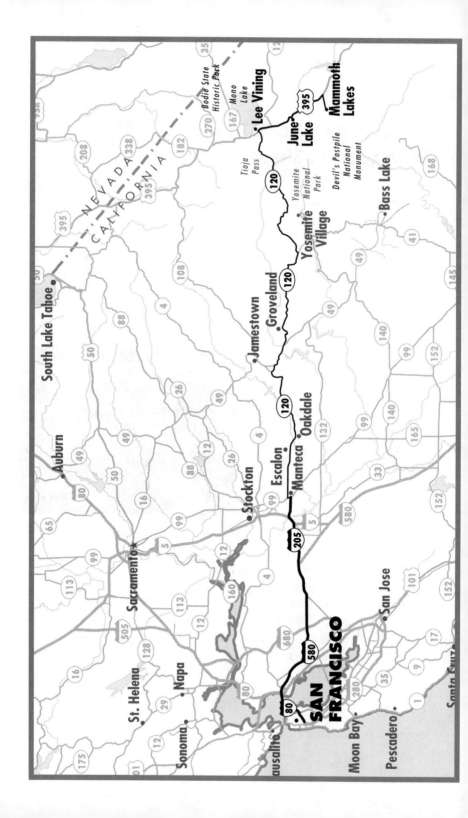

traffic, heading east from San Francisco across the Oakland Bay Bridge. Take Highway 580 to 205 east to 5 north to 120 east. Highway 120 is a two-lane country road through the farming towns of Manteca, Escalon, and Oakdale. Stop in Groveland and pick up food for a picnic lunch, as the grocery store in Yosemite has limited supplies. Enter Yosemite National Park where 120 takes you over the Sierra crest on Tioga Pass through the beautiful Yosemite high country. You pass Tuolumne Meadows, mountain-size granite domes, and the Olmstead Point overlook.

LUNCH: Enjoy a lakeside picnic at deep blue Tenaya Lake.

Afternoon

Continue on 120 until you reach Highway 395, then head south for 25 miles and exit at **Mammoth Lakes,** Highway 203. (From November to May, when Tioga Pass closes, take Interstate 80 or Interstate 50 to Highway 395 south to the Mammoth Lakes exit. It's about 320 miles.) Turn right on Highway 203 and left at Meridian Boulevard where in a few miles an impressive lodge rises at the end of the road. As a result of $100 million invested in the town in the last four years, this multisport mecca has gained four- and five-star lodging.

After settling in at Juniper Springs Lodge, adjust to the high altitude by taking a stroll along the paved path behind the lodge. You pass the Valentine Reserve, a Jeffrey Pine forest, and cross a footbridge. The path then winds through Snowcreek Meadow along a sparkling creek before rejoining the paved path that leads to **Mammoth Creek Park** (on Old Mammoth Road), the site of an evening farmers market. **Mammoth Museum & Historical Preserve** (off Old Mammoth Road, 5489 Sherwin Creek Road; 760–934–6918), housed in a handcrafted log cabin, is steps from the path.

Evening

DINNER: Settle into a wooden booth at **The Stove** (644 Old Mammoth Road, Mammoth Lakes; 760–934–2821) a short walk up the road. Prime rib, chicken potpie, salads, whatever you order it will be a generous portion. Finish with a slice of homemade lemon meringue pie.

After dinner you may wish to continue on the trail as it swings out to a meadow overlooking the Owens Mountain Range and the Long Valley Caldera.

LODGING: Against the regal backdrop of the Sherwin Mountains and Mammoth Mountain, **Juniper Springs Lodge** (4000 Meridian Boulevard, Mammoth Lakes; 760–924–1102 or 800–626–6684) fulfills what one hopes to find in such a setting. From the two-story hearthroom, you look out onto the heated patio, fire pit, outdoor pool, whirlpool spas, and the forested slopes of the Sherwins. A one-bedroom condominium suite is furnished with an overstuffed sofa and chair in rich natural tones, and has a full-sized kitchen, a dining area, a living room, and a furnished deck. As a full-service hotel, the lodge offers bell staff assistance, free ski/snowboard valet service, daily housekeeping, underground parking, and concierge service. The staff can get you set up at Sierra Star Golf Course and orient you to Mammoth's extensive network of hiking and biking trails.

Day 2 / Morning

BREAKFAST: Have breakfast in your condominium suite, or at **Talons** in Little Eagle Restaurant and Bar, Mammoth Mountain's on-hill dining establishment at Juniper Springs. After breakfast, it's time to tee-up at Mammoth's only eighteen-hole golf course.

Cal Olson, one of California's most notable golf-course architects, incorporated lush, tree-lined fairways, well-trapped greens and numerous lakes, ponds, waterfalls and streams in the **Sierra Star Golf Course and Clubhouse** (off Meridian Boulevard; 2001 Sierra Star Parkway; 760–924–4653). The five tee locations at each hole make the course challenging for the experienced golfer and enjoyable for the novice. Each hole offers a unique view of the surrounding Jeffrey pine and white fir trees.

If you brought hiking boots rather than golf clubs, you'll find several trailheads in the glacial lakes above town. Stop at Von's in Mammoth Lakes and buy sandwiches for a picnic lunch. Drive up Lake Mary Road, passing Twin Lakes, Lake Mary, Lake Mamie, Twin Falls, and Horseshoe Lake. Take the Lake George turnoff and park. Take the Crystal Lake Trailhead from the parking lot and hike uphill through Jeffery pine and Juniper pine to Crystal Lake, or for a longer trip, take the turnoff to Mammoth Crest.

For an easier hike on level terrain, hike out to Mammoth Rock. The trailhead is off Old Mammoth Road. As you come down Lake Mary Road from the Lakes Basin, turn right onto Old Mammoth Road and in less than a mile, look on your right for a small parking area in the bend of a sharp turn. The trail begins here.

Skiers at Mammoth Mountain.

LUNCH: Have lunch at the Sierra Star Golf Course Clubhouse overlooking the fairway or enjoy a picnic lunch on the beach at Crystal Lake or at Mammoth Rock.

Afternoon

Many activities begin at **Mammoth Mountain Ski Area** (Highway 203). From Juniper Springs Lodge, drive down Meridian Boulevard to the signal at Minaret Road, turn left and continue three miles. In summer and early fall, the Mammoth Mountain Ski Area is transformed into the **Mammoth Mountain Bike Park** with more than 80 miles of single-track, access to the 11,053-foot summit, and the black-diamond Kamikaze Downhill. But the trails accommodate all abilities: You can even hitch a ride on the bike shuttle at the Village at Mammoth and enjoy another downhill ride. Ask at the rental deck about guided rides, skills clinics, and special ticket/rental packages.

Biking isn't your only option. The **Panorama Gondola** at Panorama Station, directly across from the Main Lodge, whisks you to Mammoth's summit. Disembark at the summit and peer down Mammoth's legendary steeps. Mammoth Mountain was formed 200,000 years ago as the result of a series of volcanic eruptions, the most recent of which occurred 50,000 years ago. The views of the Ritter Range, Inyo Craters and Domes, and the Long Valley Caldera are spectacular. Be prepared for cooler air. Follow the hiking trail down from the summit or ride back down on the gondola.

Trailheads for wilderness hiking are located off the parking lots at Agnew Meadow and Red's Meadow. During the summer between 7:30 A.M. and 5:30 P.M. a shuttle departs from Mammoth Mountain Ski Area every half hour, talking you down to Red's Meadow. The geologic wonder of **Devils Postpile** and the misty arch over **Rainbow Falls** are both short hikes from shuttle stops. Other easy hikes include the self-guided nature trail at Sotcher Lake and the wildflower walk at **Agnew Meadow.** If you are geared up for an all-day hike, Agnew Meadow leads right into the **Ansel Adams Wilderness** where you can hike into the backcountry along the San Joaquin River.

DINNER: Lakefront Restaurant (Old Mary Road, at Tamarack Lodge, Mammoth Lakes; 760–934–3534) fronts on Twin Lakes and has been serving guests since 1924. Look for historical photos: cutting ice blocks from Twin Lakes before the spring thaw; a man driving a dogsled; a Tamarack caretaker digging out a cabin during a long winter; and young Dave and Roma McCoy celebrating Easter on skis. The Lakefront Restaurant caught the attention of *Bon Appétit* for its California-French cuisine. You can sample local and regional ingredients in such dishes as smoked trout, wild mushroom strudel, and pan-seared veal tenderloin and sea scallops. The rack of lamb is oven-roasted with thyme and finished with Merlot jus, tomato, and black niçoise olive tapenade. Also recommended is the wild blueberry tart.

LODGING: Condominium suite at Juniper Springs Lodge.

Day 3 / Morning

BREAKFAST: Have breakfast in your condominium suite, or at Talons, the restaurant in the adjacent Little Eagle base lodge.

Stop at Von's in Mammoth Lakes and stock up on sandwiches and supplies for a picnic lunch. Take Meridian Boulevard to Highway 203, turn right and travel on U.S. 395 north 55 miles. After the Conway Summit watch for the turnoff to **Bodie State Historic Park** (760–647–6445). Turn right and follow the partially paved road 13 miles to the entrance. Pay the admission and receive a town map. Join a guided tour so you gain access to the Bodie jail, and hear the legends and lore surrounding this mining town, which once sustained a population of 10,000.

LUNCH: Have a picnic lunch at the picnic area. Or stop by **Mono Inn Restaurant** (Highway 395, Lee Vining; 760–647–6581), which serves brunch, lunch, and dinner from May 1 through early fall. Mono Inn is known for its Sunday brunch and great views of Mono Lake. Look for the restaurant on your left, before the Mono Lake Visitors Center.

Afternoon

Take U.S. 395 south to Mono Lake to the **Mono Lake Visitors Center,** 51481 Highway 395, Lee Vining; (760) 647–6331. An ancient inland sea with spectacular "tufa towers," Mono Lake is a rich source of marine life for millions of migrating birds. The Mono Lake Paiute inhabited the area for roughly 1,000 to 1,500 years. You can hike out to the South Tufa area, from the parking lot located 5 miles south of the visitors center off U.S. 395. Turn right (east) and drive another 5 miles on Highway 120. Tufa line the shores and beach area.

Amid the wealth of adventures, it's difficult to top soaking outdoors in a natural hot spring. Resting in a hot pool after a hard hike is the rarest of outdoor pleasures. To reach **Hot Creek Geological Site** take Highway 395 south to Hot Creek Hatchery Road. Park at the farthest parking lot, where you'll find changing rooms and a trail leading to two bubbling pools and steaming fumeroles. Head for the second pool which has a shallow, sandy bottom.

DINNER: Located just 20 miles north of Mammoth on Highway 395, June Lake is tucked away in a protected nook of the Sierra. The 15-mile loop from the highway blazes in golden yellow aspens in the fall. The **Eagle's Landing Restaurant** (at Double Eagle Resort and Spa, P.O. Box 736, June Lake 93529; 760–648–7004) offers mountain and waterfall views from every seat in the restaurant. During the summer, you may want to dine outdoors on the deck. The menu features lemon–herb rotisserie-roasted chicken, halibut, ribs, steaks, plus nightly chef's specials and a variety of fresh specialty salads. Open daily for breakfast, lunch, and dinner.

LODGING: A condominium suite at Juniper Springs Lodge.

Day 4 / Morning

BREAKFAST: The next morning, before returning to the Bay Area, stop for breakfast and provisions at **Paul Schat's Bakery,** 3305 Main Street, Mammoth Lakes; (760) 934–6055. At the counter you can pick up pizza tarts and croissant sandwiches and if you want a hearty breakfast, have a seat in the dining room. The Dutch baby pancake is a toothsome farewell to Mammoth.

There's More

Fly fishing. Mammoth is a fishing enthusiast's haven, with crystal-clear lakes and streams teeming with trout, providing ideal conditions for fly-fishing. Orvis Mammoth Lakes School (800–MAMMOTH), the country's premier fly-fishing school, provides instruction and retail operations. Orvis instruction focuses on casting techniques, essential knots, stream entomology, fly selection, water reading, and how to play, land, and safely release fish. Instructors have the knowledge and on-water experience to turn novices into accomplished fly-fishers. Whether stalking the legendary golden trout in the High Sierra or fishing the challenging Owens River, the Orvis Mammoth Lakes School provides the skills necessary to enjoy the fly-fishing experience and, of course, catch fish. Classes are in session June through October, with discounted lodging for Orvis students at Juniper Springs Lodge.

Shopping. In December 2002, Mammoth gained a new center of town, the Village at Mammoth. The pedestrian lanes hum with people taking in the distinctive atmosphere of cafes, boutiques, and restaurants. Browse the other shops scattered around town.

Mammoth Gallery, 452 Old Mammoth Road in the Sierra Center Mall; (760) 934–3239. Browse among a large selection of Nina Kelley watercolors, Galen Rowell photography, and historic ski photographs. Also for sale: sun-catcher crystals.

Mammoth Premium Outlets, 3393 Main Street; (760) 934–9771; www. PremiumOutlets.com. Discount goods from Coach, Polo Ralph Lauren, Bass, Van Heusen, and others.

Mammoth Sporting Goods, Old Mammoth Road, at Meridian Boulevard in the Sierra Center Mall; (760) 934–3239. Mammoth's largest full-service mountain bike shop: sales, service, rentals, demos.

Round Dance Indian Art Gallery, 126 Old Mammoth Road in the Mammoth Mall; (760) 924–7838. The largest American Indian craft store in the Eastern Sierra. Good selection of Pendleton blankets and bags, apparel, wool rugs, home decor, books and music, jewelry.

Winter recreation includes cross-country ski centers, snowmobile rentals, sledding, tobogganing, outdoor ice skating, snowshoeing, sleigh rides, dogsled rides.

Area Shuttle. During winter months, Mammoth Mountain operates a free shuttle that runs throughout the town of Mammoth and to the Tamarack Lodge, Main Lodge, Canyon Lodge, and Juniper Springs (Little Eagle) areas.

Guided mountain tours. Skiers and boarders interested in learning about Mammoth area geology, history, flora, and fauna can join USDA Forest Service and Ski Area naturalists for an easy tour of the mountain. Uniformed hosts are also available to answer questions. The naturalist tours are offered twice daily.

Mammoth Snowmobile Adventures offers over 75 miles of snow-covered trails and wide snowfields to explore. Experienced guides lead one-hour, two-hour, or half-day tours of the majestic Mammoth area. Tours depart from the Mammoth Mountain Inn and head toward Inyo Craters, where a virtually untouched natural playground awaits. For more information, call (800) MAMMOTH or visit www.MammothMountain.com.

Snowshoeing. From novice to advanced, snowshoers will enjoy beautiful scenery and the tranquility of a quiet walk through the forest on any one of four trails starting at the Main Lodge. Snowshoes are available for rent at the Main Lodge rental shop.

Tamarack Lodge and Resort cross country center is one of the most popular and scenic areas in the West. Offering over 20 miles of machine-groomed tracks and ski-skate lanes, Tamarack guests may ski or snowshoe to scenic alpine lakes surrounded by glacier-carved peaks while getting the ultimate aerobic workout.

Special Events

January. Mammoth Mountain Concert Series, Mammoth Mountain Music; (760) 934–0606.

February. Presidents Arts & Craft Show, Mammoth Art Guild; (760) 872–1554.

March. Dave McCoy College Classic, Junior Olympics, USASA National Snowboard Championships, at Mammoth Mountain Ski Area; (760) 934–2571.

St. Patrick's Day Party, Mammoth Lakes Celtic & Renaissance Festival; (760) 934–2581 ext. 2224 or (760) 934–2156.

Mammoth Winter Festival; (760) 934–6643.

April. USSA/FW Grand Prix Finals, Mammoth Mountain Ski Area; (760) 934–2571.

Opening Day of the Fishing Season, Dept. of Fish and Game; (760) 934–2664.

May. Mule Days in Bishop, Bishop Chamber of Commerce; (888) 395–3952.

June. Mammoth College Golf Classic at Sierra Star Golf Course; (760) 934–3781.

July. Mammoth Lakes Jazz Jubilee; (760) 934–2478.

Mammoth Lakes Celtic & Renaissance Festival; (760) 924–3670.

Mammoth Lakes Chamber Music Festival; (760) 934–7015.

August. Crowley Lake Fish Camp Perch Derby; (760) 935–4301.

Mammoth Festival of Beers & Bluesapalooza, Mammoth Mountain Music; (760) 934–0606.

Western Dance & BBQ, South Mono Historical Society; (760) 934–6157.

September. By God, to Bodie! Interpretive Historical four-wheel-drive tour; (818) 352–9489.

Millpond Traditional Music Festival, Inyo County for the Arts; (760) 873–8014 or (818) 352–9489.

Double Haul in the Fall Trout Derby, Western Outdoor News; (714) 546–4370.

Harvest Festival Octoberfest, Mammoth Lakes Chamber of Commerce; (760) 924–2360.

November. Mammoth Mountain Ski Area Opening Day Celebration; (800) MAMMOTH.

Mammoth Lakes Ice Rink Opens for the Winter Season, Mammoth Lakes Parks & Recreation; (760) 934–8989 ext. 222.

Town Christmas Tree Lighting Ceremony, Mammoth Lakes Parks and Recreation; (760) 934–8989 ext. 222.

December. Ski & Race Week, Mammoth Mountain Ski Area; (760) 934–2571.

Christmas Celebration, Music Society of the Eastern Sierra; (760) 924–3650.

Chamber Magic, Mammoth Lakes Chamber of Commerce; (760) 934–3068.

US Snowboard Grand Prix, Mammoth Mountain Ski Area; (760) 934–2571.

Winter Tales "Stardust" Family Concerts, Mono County Arts Council; (760) 934–3342.

Evening of Celtic & Christmas, Wild Mountain Tyme Band; (760) 924–2755.

Other Recommended Restaurants and Lodgings

Mammoth Lakes

Giovanni's Restaurant, 437 Old Mammoth Road in the Minaret Shopping Center; (760) 934–7563. Voted best pizza in town. Gourmet pizzas, salads, classic Italian dinners, sports bar.

Mammoth Mountain RV Park, Highway 203, across from the Mammoth Visitors Center and Ranger Station; (760) 934–3822.

McCoy Station, at Mammoth Mountain; (800) MAMMOTH. In the winter, have lunch at this new, full-service, sit-down restaurant, located mid-mountain, with a Marketplace food court and Steeps, an outdoor bar and barbecue.

Mill Cafe, at the base of Stump Alley Express and Gold Rush Express on Mammoth Mountain; (800) MAMMOTH. Has an outdoor bar and fire pit; hearty lunch entrees. On snowy days the indoor fireplace is ideal for snuggling up with hot chocolate.

For More Information

Mammoth Lakes Chamber of Commerce handles lodging reservations for the entire town of Mammoth. Call (760) 934–2712 or (888) GO–MAMMOTH.

Mammoth Lakes Visitors Center and Ranger Station, Highway 203, Mammoth Lakes, CA 93546; (760) 934–2712 or (888) GO–MAMMOTH; www.visitMammoth.com.

Mammoth Mountain, winter and summer activities, (760) 934–0745 or (800) MAMMOTH; www.MammothMountain.com.

24-hour snowphone: (760) 934–6166 or 888–SNOWRPT.

The Big Valley

2 Nights

Native Americans called it Ahwahnee, or "Deep, Grassy Valley." John Muir saw it as a "great temple lit from above." You'll wax poetic in Yosemite Valley when a setting sun paints a shining 4,000-foot curtain across the face of Half Dome and glitters like a crown on snowcapped peaks.

Americans have camped and hiked below the granite monoliths of Yosemite Valley since before Abraham Lincoln dedicated the valley and the Mariposa Big Trees to the state in 1864; sixteen years later, the national park was created.

Today Yosemite Valley is an international tourist attraction, jam-packed with visitors in summertime. Eighty percent of them stay in the valley, where most of the public facilities and the best-known postcard views are found; nevertheless, it's just 1 percent of the park.

Fall is a good time to come. Kids are back in school, and the Merced River becomes a stream of molten gold, bright maples reflecting in its chilly waters. Crisp breezes rustle hauntingly through the aspen groves. In spring the wildflowers are a riot of color, and the valley's famous waterfalls are at their booming best. Nowhere in the world are so many high falls concentrated in so small an area as the 7 square miles of Yosemite Valley. And a winter weekend at Yosemite can be unforgettable, whether you cross-country ski on silent forest trails or view a white wonderland through the tall windows of the old Ahwahnee Hotel.

☐ Waterfalls and wildflowers

☐ Historic hotels

☐ Hetch Hetchy

☐ Trailside picnics

☐ Mountaintops, monoliths

☐ Sequoia groves

Day 1 / Morning

Drive from the Oakland Bay Bridge east on Highway 580 to 205 east to 5 north to 120 east, connecting with 99 north to Manteca, then 120 east to the Big Oak Flat entrance to **Yosemite National Park,** a four-hour

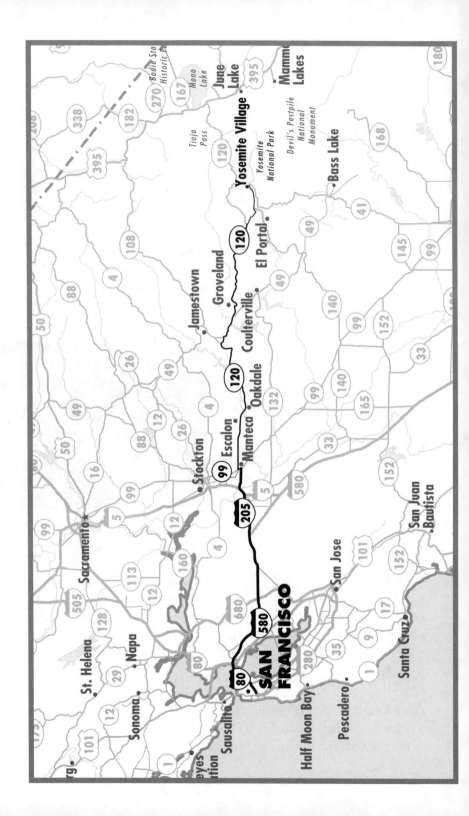

drive. The highway narrows here, ducking under huge overhanging boulders before emerging above the boiling Merced River into the valley, at an elevation of 4,000 feet. At the **visitors center** in the Yosemite Village Mall at midvalley (209–372–0299), outfit yourself with a map and the *Yosemite Guide*, a free tabloid of maps, theater and slide shows, ranger programs, trails, classes, and much more. Depending on the weather and the season, plan explorations on foot and by shuttle. If you are first-time visitors with only a half day to spare, take the two-hour, 26-mile valley floor narrated tour to see the main attractions, in an open-air tram or enclosed motorcoach, depending on the weather.

If you plan to take an extensive hike or backpack trip now or in the future, stop at the **Wilderness Center** (209–372–0740) next to the post office. Here you will find pre-trip planning stations for hikes and backpacks and a wilderness skills trail to test your knowledge of the wilderness and camping techniques. You can also obtain wilderness permits and purchase maps and guidebooks specifically for wilderness travel and education.

Sight-seeing in the valley is best done on foot, on 9 miles of bike trails, on a tour bus, or on free shuttle buses—in other words, without your car.

LUNCH: Degnan's Deli, Degnan's Pasta Plus, or **Degnan's Fast Food** in Yosemite Village; sandwiches and salads, fresh pasta, roasted chicken, kabaobs, pizza.

Afternoon

Jump on the shuttle bus and tour the valley. At stop #7 walk a short path to the base of **Yosemite Falls,** three cascades dropping 2,425 feet, the third highest waterfall in the world. (At stop #8 is the trailhead for a six-hour, strenuous hike to the top of the falls.)

For an hour's easy walk in the meadows around **Mirror Lake,** with wonderful views of Half Dome and Mount Watkins, get off at stop #17. The **Tenaya Zig Zags/Snow Creek Trail** is a little-used, 3.5-mile route to the rim of the valley, beginning east of Mirror Lake—not an easy hike, but views are eye-popping.

You can leave children at **Happy Isles** at shuttle stop #16 for free one-hour walks and talks on nature, birds, and forest lore. Happy Isles is the start of several trails, including the 1.5-mile (one-way) **Mist Trail** to **Vernal Falls,** an exciting route but too strenuous and slippery for kids younger than age seven or eight. This is the most popular hike in the valley because the rewards are a breathtaking close-up view of the falls dropping over a 317-foot cliff, plus knockout vistas of many peaks, domes, and water cascades.

Now that you're warmed up to Yosemite, go into the **Ansel Adams Gallery** (559–372–4413), near the visitors center; since 1902 the place has been a camera store and gallery of signed Adams photos, prints, and posters of the valley in its seasonal raiments. Free two-hour photography workshops with professional teachers are conducted here. There are also Sunrise Camera Walks from Yosemite Lodge (209–372–0299).

DINNER: Ahwahnee Hotel Dining Room, Yosemite Village at mid-valley; (559) 252–4848 or (209) 372–1488; www.yosemitepark.com. With a 24-foot-high ceiling and baronial chandeliers, the 130-foot-long dining room is world famous for its beauty and views through the sky-high windows. A pianist plays for dinner, and the food is better than it has ever been in the history of the hotel—top-notch California cuisine and a good wine list, plus choices that kids like. The dining room is elaborately decorated and glowing with candles and merriment every Christmas season, when the Medieval-style Bracebridge Dinners are held. Gala Vintners' Holidays and Chefs' Holidays are popular in the wintertime.

LODGING: Ahwahnee Hotel, (559) 252–4848. Standing gloriously aloof in a woodland setting, with granite cliffs rising behind, the art deco hotel is in perfect shape, with painted beams, decorated floors, and stained-glass windows faded into subtle Indian colors. Sofas, armchairs, and fabulous old oriental rugs are arranged by a huge fireplace in the Great Lounge. Built in 1927, the place still has a halcyon-days atmosphere and is museumlike, enriched with paintings, photos, and priceless Native American baskets. When fall leaves blow along the footpaths and wood smoke curls silently into a twilight glow, the spirit of summers past comes alive at the Ahwahnee. The gift shop is a good place to shop for souvenirs and books. Light meals are served on the outdoor terrace, and afternoon tea in the Great Lounge. You can walk or bike from here, or take the shuttle, to all valley sights.

Rooms have been redone and they are fabulous, with king beds, cushy fabrics, upscale mountain- and Indian-theme decor, sitting areas, and huge windows with spectacular views. Now that the food and the accommodations are the tops, the Ahwahnee lives up to its spectacular outdoor setting and atmospheric interiors.

A view of Bridalveil Fall from Wawona Tunnel.

Day 2 / Morning

BREAKFAST: An American breakfast in the Ahwahnee Hotel Dining Room.

Purchase picnic goodies and set off on the 32-mile drive on Glacier Point Road to **Glacier Point,** atop the sheer southern wall of the valley. Some 3,200 feet above the valley, the view is of several waterfalls, **Half Dome, El Capitan,** and other famous pinnacles, and the Merced River snaking along. With binoculars you may see climbers making a several days' ascent to the dizzying 2,850-foot summit of El Capitan. A vertical wall of granite four times as large as Gibraltar, "El Cap" is a memento of glaciers that tore off and ground into little pieces great sections of mountain. The faint thundering sound you hear in springtime is **Nevada Falls,** 2 miles away.

New at Glacier Point are a 150-seat granite amphitheater, campfire programs and ranger talks, viewing terraces, and a beautiful stone-and-timber building where food and gifts are sold. In wintertime the building is a bunkhouse for guided cross-country ski tours. The "Stars Over Yosemite" experience here on weekend nights gives you a chance to see the incredibly starry sky and the moon-washed monoliths through an astronomer's telescope.

A relaxing way to get to and from Glacier Point is on a narrated bus tour that runs three times a day from the valley. You can also take a hikers' bus to Glacier Point and walk down to the valley, 4.8 miles, a three- to four-hour hike. Robust climbers trek to the top of Half Dome by hiking the John Muir Trail or Mist Trail to Little Yosemite Valley, where they camp overnight. The next day, the climb is made with the aid of cables that were permanently installed on the 8,892-foot monolith in 1919. Every year more than 10,000 people climb Half Dome.

Along Glacier Point Road are several memorable stops to make. **Dewey Point,** at 7,385 feet and overlooking **Bridalveil Fall** and El Capitan, is accessible by a beautiful 7-mile round-trip trail just west of Bridalveil Campground. According to the time of year, the path may be bordered with sky-blue lupine, Indian paintbrush, or 6-foot-tall rose-colored fireweed. Crossing a footbridge over a creek, bear left around **McGurk Meadow,** where mule deer graze in grasses sprinkled with shooting stars and goldenrod.

To reach **Mono Meadow** and **Mount Starr King View,** park 2.5 miles beyond Bridalveil Campground and take the trail east, dropping for 0.5 mile to the meadow, continuing to a spectacular view 1 mile farther on: 3 miles round-trip.

LUNCH: Have a picnic on top of the world at Glacier Point or on a nearby nature trail.

Afternoon

Explore some of the 800 miles of hiking trails in the Yosemite backcountry or amble along the banks of the Merced River, trying your luck at trout fishing. Lie about on a sunny beach or take a swim in the river or at the Ahwahnee. Rent kayaks, rafts, and life jackets at Curry Village. If you've become fascinated by the history and geologic wonders of the park, you may wish to get in on one of the many seminars, lectures, theater presentations, and tours offered throughout the year.

DINNER AND LODGING: At the Ahwahnee Hotel.

Day 3 / Morning

BREAKFAST: At the Ahwahnee Hotel Dining Room.
Take Big Oak Flat Road to the **Merced Grove** of giant sequoias. It's a 2-mile walk into the grove from the road; few people take this hike, thus giving you the opportunity to be alone with the big beauties.

If you'd rather drive, take the steep, narrow, 6-mile road to **Tuolumne Grove,** a magnificent stand of sequoias that includes the famous "Dead Giant" drive-through tree.

LUNCH: Purchase picnic fixings at Yosemite Village and have a picnic amid the sequoia groves.

Afternoon

Proceed to the Big Oak Flat entrance to Yosemite (trail maps here), then go north on Evergreen Road to the **Hetch Hetchy Valley and Reservoir,** where there is much to see. The drowning of the spectacular valley in the 1930s was vigorously opposed by John Muir and the Sierra Club, but the dam was built; today the reservoir continues to supply San Francisco with water and power.

A sun catcher, the valley is quite hot in summer but delightful for hiking in fall and spring. Hetch Hetchy Reservoir is 8 miles long, ringed with granite domes and dramatic cliff faces, a habitat for a great variety of wildlife; fishing is good, although swimming and boating are not allowed. From the top of the dam, take the flat trail through the tunnel and along the north edge of the reservoir; about 2 miles beyond, **Tueeulala Fall** and **Wapama Falls** thunder down, the latter so enthusiastic that it sometimes washes out the trail. And at 6.5 miles out, **Rancheria Falls** are misty and refreshing.

Return to the Big Oak Flat entrance and take Highway 120 east through Oakdale to 99, crossing Highway 5 to 205, connecting with 580 to the East Bay.

There's More

Complimentary shuttle-bus service is provided year-round to points in the eastern end of Yosemite Valley. In summer it also runs from Wawona to the Mariposa Grove and between Tenaya Lake and Tuolumne Meadows Lodge. In winter, buses run from valley hotels to the Badger Pass Ski Area. The shuttle serves most of the valley trailheads and all of the major buildings and attractions in the valley.

Dog Lake is the closest lake to Tuolumne and the warmest of the chilly lakes at this altitude. It's a 1.5-mile, one-way trek, a little steep at first but easy enough for all ages, and there's good swimming and fishing at the end.

Rafting. Ahwahnee Whitewater Expeditions, P.O. Box 1161, Columbia 95310; (209) 533–1401. Rafting on the Merced, Tuolumne, Stanislaus, and Carson Rivers.

Tuolumne Meadows, at 8,600 feet, is the largest open meadow in the Sierras at the subalpine level, bordered by the snow-fed Tuolumne River and surrounded by peaks and glacier-polished domes. The nearest access is by Tioga Road near the town of Lee Vining, on the northeasern side of the park, a road that is closed for about half the year due to snow. You can also take the beautiful drive up from the valley (also closed during wintertime).

A hub for backpacking trails, 2.5-mile-long Tuolumne Meadows may sparkle with frost or be awash in purple nightshade, golden monkeyflowers, and riots of magenta lady-slipper orchids. You can drive to the rustic Tuolumne Meadows Lodge (209–252–4848) and the Tuolumne Meadows Campground (800–365–2297), the largest in the park, with 325 sites; the most desirable sites are on the east side near the river. Campfire programs are held most nights. Within walking distance of the campground are a grocery store, stables, and a restaurant that serves substantial American fare. Tent cabins with woodstoves are located in a picturesque setting near the river.

A variety of guided walks begin at Tuolumne Meadows. The "Night Prowl," an after-dark caravan around the meadow, turns up great gray owls, spotted bats, and other nocturnal denizens of the High Sierras.

Between Tuolumne and the valley off Tioga Road, **White Wolf,** a summertime-only headquarters for backcountry trails, has rustic tent cabins, a "first-come" campground, store, stables, and a lovely old clapboard dining hall that serves simple meals all day.

Winter fun in Yosemite. Although frosty white on the clifftops and often in the valley, winter weather is usually mild. The valley gets about 29 inches of snow, Badger Pass Ski Area about 180 inches. The outdoor skating rink at Curry Village is a cozy place to be, with a warming hut, skate rentals, hot drinks, and views of Half Dome. Badger Pass is the oldest ski school in the state and still one of the best, with low prices for everything. Except on holiday weekends, you won't wait in lift lines; the dining decks and all facilities are just steps away from the lifts and school meeting places. Take the comfortable shuttle buses from your accommodations up the (sometimes icy) hill to Badger. There are six lifts to the 8,000-foot summit. Nordic skiing on 350 miles of trails and roads, and 23 miles of machine-groomed track and skating lanes. A two-hour, ranger-guided, narrated snowshoe hike is only $3.00, including equipment. There is a popular overnight ski hike to a rustic lodge, including meals. Junior Snow Ranger program, winter field trips for photographers and artists. Snow-play areas at Crane Flat on state Route 120 and just outside the southern entrance on state Route 412 near Fish Camp.

Yosemite High Sierra Camps Saddle Trips; (209) 372–1445. Four-and six-day saddle trips to camps between 7,150 and 10,300 feet. Camps are 8 miles apart, and each provides tents, beds, linens, and blankets. Breakfast and dinner are served in a heated dining tent. Groups are limited to ten people and are accompanied by an experienced guide. Personal belongings are carried on a pack mule.

Special Events

January–February. Chef's Holidays, Ahwahnee Hotel and Yosemite Lodge; (209) 454–0555. Demonstrations, seminars with prominent chefs, gala banquets.

February. Yosemite Renaissance, Yosemite Valley Visitor Center; (209) 372–0299. National juried art show with Yosemite as the theme; paintings, photography, sculpture, lithography.

November–December. Yosemite Vintners' Holidays; (209) 454–2020. Banquets and seminars with prominent vintners.

December–January. The Bracebridge Dinners, in the Ahwahnee Hotel Dining Room; (209) 372–1489. The Renaissance is re-created at elaborate performances and monumental banquets; reservations by lottery.

Other Recommended Restaurants and Lodgings

Accommodations in the National Park at the Ahwahnee Hotel, Yosemite Lodge, Wawona Hotel, White Wolf Lodge, Curry Village, and in tent cabins and cabins without baths can be arranged by calling (559) 252-4848; or writing to P.O. Box 577, Yosemite, CA 95389; www.yosemitepark.com. The Curry Village area of the valley offers a variety of accommodations, from tent cabins to hotel rooms and loft rooms sleeping six or more; all are clean and quite basic; some can be noisy. Nearby, Yosemite Lodge has 484 units from hotel-type rooms with balconies to rustic cabins, with or without baths, in a compound that includes a cafeteria and restaurants with good, plain food; post office, gift shops, swimming pool, outdoor theater, and tour desk; free nightly programs.'

Camping: Large, usually crowded, valley campgrounds—Lower and Upper River, and North, Upper, and Lower Pines—can be noisy with road traffic and RV generators, but they're convenient for walking and biking to most public places and trailheads. If you are interested in the wide variety of classes, interpretive hikes, and performances scheduled throughout the high season, a valley campground may be your best choice (800- 436-7275). Hot showers are available to the public twenty-four hours a day at Curry Village and Housekeeping Camps; a small fee includes towel and soap.

A compromise between accessibility to the valley and a quieter, prettier place to camp is found at **Bridalveil Creek Campground,** 25 miles from the valley on the Glacier Point Road at an elevation of 7,200 feet. Each of the one hundred tent and RV sites here and at other higher-elevation camps are provided with "bear lockers," secure boxes where your food can be kept safe from black bears.

Coulterville

Hotel Jeffery, 1 Main Street; (209) 878-3471. Gloriously restored, circa-1850 twenty-room hotel; garden patio, saloon, restaurant.

El Portal

Yosemite Cedar Lodge, 8 miles from Yosemite; (800) 321-5261. Two hundred deluxe and moderate rooms, some family units and suites, a restaurant, swimming pools, access to the Merced River.

Groveland

Groveland Hotel, 18767 Main Street; (800) 273–3314; www.groveland.
com. Named one of the top ten country inns in the country; seventeen
guest rooms with antiques and down comforters, suites with fireplaces and
spa tubs. Fine dining.

Iron Door Saloon, 18761 Main Street; (209) 962–6244. Oldest saloon in
the state, open 365 days a year; good food and soda fountain. Live weekend music.

For More Information

YARTS (Yosemite Area Regional Transportation System); (877)
98–YARTS; www.yosemite.com/yarts. A new motorcoach service from
Merced, Coulterville, Mariposa, and Mammoth, with bike racks, makes
personal vehicles unnecessary. Fare includes park admission. You can also
take an Amtrak train to Merced, transferring to a motorcoach to the park
(888–PARK–BUS).

Yosemite National Park, P.O. Box 577, Yosemite, CA 95389. General information: (209) 372–1000, (209) 372–0265 or (209) 372-0264. Reservations:
(559) 252–4848.

Yosemite Web Sites. www.yosemitepark.com. Yosemite Concession Services
site with information on lodging, shopping, dining, activities, and links.

www.nps.gov/yose/. Official National Park site.

www.reservations.nps.gov. Camping reservations.

www.yosemite.com. Travelers' information, lodging, roads, and weather.

www.yosemite.org. Yosemite Association, visitors information, bookstore,
classes and seminars, weather and live-camera views.

Advice: Hikers and campers should keep in mind that sudden storms are
not uncommon in Yosemite any month of the year. Weather changes
rapidly in the Sierras, and snow can fall as early as September.

Southern Sierra 4

Wawona and the Lake Country

2 Nights

The southern part of Yosemite National Park, called Wawona, is the place to go in midsummer, when Yosemite Valley is crowded with cars and people. Wilderness trails are silent, except for the crunch of your own footsteps and the prattle of squirrels and Steller's jays.

The historical heart of the park, Wawona is anchored by the gracious old Wawona Hotel, riding the edge of magnificent Wawona Meadow like an aging but still glistening white ocean liner.

☐ Walks in the woods

☐ Sequoia giants

☐ Fireside chats

☐ Yosemite history

☐ Railroad ride

☐ Lunch at the lake

Between Yosemite and Kings Canyon National Park, the lake country of the central Sierras remains relatively undiscovered by Californians. Some 700 miles of trout streams and numerous lakes, reservoirs, and campgrounds make this an area you'll want to explore on many weekends. Just off Highway 41, at an elevation of 3,400 feet and situated on the 1,000-acre blue sparkler of Bass Lake, are a luxury resort; cabins, condos, and campgrounds; marinas for sailing, fishing, and waterskiing boats; and endless hiking trails in the surrounding Sierra National Forest.

Day 1 / Morning

It's 200 miles from the Bay Area to Yosemite. From San Francisco take the Oakland Bay Bridge to Highway 580 east to 205 east to 5 north to 120 east to Highway 99, turning south to Merced, then going east on Highway 140 to Mariposa, then south on Highway 49 to **Oakhurst,** an antiques center and busy gateway to Yosemite and the recreational lakes country.

On a quick shopping stop in Oakhurst, look for the **Alko Rock Shop** for crystals, minerals, fossils, and beads (40761 Highway 41; 559–683–0345). In a Victorian setting, **The Purple Cow** sells wood toys, tole paintings, stained glass, and cows, cows, cows (39935 Highway 41;

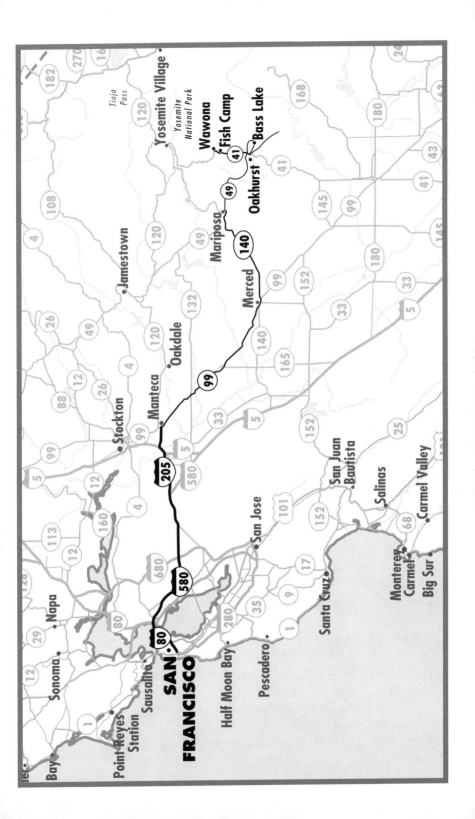

559–683–2112). **Timberline Gallery** shows works by dozens of local and nationally known artists (40982 Highway 41; 559–683–3345).

Stretch your legs on the **Oakhurst River Parkway,** an oak-shaded, 3-mile loop trail along the Fresno River and Oak Creek in Oakhurst Community Park (559–683–7766).

Take Highway 41 north from Oakhurst, for twenty minutes, to the right turn onto Highway 222; it's now 4 miles to Bass Lake. (On the way to Bass Lake, stop in at the **Old Corral Grocery and Tackle Shop** for bait, rod and reel rentals and sales, fishing licenses, and picnic fare; 41872 Road 222; 559–683–7414.)

A warm-water lake that reaches seventy-eight degrees in summer, **Bass Lake** is good for fishing in spring and fall for trout, bass, catfish, and bluegill; it's also popular for all types of water sports and camping. You can rent sailboards and boats for canoeing, sailing, rowing, and waterskiing. For a short, easy walk at the lake, take the 0.5-mile **Way of the Mono Trail,** along Road 222. You'll learn some Native American history and see some great views. Once a day in summer, the *Bass Lake Queen* takes fifty passengers on an open-air tour of the lake (559–642–3121). Don't miss **Bullwinkel's Gifts and Antiques** in Pine Village on the lake, a big antiques and country gifts emporium (54331 North Shore Drive; 559–683–2018).

LUNCH: Ducey's on the Lake, Bass Lake; (559) 642-3131. Dine on a sunny deck overlooking Bass Lake. Grilled chicken, salads, burgers, fresh fish, pasta.

Afternoon

It's 14 miles on Highway 41 to **Marriott's Tenaya Lodge at Yosemite,** 1122 Highway 41, Fish Camp (559–683–6555 or 888–514–2167; www. tenayalodge.com)—a destination resort overlooking forested mountains and valleys and located five minutes from Yosemite Park. The two-story atrium lobby and the restaurants, lounge, and public areas have a casual but luxurious feel and are decorated with Indian artifacts and Western-style furnishings. Tours from the hotel get you into the park and to the Badger Pass Ski Area. There are a fully staffed children's day camp program here and, nearby, many trailheads for walks, hikes, and mountain-bike rides through pine forests and along streamsides.

Try the **Lewis Creek National Recreation Trail,** 5 miles south of the Yosemite Gate, a 3.5-mile path through dogwood, azalea, and pine with two waterfalls and some fishing holes in Lewis Fork Creek.

Bikes are available at the hotel. Five minutes away is a stable for guided horseback rides. You can cross-country ski right from the lodge and rent equipment here, skiing on your own or taking the guided tour.

DINNER: At the **Sierra Restaurant,** in Marriott's Tenaya Lodge at Yosemite. Fresh fish, local produce, California and Northern Italian cuisines, fireplace, mountain views.

LODGING: At Marriott's Tenaya Lodge, a 242-room resort hotel. The spacious, upscale rooms were delightfully renovated recently and include many amenities: ironing boards, coffeemakers, Nintendo; some have two double beds and sitting area with sofa bed. Recreational facilities include a full-service spa and fitness center, saunas, indoor and outdoor pools, and a playground. Barbecue evenings start with a horse-drawn wagon ride to the cookout, with campfire singing and marshmallow roasting with cowpokes. Kids check in at their own station at the front desk and pick up an activity pack. "Camp Tenaya" supervised play camp is popular with five- to twelve-year-olds.

Day 2 / Morning

BREAKFAST: At the **Parkside Restaurant,** in the lodge. All-American breakfasts. Have the Parkside Deli put together sandwiches, salads, and giganto brownies for a picnic.

Drive or bike 7 miles on Highway 41 into the park to **Mariposa Grove** and take the tram through the grove to see the 209-foot, 300-ton **Grizzly Giant;** the **Columbia** (290 feet); and hundreds more 2,000-year-old giant sequoias. This is the largest and most impressive of three sequoia groves in the park. At several tram stops you can hop off and wander along nature trails, the best way to enjoy these magnificent beings, the largest living things on Earth. A vista point, accessible by a short walk from the top of the grove, overlooks the entire Wawona basin. In the **Mariposa Grove Museum** are displays about the big trees and the flora and fauna of Yosemite. Instead of taking the tram back to the parking lot, you can wander the 2.5-mile, easy downhill route on footpaths beneath the fragrant cedar and pine branches. In the wintertime, you can park at the bottom of the hill and snowshoe up to the grove, a relatively easy, absolutely beautiful route.

Back on Highway 41 in Wawona, park at the Yosemite Pioneer History Center, and take the easy, flat trail over the covered bridge and about 200 yards along the Merced River until you come to a picnic spot beside the river or a flat, sunny boulder in the middle of the river. You'll find places to wade and swim.

LUNCH: Picnic beside the Merced River behind the Yosemite Pioneer History Center.

Afternoon

The **Yosemite Pioneer History Center** is a compound of historic buildings and vintage vehicles. Here costumed docents play the parts of residents from bygone days.

Stroll around **Wawona Meadow,** across from the hotel, a flat route through the pines around the huge wildflower-strewn meadow, ending behind the hotel, a 3-mile round-trip. This is one of several meadows that make Wawona a popular area for cross-country skiing.

A more challenging hike is to **Chilnualna Falls,** a steep, 8-mile round-trip through pines, cedars, and manzanitas to a jetting avalanche of water, refreshing when you jump in the icy pool at the base of the upper falls. The trailhead is located 1.7 miles east of the main road, on Chilnaulna Falls Road.

Beaches and swimming spots are easily accessible on the south fork of the **Merced River** as it runs through Wawona.

DINNER: Wawona Hotel, Highway 41 near the southern gate of Yosemite National Park; (559) 252–4848; www.yosemitepark.com. The beautiful Victorian dining room, open for all meals, now has a fabulous chef, and the menu is a cross between California cuisine and American comfort food, with seasonal specials; don't miss the pine-nut pie and the summer barbecues.

LODGING: Wawona Hotel, the oldest resort hotel in the state, was built in the 1870s and is in fabulous shape. Rooms in several beautiful vintage buildings and cottages vary in size, and many have been redone in sumptuous fabrics, with armoires, new furnishings, and nice bathrooms with amenities. Evenings by the fireplace in the lobby are sweet, while a honky-tonk pianist plays and spins tales of old Yosemite. There is a beautiful pool, sweeping lawns, a nine-hole golf course, wonderful walking trails, tennis, horseback riding, and the Merced River is nearby for swimming and fishing. Or, you can just sink into a rocker on the covered porch. You don't need a car: just jump on the free shuttles to the valley, Badger Pass, and the Mariposa Grove, year-round. Ask about ski packages.

Day 3 / Morning

BREAKFAST: Wawona Hotel.
Right outside the park on Highway 41 is the **Yosemite Mountain Sugar Pine Railroad** (559–683–7273; www.ymsprr.com), set in a lovely wooded glade. An eighty-four-ton vintage locomotive, the largest ever built for a narrow-gauge track, pulls open cars 4 miles through forestlands into **Lewis Creek Canyon.** Steam rolls out from under the great engine, black smoke belches up into the sky, and a conductor spins tales of when the railroad hauled millions of board feet of lumber out of the Sierras. From June through September, a "Moonlight Special" evening train excursion ends with a steak barbecue and live music around a campfire. There's a beautiful picnic spot here, and cross-country skiing is excellent throughout the Sugar Pine area.

LUNCH: Narrow Gauge Inn, 48571 Highway 41, next to the railroad station, Fish Camp; (559) 683–7720. The Victorian era and the Old West are combined in the dining hall and Bull Moose saloon; cozy in cool weather, when logs burn in the big stone fireplaces.

Afternoon

Retrace your route back to the Bay Area.

There's More

Fresno Flats Historical Park, a mile from Oakhurst on Road 427; (559) 683–6570. Re-created Western community from the region's early timber and ranching era. Old buildings have been moved from all over the county, including jails, schools, barns, wagons, buggies, and a furnished home from the nineteenth century.

Horseback riding. Yosemite Trails Pack Station, P.O. Box 100, Fish Camp 93623; (800) 635–5807. Guided trips into Mariposa Grove and other parts of the park. Inquire at Marriott's Tenaya Lodge.

Nelder Grove. Ten miles north of Oakhurst on Highway 41—take Sky Ranch Road 6 miles; also accessible by vehicle from Tenaya Lodge via several miles of dirt road. One of the largest trees in the world, the Bull Buck, rests in a wilderness grove of more than a hundred specimen sequoias; a 1-mile, self-guided trail runs through the grove along the banks of Nelder Creek.

Pets in Yosemite National Park. Pets are allowed on paved areas only. They must be leashed and attended at all times and are not allowed on trails, in the backcountry, in lodgings, or in public places. Kennels are available: (559) 372–1248.

Sierra Mono Museum, at Malum Ridge Road (Road 274) and Mammoth Pool Road (Road 225), between North Fork and South Fork; (559) 877–2115. Major exhibition of Native American artifacts and California wildlife displays.

Southern Yosemite in winter. Guided snowshoe walks with a park ranger/naturalist are scheduled at the Mariposa Grove; a developed snow-play area is located at Crane Flat on Route 120, just outside the southern entrance to the park; at the Pioneer History Center, costumed docents talk about early Yosemite winters. There is caroling by candlelight and hot cider and cocoa in the old barn. For snowmobiling, head for Beasore Road near Pine Village at Bass Lake.

Yosemite High Country Wilderness Tours; (559) 683–4013. Four-wheel-drive treks in the Sierra National Forest, fabulous views, knowledgeable guides, air-conditioned vehicles, snacks and deli lunch.

Special Events

April. Oakdale Professional Rodeo, Oakdale; (559) 847–2244. One of the state's top rodeos; a week of events, parade, dance, World Champion Cowboys.

Yosemite Spring Ski Festival, Badger Pass Ski Area; (559) 372–1000. Winter carnival, racing, costumes, entertainment.

May. Mountain Peddlers' Fair, Oakhurst; (559) 683–7766. Some 500 antiques dealers.

June. Pioneer Wagon Train, Wawona Pioneer Center; (559) 742–6231. Program, campfire, wagon procession with costumed riders.

Custom and Classic Car Show, Bass Lake; (559) 642–3676. Fifties weekend, barbecue, dance.

September. Sierra Mountaineer Days, Oakhurst; (559) 683–8492. Parade, carnival, dance.

December. Yosemite Pioneer Christmas; (559) 372–0265. Special programs at the Wawona Hotel, caroling, candlelight tours.

Other Recommended Restaurants and Lodgings

Bass Lake

Ducey's on the Lake, P.O. Box 329, Bass Lake 93604; (800) 350–7463. Luxury suites on the lake in a mountain lodge, with a lakeside pool, hot tub, and sauna; adjacent is a marina that rents jet skis, water skis, party barges, and fishing boats.

The Pines Resort, P.O. Box 109, Bass Lake 93604; (800) 350–7463; www.basslake.com. Rustic condos, chalets, and luxury suites at the lake; tennis, sauna, hot tub.

Yosemite Forks Mountain House Restaurant, Highway 41 at the Bass Lake turnoff; (209) 683–5191. Casual dining in a mountain setting; pasta, steaks, sandwiches, salads, espresso, microbrews; breakfast, lunch, and dinner.

Fish Camp

Karen's Bed and Breakfast Yosemite Inn, 1144 Railroad Avenue; (800) 346–1443. One mile from the park on Highway 41. Charming country-style accommodations with TLC from Karen, plus big breakfasts; very close to the park.

Summerdale Campground, operated by the USDA Forest Service; (559) 683–4665. Nice, small, streamside sites.

Oakhurst

Best Western Yosemite Gateway Inn, 40530 Highway 41; (559) 683–2378 or (800) 545–5462. Has 118 rooms in a parklike setting; mountain views; indoor and outdoor pools; some kitchens; restaurant; bar.

Castillo's, 49271 Golden Oak Loop; (559) 683–8000. Terrific tacos and homemade Mexican food. It's a cantina, too—try the blackberry margaritas!

Erna's Elderberry House Restaurant, 48688 Victoria Lane, off Highway 41; (559) 683–6800. European and California cuisine extraordinaire in elegant country French surroundings; lunch and dinner. Also Château du Sureau, Erna's out-of-this-world European-style inn, a castle with luxurious suites; pricey, a place for honeymoons. Expect feather beds, French iron balconies, oriental rugs, antique furnishings throughout, bubbling fountains, and more opulence and finery—Robert DeNiro, Kevin Bacon, and friends love the place. In the 2,000-square-foot, two-bedroom villa, you will have your own butler, silk-and-satin bedding and draperies, lavish marble bathrooms with oversized Jacuzzi tubs and steam showers, fireplaces, antiques, and private outdoor spaces. It is nothing short of astonishing that the Château exists anywhere, let alone in the laid-back little town of Oakhurst.

Wawona

Redwoods Cottages, P.O. Box 2095, Wawona 95389; (559) 375–6666. One hundred privately owned cabins to rent.

Yosemite West

Yosemite's Four Seasons, 7519 Henness Circle, near the south entrance to the park; (800) 669–9300. Rooms, studios, homes, apartments to rent; simple to luxurious.

For More Information

Bass Lake Chamber of Commerce, P.O. Box 126, Bass Lake, CA 93604; (559) 642–3676; www.basslake.com.

Campground reservations: (800) 436–7275.

Yosemite National Park, P.O. Box 577, Yosemite, CA 95389. General information: (209) 372–1000, (209) 372–0265, or (209) 372–0264; www.yosemite park.com. Reservations: (559) 252–4848.

Yosemite Sierra Visitors Bureau, 40637 Highway 41, Oakhurst, CA 93644; (559) 683–4636; www.yosemite.sierra.org.

Morro Bay 5

Central Coast Getaway, Castle Country

2 Nights

One of California's last undeveloped stretches of coastline offers a long weekend of outdoor recreation by the sea, a stay in a cozy seaside inn, and an impressive cultural attraction, Hearst Castle. Discover the hearty Rhone varietal wines that are unique to the Central Coast. Stroll the garden lanes and browse the art galleries of a sweet little burg of Cambria, and the tiny village of Harmony. Beachcomb on miles of warm sand. Kayak and bird-watch in the habitat of the great grey heron on quiet Morro Bay. Discover the kingdom of Nipomo Dunes.

☐ Sea breezes, seafood

☐ Hearst Castle

☐ Adventure in the dunes

☐ Biking and hiking

☐ Winery tours

☐ Antiques and art

On your scenic 12-mile drive from San Luis Obispo to Morro Bay, notice the chain of volcanic "plug dome" peaks. They are called the "Seven Sisters"; the seventh is **Morro Rock,** a looming sentinel guarding Morro Bay.

Day 1

From San Francisco, take Highway 280 south to Highway 85, connecting to Highway 101 south to San Luis Obispo, about 3.5 hours altogether. Proceed 12 miles to **Morro Bay.**

LUNCH: Great American Fish Co., 1185 Embarcadero, Morro Bay; (805) 772–4407. Enjoy the sea breezes and seafood.

On Embarcadero in Morro Bay is an unassuming line-up of art galleries, souvenir and gift shops, and seafood restaurants.

Afternoon

Drive a short distance from Embarcadero, south on State Park Road to the Museum of Natural History at **Morro Bay State Park** to get an overall

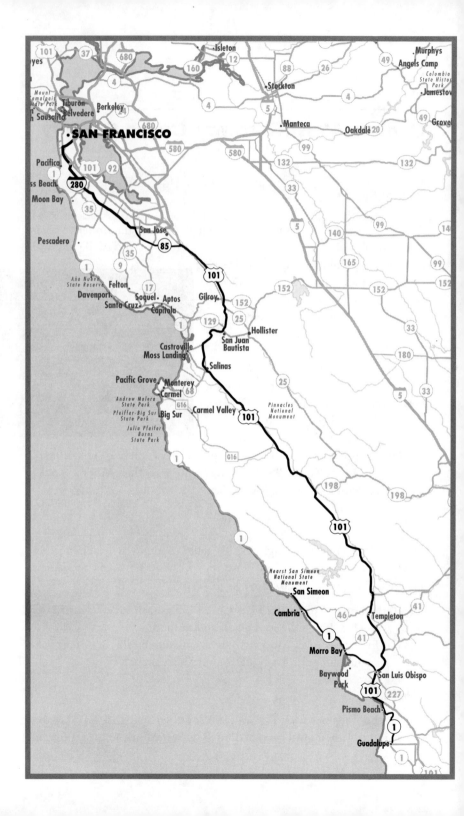

perspective of the bay and surroundings; take advantage of the docent walks, natural history and environmental exhibits, and guidebooks and maps of the area (800–544–5437; www.mbspmuseum.org). Just below the museum on the south side is a small boat harbor, a cafe, canoe and kayak rentals, a campground, and a picnic area. The 1.5-mile Black Mountain biking/hiking trail winds through the hills.

For a long beach walk, take the brief drive to **Morro Strand State Beach** on the south end of the bay. This 3 miles of powdery sand is popular for fishing, sailboarding, and strolling in the sea air. Kayaking on serene **Morro Bay** is the best way to see hundreds of shore- and seabirds that stop here on the Pacific Flyway, the migratory path from Alaska to South America. One of a handful of natural coastal estuaries that still exist in this country, the best preserved wetland between San Francisco and Mexico, the bay shelters more than two dozen endangered and threatened species, including the peregrine falcon and the beautiful sand-colored snowy plover. Among literally hundreds of birds, you will likely see belted kingfishers, snowy egrets, brown pelicans, and three types of elegant grey-and-white terns with black heads.

California gray whales migrate near the coastline January through March. The best vantage points on this coastline are Point Sal, Montana de Oro State Park, Cambria, San Simeon, and Piedras Blancas.

DINNER: The Dining Room at the Inn at Morro Bay, 60 State Park Road, Morro Bay; (805) 772–5651 or (800) 321–9566; www.innat morrobay.com or www.coastalhotel.com. Have a cocktail in the romantic lounge while the sun sets over Morro Rock, then proceed to the casually elegant bayside dining room for California cuisine and Mediterranean specialties, with a focus on fresh seafood and Central Coast wines and produce. The chef's classic French approach is evident in subtle sauces, his creative California style in lavish presentation. Don't miss the local abalone, a rare treat.

LODGING: Inn at Morro Bay. In a lyrical garden setting right on the bay, a charming complex of Cape Cod–style buildings. Rooms have either a sundeck or private balcony, and each has a sea view or a garden or pool terrace view. Cozy and luxurious at the same time, rooms are deliciously outfitted with feather beds and imported linens, plantation shutters, fireplaces, and, best of all, private balconies with hot tubs! And there is a bayside cottage for honeymooners. There are an on-site massage center and heated swimming pool; bikes and binoculars are available to borrow.

The **Morro Bay Golf Course** (805–782–8060) is across the road. Located within the Morro Bay State Park and a large heron rookery, the inn is perched above a mile-long sand dune above Morro Bay, with glorious views of the sea and Morro Rock.

Day 2 / Morning

BREAKFAST: The Conservatory at the Inn at Morro Bay, a casual bayview restaurant at the inn that serves breakfast, lunch, and dinner.

Drive north on Highway 1 for a half hour to **Hearst Castle** (750 Hearst Castle Road, Highway 1, San Simeon; 805–927–2020), a monumental Mediterranean Revival palace in a stunning mountaintop setting. Designed by famed architect Julia Morgan and built for the pleasure-filled life of William Randolph Hearst, a stupendously wealthy San Francisco newspaper publisher, the castle and grounds comprise one of the most spectacular estates in the world, the scene of legendary Hollywood parties and weekend retreats in the 1920s and '30s. Priceless European art and antiques fill 165 elaborately decorated rooms—from hand-carved and painted ceilings to marble sculptures, Flemish tapestries, cathedral-size drawing rooms, gilded chandeliers, spectacular indoor and outdoor swimming pools, and hundreds more museumlike details and furnishings.

The gardens, terraces, and pools create a tropical paradise on the mountaintop, with wide views of the surrounding landscape and the sea.

Although this is one of the most popular tourist destinations in the state, the flow of visitors at the castle is managed gracefully. You park below at the visitors center, take time, if you wish, to see the fascinating, forty-minute IMAX film of the history and building of the castle, then hop onto a comfortable, air-conditioned bus to ride up into the hills; historical narration sets the scene for your arrival, whereupon your bus group is then guided around the grounds and buildings, depending on which tour you elect to take (first-timers usually take Tour 1, which includes the gardens, main house, and main guest houses; other tours focus on the private upper levels, more guest houses, or evening tours with docents in period dress; tours are just short of two hours). Call (800) 444–4455 for tour reservations. Wear your walking shoes for the 0.5-mile walk, which includes 150 to 400 stairs. A snack bar and espresso bar are at the visitors center.

Across Highway 1 from Hearst Castle are two beaches less frequented than most: **San Simeon State Beach,** with campgrounds, fishing, tidepools, and swimming; and **William R. Hearst Memorial State Beach,** with protected swimming, a fishing pier, and a picnic area in a eucalyptus grove (805–927–2020). Just north of San Simeon is the southernmost resting and mating beach for elephant seals; they are here most of the year, and you can get quite close (not too close!).

LUNCH: Robin's, 4095 Burton Drive, Cambria; (805) 927–5007; www. robinsrestaurant.com. Sit under the vines on the patio and enjoy a grilled fish sandwich, fish tostadas, burgers, a luscious salad sampler, and more healthy, delicious fare. On the dinner menu are Thai curry, Indian Tandoori, homemade pasta, and Mexican-inspired specialties.

Afternoon

Amble around the tiny town of **Cambria.** Tucked into a Monterey pine forest, the few streets are wall-to-wall antiques shops and galleries. At the **Country Collectibles and Antiques Mall,** twenty-eight dealers buy "junque" and sell antiques (2380-E Main Street; 805–927–0245). If you don't get a chance to tour the wineries, stop in at **Fermentations** (4056 Burton Drive; 805–927–7141 or 800–446–7505; www.fermentations.com) to taste and purchase a wide variety of local wines. **Heart's Ease Herb Shop and Gardens** (4101 Burton Drive; 805–927–5224) is a showplace of cottage gardens and exotic herbs, botanic prints and antique books. Stunning glass creations by nearly 200 American glass artists are on display at **Seekers Collection and Gallery** (4090 Burton Drive; 800–841–5250; www.seekersglass.com).

Cambria is a stone's throw from a nice mile-long beach with tidepools, surf fishing, beachcombing for moonstones and driftwood, and picnic areas. Just down the Highway from Cambria, the village of Harmony is worth a stop to see artisan glassblowers in action at **Phoenix Glass** (805–927–4248; www.phoenixglass.com) and a huge array of hand-thrown pottery at **Harmony Pottery** (805–927–4293).

DINNER: Galley Restaurant, 899 Embarcadero, Morro Bay; (805) 772–2806. On a waterfront dock; fresh, fresh seafood; nice background music; casual atmosphere.

LODGING: Inn at Morro Bay. Lovely nature walks begin at the inn, and you can watch herons flying to and from their nests in the Monterey pines adjacent to the inn; this is a major great blue heron rookery. The dramatic courtship of the herons begins in January, when males strut and battle for their mates and build their nests.

Day 3 / Morning

BREAKFAST: Inn at Morro Bay.

Drive south on Highway 1 to Guadalupe to the **Dunes Discovery Center** (951 West Main Street; 805–343–3455) to see excellent exhibits and get maps and information about **Nipomo Dunes,** a huge, otherworldly, active sand-dune system; you can take a guided tour or explore on your own. Drive 1.5 miles north of town to the access road. Near the parking lot, a boardwalk snakes through a mysterious, swampy, and beautiful freshwater lake, where willows and cattails shelter bird life. You may see marsh wrens, ruddy cinnamon ducks, and even red-legged frogs. The dunes trail stretches beyond the boardwalk over silky, golden sands; a surprising variety of shrubs and wildflowers cling to the windy swales. As far as the eye can see, the dunes seem an endless ocean of tilting, whirling sand hills. You can lie here on the beach and watch the cormorants and Harrier hawks fish or hike over the dunes, discovering small creeks and blooming wildflowers: blood-red poppies, pale lavender sea rocket, and sun-yellow coreopsis.

LUNCH: **Far Western Tavern,** 899 Guadalupe Street, Guadalupe; (805) 343–2211; www.farwesterntavern.com. A local landmark for decades, Far Western is famous for Santa Maria barbecue and a real Western saloon and dining room with cowhides for drapes; steer, moose, and deer heads; and branding irons on the walls. Don't miss the Sweet Tumbleweed Onion appetizer and the house special—Bull's Eye Steak.

After you've had your fill, retrace your route north to San Francisco.

There's More

Kayaking Morro Bay. A calm, easy place to kayak, even for first-timers and children, the estuary/bird sanctuary is best enjoyed soon after dawn when the sky is pink, the air is fresh and cool, and the birds are active. Explore the mud flats, eel grass beds, tidal wetlands, and open water where scores of shore- and seabirds fly, fish, and putter about. You will likely see harbor seals and sea lions, too. Located right on the edge of the bay, Kayak

Horizons 551 Embarcadero, Morro Bay; (805) 772–6444. Rents all the necessary gear and gives free instruction and guided tours.

Montana de Oro State Park. The visitors center is 10 miles south of Morro Bay off Los Osos Valley Road on Pecho Valley Road; (805) 528–0513. In diverse natural habitats from rocky beaches and tidal pools to rolling hills and riparian streams, there are 50 miles of trails. The 3-mile bluff trail winds along the edge of the ocean and is a good bird-watching route; at several points you can access secluded coves. The 4-mile-long sand spit on the west side of Morro Bay is accessible on foot from the parking lot above the south end of the spit.

Pismo Beach. Six miles of wide, sandy beach, for decades a famous place where clammers dug for abundant Pismo clams—which no longer exist here in legal sizes. A popular beach with seaside resorts, surf fishing, swimming, fishing pier, camping. In the State Vehicular Recreation Area here, you can rent all-terrain vehicles and drive on the beach.

Thursday Night Market. Every Thursday, San Luis Obispo throws a party. Higuera Street is blocked off and filled with farmers and vendors selling fresh produce, flowers, prepared food, and arts and crafts, and there is barbecue and live music. The shops are open late.

Tiger's Folly II. Enjoy a bay tour on an authentic paddlewheel boat. Sunday Champagne brunch, harbor cruises, private charters; (805) 772–2257.

Wineries. Countywide winery open houses, special tastings, food and music at annual festivals held the third weekends of March, May, and October. Call for a schedule of events and winery map: (805) 239–8463 or (800) 549–WINE; www.pasowine.com.

Eberle Winery, Highway 46, 3.5 miles east of Paso Robles; (805) 238–9607. Picnic patio with view, cave tours. The Syrah is as good as it gets, anywhere, and the Chardonnays are medal winners.

Edna Valley Vineyard, 2585 Biddle Ranch Road, San Luis Obispo; (805) 544–5855; www.ednavalley.com. Producer of some of the best Rhone-variety wines in the state. Big, beautiful gourmet marketplace; gift shop and tasting room with wide views of the vineyards; picnic area. Lively schedule of classes and events, and "Wine Downers," late-afternoon food and wine open house on Friday in the summertime.

EOS Estate Winery, 5 miles east of Highway 101 on Highway 46, Paso Robles; (800) 249–WINE; www.eosvintage.com. Large tasting room and retail shop with gourmet foods, beautiful pottery, and gifts. Rose garden, picnic area, guided and self-guided tours.

7 Peaks Winery, 5828 Orcutt Road, San Luis Obispo; (805) 781–0777. In a beautiful Victorian schoolhouse, a great retail shop and tasting room. The notable Shiraz and Chardonnay are produced by a joint venture of Australian and California winemakers.

Tobin James Cellars, 8950 Union Road, Paso Robles; (805) 239–2204. Destined to be the highlight of winery touring, a "must-see" winery seemingly lost in another era. Belly up to the 1860s mahogany bar to taste Syrahs, Cabs, and Zins while being regaled by a wise-cracking, Stetson-wearing staff of fun-lovers. The place is chock-full of Wild West memorabilia, from six-shooters to saddles to John Wayne, himself, and a slew of gold medals and blue ribbons for fine wine. Unique here are the dessert wines: Late Harvest Zinfandel "James Gang Reserve" and the Late Harvest "Charisma," otherwise known as "Love Wine."

Special Events

January. Winter Bird Festival, Morro Bay; (800) 231–0592. Guided tours of the estuary and surrounding area. Attracts 500 birders.

March. Jazz Festival, Morro Bay; (805) 772–4467; www.morro-bay.net/jazz. Zydeco, Big Band, Swing, Dixieland.

Zinfandel Festival, Paso Robles; (800) 549–WINE; www.pasowine.com.

April. Cruisin' Morro Bay, Morro Bay; (805) 772–4467. Fifties cars and music. Wear your poodle skirt.

May. Wine and Jazz Fest, Cambria; (805) 927–3624.

Wine Festival, Paso Robles; (800) 549–WINE; www.pasowine.com.

July. Renaissance Festival, San Luis Obispo; (805) 541–8000 or (800) 634–1414.

Fourth of July in Morro Bay; (805) 772–4467.

KCBX Wine Classic; (805) 781–3026; www.kcbx.org. Annual weeklong fund-raiser, wine symposia, special tastings, wine-maker dinners, black-tie event, live auction, famous chefs; events at Inn at Morro Bay, wineries, Hearst Castle, and other locations.

September. International Orchid Show, Morro Bay; (805) 772–4467. Central Coast Wine Festival, San Luis Obispo; (800) 549–WINE; www. pasowine.com.

October. Harbor Festival, Morro Bay; (800) 366–6043. Seafood fair, wine tasting, barbecue, ship tours, heritage displays, entertainment, and exhibits. Harvest Wine Affair, Paso Robles; (800) 549–WINE; www.pasowine.com.

November. Edna Valley Vintner's Harvest, Arroyo Grande; (800) 549–WINE; www.pasowine.com.

December. Lighted Boat Parade, Morro Bay; (805) 772–4467.

Other Recommended Restaurants and Lodgings

Baywood Park

Baywood Inn, 1370 Second Street; (805) 528–8888; www.baywoodinn. com. A small bed-and-breakfast inn with fireplaces and sea views on the southern end of Morro Bay. You can kayak from right across the street. Rooms vary in decor, from French country to early American to California beach house, and each has a separate entrance, microwave, and refrigerator. Full breakfast and afternoon wine.

Cambria

Blue Whale Inn, 6736 Moonstone Beach Drive; (805) 927–4647; www. blue-whaleinn.com. A small, cozy bed-and-breakfast inn; each room has dazzling sea views, canopy beds, antiques, luxurious amenities, and fireplaces.

Morro Bay

Ascot Suites, 260 Morro Bay Boulevard; (805) 772-4437; www.AscotInn. com.

Harbor Hut Restaurant, 1205 Embarcadero, Morro Bay; (805) 772–2255. Fine dining on the water.

Pismo Beach

SeaVenture Resort, 100 Ocean View Avenue; (800) 662–5545; www.sea venture.com. Luxurious rooms with fireplaces and feather beds, private balconies with spas, white plantation-style decor, complimentary continental breakfast, a nice oceanfront restaurant, on-site massage center—all right on the beach, one half hour south of Morro Bay.

Templeton

A. J. Spurs, 508 Main Street; (805) 434–2700. Big, noisy, and popular, a Wild West saloon and dining hall that specializes in steak, ribs, Cajun fish and chicken, and "Sidebuster" combos of all of the above. The 1886 building is crowded with interesting Western memorabilia, art, and antiques. Prepare to have fun here!

For More Information

Airlines: Seven major airlines fly into San Luis Obispo County Airport (805–781–5205), offering more than forty flights a day.

Cambria Chamber of Commerce and Visitors Bureau, 767 Main Street, Cambria, CA 93428; (805) 927–3624.

Morro Bay Visitors Center, 880 Main Street, Morro Bay, CA 93442; (805) 772–4467; www.MorroBay.org.

San Luis Obispo County Visitors Bureau, 1037 Mill Street, San Luis Obispo, CA 93401; (805) 541–800 or (800) 634–1414; www.SanLuisObispo County.com or www.VisitSLO.com.

INDEX

ABOUT THE AUTHOR

Karen Misuraca is a golf, travel, and outdoor writer and the author of six regional guidebooks. She lives in Sonoma, California, and explores northern California's outdoors with her partner, Michael Capp.